MORAL PHILOSOPHY
Theories, Skills, and Applications

ANTHONY F. FALIKOWSKI

Sheridan College of Applied
Arts and Technology

Prentice Hall, Englewood Cliffs, New Jersey 07632

Falikowski, Anthony.
    Moral philosophy : theories, skills, and applications / Anthony
Falikowski.
        p.   cm.
    Bibliography: p.
    Includes index.
    ISBN 0-13-600883-6
    1. Ethics.   I. Title.
BJ1012.F34   1990
170--dc20   89-31907
                                                                CIP

Editorial/production supervision: Linda B. Pawelchak
Cover design: Wanda Lubelska
Manufacturing buyer: Peter Havens/Carol Bystrom

© 1990 by Prentice-Hall, Inc.
A Division of Simon & Schuster
Englewood Cliffs, New Jersey 07632

Printed in the United States of America
10 9 8 7 6 5 4 3 2 1

ISBN   0-13-600883-6

Prentice-Hall International (UK) Limited, *London*
Prentice-Hall of Australia Pty. Limited, *Sydney*
Prentice-Hall Canada Inc., *Toronto*
Prentice-Hall Hispanoamericana, S.A., *Mexico*
Prentice-Hall of India Private Limited, *New Delhi*
Prentice-Hall of Japan, Inc., *Tokyo*
Simon & Schuster Asia Pte. Ltd., *Singapore*
Editora Prentice-Hall do Brasil, Ltda., *Rio de Janeiro*

Dedicated with love to
my dear wife Pamela,
my daughters Heather and Michelle,
and to my son Michael, who always asks,
"Why, Daddy?"

CONTENTS

Social Morality

4

JEREMY BENTHAM AND THE PRINCIPLE OF UTILITY   45

5

JOHN STUART MILL AND THE GREATEST HAPPINESS PRINCIPLE   55

6

IMMANUEL KANT'S CATEGORICAL IMPERATIVE AND DUTIES TO OTHERS 66

7

JOHN RAWLS: MORALITY AND SOCIAL JUSTICE 76

PART THREE: APPLICATIONS

Abortion

11

12

Capital Punishment

13

14

"THE FOLLY OF CAPITAL PUNISHMENT"   179
Arthur Koestler

Sexuality

15

"THE JUSTIFICATION OF SEX WITHOUT LOVE"   191
Albert Ellis

16

"CHRISTIAN SEXUAL ETHICS"   200
Lewis B. Smedes

Business Practice

17

"PROFITS AND LIBERTY"   213

John Hospers

18

"BUSINESS ETHICS: PROFITS, UTILITIES, AND MORAL RIGHTS"   222

Alan H. Goldman

World Hunger

19

"LIVING ON A LIFEBOAT"   239

Garrett Hardin

20

"KILLING AND STARVING TO DEATH"   256
James Rachels

Pornography

21

"IS PORNOGRAPHY BENEFICIAL?"   274
G. L. Simons

22

"PORNOGRAPHY AND RESPECT FOR WOMEN"   284
Ann Garry

War

23

"IN DEFENSE OF WAR"   295

William Earle

24

"NUCLEAR ILLUSION AND INDIVIDUAL OBLIGATIONS"   315

Trudy Govier

Appendix

HOW TO WRITE A MORAL PHILOSOPHY PAPER   327

PREFACE

This work is designed as an introductory textbook in the field of moral philosophy and applied ethics. It is best suited for junior and community college students who wish to gain some background in moral theory and its practical applications without having to specialize in a four-year degree program in philosophy. This book may also be useful to some university ethics professors who teach moral philosophy as a liberal-arts course requirement or general-education elective to those specializing outside the field. Most students using this book will regard their ethics elective as an enrichment course and probably a terminal point in their formal philosophical training. In view of this, the material included here will cover the "basics" of moral philosophy and applied ethics without going into much of the subtlety, detail, and theoretical criticism more appropriately reserved for philosophy majors.

The book is comprised of three parts: (1) Theories, (2) Skills, and (3) Applications. In Part One, after providing a brief preliminary explanation of morality, some traditional ethical theories are discussed in terms of the distinction between individual and social morality. The basic moral ideas of Plato, Aristotle, Jeremy Bentham, John Stuart Mill, Immanuel Kant, and John Rawls are distilled, paraphrased, and discussed. The discussion of moral theory is not comprehensive. For example, since morality is treated as a rational, human construction, religious morality is not addressed directly. The question of whether or not religion ought properly to belong to the moral realm in the first place introduces a highly complex, metaethical problem that falls outside the restricted concerns of this introductory text. What Part One does contain are many of the essential elements of consequentialism, social contract theory, Greek humanism, and deontology—likely the most significant and influential movements in the history of ethical theory. The material in Part One should provide beginning students with a solid theoretical foundation upon which practical moral issues can be analyzed and debated. It should also cultivate in students an appreciation for a few of the various styles of moral thinking and methods of ethical justification which are possible.

In Part Two, the nature of ethics is further clarified in terms of how science and philosophy differ in their approaches to moral inquiry. Students will learn to recognize the different kinds of claims (for example, empirical versus normative) one can make about morality, how such claims should be understood, and whether it is appropriate to speak about verification or justification in their regard. In this "skills" section, students are also introduced to the basic forms of logical thinking needed to construct, analyze, and evaluate moral arguments. They are acquainted in addition with several tests that can be used to judge the value principles upon which moral arguments are based. Errors in reasoning are explained under the subject of logical fallacies. Complementing Part Two is the appendix, "How to Write a Moral Philosophy Paper." Here, the formats for different types of papers and the steps in writing a moral thesis are explained; students are assisted in completing an "argument assembly chart," which can be used in the organization and preparation of a first moral philosophy paper. And whether or not a paper is a course requirement for the student, the appendix is useful as an illustration of the dialectical nature of moral argument. It can help students to organize their thoughts and to prepare their arguments and rebuttals in debating particular controversial issues.

Part Three is the applied section of the book. Contemporary moral problems of abortion, capital punishment, business practice, sexuality, world hunger, pornography, and war are featured. Accompanying the original works of authors writing on these topics are learning aids designed to enhance comprehension and mastery of the material covered. While the text can be used in a variety of ways, it is recommended that Part Three be taught by instructors only after covering Parts One and Two, in either order they prefer.

Before students can constructively debate issues of moral philosophy, they must first acquire a basic understanding of moral theory and master the fundamental skills of moral reasoning. Of course it is possible that students will have had prior logic courses before taking ethics. In this event, Part Two on "skills" may be glossed over or skipped entirely. Some students will bring to the course previous knowledge of ethical theory. In this case the instructor may wish to concentrate on skills and applications. A major advantage of this text is that its use can be adapted to fit the varied needs and backgrounds of both teachers and students.

This book is significantly different from others in the field of ethics. It incorporates and improves upon the "SQ3R" teaching methodology used so successfully in many introductory psychology texts; see, for example, Lefton and Valvatne, *Mastering Psychology* (3rd ed.; Boston: Allyn and Bacon, 1988). The acronym SQ3R stands for *survey, question, read, recite,* and *review.* SQ3R tends to be descriptive and primarily concerned with assimilating information and with understanding and applying concepts. I call my modified version of SQ3R "Philosophy with S.O.U.L." which refers to the "Student Orientation for Understanding and Learning" built into my approach. The S.O.U.L. system goes beyond SQ3R by including elements such as reasoning charts, analytical questions, and evaluative exercises. The S.O.U.L. system includes ten learning aids:

1. Chapter overviews
2. Educational objectives
3. Focus questions
4. Numbers in the margins to indicate where learning objectives are addressed
5. Highlighted key terms
6. Progress checks
7. Study Exercises
8. Self-tests
9. Summaries and synopses
10. Further readings, references, and notes

It should be emphasized that the S.O.U.L. system in no way detracts from the built-in versatility of the text. The content of the book can be quite adequately covered without explicit reference ever being made to the S.O.U.L. apparatus which may be used as little or as much as the users of the book see fit. Students experiencing difficulties may wish to make extensive use of the S.O.U.L. aids. Others may find them overly structured and wish to dispense with some or all of them. While personal experience indicates that the S.O.U.L. system is quite he'pful, it is not indispensable. The fact is, this book offers the luxury of choosing ether or not to use what in effect is a built-in student study guide.

This text differs greatly from many others by virtue of another innovation. Most texts deal exclusively either with theory or application. Some books make an attempt at integration by bringing theories and applications together. This text offers yet a third component, however, dealing with moral-reasoning skills. This innovation facilitates the rational application of moral theory to practical ethical problems by cultivating better logical thinking. Without such a treatment of logic, it is unlikely that the gap between theories and applications can be bridged successfully. Recognizing this, many teachers instructing first-time philosophy students in ethics already find themselves having to provide a minicourse in logic even before introducing the concepts of ethical discussion and argument. By covering some of the basics in logic within a moral context, this book thereby kills two birds with one stone. It has the advantage of not forcing teachers to assign other logic texts for reading which are only tangentially related to the ethical concerns central to the course of study. Concepts of logic are covered in such a way that they seem an integral part of morality and moral inquiry.

HOW TO USE THE S.O.U.L. SYSTEM

Built into the structure of this textbook is a student study guide called the S.O.U.L. system, a label which refers to the Student Orientation for Understanding and Learning. See the Preface for a general explanation of the reasoning behind the S.O.U.L. system as a potent learning aid. Continue reading here to learn the specifics of using this system.

This text facilitates students' learning by introducing activities that enhance knowledge acquisition, comprehension, analysis, application, and evaluation of the information presented in each chapter. As a student using the S.O.U.L. system, you are asked to begin each chapter by first glancing at the overview. You should then look over the educational objectives. Once you have finished studying a particular chapter, you should be able to do everything listed in that chapter's objectives. To facilitate mastering the objectives, read the section entitled Focus Questions before reading the body of the text. The questions posed there will serve to help direct your attention while you read through the main content. They will also help you become involved in the material and identify what is particularly important. After reading, you should complete the progress checks and do any exercises that are included. If you encounter difficulty with a particular question, you should refer to the appropriate educational objective and find its numbered location in the body of the text. The problematic section should then be reread. You will want to pay special attention to highlighted key terms and definitional statements. Your ethics teacher will have answers to all progress checks, self-tests, and learning exercises in this text's accompanying instructor's manual. The answers may be provided in advance so that students can make their learning self-paced. Providing answers in class while taking up assignments is also an option.

Once all of the correct answers are obtained, you should review to yourself the relevant points covered and then memorize them by rote, if necessary. To avoid parroting meaningless statements, you should paraphrase important concepts from the text and express them in your own words. Summaries and synopses should be referred to when you are reviewing the chapter as a whole. Be sure to take notes to help in your studying later on. And if you have an interest to pursue a particular point or to read an author in the original, direct your attention to the "References" and "Notes" sections at the end of each chapter. Once you begin Part Three, you should have the requisite theoretical background and reasoning skills needed to approach controversial ethical issues in a rational and informed fashion.

INTRODUCTION: WHAT IS MORALITY?

Despite what one's handy pocket dictionary may say, morality is not something that permits easy and simple explanation. Over the centuries, many elaborate views have been developed which present different and sometimes conflicting conceptions of what is meant by morality. Recognizing this fact, the first part of the text approaches the understanding of morality by focusing attention on several contrasting normative theories. Exhaustiveness is not the intent. The normative theories described here were selected because they represent what are probably the most important historical movements within the field of moral philosophy. They should be regarded as a springboard, as it were, for further study and thought.

A **normative theory** of morality represents a type of conceptual ethical framework. In many ways it can be seen as an extended definition of morality. Typically normative theories are based on a principle (for example, Kant's Categorical Imperative) or on a set of principles (for example, rationality and moderation) which can be called upon when deciding what, morally speaking, ought or ought not to be done. Normative theories are therefore not descriptive of what is true or likely to be the case about moral experience. They are **prescriptive** at a general level. They suggest to us how morality ought to be understood and implemented. Normative moral theories provide supporting reasons and justifications for adopting the principles which they uphold for acceptance and application in real life. Normative moral theories recommend, in effect, different "styles" of thinking on ethical matters. They are helpful to individuals insofar as they provide signposts for choosing the ethical directions their lives will take when matters of extreme moral importance are at issue. Another way of putting it is that normative theories of morality offer strategies and priority recommendations for dealing with difficult ethical choices, decisions, and conflicts as such events enter into the drama of our daily lives. General normative theories do not usually condone or condemn specific actions, but rather focus on providing ways and means of understanding those actions, determining the moral worth of alternative courses of action, and providing a justification for actions deemed to be most morally acceptable.

In many respects, the basic ingredients of normative moral theories reflect the contents of morality itself. For example, normative theories are frequently grounded on a number of **beliefs about the nature of man.** Human beings may be conceptualized as rational and autonomous (John Rawls), or they may be regarded as essentially irrational and conditioned by psychological, economic, and other environmental factors. Whether we see people as free or determined will profoundly influence our understanding of morality and the role it plays in daily life. If people are regarded as simply the products of conditioning, then morality may be conceptualized as little more than a mechanism of social control. On the other hand, if people are viewed as independent and self-governing, then morality may be defined as a vehicle for self-realization and personal growth. The definition one assigns to morality is clearly influenced by the conception of human nature which is presupposed.

Definitions of morality, like normative theories, are also tied to fundamental ideals and beliefs about what is good—and to beliefs about what is desirable or worth pursuing for its own sake. For example, utilitarians like Jeremy Bentham and John Stuart Mill believe that pleasure and happiness are ultimately valuable and that the morally right action in a particular situation is the one which produces the greatest pleasure or happiness. Morality, for them, is therefore a means of maximizing utility. By contrast, Immanuel Kant believes that only the human will is good in itself and that the object of morality is to have the rational will choose in ways that conform with the demands of universal and prescriptive principles such as respect for persons. Thus, Kant does not see morality as an attempt to maximize happiness or pleasure but as an exercise of rational will. Again, it is evident that definitions of morality will vary according to beliefs and assumptions—in this case about what is ultimately good.

Despite their differences, normative theories do appear to share some common ground with respect to how morality is conceptualized. For example, all of the theories to be discussed in this book regard morality as something involving **human life** and **interpersonal relations.** While it is a debatable point whether or not humans have moral responsibilities toward animals and the environment, it appears clearly evident that morality does indeed involve responsibilities we have toward ourselves as persons and to other human beings. It also seems intuitively obvious that nonhuman creatures such as animals like foxes or snakes do not possess morality, at least not by any conventional definition of the term. On the subject of responsibility, it would also seem evident that all the theories and definitions of morality incorporate some notion of **duty** or **obligation.** This is demonstrated by the fact that normative moral theories lay down core principles (for example, Aristotle's Golden Mean) for determining how life should be lived and for deciding what ought or ought not to be done. Whichever way morality is conceptualized, there always appear to be elements of "Do's" and "Don'ts" or "Thou shalt's" and "Thou shalt not's." Morality has a way of pressuring us through the experience of obligation. For instance, the anxiety or the expectation of guilt arising from moral conscience may dissuade us from doing what we know ought not to be done. On the positive side, personal ideals and visions of the morally good life may pull us forward or impel us to do things which we know ought to be done because they are praiseworthy or because they lead us closer to character perfection.

Of course, deciding what ought to be done or refraining from doing what ought not to be done involves **choice.** This appears to be another essential characteristic of morality. The choices made are of the sort typically found in situations of **dilemma.** In these situations different alternatives are possible, but only one can be selected. The selection of one alternative either precludes the selection of another or else it somehow compromises or violates the moral principles underlying the other alternative(s). Yet, a choice must nonetheless be made. For this reason, morality is intimately related to **conflict** as well, either personal or social. Difficult and sometimes unpleasant decisions must be made in ethical contexts. The conflict may be psychological, for instance. There can exist an opposition between inclination and duty. An individual may not be inclined to do what ought to be done or may be inclined to do what ought not to be done. Moral conflict may also be social or interpersonal. Freedoms and liberties could be in dispute as one group might unilaterally decide to limit or infringe upon the rights of another group, for example, causing strife and perhaps even open warfare.

Whatever form the moral conflict takes, it will always revolve around **normative** or **value-related** considerations. Moral disputes are not scientific debates about what is factually true about the physical universe. They are arguments based on rival ideals, beliefs, goals, values, and principles. Such things pertain to matters of what is right and wrong, good and bad, or praiseworthy and blameworthy. These matters are not trivial. They strike at the very core of human existence, exposing fundamental assumptions about liberty, equality, justice, fairness, goodness, human dignity, self-realization, happiness, respect for persons, benevolence, self-interest, and all the other value-related issues concerned with living a decent moral life within an ethically acceptable social system. Morality, then, is something which impinges on **human interests** in very important ways.

Before moving on to the more elaborate explanations of morality which follow, perhaps a brief tentative definition can be offered at this point for the reader's benefit, even at the risk of introducing yet another controversial theory. In the broadest of terms, one could say that morality is a distinctive human phenomenon, often involving conflicting choices which are based on fundamental normative considerations and obligations that affect human interests in important ways. Actions that have little or no effect on people's lives, those which are not freely or consciously chosen, and those which involve no conflict or normative considerations are not likely to be relevant to morality and probably do not belong to the moral domain. The working definition of morality presented in this introduction is not doubt incomplete and in need of further elaboration and justification. It can nonetheless serve as an initial perspective from which the following major theories can be viewed and interpreted.

Individual Morality

1

PLATO, MORALITY, AND THE HARMONIOUS PERSONALITY

OVERVIEW

1. Plato (427–347 B.C.)
2. Types of Corrupt Moral Character
3. The Just Person or Philosopher Ruler
4. Progress Check
5. Summary
6. References
7. Notes

EDUCATIONAL OBJECTIVES: After reading this chapter the student will be able to:

1.1 Provide two basic questions with which Plato's self-realization ethics is concerned.
1.2 Define the concept of teleology.
1.3 Explain the tripartite division of the human soul.
1.4 List the target objects of each part of the soul.

1.5 Explain the cause of moral evil and human unhappiness.

1.6 Understand and appreciate the difference between appearance and reality.

1.7 Describe the four types of corrupt moral character.

1.8 Provide a personality profile of the just person exemplified by the philosopher ruler.

FOCUS QUESTIONS

1. On what aspects of morality does Plato's theory focus?
2. How is goodness defined by Plato? On what is it based?
3. How does Plato conceptualize human nature?
4. How should the soul function?
5. What is the cause of immorality and unhappiness in moral life?
6. What are various ways in which we can fall short of Plato's ideal of moral perfection?
7. What is the inner peace or tranquility to which Plato alludes?
8. What is the ideal moral person like, according to Plato? Do you agree with his depiction? Why or why not?

PLATO (427–347 B.C.)

Plato lived from 427 to 347 B.C. He was born into a wealthy family that was both aristocratic and politically influential. His importance to intellectual history was underscored by Alfred North Whitehead, who once stated that all of western philosophy is but a series of footnotes on the work of Plato.

When Plato was 40, he founded the "Academy," an independent institution of learning which continued to exist for almost nine hundred years until the Roman Emperor Justinian closed it in 529 A.D. The Academy was a quiet retreat where teachers and students could meet to pursue knowledge in a disinterested fashion. Students throughout Greece enrolled to partake in the adventure of learning and to experience personal growth toward wisdom. The Academy can be regarded as the precursor of today's modern university.

Plato himself studied under Socrates, once described by the Oracle at Delphi as the wisest man in Athens. Fifteen years after the tragic trial and death of Socrates, Plato began to write "dialogues" in which Socrates was the principal speaker. The dialogues explored moral, political, logical, religious, and cosmological topics. Though Socrates never actually recorded his ideas, we derive from the dialogues a profile of Socrates' personality and a statement of his doctrines which likely bear a very close resemblance to his actual philosophy and the historical figure himself. When reading Plato it is sometimes difficult, therefore, to determine what is attributable to Plato and what comes from Socrates. Some argue that the early works of Plato are more reflective of Socratic thinking, while the later works begin to reflect Plato's own philosophical investigations. Plato's most famous work is likely *The Republic*. Other works by Plato include *The Apology, Crito, Phaedo,* and *Symposium.*

1.1   Plato's moral theory reflects a type of **self-realization ethics.**[1] Concerned with betterment of human character, Plato asks questions like, "What constitutes the good life?" and "What sort of individual should I strive to become?" Such questions frequently entail personality considerations. They address themselves to the intentions, goals, dispositions, and mental states of persons. These questions call for answers about how one's life ought to be lived and what is ultimately important and worth pursuing.

1.2   Essential to an understanding of Plato's ethics is the concept of **teleology.**[2] The doctrine of teleology states that the development of anything follows from the fulfillment of the purpose for which it was designed. As a teleologist, Plato believes that everything in the world has a proper function within a **harmonious hierarchy** of purposes.[3] For him, anything is good to the extent that it performs its proper function.[4] Thus, a pen is good if it writes smoothly and without blotting. Given the function of a pen, however, one should not expect it to perform well as a weapon of self-defense or to work adequately as a drill press, for example. We should demand from a pen nothing more than that it allow ink to flow smoothly and neatly through its tip. As human beings, we too have a function in living. This function is based on our human nature. We live the morally good life insofar as we perform our distinctively human function. In order to understand what our distinctively human function is, Plato defines human nature for us.

1.3
1.4   Plato conceptualizes human nature in terms of a tripartite division of the soul. The three parts of the human soul are labeled **reason, spirit, and appetite.**[5] Each part of the soul has its own particular objects or targets toward which it strives. Appetite is that element of human nature which is largely biological and

instinctive. The appetite has as its targets those pleasures relating to our physical being such as food, drink, and sex. Acquisitiveness or the desire for material possessions is also part of appetite. Spirit represents the drive toward action. It is that psychological faculty which serves as the source of courage, determination, and indignation.[6] It has things such as glory, honor, and fame as its target objects. Finally, reason gives us the ability to think, measure, and understand before we act. Reason permits us to calculate and make decisions with rational foresight. As the faculty of decision making, it aims at knowledge and wisdom.

1.5   The three parts of the human soul are constructed in such a way that they should in principle be able to work harmoniously together. Unfortunately the soul sometimes becomes disordered, and when this occurs **human unhappiness** results. **Disorder** in the soul arises when certain elements (for example, the appetite) assume undue importance and influence, or when subordinate elements (for example, spirit) fail to be restrained by other higher faculties (for example, reason) in the hierarchy of human functioning. While no one element or faculty should be denied its proper target objects, and whereas no one **psychological faculty** should be totally suppressed and denied expression, neither should it become unduly powerful or enslaving. Each faculty of the soul has its proper purpose and place in the harmoniously functioning personality.

1.5
1.6   For Plato, disorder of the soul is at bottom a product of **ignorance.** Ignorance is what results when reason is not given its proper place as the controlling faculty of the soul. If the passions of the spirit and desires of the appetite are left unchecked, they will lead the individual into a fantasy world of deception. If passions and desires are allowed to override reason, **appearance** becomes confused with **reality.** People who succumb to their physical appetites and vain ambitions may come to believe that transitory and material pleasures will bring happiness, when in fact this is a delusion. Wealth and power, for example, do not guarantee happiness. Rich, powerful, and influential people frequently die unhappy and alone. The physical pleasures derived from one's sexual exploits may be momentarily satisfying or titillating, but they eventually can become empty or emotionally bankrupt and, therefore, unfulfilling in the long run. According to Plato, the belief that appetites and passions are ultimately the source of happiness is **false knowledge,** reflecting an ignorance which contributes to disharmony and moral evil in one's life. True knowledge, happiness, and a harmoniously functioning personality can result only when reason is given primacy of place in life.

1.7   TYPES OF CORRUPT MORAL CHARACTER

In *The Republic,* Plato presents a number of character profiles that reflect the various ways in which people can fall short of the ideal moral personality. These characters are given descriptive, political labels. Plato believes that there is a kind of parallel between society and the individual. Corresponding to each type of imperfect society, there is a certain type of morally degenerate individual or inferior character type. The four imperfect types of society include timarchy, oligarchy, democracy, and tyranny.[7] The corresponding individuals have either timarchic, oligarchic, democratic, or tyrannical characters. A description of each type of character is given below.

1.7   Timarchic Character

The dominant force in the **timarchic character** is spirit. Such an individual is highly ambitious, energetic, and athletic.[8] The "jock" who thinks of nothing but winning and displaying athletic prowess is typical of the timarchic character. Such an individual is also very self-willed and confident in external appearance. The person is usually less well-educated, though, and only superficially cultivated. This kind of person seems ready to listen but displays an inability to express himself or herself. Such an individual is polite and obediant to authority but, due to an imperfect education, lacks a proper sense of superiority toward subordinates. The timarchic person is not truly happy. Beneath the external veneer of confidence and prowess, one finds in the timarchic character inner uncertainty and conflict. One could well imagine how a life ruled by the passions of pride and ambition could be riddled with insecurity. For example, people at the top of the ladder of success may perceive only one way to go — down. They may also become jealous and begrudge the success of others. Having achieved ambitious goals, people may find that their single-minded pursuits have left them financially unstable or poverty-stricken, lacking the necessities of a comfortable economic existence. The important point here is that the timarchic person is destined to have a disordered soul. The apparent happiness produced by success and ambition is ultimately undermined by underlying fears, jealousies, and insecurities. A life governed by passion or spirit, that is, one which feeds off of things like success, glory, and honor, is ultimately doomed to unhappiness.

1.7   Oligarchic Character

A second way of falling short of Plato's moral ideal is by developing an **oligarchic character.** In *The Republic*, Plato illustrates how children could develop this type of personality structure. He points out how easy it is for offspring of the timarchic character to become disillusioned. Ambitious parents pursuing success and honor may struggle an entire lifetime only to meet with political ruin or financial disaster. As a result, children of the timarchic character may dethrone courage and ambition as idols of worship. Desire, profit seeking, and acquisitiveness may replace them and be elevated to the throne. When individuals become motivated primarily by appetite and a desire to earn a fortune, they fall under Plato's category of oligarchic character. According to Plato, there is no transition quicker or more violent than the one from **ambition** to **avarice.**

People possessing an oligarchic character are interested in satisfying only **necessary** wants. They do not indulge in other **unnecessary** expenses. Such people may be said to have a mean and wretched character. One can expect them always to be "on the make," putting something by another. The oligarchic character represents, nevertheless, a type of personality which is widely admired in a materialistic, business-oriented society. For example, many people today stand in awe of those who have the manipulative skills to "sell snow to an Eskimo." Because money and profit are the basic driving forces of the oligarchic character, the person will be dishonest when able. The only deterrent is fear of punishment. There is certainly no **moral conviction** or taming of desire by reason.

The problem with having an oligarchic character is that one is never really at **peace** with oneself. Though this character enjoys a certain degree of respectability in society, the person does not really experience the **inner tranquility** of an integrated and balanced personality. The oligarchic character is a poor competitor and is unwilling to spend in order to pursue nonmonetary ambitions. Though this character's personal ambitions or achievements in public life never amount to much, neither do his or her financial losses. In the end, the oligarchic character is able to save or invest money and, hence, to increase his or her net worth.

1.7   **Democratic Character**

In contrast to the oligarchic character who distinguishes between necessary and unnecessary desires, the **democratic character** does not. All desires or appetites are treated equally. Thus, the person having this character profile spends as much money, time, and trouble on the necessary desires as on the unnecessary ones. For the democratic personality, no pleasure is underprivileged as each gets its fair share of encouragement. This type of character lives from day to day, indulging in any momentary pleasure which presents itself. The pleasures are varied. Plato says:

> One day it's wine, women and song, the next water to drink and a strict diet; one day it's hard physical training, the next indolence and careless ease, and then a period of philosophic study. Often he takes to politics and keeps jumping to his feet and saying or doing whatever comes into his head. Sometimes all his ambitions and efforts are military, sometimes they are all directed to success in business. There's no order or restraint in his life, and he reckons his way of living is pleasant, free and happy, and sticks to it through thick and thin.[9]

People displaying a democratic character are versatile. This is because they lack principles. The problem is that if people do not live a rational principled life, then diverse and incompatible pleasures, appetites, and passions can pull them in different directions at the same time. Their personalities are consequently not integrated and functioning harmoniously. Individuals with a democratic character are torn apart inside. As Plato says, there is no order or restraint. Rather, there is disorder and lack of control. Persons obsessively pursuing different and sometimes conflicting pleasures cannot avoid becoming disorganized and fragmented. Their lives exhibit a definite lack of rational coherence and direction. Democratic people are like children in a candy store. They are excited but torn apart inside because they want everything in the store at the same time — and this is impossible.

Plato speculates about how the democratic character is formed. He believes that people raised in a strict oligarchic household, for example, where unnecessary pleasures have been denied, eventually may be lured by those people outside the family who do enjoy them. A basic diet for instance becomes no longer sufficient or satisfactory. A desire grows for luxurious or exotic food. Simple tastes are replaced by sophisticated and extravagant tastes. Unnecessary desires, immediate pleasures, and extravagant tastes eventually transform the oligarchic person into a democratic character. Plato writes:

> When a young man, brought up in the narrow economical way we have described, gets a taste of the drones' honey and gets into brutal and dangerous company, where he can be provided with every variety and refinement of pleasure, . . . the result [is] that his internal oligarchy starts turning into a democracy.[10]

1.7 Tyrannical Character

According to Plato the **tyrannical character** is the worst, being the most unhappy and undesirable. It is essentially similar to the criminal personality. People with a tyrannical character suffer from a kind of mania. They possess one **master passion** which controls all other idle desires. This master passion becomes so powerful that it runs wild, causing madness in the individual. The object of this passion may be sex, alcohol, or other drugs. In the tyrannical personality, no shame or guilt is experienced. All discipline is swept away and usurped by madness. Thus, tyrannical people are lawless, immoral individuals driven by drunkenness, lust, and craziness. While all of us have aggressive and bestial desires, evidenced especially in dreams, most people are able to control them — not so, however, with the tyrant.

If and when tyrants have spent all of their money enabling them to indulge in their master passion, they will start borrowing to satisfy it. When no longer able to borrow, they may then proceed to rob, commit fraud, or engage in acts of violence. Tyrannical characters become thieves, pick-pockets, and kidnappers and may even sink so low as to become church robbers or murderers.

1.8 THE JUST PERSON OR PHILOSOPHER RULER

The ideal moral character is exemplified by Plato's notion of the **just person** who, in *The Republic's* utopian society, functions as one of the **philosopher rulers**. The philosopher ruler is a morally virtuous person. Such an individual is **temperate**. No physical appetites or material desires become enslaving for that individual. The just person is his own master. Appetites are regulated by rational understanding. The morally virtuous philosopher ruler also displays the virtue of **courage**, a passion which supports reason in its judgments and decisions to act. Plato says,

"He is deemed courageous whose spirit retains in pleasure and in pain the commands of reason about what he ought or ought not to fear . . ."[11] For Plato, the morally virtuous person is also **wise**. A wise person is one who governs the soul by reason. This individual knows what is best for each of the three elements of the human character. A wise person "has in him that little part which rules, and which proclaims these commands [of reason]; that part too being supposed to have a knowledge of what is for the interest of each of the three parts of the whole . . ."[12] Finally, the philosopher ruler is **just**. In the context of personality functioning and moral character, the notion of being just does not entail considerations of social rights or the treatment of others. Rather, it pertains to a state of inner being. Just people have integrated personalities. Within them, reason, emotion, and desire function harmoniously together. There is no inner rebellion or disorder of the soul, but rather tranquility and calm. The just person does not allow the three elements of the soul to interfere with one another. The philosopher ruler has reason as the controlling faculty of the soul. As a consequence, he or she is able to distinguish between appearance and reality. The morally virtuous ruler possesses a knowledge of true goodness. Informed by such knowledge, this person appreciates those things which bring genuine and lasting happiness. The philosopher ruler is not lured by the "drone's honey" or seduced by the power monger's prestige and influence. The philosopher ruler understands well how a life dominated by passions (spirit) and desires (appetite) ultimately ends in unhappiness, anxiety, and despair. Only a life of reason and a disinterested pursuit of truth and goodness is fulfilling in the end. It is by living a life of reason that we fulfill our distinctive function as human beings and live the morally good life. Reason allows us to acquire knowledge of goodness, the ultimate basis of moral virtue. The point should be underscored here, then, that ignorance leads to moral corruption and unhappiness, while knowledge of goodness leads to moral virtue and happiness. Once people know what is good, they will do what is good. A problem for seekers of knowledge of goodness is that it does not permit direct statement. Plato says that just as sight needs not only the eye and the object of sight, but the sun as well, so too understanding requires not only the mind and objects of understanding, but also the **good,** which acts as the source of intelligibility. Truth can only be perceived and known when illuminated by the good.[13]

A person who knows true goodness and acts upon that knowledge does not preoccupy himself or herself with matters of beauty, strength, health, riches, and power. The ideal moral person will focus attention upon the soul, regarding it as most important. The just person will regulate bodily habits and training. Such individuals will not surrender to brutal and irrational pleasures; nor will they allow themselves to be flattered or dazzled by the foolish applause and adulation of the world, while building up riches to their own harm.[14] The just person "will gladly accept and enjoy such honors as he deems likely to make him a better man; but those, whether private or public, which are likely to disorder his life, he will avoid."[15] The philosopher ruler will take care to ensure that there is no disharmony within his or her soul.

PROGRESS CHECK 1.1

Instructions: *Fill in the blanks with the appropriate responses below.*

reason
teleology
spirit
knowledge
ignorance
idols of worship
inner peace
timarchic character
oligarchic character
philosopher ruler

self-realization ethics
appetite
ambition
tripartite
disorder
appearance
avarice
democratic character
tyrannical character
master passion

1. According to Plato, the cause of moral evil and personal unhappiness is _____.
2. In the development of an oligarchic character, one experiences a transition from ambition to _____ as the dominant motivating force in life.
3. Plato's ideal moral personality type is exemplified by the _____.
4. The faculty of the soul having success, glory and honor as target objects is called _____.
5. The faculty of the soul which aims at goals like sexual gratification and the accumulation of material possessions is called _____.
6. The tyrannical character is driven by a _____.
7. Plato conceptualizes the human soul in terms of a three-part or _____ division.
8. The fact that Plato focuses on matters of developing personal character and states of mental being makes his moral theory a type of _____.
9. Ignorance causes us to confuse _____ with reality.
10. The most unhappy and corrupt personality type for Plato is the _____.
11. The doctrine of _____ holds that things develop along the lines of the purposes for which they were designed.
12. The object of reason is _____.
13. Tranquility or _____ is a major goal of self-realization.
14. The _____ makes no distinction between necessary and unnecessary desires.
15. Disharmony or _____ of the soul produces unhappiness in the individual.
16. The _____ has spirit as the dominant motivational force in life.

17. Money, profit seeking, and acquisitiveness are essential ingredients in the
_____.

18. Money, sex, drugs, alcohol, fame, glory, and honor are all _____.

19. The faculty of _____ is the controlling factor in the ideal moral personality.

20. Having _____ may be essential in success, but it does not guarantee economic security.

SUMMARY

1. Self-Realization Ethics
   Reflected by Plato's moral theory
   Concerned with human character
   Asks "What constitutes the good life?" and "What sort of individual should I strive to become?"

2. Teleology
   Doctrine stating that the development of anything follows from the purpose for which it was designed

3. Tripartite Division of the Soul
   Elements include reason, appetite, and spirit
      Appetite: biological, instinctive, desire for possessions
      Spirit: drive toward action; target objects include success, fame, glory, and honor
      Reason: ideally the ruling faculty; target objects are knowledge and wisdom

4. Ignorance
   Intimately related to disorder of the soul, unhappiness, and moral evil
   Causes one to confuse appearance with reality
   Produces false knowledge

5. Types of Moral Character
   Timarchic character: spirit dominated jock-type; insecure; superficially cultivated
   Oligarchic character: dominated by desires for money, profit, and acquisitions; disillusioned by goals of timarchic character; replaces ambition with avarice; seeks only necessities; dirty and wretched; lacks moral convictions; lacks inner peace
   Democratic character: all desires and appetites treated equally; versatile but lacking in principles; lacks order and restraint; has extravagant tastes
   Tyrannical character: most unhappy and undesirable criminal personality; ruled by one master passion; discipline usurped by madness, lawless

6. The Just Person or Philosopher Ruler

    Virtuous: temperate, courageous; wise, and just

    Controlled by reason

    Actions and judgments informed by knowledge of goodness

    Not attracted by idols of worship

    Most concerned with perfection of the soul

    Possesses harmonious personality

REFERENCES

Albert, Ethel M., Theodore C. Denise, and Sheldon P. Peterfreund. *Great Traditions in Ethics*, 5th ed., Belmont, CA: Wadsworth, 1984.

Plato. *The Republic*. (trans.) Desmond Lee, 2nd ed. Harmondsworth, England: Penguin Books, 1976.

Runkle, Gerald. *Ethics: An Examination of Contemporary Moral Problems*. Toronto: Holt, Rinehart and Winston, 1982.

NOTES

1. Gerald Runkle, *Ethics: An Examination of Contemporary Moral Problems* (Toronto: Holt, Rinehart and Winston, 1982), p. 3.
2. Ethel M. Albert, Theodore C. Denise, and Sheldon P. Peterfreund, *Great Traditions in Ethics*, 5th ed. (Belmont, CA: Wadsworth, 1984), p. 10.
3. Ibid., p. 10.
4. Runkle, *Ethics*, p. 3.
5. Plato, *The Republic*, 2nd ed., trans. Desmond Lee (Middlesex, England: Penguin Books, 1976), p. 218.
6. Ibid., p. 207.
7. Plato, *The Republic*, pp. 356–420.
8. Ibid., p. 364.
9. Ibid., p. 381.
10. Ibid., p. 378.
11. Plato, cited in Albert, Denise, and Peterfreund, *Great Traditions in Ethics*, p. 20.
12. Ibid.
13. Albert, Denise, and Peterfreund, *Great Traditions in Ethics*, p. 24.
14. Ibid., p. 26.
15. Ibid.

2

ARISTOTLE
AND
MORAL CHARACTER

OVERVIEW

1. Aristotle (384–322 B.C.)
2. Definitions of the Good Life
3. The Distinctive Function of Man
4. The Definition of Virtue and Aristotle's Golden Mean
5. Progress Check
6. Summary
7. References
8. Notes

EDUCATIONAL OBJECTIVES: After reading this chapter the student will be able to:

2.1 Define the concept of teleology.
2.2 Explain how teleological considerations influence Aristotle's ethical perspective.
2.3 Describe different conceptions of happiness and the good life.

2.4 Distinguish between intrinsic and instrumental ends.

2.5 Identify the distinctive function of man.

2.6 Distinguish between professional functions and human functions.

2.7 Define virtue.

2.8 Explain how virtue is related to states of character.

FOCUS QUESTIONS

1. If morally right conduct is not determined by reference to ends, then how else could it be interpreted?
2. Where is man's ultimate good found, in concrete experience or in some transcendent realm? Explain.
3. How is it that the "masses of men" fail to discover what truly leads to happiness?
4. Do you agree with Aristotle's conception of happiness? Why?

ARISTOTLE (384–322 B.C.)

Aristotle was born in Stagira in 384 B.C. He was the son of a physician who lived and worked at the royal court of Amyntas II, king of Macedonia. At the age of 17, Aristotle went to Athens to enroll at the Academy. For 20 years he worked and studied under Plato, for whom he had respect as a philosopher and good feelings as a friend. Upon the death of Plato, Aristotle left Athens and spent a number of years in Asia Minor, where he married Pythias, the niece of a local king. Aristotle eventually returned to Macedonia in order to become tutor to the heir of the throne, namely Alexander, who later became known as Alexander the Great. After an 8-year stay in Macedonia, he left again for Athens in 335–334 B.C. In Athens, Aristotle established a new school called the Lyceum. It was patterned after Plato's Academy insofar as community life, friendliness, intent on learning, and dialogue were emphasized. Many of Aristotle's dialogues with students were conducted while strolling down a garden path (peripatos). In view of this, followers of Aristotle have come to be known as "peripatetics." In 323 B.C. Aristotle felt compelled to leave Athens again. Alexander the Great died suddenly while returning from one of his Asian conquests. The Athenians, who were under the yoke of Alexander, regarded his death as an opportunity to rid themselves of Macedonian control. Knowing his Macedonian ties and fearing the prospect of having to stand trial for impiety like Socrates, Aristotle fled Athens. He died in exile one year later in 322 B.C. Aristotle's wife died somewhat earlier. Aristotle's son, Nichomachus, after whom *Nichomachean Ethics* is named, was born as a product of a domestic union with Herpyllis.

Aristotle wrote on subjects as varied as logic, ethics, aesthetics, metaphysics, biology, physics, psychology, and politics. He had a profound influence on medieval Hebrew, Arabic, and Christian philosophers, most notably Saint Thomas Aquinas and his later scholastic followers who helped to formulate the official moral theology of the Catholic Church. Works by Aristotle include: *Categories, Prior and Posterior Analytics, Physics, On the Heavens, On the Soul, Metaphysics, Nichomachean Ethics, Politics, Rhetoric,* and *Eudemian Ethics.*

2.1 DEFINITIONS OF THE GOOD LIFE
2.2
2.3

Aristotle's philosophy emphasizes the supremacy of our rational capacities. As a **teleologist,** Aristotle believes that everything in nature, including man, has a distinctive end or purpose to achieve. Interpreting morality within a teleological framework, the basic moral question becomes for him: "What is the good at which human behavior aims?"[1]

Aristotle's teacher, Plato, maintained that knowledge of man's good had to be discovered apart from the concrete world of everyday experience. One was forced to go beyond the tangible world where things are imperfect and transitory to a world of intelligible unchanging forms. Knowledge of man's true good required for Plato a rational acquaintance with a supernatural realm. By contrast, Aristotle believes that man's good can be discovered by studying his essential nature and by examining his behavior in daily living.

Aristotle contends that if one focuses on the experience of people, one will find that both the masses and men of culture agree that **"happiness"** is the ultimate good. It is the end toward which all of human behavior is directed. We all wish to find happiness in our lives. The problem, however, is that happiness can be defined in a variety of ways by different people. There appears at first glance to be no consensus.

2.4 To help us get a handle on the definition of happiness as the end of mankind, Aristotle makes a distinction between two types of ends: **instrumental** and **intrinsic.** Acts performed instrumentally are acts done as a means to other ends. Acts performed for their intrinsic worth are acts done for their own sake. They are valued in themselves, not because of what they produce or not because of that to which they lead. To explain what he means by this distinction, Aristotle uses an illustration from war. In war, one finds a number of different activities being performed. Many of these activities, however, when completed turn out to be only means by which other, more distant ends are achieved. Take the bridle-maker, for instance. When the bridle is finished, the craftsman has achieved his end. But the bridle turns out to be a means for the horseman to guide his horse into battle. Similarly, when a carpenter builds a barrack, that goal is attained. The barrack, though, is intended as a means to provide shelter for soldiers. Even attempting to achieve victory in war is not an end in itself; rather, it is a means to create the conditions by which men, as men, can fulfill their purpose.[2]

The failure by men to distinguish between intrinsic and instrumental ends has in part led them to define the good life erroneously. The masses have a tendency to believe that happiness is found in a **life of enjoyment and pleasure.** They believe that happiness can be achieved once sufficient money is accumulated, for example. Aristotle rejects this definition of goodness by pointing out that money is only a **means** to something else, not an end in itself. Money allows people to buy goods and to do various things. Printed bills have little if any worth in themselves. More importantly, a life of materialistic pleasure entails enslavement to the appetites and an existence on the level of brutish beasts. Aristotle also rejects the **life of the statesman** as embodying happiness. The honor and glory sought by the statesman hinge on the approval of others—an approval that can be withdrawn at any time. The pursuit of honor provides a very insecure foundation for lasting happiness. In addition, honor is really only a means. One seeks honor because one believes it will make one happy. If it didn't make one happy and if, say, misery were its result, then honor would likely cease to have any value or desirability. Honor and pleasure are sought for the sake of happiness. Happiness is not sought for the sake of honor and pleasure. Happiness is intrinsically valuable. Honor and pleasure are instrumentally valuable.

If happiness is not to be found in the life of pleasure or in the life of the statesman, then the question remains unanswered as to where in fact it is to be found. Whatever end represents happiness, Aristotle believes it must fulfill three conditions. First, the **ultimate end** for people must be **self-sufficient.**[3] This end must make life desirable and it must lack nothing. Second, this end must be **final.** It must be desirable in itself. In this sense, man's ultimate good is intrinsically, not instrumentally, valuable. Finally, this end must be **attainable.** A goal that cannot be achieved or which is unattainable in principle is likely to lead to frustration and despair. Though all agree that happiness is man's ultimate good, its precise definition is still elusive for the moment.

2.5   THE DISTINCTIVE FUNCTION OF MAN
2.6

Aristotle embarks on his pursuit of man's ultimate good by looking through his "teleologically colored" glasses. According to Aristotle, the "good" of anything refers to the **special function** of that thing. For example, a good pen is one which writes smoothly without skipping or blotting. A good light is one which provides sufficient illumination. Lights and pens have their special functions and how good they are depends on how well they perform their function. Similar is the case with man. In order to discover the ultimate good of man (that is, that which makes him happy), one must identify the unique or distinctive function of human nature. One will lead the good life to the extent one performs his function well. Aristotle's hunt for man's distinctive function begins with a comparison between plants and people. He finds that plants and people have life in common. They both require nourishment and both grow. Aristotle thus concludes that the sort of existence based on nutrition (eating, drinking) and growth is not peculiar to man. Aristotle also compares humans and animals. Humans share with animals a sensory capacity to experience the world. Thus, the life of sensation (sensuality and appetite gratification) is not befitting of humans for it is the life of cattle, horses, and sheep. According to Aristotle, man's peculiar quality is found in reason. Humans can measure, make calculations, evaluate, and plan for the future. Animals and plants cannot do such things. Thus, the fulfillment of man's distinctive function involves the exercise of his **rational capacities.** Happiness is not found in the hedonistic pursuit of pleasure, nor in the glory seeking of the statesman, but in a life of rational contemplation. On this note, the point should be made that one must, for Aristotle, separate a person's craft, profession, or occupation from his or her activity as a human being. One can be a good lawyer without being a good person. Conversely, one can be a good person without being a good lawyer. When the moral question is asked: "What is the good at which human behavior aims?," the good refers not to the functions of different craftsmen or professionals, but to the distinctive quality of man, functioning **as man.** While the occupational functions of lawyers, doctors, and plumbers are different, they all share humankind's unique function of rationality. Understanding this, the good of man becomes the exercise of his rational faculties in accordance with excellence or virtue. Aristotle writes in *Nichomachean Ethics:*

> Man's function then being, as we say, a kind of life—that is to say, exercise of his faculties and action of various kinds with reason—the good man's function is to do this well and beautifully [or nobly]. But the function of anything is done well when it is done in accordance with the proper excellence of that thing. If this be so the result is that the good of man is exercise of his faculties in accordance with excellence or virtue, or, if there be more than one, in accordance with the best and most complete virtue.[4]

2.7 THE DEFINITION OF VIRTUE AND ARISTOTLE'S GOLDEN MEAN

Saying that the good of man entails an activity of reason in accordance with virtue requires that one understand what is meant by **virtue.** Virtue, here, does not refer to an excellence of the body but of the soul. There are two kinds of virtue: **intellectual** and **moral.** Intellectual virtues involve our ability to think. They deal with rational principles. The practice of intellectual virtue leads to such things as philosophical wisdom and understanding. By contrast, moral virtues entail acting correctly in accordance with reason. Moral virtue neither comes by nature nor is opposed to nature. Rather, nature provides the capacity for acquiring virtue through appropriate training. For example, people become just by performing just acts. Virtues like temperance and courage are not inborn or innate. They are cultivated and perfected by the development of specific habits.

Aristotle clarified further what he means by moral virtue by breaking down human personality into three elements.[5] These elements include the (1) **passions,** (2) **faculties,** and (3) **states of character.** Passions include emotions such as anger and fear while faculties are the abilities to feel such things. Since anger and fear or their respective faculties are not praiseworthy or blameworthy in themselves, Aristotle concludes that moral virtue must rest in one's state of character. More precisely, moral virtue becomes for Aristotle a state of character enabling people to perform their functions by aiming at intermediary points between opposing extremes of excess and deficiency. The person who could be described as morally virtuous is the one who lives according to the **Golden Mean.** Aristotle writes:

2.8   Virtue, then, is a state of character concerned with choice, lying in a mean, i.e., the mean relative to us, this being determined by a rational principle, and by that principle by which the man of practical wisdom would determine it. Now it is a mean between two vices, that which depends on excess and that which depends on defect; and again it is a mean because the vices respectively fall short of or exceed what is right in both passions and actions, while virtue both finds and chooses that which is intermediate. Hence in respect of its substance and the definition which states its essence virtue is a mean, with regard to what is best and right an extreme.[6]

The fact that one has performed a virtuous act is no guarantee that one is actually virtuous. For instance, a fighting soldier may run into battle because he is more afraid of his commanding officer than he is of the enemy. Such an act would not be indicative of courage, though running into battle is something the courageous man would do. Likewise, a person may avoid stealing because of fear of punishment, not because of any virtuous trait. For Aristotle, the virtuous person must enjoy being virtuous. The virtuous individual chooses to be virtuous and does not regret it. Virtue becomes its own reward. Thus, charitable behavior is displayed cheerfully and joyfully, not with bitterness and reluctance. In the context of physical pleasure, Aristotle writes:

He who abstains from the pleasures of the body and rejoices in the abstinence is temperate, while he who is vexed at having to abstain is profligate; and again, he who faces danger with pleasure, or, at any rate, without pain, is courageous, but he to whom this is painful is a coward. For moral virtue or excellence is closely concerned with pleasure and pain. It is pleasure that moves us to do what is base, and pain that moves us to refrain from what is noble. And therefore, as Plato says, man needs to be so trained from his youth up as to find pleasure and pain in the right objects. This is what sound education means.[7]

Not only must temperate acts be performed gladly or without pain and regret if they are to be considered virtuous, they must also fulfill certain other conditions. First, individuals must **know** what they are doing. Second, they must consciously and deliberately **choose** to perform "virtuous" acts. Third, they must **perform them for their own sake.** And finally, the action performed must not be an isolated incident but rather a manifestation of an **enduring state** of character. One donation does not a charitable person make. Nor is giving only to enhance one's reputation or to reduce one's taxable income a virtue according to Aristotle. The act of giving must be performed for itself. If one buys a desired item at an auction and then discovers later that the proceeds will be forwarded to some charitable cause, one has not acted virtuously, but rather self-interestedly or materialistically.

Virtue does not apply to all activities, and a proper mean does not exist for some types of behavior. While one may drink or eat in moderation, one cannot behave virtuously by murdering, stealing, or committing adultery in moderation; nor can one establish a virtuous level of hatred, envy, or spite. These attitudes and behaviors are bad in themselves. Since these things are always wrong, it is absurd to look for moderation or excess where they are concerned.

In his *Nichomachean Ethics*, Aristotle provides a list of virtues representing means and vices representing extremes. Courage, for instance, is the virtuous mean between the vices of cowardice and foolhardiness; modesty is the mean between bashfulness and shamelessness; righteous indignation is the middle between envy and malice; while aspiration is the virtuous point between ambition and laziness.[8]

In closing, the point should be stressed that Aristotle defines good not so much in terms of following a system of ultimate principles, obeying rules, or calculating pleasurable consequences, but rather in terms of human excellence. One lives the good life by developing a particular state of character—one is predisposed to choose the Golden Mean between deficiency and excess.

PROGRESS CHECK 2.1

Instructions: Fill in the blanks with the appropriate responses listed below.

intellectual   teleologist
virtue   honor

happiness

special function

moral

the Golden Mean

instrumentally

intrinsically

states of character

1. A philosopher who determines the goodness or rightness of some action or person by reference to ends and purposes could be described as a _____.
2. Actions performed for the sake of something else are _____ valuable.
3. Actions performed for their own sake are _____ valuable.
4. The statesman's life is one based on a pursuit of _____.
5. Aristotle contends that both the masses and men of culture agree that _____ is the ultimate end of humankind.
6. One can determine the ultimate good of anything by making reference to its _____.
7. Courage, modesty, and righteous indignation are all examples of _____.
8. Living the good life, for Aristotle, is less concerned with following rules and principles and more concerned with cultivating appropriate _____.
9. If one lived one's life in moderation, avoiding excess and deficiency, one would live according to _____.
10. There are two types of virtue: _____ and _____.

SUMMARY

1. Teleology

   Everything in nature including man has a distinctive end or purpose to achieve.

2. Happiness

   It is concerned with the ultimate good.

   It is the end toward which human behavior is directed.

3. Types of Ends

   Intrinsic ends are valuable in themselves.

   Instrumental ends are valuable as a means to something else.

4. Lifestyles

   Life of Enjoyment: materialism, physical pleasure

   Life of the Statesman: honor, glory, ambition

   Life of Contemplation: exercise of reason in accordance with virtue

5. Criteria of Ultimate End

   Self-sufficient

   Final

   Attainable

6. Special Function of Man

It is found in his rational capacities, that is, in his ability to evaluate, measure, and calculate

7. Two Types of Virtue

Intellectual: ability to think; deals with rational principles; leads to philosophical wisdom

Moral: deals with correct conduct, developed initially through habit; involves a state of character; is a mean between excess and deficiency

8. Conditions of Virtue:

Virtuous/temperate acts must be performed gladly.

One must know what one is doing.

One must deliberately choose to perform virtuous acts.

Virtuous acts must be done for their own sake.

9. A Partial List of Virtues:

Courage: cowardice vs. foolhardiness

Modesty: bashfulness vs. shamelessness

Righteous Indignation: envy vs. malice

Aspiration: ambition vs. laziness

REFERENCES

Albert, Ethel, Theodore Denise and Sheldon Peterfreund, *Great Traditions in Ethics*. Belmont, CA: Wadsworth, 1984.

Allan, D. J. *The Philosophy of Aristotle*. Toronto: Oxford University Press, 1963.

Aristotle. *Nichomachean Ethics*. trans., Terence Irwin, Indianapolis: Hackett Publishing, 1985.

Hardie, W. F. R., *Aristotle's Ethical Theory*, 2nd ed. Toronto: Oxford University Press, 1980.

Solomon, Robert. *Morality and the Good Life: An Introduction to Ethics through Classical Sources*. Toronto: McGraw-Hill, 1984.

Stumpf, Samuel. *Philosophy: History and Problems*. Toronto: McGraw-Hill, 1983.

NOTES

1. Samuel Stumpf, *Philosophy: History and Problems* (Toronto: McGraw-Hill, 1983), p. 96.
2. Ibid., pp. 91–97.
3. Aristotle, *Nicomachean Ethics*, trans. Terence Irwin (Indianopolis, IN: Hackett Publishing, 1985), pp. 53–57.
4. Aristotle, quoted from Robert Solomon (ed.) *Morality and the Good Life* (Toronto: McGraw-Hill, 1984), p. 62.
5. Aristotle, *Nichomachean Ethics*, as translated in Ethel M. Albert, Theodore C. Denise, and Sheldon P. Peterfreund, *Great Traditions in Ethics*, 5th ed. (Belmont, CA: Wadsworth, 1984).
6. Aristotle, *Nichomachean Ethics*, quoted from Ethel M. Albert, Theodore C. Denise, and Sheldon P. Peterfreund, *Great Traditions in Ethics* p. 41.
7. Aristotle, *Nichomachean Ethics*, quoted from Solomon, *Morality and the Good Life*, p. 73.
8. See Solomon, *Morality and the Good Life*, p. 78.

3

IMMANUEL KANT
AND
DUTIES TO ONESELF

144,420

EDUCATIONAL OBJECTIVES: After reading this chapter the student will be able to:

3.1   Explain why Immanuel Kant believes the concept of individual morality is important.

3.2   Elucidate Kant's position on the basis of self-regarding moral duties.

3.3   Define "proper self-respect."

3.4   Explain how conscience acts as a type of sanction.

3.5   Distinguish among the concepts of self-love (Philautia), arrogance, and self-esteem.

3.6   State why self-mastery is important in the context of individual morality.

3.7   Explain how self-mastery may be achieved.

3.8   Discuss some of the obstacles interfering with the development of self-mastery.

3.9   Distinguish between good intentions and good actions.

3.10 Comment on the difference between ills and wickedness.

3.11 Outline the duties we have toward ourselves and our bodies.

3.12 Provide Kant's explanation for why work is essential to life.

3.13 Distinguish between necessities and amenities and explain Kant's views on them.

3.14 State the dangers of living a life of comfort.

FOCUS QUESTIONS

1. Do you believe that morality is exclusively a "social" concept and that it deals only with interpersonal relations? Why or why not? Does Immanuel Kant make room in his philosophy for a personal or individual morality?

2. In what sense are "duties to oneself" prerequisites for social morality?

3. How are humans capable of lowering themselves below the level of animals?

4. What is the distinction between duties of prudence and duties of morality?

5. What exactly is meant by the concept of proper self-respect?

6. Is Kant in favor of individuals humbling themselves before others? Why or why not?

7. What is the problem with deathbed confessions and repentences?

8. How can conscience assist in the regulation of moral conduct?

9. In what respect, if any, can it be said that it is better to be worthy of self-esteem than love?

10. How is self-mastery important to individual morality? What must we do in order to gain more of it?

11. Why must we be wary of imagination in our lives?

12. Morally speaking, are we free to do with our own bodies anything that we wish? Why or why not?
13. What is involved in the proper maintenance of the body, according to Kant?
14. Why is it suggested to us by Kant that our lives not become dependent upon comforts?
15. If you accepted Kant's moral philosophy, what specific changes would you be forced to make in your life?

IMMANUEL KANT (1724-1804)

Immanuel Kant was born in 1724 in the East Prussian town of Königsberg. Belonging to the lower middle class, his parents were deeply religious. Although throughout his life, Kant always maintained an honest respect for religion and a deep moral sense, he eventually abandoned the puritanical pietism that had been a dominating influence in his family. Immanuel Kant's life could hardly be described as eventful and is now famous for its routine. He arose the same time each day and had a fixed hour for all of his daily activities. It has been said that people could set their clocks by Kant's afternoon walks at half past three. Each day he would put on his grey coat and with bamboo cane in hand would walk down Lime Tree Avenue, now called "Philosopher's Walk" in honor of Kant. Kant never married and in contrast to many of his contemporaries who were filled with the spirit of travel, Kant never ventured more than 40 miles in any direction of Königsberg. This lack of physical travel apparently did not affect the wandering intellectual genius of Kant, however. For more than a dozen years, he lectured as a *privatdozent* at the University of Königsberg in subjects as varied as mathematics, logic, geography, history, and philosophy. He also worked as a family tutor before being appointed professor of philosophy at the University of Königsberg in 1770. Kant is considered by many philosophers today as the greatest thinker since Plato and Aristotle. His influence is evident insofar as his ethical investigations still serve as the basis for much of the debate found in contemporary moral philosophy and applied ethics. His important works include: *Foundations of the Metaphysics of Morals, The Metaphysical Principles of Virtue, Lectures on Ethics,* and *The Critique of Pure Reason.*

3.1   INDIVIDUAL MORALITY AND DUTIES TO ONESELF

In *Lectures on Ethics*, Immanuel Kant addresses the issue of individual morality. He does so by employing the concept of "duties to oneself." Although it goes almost without saying that morality involves our relations and duties to others, Kant contends that individual morality should not be an afterthought or considered an addendum to ethical inquiry. Too often moral discussions are restricted to social matters and interpersonal conflict. Kant insists, however, that "our duties towards ourselves are of primary importance and should have pride of place."[1] Arguing that we can expect nothing from a person who dishonors his own person, he maintains that, "a prior condition of our duty to others is our duty to ourselves; we can fulfill the former only insofar as we first fulfill the latter."[2] To illustrate his point, Kant asks us to consider the drunkard. Such a person may do no harm to others and, provided his own constitution is strong, he may not even harm himself. Nonetheless, Kant claims that the drunkard becomes for us an object of moral contempt. Such an individual degrades his person and loses his manhood. He loses his inner worth as a moral subject. Kant writes:

> Only if our worth as human beings is intact can we perform our other duties; for it is the foundation stone of all other duties. A man who has destroyed and cast away his personality, has no intrinsic worth, and can no longer perform any manner of duty.[3]

3.2   THE BASIS OF SELF-REGARDING DUTIES

After underscoring the importance of individual morality, Kant proceeds to discuss in his *Lectures* the basis of self-regarding duties. For him, the ultimate determining principle of his ethical system is **freedom.** This freedom is not unbridled, however. Freedom, for Kant, must be subjected to what he calls **objective determination,** which places restrictions on the exercise of freedom. These restrictions stem from rational understanding. When freedom is understood and used properly, it is subjected to the supreme rule which necessitates that one ought to restrain one's freedom so that it conforms to the essential "ends of humanity." In conforming to the essential ends of humanity, one is not merely acting according to inclination. Kant writes: "[I]f man gives free rein to his inclinations, he sinks lower than an animal because he then lives in a state of disorder which does not exist among animals."[4] Animals act by inclinations determined by biological, genetic, and hormonal factors. In their case, disorderliness is impossible. In the case of man, if we give free rein to our inclinations we are likely to degenerate into complete savage disorder. This state of disorder that cannot exist among animals places us below them. For Kant, if we are to retain our human dignity we should not enslave ourselves to our inclinations, but determine for ourselves through rational thought what those inclinations will be and what constraints will be placed upon them. In determining how we should act, Kant says, "The supreme rule is that in all the actions which affect himself a man should so conduct himself that every exercise of his power is compatible with the fullest employment of them."[5] In conducting himself in this fashion, man is acting in a way consistent with the essential ends of humanity. Any actions which incapacitate us or make us incapable of using our freedom and our powers fully are wrong. For example, if one drinks too much, one's thinking becomes impaired and one's physical coordination deteriorates. Under these circumstances, one cannot exercise full freedom as one's physical and psychological powers are weakened.

Self-regarding duties are consistent with the ends of humanity, not only in the sense that they allow for the fullest use of freedom, but in the sense that they are in keeping with the worth and dignity of man. These duties are not prudential. They are not determined by what is simply advantageous to ourselves. For Kant, "not self-favor but self-esteem should be the principle of our duties towards ourselves. This means that our actions must be in keeping with the worth of man."[6]

With respect to action per se, Kant claims there are two grounds for it. First of all, as already noted, there is inclination. This belongs to our animal nature. Second, there is humanity, something to which our inclinations must be subjected. In Kant's view, "Our duties to ourselves are negative; they restrict our freedom in respect of our inclinations, which aim at our own welfare."[7] Kant draws a parallel here between law and negative self-referring duties. He points out that just as the law places constraints on our freedom in our relations with others, so do our duties to ourselves restrict our freedom in dealing with ourselves. As moral subjects, we must not become unworthy. Our actions must be in keeping with humanity itself.

3.3 PROPER SELF-RESPECT

If we are to maintain our human worth and dignity, we must develop proper self-respect, which is comprised to two components: (1) humility and (2) noble pride.[8] At first glance, these two components of self-respect may appear to be incompatible or inconsistent, but this is not so. We display noble pride when we consider ourselves equals in comparison with other human beings. We do not see ourselves as their superiors, but neither do we have a low opinion of ourselves when we measure ourselves against others. According to Kant, **self-deprecation** in comparison to others is in fact a disguised form of pride that does not represent true humility at all. It may even represent servility and lack of spirit. For Kant, we have a right to consider ourselves just as valuable as any other individual. Since we are all representatives of humankind, we all ought to hold ourselves in high esteem. We should all have noble pride.

Humility, then, comes not from having a lower opinion of ourselves than of others but from something else. We are humbled when faced with the moral law. Recognizing our imperfections in view of the perfect moral law, we curb our self-conceit and develop true humbleness. If we develop a low opinion of ourselves, this low opinion should derive from a recognition that we are weak in our transgressions of the law. We should not, however, become dejected or despairing because we do not feel strong enough to follow the law. The remedy for dejection is found in God. Our "weakness and infirmity will be supplemented by the help of God if we but do the utmost that the consciousness of our capacity tells us we are able to do."[9] Through faith and prayer, we can find hope and the necessary strength to act in accordance with the moral law.

Though we should, as imperfect beings, be humbled before the moral law, we may nonetheless possess self-esteem. This self-esteem comes from self-love. It contributes to a certain favoritism and partiality toward ourselves. Kant labels this type of self-esteem "pragmatic self-respect."[10] It is based on rules of prudence and is valuable to us insofar as it helps to promote confidence in ourselves.

Kant distinguishes between pragmatic self-respect and moral self-esteem. The latter is grounded not in comparisons with others or on prudential rules, but in human worth. We base our moral self-esteem on how well we act in accordance with the moral law. In other words, we develop moral self-esteem in conforming to the moral law. It acts as a standard of ethical evaluation. Rather than taking pride in comparisons with others (who may be degenerate), self-satisfaction is gained by acting according to the perfect moral law.

3.4   CONSCIENCE

When moral duties are violated in the social realm of experience, a number of sanctions may be imposed. For example, moral wrongdoers such as thieves may be incarcerated. They may also be ostracized from a particular community or group of persons. Recognized authorities may pass judgments and impose sentences of punishment. In the case of individual morality, however, where self-regarding duties are at issue, it is not usually the case that external sanctions are imposed by social authorities. Rather, moral judgments and sanctions are more typically self-imposed by **conscience.**

Immanuel Kant defines conscience as "an instinct to pass judgment upon ourselves in accordance with moral laws."[11] Conscience is like a judge insofar as it acquits us of any wrongdoing or accuses us for violations of the moral law.

When we evaluate our actions as right or wrong, good or bad, we should be careful to distinguish between **judgments of prudence** and **judgments of conscience.** In the former case, there is a semblance of conscience, but only that. What appears sometimes as a judgment of conscience is really not. As an example, Kant uses deathbed repentance. He contends that such repentance is not truly remorse for the immorality of previous acts, but is more likely fear of the eternal punishments soon to come. Were death not imminent, there would be no fear and, hence, no remorse. Kant writes: "He who goes in fear of being prosecuted for a wicked deed, does not reproach himself on the score of the wickedness of his misdemeanor, but on the score of the painful consequences which await him; such a one has no conscience, but only a semblance of it."[12] To have a conscience, then, one must have a sense of the inherent wickedness of the act being contemplated or committed, irrespective of the consequences which flow from the act. A gambler may become enraged and reproach himself for his folly in losing his wealth and property. However, he may have no qualms about his immoral vice per se, only the unfortunate consequences of it. Kant concludes therefore that, "We must guard against confusion here: reproaches for the consequences of imprudence must not be confused with reproaches for breaches of morality."[12] On this note, Kant makes a recommendation to teachers. He cautions them to look and see whether students repent immoral deeds from a true sense of their wickedness, or whether they feel remorse only because they must face a punishing judge.

Appreciating the inherent wickedness of immoral acts is not enough for conscience. If its moral judgments are to have validity, they must be felt and enforced. There must be moral repentance, regret, or penitence. Whining and lamentation are not enough though. There must also be an effort put forward to do what is demanded to satisfy the moral law. Penitence alone is vain as long as we do not satisfy the debt we owe to the moral law. We must, for example, endeavor to remedy any injustices committed against others. Without this effort our moral conscience sits idle. (Complete Progress Check 3.1.)

3.5 SELF-LOVE

Given that Christian morality, for example, commands us to love our neighbors, the question arises in the context of individual morality as to whether or not we have a duty to love ourselves. Addressing this issue, Kant defines one form of self-love as "an inclination to be well-content with ourselves in judging our own perfection."[14] He calls this self-love **philautia.** For Kant, philautia must be distinguished from arrogance. With **arrogance,** there are unwarranted claims to merit. Typically a narrow and indulgent view of the moral law is taken by the arrogant individual. The individual's moral conscience is therefore not impartial in its judgments and evaluations. By contrast, self-loving persons do not pretend to possess more moral perfections than they actually have. They are merely self-satisfied and do not take themselves to task. According to Kant, both philautia and arrogance are undesirable. As was intimated, arrogance is harmful in its partiality. About self-love, Kant writes: "Moral philautia, which gives a man a high opinion of himself in respect of his moral perfections, is detestable; it springs up when we preen ourselves upon the goodness of our disposition, and think to promote the welfare of the world by empty wishes and romantic ideas."[15] What we should cultivate, according to Kant, is self-esteem. If the choice we have is between either becoming an object worthy of esteem or of love, then we should pick the former. Kant writes:

But a man is required to be worthy, not so much of love, as of respect and of esteem. A conscientious and righteous man who is impartial and will accept no bribe, is not an object of love, and because he is conscientious in the matter of what he accepts, he will have few opportunities to act with magnanimity and love, and he will consequently not be thought lovable by his fellows. But he finds happiness in being considered by his fellows worthy of esteem; virtue is his true, intrinsic worth. A man might therefore be an object of esteem without being an object of love, because he refuses to curry favor. We can also love a bad man without in the least respecting him. Whatever increases self-love ought to be rejected from moral philosophy, and only that ought to be commended which makes one worthy of respect, e.g., doing one's duty to oneself, righteousness and conscientiousness; these things may not make us objects of love, but we can hold our head high, though not defiantly, and look men straight in the eye, for we have worth.[16]

3.6   SELF-MASTERY

Earlier it was stated that a prior condition of our duties to others is our duty to ourselves. If we are to obey our self-regarding duties, we must develop **self-mastery.** This is the objective condition of morality to which Kant alludes. This self-mastery involves discipline. It reflects in its discipline respect for one's own person in relation to the essential **ends of humanity.**

Immanuel Kant distinguishes between **moral discipline** and **pragmatic discipline of prudence.** Rules of prudence serve our sensibilities. Our rational understanding is used as a means to satisfy our inclinations; the understanding is thus subordinated to the ends of sensibility. Moral discipline, on the other hand, endeavors to master and control our sensibilities and sensuous acts not by prudence but by moral laws. For Kant, self-mastery is one's highest duty to oneself.[17] In mastering ourselves through moral discipline, we subject all our principles and faculties to free will.

The biggest problem facing our development of self-mastery is affect. The moral law contains precepts but lacks a **motivational component.** What is absent is the compelling force of moral feeling. Without the appropriate moral sentiments, we can exercise sound moral judgment in recognizing that an act is evil and deserves punishment, for example, but may commit that act nonetheless.

3.7   In order to gain self-mastery, we must weaken the opposing forces which militate against the development of moral feelings. We must extinguish those tendencies which emanate from sensuous motives. This is done by **self-scrutiny.** We must observe ourselves and present to our internal judge, that is, our conscience, a regular account of our actions. Through continual practice we will strengthen our moral impulses. Through self-cultivation we will develop a habit of desire and aversion toward what is morally good or bad, respectively. In time, moral strength and motivation will emerge. Our sensuous inclinations will be weakened and eventually overcome. In disciplining our inclinations and gaining mastery over them, we become lords over ourselves.

In mastering and developing ourselves morally, we are not seeking to perfect our skills or maximize our personal powers. Doing our best in business or sport involves acting on rules of prudence which are pragmatic. Acting on these rules is conducive to furthering our self-interests and personal welfare. By contrast, moral perfection of oneself for Kant entails excluding everything which has no bearing on our inner worth and human dignity. Striving to achieve moral perfection entails subjecting "everything to our own will, insofar as our will directs our actions in conformity with the essential ends of humanity."[18]

3.8   According to Kant, **moral self-perfection** requires that we develop a healthy mind and body. The physical state of the body affects the condition of the mind, which in turn influences the thinking, giving rise to moral conduct. **Imagination** is one power of the mind which impacts on human conduct. The imagination is capable of producing in our minds very vivid and attractive images. As a result, it gives rise to **temptations.** The temptations, images, and related fantasies frequently cause us to offend ourselves and transgress in our duties toward ourselves. Vices may be created, for instance, if we give free rein to our imaginations in titillating us with images of sensual pleasure. Kant suggests that our imaginings actually intensify the allurement of morally prohibited objects and activities. Thus the rational understanding must take control over our imaginations which serve to cast evil spells over us. We must subdue and control our imaginations and not allow our imaginations to control and subdue us.

Self-perfection is a goal which demands that we be wary of our senses as well as of our imaginations. The reason is that the senses have a tendency to betray the understanding; things are not always as they appear. Furthermore, the senses lead to our enjoyment of **base pleasures** in life. Instead of being enslaved by our physical and sensuous appetites, we should "offer to the mind an alternative entertainment to that offered by the senses. We must try to occupy the mind with ideal pleasures, with which all polite learning and literature are concerned."[19]

3.9   Being on guard against the deceptions of sensory experience and the fascinations of the imagination requires **self-observation.** In fact, self-observation is for Kant a duty to oneself. He argues that in our self-observations we should distinguish between our good intentions and our good actions. Greater significance should be attributed to the latter. Kant writes:

> The supreme rule is this: Give good, practical proof of yourselves in your lives by your actions; not by set prayers, but by doing good acts, by work and steadiness, and in particular by righteousness and active benevolence towards your neighbor; then you can see whether you are good.[20]

For Kant, **good intentions** alone are "cheap." We are all capable of having them. We can all have favorable opinions of ourselves by our good intentions. The real test, though, comes when we are confronted with situations demanding action. In these situations we discover the most about ourselves. We may be inclined to take a particular action (for example, helping a neighbor in need), but we will never know whether we could actually perform it until we are required or called upon to do so.

Another dimension of self-mastery includes **suspension of judgment.**

People who suspend judgment do not react spontaneously, that is, thoughtlessly and in a reflexive way, to strong emotions like anger. Reactions are delayed by the control and autocracy of the mind. This same autocracy also enables us to delay our decision making until an issue is fully considered and analyzed.

A strong mind displaying autocracy remains active and efficient when burdened with work, regardless of its nature. The mind is aware of its strength to overcome the discomforts of work. Accepting the work which must be carried out and doing so without vexation or bitterness and resentment reflects a life of dignity. **Mental attitude** and **steadfastness of mind** are thus important ingredients in self-mastery. Though we have distasteful tasks to perform and displeasures to experience, we can still preserve our dignity as humans by our responses to these things.

3.10   In the context of discussing our human responses to the world, Kant draws our attention to the distinction between "ills" and "wickedness." The opposite of ills is well-being. The opposite of wickedness is good conduct. While ills are typically produced by nature, wickedness results from the improper exercise of our freedom and is produced entirely by our conduct. Having very little or no control over the ills produced by nature, we ought to show ourselves to be steady, resolute, and calm of mind. With respect to wickedness, on the other hand, we ought to experience spiritual pain. We should not remain calm and composed but rather disturbed at the sight of evil. Only profligate minds and infamous characters are apathetic when faced with moral wrongdoing.

For an individual to develop **steadfastness of mind,** he or she should not surrender to physical ills. That person should not be pushed and pulled as a toy of accident and unforeseen circumstance. This would be contrary to human dignity. The individual must in his or her character find the source of strength which will allow for the enduring of all ills.

Steadfastness of mind requires as well that we remove **false appearances** and **vain hopes.** We must not search for contentment and peace in physical objects and material possessions which many believe lead to happiness. We should not compare ourselves with our neighbors, for this is very disquieting. Kant says, "The greatest source of happiness and unhappiness, of well-being and wretchedness, of satisfaction and dissatisfaction is to be found in the comparison with other men."[21] Kant offers us an illustration to support his point. He maintains that if everyone in our community had nothing but bread and water for food and drink, one would be satisfied with such a simple diet; one would be cheerful. If everyone else were able to enjoy exotic foods and sumptuous repasts, however, one would likely become unhappy and regard one's life as a misfortune. In view of this Kant argues that, "good and ill-fortune depend upon ourselves and upon the mental attitude we adopt towards them."[22]

3.11   DUTIES TO OUR OWN BODIES IN REGARD TO LIFE

With respect to our moral treatment of ourselves, the question arises, "What are our powers of disposal over our life?"[23] As free, rational individuals, can we not decide how our own bodies should be treated? According to Kant, we cannot justifiably dispose of our own life if we choose; nor do we have complete freedom in choosing how to treat ourselves physically. The reason for this is simple. Our (moral) life and exercise of free will depend on the body. Kant says, "We cannot make use of our freedom except through the body."[24] To use our rational wills to destroy our bodies is illogical. Kant explains, "If a man destroys his body, and so his life, he does it by the use of his will, which is itself destroyed in the process. But to use the power of a free will for its own destruction is self-contradictory."[25] Freedom cannot be employed, therefore, to abolish life and destroy itself. Using life for life's own destruction is irrational.

In his *Lectures on Ethics,* Kant considers plausible arguments in favor of suicide and rejects each in turn. Kant opposes the argument that suicide can sometimes be noble or virtuous. He also rejects the idea that suicide can be the best solution to human pain and suffering. External circumstances and contingent conditions cannot place a value on life or its preservation. In this vein, Kant argues that, "Misery gives no right to any man to take his own life, for then we should all be entitled to take our lives for lack of pleasure."[26] If misery did justify suicide, then duties to ourselves would be directed toward happiness. Such duties would be prudential, not moral. "No chance or misfortune ought to make us afraid to live; we ought to go on living as long as we can do so as human beings and honorably."[27]

Though Kant does not condone suicide in cases where people are tormented and suffering, he does allow for suicide when one can no longer live honorably. Kant says, "If a man cannot preserve his life except by dishonoring his humanity he ought rather to sacrifice it; it is true that he endangers his animal life, but he can feel that, so long as he lived, he lived honorably."[28] For Kant, then, it is better to die honorably and respectfully than to prolong one's life in disgrace, unworthy of human respect. "The preservation of one's life is, therefore, not the highest duty, and men must often give up their lives merely to secure that they have lived honorably."[29]

3.11 DUTIES TOWARD THE BODY ITSELF

Given that we have a duty to preserve and maintain an honorable life, the question arises as to how we should treat our bodies. What duties toward the body itself do we have? According to Kant, the body must be **disciplined.** The body can affect the mind and the mind's condition. Kant says, "The mind must gain such mastery over the body that it can guide and direct it in accordance with moral and pragmatic principles and maxims."[30]

The discipline demanded by the mind is negative. The mind need only ensure that the body not exert any compulsion upon it. If bodily habits are left unchecked, and if they become necessities in life, the mind may not be able to suppress the inclinations of the body. The body can thereby gain dominance over the mind.

In recommending that we gain control over the body, Kant does not favor **"mortification of the flesh."** There is no virtue for Kant in robbing oneself of all sensuous pleasures. It is wrongheaded to believe that by divesting ourselves of all sensibility, we approach more closely the spiritual life. Penance and fasting simply waste the body. If we are to discipline the body properly, we should not practice fanatical and monkish virtues. Disciplining the body involves living in conformity with one's purpose.

If we are to treat the body properly, then we must strengthen and harden it. We should take care of it without pampering. The body must be made able to dispense with everything that is not necessary. Kant contends that, "The less man needs for the upkeep of his life-strength, the more he is conscious of living."[31] In short, our duty is to make the body frugal in its needs and temperate in its pleasures.[32] Kant maintains, "it is better to keep within the limits of these needs, and even to fall a little short of them, than to go beyond them and enfeeble the body and sap its powers."[33]

We abuse our bodies through **vices.** Two kinds of vice which cannot be tolerated are **"bestial"** and **"satanic"** ones. Bestial vices place humans below the level of animals. Such vices include gluttony, drunkenness, and crimes against nature. Satanic vices involve envy, ingratitude, and malice.

3.12 OCCUPATION

According to Kant, occupation is comprised of either work or play. Of the two, work is preferable, though it is better to be engaged in play than not to be occupied at all. At least in play, we are energized. Without some form of occupation, we lose our life force and become indolent by degree. If we remain idle too long, we may find it difficult to regain our former energy of mind. "Without occupation man cannot live happily."[34]

As Kant saw it, it is **work** that sustains life. It is through our work activities and not by idle enjoyment that we feel we are alive. Spare time is in fact disagreeable. Pleasures fill the moment, but memory finds such pleasurable moments empty. If we have filled our time with idleness and play, the appearance of fullness will be confined to the present. In reviewing our lives we will become amazed by how quickly they have passed. By contrast, when engaged in work activity, the moments fly by quickly, but in retrospect there is so much more to remember. Faced eventually with the prospect of death, we experience a greater fullness of life, a greater sense of personal achievement.

3.13 SELF-REFERRING DUTIES IN RESPECT OF EXTERNAL CIRCUMSTANCES

As human beings, we cannot totally divorce ourselves from the material world. We must live in this world. The morally relevant question is, "How should we interact with or relate to things in the external world?"

Kant answers this question first by highlighting the point that external physical objects are a means and condition of our well-being. External things can be classified into two categories: **necessities** and **amenities.** Necessities are those things which serve to support life. Our contentment as individuals depends on our obtaining bare necessities like food and clothes. Contentment can be achieved if we manage to find the minimal requirements of subsistence. Kant thus regards contentment as negative. Comfort, on the other hand, is positive. Life is made more comfortable as the number of amenities we enjoy increases. While we can live without amenities, we cannot do without necessities.

3.14   Kant believes that pleasure in living can be found, even if one lives in poverty and lacks the comforts of life. What we must learn to do is dispense with comfort and learn to bear discomfort. This does not mean that we should impose discomforts upon ourselves. We should not try to make our lives more inconvenient or difficult; nor should we engage in useless rituals of self-mortification and self-chastisement. Rather, we should cultivate a positive frame of mind. We should develop a cheerful countenance in order that we might find the difficulties, pains, and obstacles in life bearable. Kant describes this frame of mind as **cheerful courage:** "If we bear with a cheerful mind and a happy disposition the ills which cannot be altered, we have strength of mind."[35] On the other hand, we should not become dependent upon the amenities of life. Kant recommends that "all comforts and pleasures should be enjoyed in such a way that we can dispense with them; we ought never to make necessities of them."[36] The more our satisfaction, happiness, or contentment rely on amenities, which are nothing more than **pseudo-necessities,** the more we are insecure. Our contentment is at the mercy of external circumstances and things. Over such things we have little or no control. To base our personal happiness on what ultimately lies beyond our powers is certainly precarious. "Man must, therefore, discipline his mind in regard to the necessaries of life."[37]

If we do not discipline ourselves properly with respect to pseudo-necessities, we may fall prey to luxurious living and effeminacy. **Luxury** enslaves us. It makes us dependent on enjoyable things, which really are dispensable. If we are prevented from procuring these desired luxuries or grasping more, then we become miserable: "Luxury adds to the number of our wants and temptations and makes it increasingly more difficult to walk in the path of morality."[38] Likewise, if we wallow in excessive self-indulgence we are likely to become effeminate. Our strength will be sapped and we will become indolent.[39] (Kant's eighteenth-century examples of effeminacy and indolence include wearing silk and driving in carriages.)

Kant suggests that we remain independent of both luxury and effeminacy. He declares that, "the more dependent man is upon luxury and comfort, the less free he is and the more prone to vice."[40] For Kant, pleasure can be found in doing no wrong against oneself or another. Acting according to duty is enjoyable in itself. However, "Man cannot fulfill his duties if he cannot do without things, for he will be dulled by the temptations of his senses."[40] And if we do not also develop strength of mind, we will be less able to perform our moral duties. One cannot be virtuous if one is not resolute in misfortune. If one wishes to be virtuous, one must be able to suffer.

PROGRESS CHECK 3.1

Instructions: *Place the appropriate responses in the blanks below.*

duties to oneself   negative
ends of humanity   servility and lack of spirit
inclinations   pragmatic self-respect
prudential   noble pride
ultimate determining principle   the moral law

1. According to Kant, duties to oneself are _____ insofar as they are like the law, placing restrictions on our inclinations and behaviors.
2. Animals and humans both have _____. In the former case, biological, genetic, and hormonal factors control their expression. In the latter case, their expression is under voluntary control.
3. The _____ of Kant's notion of individual morality is freedom.
4. Having a low opinion of oneself in relation to others is not humility. This low opinion reflects _____.
5. Self-esteem which arises from self-love and which leads to favor and partiality towards ourselves is called _____.
6. Having self-respect in comparison with others means that one has _____.
7. True humility comes when we compare ourselves with _____.
8. Actions which are consistent with the _____ permit the fullest use of freedom and personal power.
9. Kant's conception of individual morality is based upon the notion of _____.
10. Actions which serve only to promote our own happiness and self-interest are _____.

PROGRESS CHECK 3.2

Instructions: *Place the responses below in the appropriate blanks.*

mental attitude   satanic
sanctions   luxury
Philautia   self-contradiction
self-mastery   conscience
moral perfection   comparison with others

imagination
steadfastness of mind
necessities
amenities
bestial
moral feeling
occupation

arrogance
moral discipline
esteem
suspension of judgment
ills
intentions
wickedness

1. Violations of moral duties are sometimes followed by _____.
2. _____ is an instinct to pass judgment upon ourselves in accordance with moral laws.
3. Another word for self-love is _____.
4. When people make unwarranted claims of merit, they are guilty of _____.
5. According to Immanuel Kant, it is better to become an object worthy of _____ than of love.
6. _____ is a prerequisite if we are to obey self-regarding duties.
7. _____ subjects our sensibilities and inclinations to moral law.
8. An obstacle to self-mastery is the absence of _____.
9. If we seek to achieve _____ we must subordinate everything to our will and act in ways which are consistent with the essential ends of humanity.
10. _____ gives rise to temptations.
11. In monitoring ourselves morally, we should distinguish between our good actions and our good _____.
12. People who always react thoughtlessly and reflexively lack _____.
13. If one accepts unpleasant or arduous work without vexation, one displays _____.
14. _____ are produced by nature.
15. _____ arises when we employ our freedom of will improperly.
16. In _____ we find the greatest source of happiness and unhappiness.
17. Kant argues that happiness and unhappiness are not found in things or in external circumstances, but in _____.
18. Using the power of free will for its own destruction is a _____.
19. There are two types of vice which cannot be tolerated. They are the _____ and _____ type.
20. _____ is comprised of either work or play.
21. We need external things as a condition of well-being. These external things are either _____ or _____.
22. _____ makes it difficult to walk in the path of morality.

LEARNING EXERCISE 3.3

Instructions: *The following statements are either normative or nonnormative. Place an "F" next to the nonnormative statements presenting factual claims and a "V" next to the normative statements containing value judgments.*

_____ 1. A drunkard is an object of moral contempt.

_____ 2. Animals act by inclinations determined by biological, genetic, and hormonal factors.

_____ 3. If we give free rein to our inclinations, we are likely to degenerate into complete savage disorder.

_____ 4. Actions which incapacitate us are wrong.

_____ 5. Self-esteem should be the principle of our duties towards ourselves.

_____ 6. Kant maintains that proper self-respect is comprised of humility and noble pride.

_____ 7. One individual is just as valuable as any other individual.

_____ 8. We should not despair if we fall short of the moral law.

_____ 9. We should not compare ourselves with others.

_____ 10. Comparing ourselves with others makes us unhappy.

_____ 11. Sanctions are sometimes imposed on individuals for wrongdoing.

_____ 12. Deathbed repentance is motivated more out of fear than out of remorse.

_____ 13. Christianity commands us to love our neighbor.

_____ 14. Having a high opinion of oneself is detestable.

_____ 15. The absence of moral feeling contributes to the difficulty of achieving self-mastery.

_____ 16. Things are not always as they appear.

_____ 17. Good intentions alone are cheap.

_____ 18. Our first inclination in controversial matters should be to suspend judgment.

_____ 19. People should develop steadfastness of mind in enduring all ills.

_____ 20. If a man cannot live except by dishonor, he ought rather to sacrifice his life.

SUMMARY

1. Duties to Oneself
   Primarily important

Part of individual morality

Prior to social morality

2. Basis of Self-Regarding Duties

Freedom

Restrictions stem from rational understanding

Consistent with the ends of humanity

3. Proper Self-Respect

Comprised of humility and noble pride

Self-deprecation represents servility and lack of spirit

Humility arises from our perception of falling short of the moral law

Does not come from comparisons with others

4. Conscience

A form of moral sanction

An instinct to pass judgment upon ourselves in accordance with moral laws

Able to appreciate the inherent wickedness of immoral acts

5. Self-love

Contrasts with arrogance and Philautia

Involves respect and self-esteem

Requires doing one's duty to oneself

6. Self-Mastery

Involves discipline

The highest duty to oneself

requires weakening forces which militate against development of moral feeling

Demands control over our imagination

Sometimes necessitates suspension of judgment

Contributes to the development of a sound mental attitude and steadfastness of mind

7. Duties to Our Own Bodies in Regard to Life

The use of rational will to destroy our own body is illogical

The value of life cannot be made contingent

Misery cannot justify suicide

One has no duty to live life if life requires dishonoring humanity

8. Duties toward the Body Itself

The body must be disciplined

The mind must gain mastery over the body

We should not practice penance and fasting as they simply waste the body

We must strengthen and harden the body

The body is abused by bestial and satanic vices

9. Occupation

Work activity sustains life

Idle enjoyment makes life empty

10. Self-Referring Duties in Respect of External Circumstances

One must learn to dispense with comfort and learn to bear discomfort, though we should not engage in useless rituals of self-mortification and self-chastisement

We should develop a cheerful countenance in order that we might find the difficulties, pains, and obstacles in life bearable

Man must discipline his mind in regard to the necessities of life

Luxury is enslaving

REFERENCES

Beck, L. W. *A Commentary on Kant's Critique of Practical Reason.* Chicago: University of Chicago Press, 1960.

Broad, C. D. *Five Types of Ethical Theory.* New York: Harcourt, Brace, 1930; chap. 5.

Kant, Immanuel. *Foundations of the Metaphysics of Morals.* Trans., Lewis White Beck. Indianapolis, IN: The Library of Liberal Arts, 1959.

———. *Lectures on Ethics.* Trans., Louis Infield. Indianapolis, IN: Hackett Publishing, 1963.

———. *The Metaphysical Principles of Virtue.* Trans., James Ellington. Indianapolis, IN: The Library of Liberal Arts, 1964.

NOTES

1. Immanuel Kant, *Lectures on Ethics* (Indianapolis, IN: Hackett Publishing, 1963), pp. 117–118.
2. Ibid., p. 118.
3. Ibid., p. 121.
4. Ibid., pp. 122–123.
5. Ibid., p. 123.
6. Ibid., p. 124.
7. Ibid., p. 125.
8. Ibid., pp. 126–129.
9. Ibid., p. 128.
10. Ibid., p. 127.
11. Ibid., p. 129.
12. Ibid., p. 130.
13. Ibid., p. 130.
14. Ibid., p. 135.
15. Ibid., pp. 136–137.
16. Ibid., p. 136.
17. Ibid., p. 138.
18. Ibid., p. 141.
19. Ibid., p. 143.
20. Ibid., p. 143.
21. Ibid., p. 145.
22. Ibid.
23. Ibid., p. 147.
24. Ibid., p. 148.
25. Ibid.

26. Ibid., p. 152.
27. Ibid., p. 153.
28. Ibid., p. 156.
29. Ibid.
30. Ibid., p. 157.
31. Ibid., p. 158.
32. Ibid., p. 159.
33. Ibid.
34. Ibid., p. 161.
35. Ibid., p. 172.
36. Ibid.
37. Ibid., p. 173. The translator uses the term "necessaries" rather than "necessities." There is no substantial difference in meaning.
38. This view of effeminacy is obviously sexist. It is based on a conception of women in the eighteenth century.
39. Kant, *Lectures*, p. 173.
40. Ibid., p. 174.

Self-Test

Individual Morality

1. Plato's moral theory addresses itself to answering two basic questions concerning self-realization. These questions ask:
   (a)
   (b)
2. How does the teleologist determine the moral worth of persons? What makes a person morally good, in other words?
3. What is characteristic about the disordered soul?
4. Plato's timarchic character is dominated by which psychological faculty?
5. What is the primary source of unhappiness for the timarchic character?
6. What is the democratic character like? Why does this character fall short of Plato's ideal personality?
7. What virtues are displayed by Plato's philosopher ruler?
8. In what respect do the moral theories of Plato, Aristotle, and Immanuel Kant resemble each other? Is there any common theme or commitment?
9. According to Aristotle, how should the *ultimate* good of man be conceptualized?
   (a)
   (b)
   (c)
10. Explain why the "life of enjoyment and pleasure" *or* the "life of the statesman" cannot provide happiness ultimately.
11. What sort of lifestyle is the one recommended by Aristotle? Elaborate.
12. What importance does "freedom" have for Kant in his conception of morality?

13. Explain what Kant means by "proper self-respect." What elements comprise it? What does each element entail?

14. What does Immanuel Kant say about "self-mastery"?

15. What does Kant say about luxury?

Social Morality

4

JEREMY BENTHAM
AND
THE PRINCIPLE OF UTILITY

OVERVIEW

1. Jeremy Bentham (1748–1832)
2. The Principle of Utility
3. The Theory of Sanctions
4. Law and Punishment
5. Measuring Utility: The Hedonistic Calculus
6. Progress Check
7. Summary
8. References
9. Notes

EDUCATIONAL OBJECTIVES: After reading this chapter the student will be able to:

4.1 State Bentham's general aims.
4.2 Define and explain the principle of utility.
4.3 Elucidate the meaning of utility.

4.4 Identify the philosophical problem underlying Bentham's acceptance of utility as the standard of moral rightness.

4.5 List and define the various types of sanctions.

4.6 Explain the role of punishment in relation to law and sociomoral reform.

4.7 Outline the conditions for the proper administration of punishment.

4.8 List the criteria included in Bentham's hedonistic calculus.

FOCUS QUESTIONS

1. What is meant by the "spirit of scientific objectivity" in the context of moral inquiry? Do you think this objectivity is possible? Why or why not?
2. How could Bentham's principle of utility be paraphrased?
3. Are there any potential problems in using the principle of utility as the standard of moral rightness?
4. How does the "is–ought" problem relate to Bentham's theory?
5. Do you think punishments are required to sanction moral behavior? Why?
6. Can you provide any criticisms of Bentham's concept of punishment and his idea of when it can be properly administered?
7. Is it possible to use realistically the hedonistic calculus? Show by means of illustration.

JEREMY BENTHAM (1748–1832)

Jeremy Bentham was born in London in 1748. As a child, he was intellectually precocious. By the age of 4 Bentham was already studying Latin grammar and, at the age of 12, he enrolled at Queen's College, Oxford. In 1763 Bentham earned the Bachelor of Arts degree and thereupon began legal studies at Lincoln's Inn. This was in compliance with his father's wishes. In that same year, he returned to Oxford for what turned out to be one of the most decisive experiences of his intellectual life. Bentham attended a number of lectures on law given by Sir William Blackstone. Blackstone presented his legal theory based on "natural rights." Regarding this theory as little more than rhetorical nonsense, Bentham began setting the stage for the development of his own utilitarian conception of law, justice, and society. Bentham earned his Master of Arts degree in 1766 and then proceeded to London. Having never really developed a fondness for the legal profession, he decided against becoming a practicing lawyer. Instead, he embarked on a literary career, the basic object of which was to bring order and moral defensibility into what he perceived as the deplorable state of the law and the social realities it made possible in his day. Jeremy Bentham can thus be regarded as a social reformer. He undertook the task of trying to modernize British political and social institutions. There is little doubt that it was due at least in part to his influence that an historical landmark was established, the Reform Bill of 1832, which transformed the nature of British politics. The control of Britain's parliament was taken away from the landed aristocracy and placed into the hands of the urban bourgeoisie.[1]

On a personal note, Jeremy Bentham was the godfather of John Stuart Mill, son of James Mill, a friend and colleague. John Stuart Mill later became the godfather of Bertrand Russell, a famous English philosopher who led the fight for nuclear disarmament in the 1960s. Starting with Bentham, an interesting philosophical lineage begins to evolve that has had political activism as essential elements.

4.1 THE PRINCIPLE OF UTILITY

Jeremy Bentham's name is almost synonymous with the moral theory of **utilitarianism.** It should be noted, however, that Bentham was not the sole inventor of this idea. Elements of utilitarianism are found in the writings of such people as Thomas Hobbes and John Locke.[2] Bentham's significant contribution to utilitarianism is that he connected its basic principles and assumptions to the problems of his time. He sought to provide nineteenth-century English society with philosophical foundations for moral thought and practical social reform. Bentham believed that ethical questions could be answered in a **spirit of scientific objectivity** and that there was no need to appeal to authority figures or religious dogmas.

4.2   In his most famous work, *Introduction to the Principles of Morals and*

Legislation (1789), Bentham outlines his objective basis for morality. He calls it the **principle of utility.** Bentham writes:

> By the principle of utility is meant that principle which approves or disapproves of every action whatsoever, according to the tendency which it appears to have to augment or diminish the happiness of the party whose interest is in question: or, what is the same thing in other words, to promote or to oppose that happiness. I say of every action whatsoever; and therefore not only of every action of a private individual, but of every measure of government.[3]

4.3   Bentham equates utility with benefit, advantage, pleasure, happiness, and goodness.[4] He also maintains that if something prevents mischief, pain, evil, or unhappiness in people's lives it too has utilitarian value. Bentham's general thesis is that everyone desires pleasure and happiness. From this fact the inference is made that moral goodness can best be understood in terms of **happiness.** According to Bentham, we can move from the fact that we actually want pleasure or happiness to the ethical judgment that we ought to pursue it. Bentham thus moves from a psychological fact about human nature to the moral principle of utility.

4.4   ### Is-ought Fallacy

As the philosophical commentator Samuel Stumpf points out, Bentham's move here appears to make him guilty of committing the **"naturalistic"** or **"is-ought fallacy."**[5] Bentham fails to offer any careful or detailed argumentation to illustrate how one can justifiably proceed to an ethical "ought" from an "is" of experience. This is important, for frequently what *is* ought *not* to be.

4.3   According to Bentham, the concept of ought must be tied to pleasure. For him, words like ought, right, and wrong possess meaning only in terms of people's happiness and of its opposites unhappiness, pain, or discomfort. This claim is based on the assumption Bentham makes about human nature. In the first chapter of the aforementioned work Bentham writes: "Nature has placed mankind under the governance of two sovereign masters, pain and pleasure. It is for them alone to point out what we ought to do, as well as to determine what we shall do."[6] Leaving the principle of utility unquestioned, Bentham justifies this action by asserting that, "that which is used to prove everything else, cannot itself be proved: a chain of proofs must have their commencement somewhere. To give such proof is as impossible as it is needless."[7]

Though Bentham does not offer any positive rationale or detailed justification for his principle of utility, he does offer some support in a negative sense. He argues that other moral theories are ultimately reducible to the principle of utility or that they are inferior to this principle owing to the fact that they are either inconsistent or lacking clarity in meaning.[8] He uses social contract theory as an example. When people contract to establish certain laws and rules, the obligation to submit to them rests ultimately upon the principle of utility. By everyone obeying the law, the greatest happiness of the greatest number will be achieved. Bentham consequently does not see the necessity of developing an elaborate contract theory of questionable scientific worth when one can conclude that obeying does more good than disobeying.[9]

4.5 THE THEORY OF SANCTIONS

Bentham not only believed that pain and pleasure give value to actions, but that they are also **causes** of our behavior. A source of pleasure or pain is called a **sanction.** According to Bentham's theory of sanctions, a sanction gives binding force to rules of conduct and to laws in society. One cannot rely exclusively on people's goodwill, sympathy, or benevolence to benefit other people. Sanctions are required. According to Bentham there are four types of sanctions: (1) physical, (2) moral, (3) religious, and (4) political. **Physical** sanctions bind one to the laws of nature. One cannot jump off the CN Tower in Toronto or the Empire State Building in New York, for example, without suffering the consequences. **Moral** sanctions bind one to public opinion. One does not consistently lie to one's best friend if one wishes to keep that friend. **Religious** sanctions may involve promises of eternal bliss in heaven or eternal damnation in hell. Thus one may obey God's will in light of the anticipated rewards and punishments. Lastly, there are **political** sanctions which entail fear of magistrates and courts. People will refrain from robbing, for instance, because they are fearful of a possible jail sentence.

Bentham was most interested in political sanctions. As a reformer, he wished to change the laws of England in such a fashion that the general welfare would be promoted by each individual pursuing his or her own advantage. He felt that the legislator's main concern should be to decide what kinds of behavior will increase the happiness of society and what sanctions would be most likely to increase that happiness. For Bentham, **laws should serve utilitarian ideals.** Laws are not necessarily right or wrong in themselves but are acceptable to the extent that they further human happiness.

4.6 LAW AND PUNISHMENT

Laws are intimately bound up with **punishments** in Bentham's scheme. For Bentham, the law should be designed to discourage those types of acts which produce evil consequences for society. He believed, however, that the English laws of his day unjustifiably controlled many matters of individual or private morality which had no significant effect on public affairs and general happiness. For example, laws prohibited people from fornication and required individuals to be members of the Anglican church if they wished to occupy certain political offices.[10] Bentham's utilitarianism required a reclassification of behaviors to establish what would and would not be appropriate for the government to regulate.

Bentham was not a **retributivist** with respect to the meting out of punishment. According to him punishment is evil in itself as it inflicts suffering and pain. Thus punishing violations of social misconduct could only be justified if the pain inflicted prevented or excluded some other greater pain. In short, the principle of utility requires the elimination of retribution. From a utilitarian perspective, no useful purpose is served by making an individual suffer because his or her act caused a victim pain.

4.7   Bentham provides us with several utilitarian guidelines for the administration of punishment beyond the one mentioned above. Punishment should not be administered where it is **groundless**. Where an offense allows for compensation and where compensation is very likely to be forthcoming, there is no need for punishment. Punishments which are **inefficacious** should be eliminated. Retroactive legislation and resulting sanctions are ineffective and thus unjustifiable. Punishing the insane or very young children is also wrong by virtue of being inefficacious, since neither group has a true sense of responsibility. Punishments also should not be inflicted where they would prove to be **unprofitable** or **too expensive**. In other words, the punishment should not create more pain or mischief than the act it is intended to prevent. Finally, punishments should be avoided where **needless**. If a mischievous act can be prevented without punishment, then no punishment should be given

When punishments are inflicted, they must outweigh the profit resulting from the offence that is committed. In situations where two different offences come in competition, the punishment for the larger offence must be sufficient to induce the individual to prefer the lesser offence. Furthermore, each offender should receive the same punishment for the same offence. The amount of punishment should never exceed the bare minimum required to make it effective. Also, the less chance there is for an offender to be caught, the greater should be the punishment. Lastly, if the individual is a repeat offender, then the punishment should outweigh the gains not only of the immediate offence, but also of the yet unknown offences committed.

Underlying Bentham's entire discussion of punishment, law, and political reform is, of course, the principle of utility. As mentioned earlier it is the cornerstone of Bentham's thinking and writing. Recall that Bentham believed that morals and legislation could be **quantified** and approached objectively and in the spirit of science. Before concluding this chapter, therefore, it is important to understand how the pleasure–pain calculation works and how utility is quantified and measured.

4.8 MEASURING UTILITY: THE HEDONISTIC CALCULUS

In his attempt to provide mathematical precision in moral and legislative deliberation, Bentham has articulated a **hedonistic calculus**. It is comprised of seven criteria of evaluation. These criteria are:

1. Intensity
2. Duration

3. Certainty or Uncertainty
4. Propinquity or Remoteness
5. Fecundity
6. Purity
7. Extent

When considering **intensity** one asks: "How much good or bad is produced for every person affected?" To determine **duration,** one considers whether the pleasure or happiness produced is short-lived or long-lasting. We must ask what is the **certainty** of the probable consequences. Greater weight is to be assigned to circumstances that are more likely to occur. Will the nearer consequences of the proposed action or policy (and the like) tend to cause or help cause more desirable consequences later on? That is, will they possess **fecundity?** What will be the **purity** of each of the alternatives? Will the consequences produced be unmixed and purely good, or mixed up with undesirable or evil results? Also, how many people will be involved? That is to say, what is the **extent** of consequences? Finally, what is either the **propinquity** or **remoteness** of the contemplated actions or policies. In other words, how close or far away are the good consequences? All of these questions are asked when using Bentham's hedonistic calculus. Plus and minus values are assigned to competing alternatives. That alternative which is likely to produce the greatest balance of good over evil is the right action.[12] This principle is one Bentham would recommend we live by all our lives.

Example

The application of the hedonistic calculus can be illustrated by an example. Let us imagine that a member of a student-union organization is attending a conference held for union members on a college campus far from his own. While socializing at the conference on a particular evening, the individual is sexually propositioned by another delegate. A choice must now be made; the invitation to sex can either be accepted or rejected. According to Bentham's utilitarian principles, the sexual acts which would result as a product of accepting the invitation are not necessarily right or wrong in themselves. It is not intuitively obvious that one should engage in such actions; nor are there any absolute unbreakable laws which prohibit them. The rightness or wrongness of the considered sexual activity will depend on the utility of each alternative. Moral dilemmas, then, can be viewed as problems of calculation, involving the addition and subtraction of pleasurable and painful consequences. In this case, the individual adds up all the pleasures and pains that anybody in the situation would experience as a result of having sex and then compares this sum with the total of pleasures and pains one would experience by not having sex. The alternative action with the greatest positive total is the morally correct one. In those cases where both alternatives result in negative totals, the action with the lesser negative total is the morally correct one.

TO ACCEPT OR NOT TO ACCEPT THE SEXUAL INVITATION: A HEDONISTIC CALCULATION

If I Accept	Units of Pleasure
Thrill and Excitement (duration, certainty, propinquity)	+100
Ego-boost (intensity, duration)	+100
Hurt and Angry Feelings of Girlfriend/Boyfriend (fecundity, purity, extent)	−500
Personal Guilt (purity, fecundity)	−100
Possibility of Contracting AIDS or VD (purity, certainty)	− 50
Total	−450

If I Don't Accept	Units of Pleasure
Loss of Physical Gratification (intensity, propinquity, extent)	−100
Feelings of Regret (duration, purity, certainty)	− 50
Risk of AIDS and VD Eliminated (certainty, purity, fecundity)	+ 50
No Guilt Feelings (purity, certainty, propinquity)	+100
Trust Relationship Reinforced (certainty, fecundity, extent, intensity, propinquity)	+500
	+500

+500 is greater than −450

Morally correct conclusion: *Don't accept invitation.*

PROGRESS CHECK 4.1

Instructions: *Fill in the blanks with the appropriate responses listed below.*

hedonistic calculus
utility
pain and pleasure
scientific objectivity
utilitarianism

happiness
social contract theory
propinquity
utilitarian ideals
sanctions

1. Bentham believed it was possible to inject an element of ＿＿＿＿＿ into moral reasoning and social reform.

2. The _____ contains seven criteria that enable one to determine which course of action is the right one in a moral dilemma.

3. Sanctions are bound up with _____.

4. That which contributes to people's benefit, advantage, or pleasure contains _____.

5. The moral theory which determines the rightness or wrongness of some action or policy, etc., on the basis of its consequences is called _____.

6. According to Bentham, all people desire _____.

7. Bentham criticizes _____ because ultimately its justification rests on utilitarian considerations.

8. The concept of _____ deals with how close or far away the good and bad consequences of an act are.

9. There are four kinds of _____: physical, moral, religious, and political.

10. According to Bentham, laws should serve _____.

SUMMARY

1. Principle of Utility
   That action which most greatly increases the happiness of the individual in question is the right one to perform.

2. Utility
   Utility can be equated with benefit, advantage, pleasure, happiness, or goodness.
   Disutility involves mischief, pain, evil, or unhappiness.

3. Is–Ought Controversy
   The concept of "ought" or moral obligation possesses meaning only in terms of people's happiness and unhappiness.
   We ought to do that which will be likely in fact to produce the greatest utility.

4. Sanctions
   Sanctions are a source of pleasure and pain.
   They give binding force to rules sand laws.
   Four types include: physical, moral, religious, and political.

5. Punishment
   It is inextricably bound up with laws.
   Punishment is not good in itself.
   It should not be administered where groundless, inefficacious, unprofitable, or needless.

6. The Hedonistic Calculus
   Calculations are made on the basis of seven criteria.
   (a) intensity

(b) duration

(c) certainty or uncertainty

(d) propinquity or remoteness

(e) fecundity

(f) purity

(g) extent

REFERENCES

Ayer, A. J. "The Principle of Utility," in *Philosophical Essays*, ed. A. J. Ayer. New York: St. Martin's Press, 1955.

Bentham, Jeremy, *An Introduction to the Principles of Morals and Legislation*. Oxford: Oxford University Press, 1823.

Glickman, Jack (ed.). *Moral Philosophy: An Introduction*, part 4. New York: St. Martin's Press, 1976.

Narveson, Jan. *Morality and Utility*. Baltimore: Johns Hopkins University Press, 1967.

Smart, J. J. C. *Outline of a Utilitarian System of Ethics*. London: Cambridge University Press, 1961.

NOTES

1. This biographical summary is adapted from Samuel Stumpf, *Philosophy: History and Problems*, 3rd edition (Toronto: McGraw-Hill Ryerson), 1983, pp. 336–338.
2. John Locke wrote: ". . . what has an aptness to produce pleasure in us is what we call good and what is apt to produce pain in us we call evil." Cited in Stumpf, *Philosophy*, p. 336.
3. Bentham, cited in Jack Glickman (ed.), *Moral Philosophy: An Introduction* (New York: St. Martin's Press, 1976), p. 528.
4. Ibid, p. 528.
5. Samuel Stumpf, *Philosophy*, p. 338.
6. Bentham, cited in Glickman, *Moral Philosophy*, p. 527.
7. Ibid, p. 529.
8. This point is highlighted by Stumpf, *Philosophy*, p. 338.
9. Ibid.
10. Gerald Runkle, *Ethics: An Examination of Contemporary Moral Problems* (New York: Holt, Rinehart, and Winston, 1982).
11. Bentham, "The Principle of Utility," in Glickman, *Moral Philosophy*, p. 534.
12. For an interesting example of how the principle of utility could be used to consider alternatives see, for example, Jeffrey Olen, *Persons and Their World: An Introduction to Philosophy* (New York: Random House, 1983), pp 40–42.

5

JOHN STUART MILL AND THE GREATEST HAPPINESS PRINCIPLE

OVERVIEW

EDUCATIONAL OBJECTIVES: After reading this chapter the student will be able to:

5.1   State Mill's personal and intellectual connection to Jeremy Bentham.

5.2 Explain the difference between "quantity" and "quality" of pleasure and how this difference distinguishes Mill's views from Bentham's.

5.3 Elaborate on the distinction between higher and lower pleasures.

5.4 Paraphrase Mill's justification for why higher pleasures are better.

5.5 Comment on the advantages and dangers of pursuing higher pleasures.

5.6 Provide a psychological explanation for why people choose lower pleasures.

5.7 Distinguish between Mill and Bentham's understandings of utility.

5.8 State Mill's "greatest-happiness principle."

5.9 Give reasons why Mill rejects Bentham's hedonistic calculus.

5.10 Name two major evils in the world and tell how they can be eradicated.

5.11 Give an explanation for why people who should be happy given their lot in life are not.

5.12 Outline the limits and restrictions which, according to Mill, should be imposed on government in a democracy.

FOCUS QUESTIONS

1. What advantages and disadvantages are there for the utilitarian in distinguishing between quantity and quality of pleasure?

2. What is so undesirable about living "the life of a pig satisfied?" Couldn't one rationally choose this lifestyle? Why or why not?

3. Why are some people bored by poetry, classical music, art, and history?

4. In what areas of life does the government have no right to intrude?

JOHN STUART MILL (1806-1873)

John Stuart Mill was born in London, England, in 1806. He was the eldest child of Harriet and James Mill, a Scotsman who was an accomplished author, friend, and colleague of Jeremy Bentham. James Mill was an intensely intellectual man. This is evidenced by the fact that he conducted an educational experiment with his son John. The young Mill was put through a rigorous program of home education by his father. At the age of 3, John Stuart was learning Greek, and by age 8 he was reading Plato and other Greek authors in the original. Along with Latin and arithmetic, extensive reading was part of Mill's rigorous curriculum. Each morning, John Stuart was expected to give a recitation of the previous day's reading to his father.

The young Mill did not become an academic by profession. His research and writing were done in conjunction with his duties as a civil servant in the East India Company. Mill imposed upon himself an onerous regimen in his position, one which eventually led to his psychological collapse at age 20. The depression associated with his "nervous breakdown" lasted several months. Mill gradually recovered from his gloomy state by allowing emotion and sentiment to grow within him. His father's unfeeling disposition had apparently impacted negatively on John Stuart's affective development and psychological health. He once wrote that he was never allowed to be a boy and to experience normal childhood friendships and playfulness. Fortunately for Mill, his one-sided, highly intellectualized personality became more balanced. His feelings for humanity were cultivated by reading Wordsworth's poetry and by developing a loving friendship with Harriet Taylor, who later became his wife.

J. S. Mill was convinced that his wife was a talented thinker who, unfortunately, was not appreciated because of the discrimination against women at that time. Acutely sensitive to the matter of discrimination, Mill addressed it in a work entitled *The Subjection of Women*. J. S. Mill's objections to sexism make him a predecessor of contemporary feminism. On this note, it should be pointed out that he was elected to Parliament in 1865. As part of his political struggle he fought for the exploited Negroes of Jamaica; and he tried to increase the power and influence of the working class in England, hoping to bring it into the country's political and economic mainstream. He also worked for the redistribution of lands in Ireland. J. S. Mill can be described as a political thinker, social reformer, activist, and moral philosopher. Selected works include: *Utilitarianism, On Liberty, A System of Logic, The Principles of Political Economy,* and *Considerations on Representative Government.*

5.1 MILL'S ACCEPTANCE AND DEFENSE OF UTILITARIANISM

As a young man, J. S. Mill was influenced by Jeremy Bentham primarily through his father. James Mill had been not only a friend to Bentham but a collaborator who assisted him in shaping his political ideas. The young Mill was particularly impressed by Bentham's *principle of utility*. Bentham tried to derive concepts of morality and lawmaking from notions like "right reason" and "natural law."[1] Mill wrote:

> The "principle of utility" understood as Bentham understood it . . . gave unity to my conception of things. I now had opinions, a creed, a doctrine, a philosophy; in one of the best senses of the word, a religion; the inculcation and diffusion of which could be made the principle outward purpose of a life.[2]

In his classic essay, *Utilitarianism*, Mill set out to defend the principle of utility against its critics. In the process, he articulated a version of utilitarianism which differed significantly from Bentham's. Bentham limited his discussions of pleasure solely to **quantity**. He argued that pleasures differ only in amount, saying things like, "pushpin is as good as poetry." For Bentham, the only criterion for goodness is the amount of pleasure which an act can produce.

5.2 QUANTITY VERSUS QUALITY OF PLEASURE
5.3

In contrast to Bentham, Mill makes a distinction between the **quantity** and **quality** of pleasure. More important than amount is the type of pleasure experienced. Mill believes that pleasures can be categorized as either **higher** or **lower** and that the former type is preferable. Mill contends that human beings possess psychological faculties which are elevated above the level of animal appetites. Once made conscious of them, people do not and will not accept any definition of happiness which does not include the gratification and development of these faculties. On this note, Mill writes:

5.4

> Now it is an unquestionable fact that those who are equally acquainted with and equally capable of appreciating and enjoying both [kinds of pleasures] do give a most marked preference to the manner of existence which employs the higher faculties. Few human creatures would consent to be changed into any of the lower animals for a promise of the fullest allowance of a beast's pleasures; no intelligent human being would consent to be a fool, no instructed person would be an ignoramus, no person of feeling and conscience would be selfish and base, even though they should be persuaded that the fool, the dunce, or the rascal is better satisfied with his lot than they are with theirs.[3]

Mill concludes, then, that higher pleasures are better — that they should be preferred because they are favored by those familiar with both types of pleasure. In *Utilitarianism*, Mill also argues for the superiority of higher mental pleasures over lower bodily pleasures on the grounds that the former possess greater **permanency, safety,** and **uncostliness.**[4] The pleasure derived from an alcoholic binge, for instance, is short-lived; it likely harms one's liver and brain functioning and may require a significant outlay of money. Once the pleasure derived from a gulp of beer has dissipated, one may even experience negative aftereffects such as a hangover and an empty wallet. By contrast, the pleasure of listening to beautiful music or appreciating nature typically costs little, if anything; it is also **ennobling, satisfying,** and **enduring.** The higher pleasures of the mind appeal to our sense of human dignity, not to our base appetites which we share with animals.

5.5 RISKS OF PURSUING HIGHER PLEASURES

A life based on the pursuit of higher pleasures is not without risk, however, Mill writes:

> A being of higher faculties requires more to make him happy, is capable probably of more acute suffering, and certainly accessible to it at more points, than one of an inferior type; but in spite of these liabilities, he can never really wish to sink into what he feels to be a lower grade of existence.[5]

The **inferior type** of individual is more likely to find contentment in the lower pleasures than the **superior type,** who perceives most sources of happiness in the world as imperfect. Nevertheless, the superior type can learn to bear these worldly imperfections and be satisfied with the exercise of his or her higher faculties.

Equating the inferior type's lifestyle with animal existence, Mill says, "It is better to be a human being dissatisfied than a pig satisfied; better to be Socrates dissatisfied than a fool satisfied."[6]

5.6 Mill recognizes, of course, that many people capable of higher pleasures occasionally (or frequently) succumb to temptation and opt for pleasures of a lower sort. This fact poses no obstacles for Mill. People are perfectly aware that their pursuit of sensual indulgence, for example, injures their health and that health is actually the greater good. Apart from moral weakness, the problem is that once people have devoted themselves to lower pleasures, they may become incapable of enjoying the other higher type. In this regard, Mill writes:

> Capacity for the nobler feelings is in most natures a very tender plant, easily killed, not only by hostile influences, but by more want of sustenance; and in the majority of young persons it speedily dies away if the occupations to which their position in life has devoted them, and the society into which it has thrown them, are not favorable to keeping that higher capacity in exercise. Men lose their high aspirations as they lose their intellectual tastes, because they have not time or opportunity for indulging them; and they addict themselves to inferior pleasures, not because they deliberately prefer them, but because they are either the only ones to which they have access or the only ones which they are any longer capable of enjoying.[7]

5.7 REVISING BENTHAM'S UTILITARIAN MORALITY

Mill's distinction between higher and lower pleasures necessitates a reformulation of Bentham's utilitarian standard of morality. In contrast to Bentham, Mill does not agree that the standard of goodness in behavior deals with the maximization of pleasure; rather, he maintains that goodness involves the fulfillment of our distinctively **human faculties.**[8] The degree to which we live the moral life is proportionate to the happiness we derive in being truly human, not in the amount of pleasure we experience.

5.8   Mill's theory differs from Bentham's utilitarianism in another respect. Mill's understanding of the utilitarian standard of morality tends to be less **egoistic** than Bentham's. In his discussions of the hedonistic calculus, Bentham says that we should decide what is right or wrong on the basis of how much pleasure is produced *for ourselves* or for the individual concerned. Supposedly, if everyone lived in a rationally self-interested way, and if we helped others to live in this way, we would secure our own happiness and the general welfare would be improved. Bentham adopts an egoistic psychology which supports this ethical position. He argues that people should act self-interestedly because by nature they are predisposed to do so anyway. In his defense of utilitarianism Mill appears to be more insistent about stressing the fact that moral acts must take into account the interests and happiness of all.[9] He writes: ". . . the happiness which forms the utilitarian standard of what is right in conduct, is not the agent's own happiness, but that of all concerned. As between his own happiness and that of others, utilitarianism requires him to be as strictly impartial as a disinterested and benevolent spectator."[10] It is possible, therefore, that the right thing to do may in a particular instance not promote the individual's immediate happiness. Mill would hope, of course, that the interests of individuals could be made harmonious with the interests of the whole (for example, society), so that the two sets of interests would be complementary, not in opposition to each other. Through proper character education, a link could be made between an individual's own happiness and the common good.[11] An indissoluble association could be made between a person's own happiness and the good of the whole. When what is in one's interest is also in the interest of society and when what is in the interest of society is in the individual's interest, then a harmonious balance is struck. The point should be stressed, therefore, that Mill interprets the utilitarian "greatest-happiness principle" to mean not simply my greatest happiness, but the greatest happiness of the greatest number.[12] Mill regards the greatest-happiness principle to be quite consistent with the golden rule of Jesus. That is, Do unto others as you would have others do unto you, and love your neighbor as yourself. For Mill, **personal sacrifice** in the interests of the common good may sometimes be required. To Bentham's principle of utility, Mill thus adds an element of **altruism.**

5.10   MILL'S REJECTION OF THE HEDONISTIC CALCULUS

A third major difference between Mill and Bentham involves the issue of calculating pleasures. Bentham believed that by means of the hedonistic calculus, one could quantify pleasures and determine objectively in a scientific spirit what alternative action or policy, or the like, results in the best consequences or greatest utility. Mill, on the other hand, does not believe that pleasure and pain can be calculated in Bentham's sense, He asks:

> What means are there of determining which is the acutest of two pains, or the intensest of two pleasurable sensations, except the general suffrage of those who are familiar with both? Neither pains nor pleasures are homogeneous, and pain is always heterogeneous with pleasure. What is there to decide whether a particular pleasure is worth purchasing at the cost of a particular pain, except the feelings and judgment of the experienced.[13]

Above we see that Mill regards pains and pleasures to be **incommensurable**. One cannot compare pain and pleasure because they are essentially different in kind. Those who are experienced with them both are able to express a **preference** for one pleasure over another but, apart from this, there is no other impartial tribunal where some kind of objective calculation can be performed.

5.10 REDUCING HUMAN MISERY

Mill believes that many of the world's evils which cause unhappiness can be eradicated. Poverty is one example. Mill contends that this ailment can be cured by the wisdom of society and the good sense of individuals. Disease, another evil, can certainly be reduced by proper physical and moral education. Mill states that:

> All the grand sources, in short, of human suffering are in great degree, many of them almost entirely, conquerable by human care and effort; and though their removal is greviously slow—though a long succession of generations will perish in the breach before the conquest is completed, and the world becomes all that, if will and knowledge were not wanting, it might easily be made—yet every mind sufficiently intelligent and generous to bear a part, however small and inconspicuous in the endeavor will draw a noble enjoyment from the contest itself, which he would not for any bribe in the form of selfish indulgence consent to be without.[14]

5.11   It is true, of course, that many rich and healthy people are still unhappy. Though they may not suffer great physical pains or mental anguish resulting from maltreatment or some kind of economic or political injustice, happiness may nonetheless elude them. Mill has a psychological explanation for this. He maintains that for people who are, "fortunate in their outward lot [and who] do not find in life sufficient enjoyment to make it valuable to them the cause generally is caring for nobody but themselves."[15] Apart from selfishness, "the principle cause which makes life unsatisfactory is want of **mental cultivation** (emphasis added).[16] The uncultivated mind is surrounded by possible sources of pleasure, yet discovers few lasting ones. The cultivated mind, by contrast, "finds sources of inexhaustible interest in all that surrounds it: in the objects of nature, the achievements of art, the imaginations of poetry, the incidents of history, the ways of mankind, past and present, and their prospects in the future."[17] Happiness, then, can be found in the satisfaction of curiosity and in the pursuit of higher intellectual interests. It can also be found in working for the common good, not simply for oneself in an egoistic fashion.

5.12   DEMOCRACY AND THE PROPER LIMITS OF GOVERNMENT AUTHORITY

In terms of implementing the standard of utility in social and political life, Mill was in agreement with Bentham that democracy is the best form of government. In his work, *On Liberty*, Mill warns of its possible dangers, however. In a democracy, things typically get done by majority rule. This allows for the possibility that the majority may choose to oppress the minority. A type of coercion may also arise involving the tyranny of public opinion. In view of this, Mill believed that a morally acceptable form of democracy must include certain safeguards. These safeguards should be designed to guard against the forces that would hinder individuals from realizing themselves and their goals in a free and open fashion. Speaking as a political reformer, and on the topic of society's rights to exercise control over the individual. Mill argues that:

> the sole end for which mankind are warranted, individually or collectively, in interfering with the liberty of action of any of their number is self-protection. That the only purpose for which power can be rightfully exercised over any member of a civilized community, against his will, is to prevent harm to others. His own good, either physical or moral, is not a sufficient warrant. He cannot rightfully be compelled to do or forbear because it will be better for him to do so, because it will make him happier, because, in the opinions of others, to do so would be wise, or even right.[18]

As an advocate of individualism, Mill was not thoroughly opposed to government intervention in people's lives. However, under certain conditions, he felt that it is best to leave the individual unhampered. For example when particular kinds of actions can be done better, more efficiently and economically, by private citizens, the government should stay out. If the government could possibly do something better than private individuals but if the action involved hinders individuals' development and education, then the government should stay out. Finally, if there is a danger of the government accumulating too much power, it should stay out of those affairs.[19] Whatever laws and policies the government does choose to enact, they should not be justified by appeals to rational intuition, absolute authority, or natural law, but by reference to utility understood as the greatest-happiness principle.

The question could be asked why anyone should act on the greatest-happiness principle either in social and political life or in one's personal life. What is the "sanction," in other words? Mill contends that it is our **feeling for humanity** that produces the ultimate sanctions of the principle of utility.[20] This feeling for humanity is internal. It is a subjective feeling in our minds—what can be called *conscience*. It is what helps us to recognize the general happiness as the ultimate moral standard. It serves to place us in unity with our fellow men and women. This feeling for humanity contributes to our recognition of others' goals and makes us sympathetic toward them in our attempts to build a happy and harmonious world.

PROGRESS CHECK 5.1

Instructions: *Fill in the blanks with the appropriate responses listed below.*

altruism	greatest-happiness
natural law	human dignity
inferior type	quality
selfishness	egoistic
higher	utilitarian

1. J. S. Mill and Jeremy Bentham are both _____ philosophers.
2. According to Bentham and Mill, actions cannot be judged right or wrong by reference to _____, but by reference to consequences or results.
3. For Mill, not all pleasures are the same. One must distinguish between quantity and _____.
4. _____ pleasures are preferable over physical pleasures, as anyone familiar with both chooses the former over the latter and because the former are more ennobling and enduring.
5. Mill's version of utilitarianism is less _____ than Bentham's.
6. Higher pleasures contribute to _____, while lower pleasures are base and vulgar.
7. People whose lot in life is quite favorable may still be unhappy due to their _____.
8. The _____ individual finds the greatest pleasure in base activities and indulgence of appetite.
9. Mill injects an element of _____ into his conception of utility. His understanding of the principle of utility is closely akin to Christianity's Golden Rule.
10. Mill's _____ principle requires that we further not only our own interests but that which is good for the majority of those concerned.

SUMMARY

1. Bentham's Influence on Mill
   Mill accepted Bentham's principle of utility as the standard of morality.

2. Quantity versus Quality of Pleasure

Some pleasures are higher or better than others, which are lower or inferior.

Pleasures dealing with the higher faculties of man are better.

Physical pleasures are inferior.

Those familiar with both kinds of pleasures prefer higher pleasures.

Higher mental pleasures possess greater permanency, safety, and uncostliness; they are also ennobling, satisfying, and enduring.

3. Risks of Pursuing Higher Pleasures

There is a greater risk of acute suffering.

Less contentment will be found in the lower pleasures.

4. Revision of Bentham's Utilitarianism

The standard of goodness does not deal solely with the maximization of pleasure, but with the fulfillment of our distinctively human faculties.

Mill's utilitarianism incorporates altruism and thus is less egoistic than Bentham's.

Mill does not believe that objective calculations concerning amounts of pleasure can be made. Only preference can be expressed.

5. Source of Unhappiness in the Rich and Successful

Selfishness can cause unhappiness.

The uncultured mind discovers few lasting pleasures in inferior activities and pursuits.

6. Happiness

It is found in the satisfaction of curiosity and in the pursuit of higher intellectual interests.

It is also found in working for the common good.

7. Democracy

There is a danger that the majority may oppress the minority.

Requires safeguards to protect the individual.

Mill's favored Government.

REFERENCES

Broad, C. D. *Five Types of Ethical Theory*. New York: Harcourt, Brace, 1930; Chap. 6.

Mill, J. S. *Utilitarianism*, in *Moral Philosophy: An Introduction*, ed. Jack Glickman. New York: St. Martin's Press, 1976.

———— *On Liberty*. In *On Liberty: A Norton Critical Edition*, ed. David Spitz. New York: W. W. Norton, 1975.

Stumpf, Samuel Enoch. *Philosophy: History and Problems*. 3rd ed. Toronto: McGraw-Hill 1983; see book 1, chap. 18, and book 2, chap. 14.

NOTES

1. Samuel Enoch Stumpf, *Philosophy: History and Problems*, 3rd Ed. (Toronto: McGraw-Hill, 1983), p. 344.
2. J. S. Mill, *Utilitarianism*, quoted from Stumpf, *Philosophy*, p. 344.
3. Mill, quotation taken from Jack Glickman (ed.), *Moral Philosophy: An Introduction* (New York: St. Martin's Press, 1976). pp. 541–542.
4. Ibid., p. 541.
5. Ibid., p. 542.
6. Ibid.
7. Ibid., p. 543.
8. This clarification is provided by Stumpf, *Philosophy*.
9. Gerald Runkle, *Ethics: An Examination of Contemporary Moral Problems* (Toronto: Holt, Rinehart, and Winston, 1982), pp. 35–36.
10. Mill, *Utilitarianism*, quoted in Stumpf, *Philosophy*, p. 348.
11. Mill, *Utilitarianism*, in Glickman, *Moral Philosophy*, p. 548.
12. Stumpf, *Philosophy*, p. 348.
13. Mill, *Utilitarianism*, in Glickman, *Moral Philosophy*, p. 543.
14. Ibid., pp. 546–547.
15. Ibid., p. 545.
16. Ibid., p. 545.
17. Ibid.
18. Mill, *On Liberty: A Norton Critical Edition*, David Spitz (ed.) (New York: W. W. Norton, 1975), pp. 10–11.
10. This summary of Mill's position is adapted from Stumpf, *Philosophy*, p. 350.
20. Ethel Albert, Theodore Denise, and Sheldon Peterfreund clarifies this point in *Great Traditions in Politics*, 5th ed. (Belmont, CA: Wadsworth, 1984), p. 223.

6

IMMANUEL KANT'S CATEGORICAL IMPERATIVE AND DUTIES TO OTHERS

OVERVIEW

EDUCATIONAL OBJECTIVES: After reading this chapter the student will be able to:

6.1 Identify Kant's basis for morality.
6.2 Give reasons why Kant chooses the basis of morality which he does.

6.3 Name what, in Kant's view, is the only thing good-in-itself and explain why.

6.4 Distinguish between acting "for the sake of duty" and "in accordance with duty."

6.5 Explain what role, if any, "inclination" plays in morality.

6.6 Define *duty* and *maxim*.

6.7 Provide two formulations of the categorical imperative.

6.8 Explain how Kant's theory challenges the thesis that morality is subjective and relative.

FOCUS QUESTIONS

1. Why is it important to establish a foundation or basis for morality? What is Kant's basis? Why does he reject other possible foundations?
2. What is meant by the concept of the "good will"?
3. In what important respects does Kant's moral theory differ from utilitarianism and Aristotle's Greek humanism?
4. Could Kant's interpretation of "inclination" lead to any silly conclusions?
5. Kant is sometimes described as a formalist. What does this mean?
6. Does Kant's second formulation of the categorical imperative remind you of any other moral absolute?
7. We all live by maxims or rules of conduct. How do we decide which ones are moral?
8. Why isn't morality relative and subjective for Kant?

"Nothing in the world—indeed nothing even beyond the world—can possibly be conceived which could be called good without qualification except a good will."

6.1 THE RATIONAL BASIS OF MORALITY

Although Immanuel Kant's theory of ethics includes a conception of individual morality, it nonetheless represents a challenge to the idea that morality is purely personal. In Kant's account, morality is not simply a matter of subjective preference or emotional expression. Kant also refuses to accept the notion that morality is relative to a particular culture, place, or time. In the Kantian scheme there is ultimately only one basis of morality. This singular basis provides absolute principles of moral conduct which are **binding** on all men regardless of individual characteristics or idiosyncracies. Kant even identifies "moral duties to oneself" which he argues all individuals must observe by virtue of being human beings. For example, Kant provides arguments for why suicide is morally wrong for everyone. Thus one such "self-referring duty" we all share is to preserve life.[1]

6.1
6.2
Philosophers, before and after Kant, have sought the ultimate basis of morality in a variety of places. Utilitarians like Bentham believed that the morality of actions could be determined by reference to their pleasurable **consequences.** Plato sought moral goodness in the **transcendent realm of forms.** Aristotle attempted to ground morality in human nature and man's pursuit of **happiness.** By contrast, Kant does not try to establish the basis of morality in some other world or in the experiential contents of people's lives. Since what people actually do, say, experience, believe, think, and feel vary, no **moral certainty** can be found there. If morality is to be considered binding on everybody and if particular moral principles are to be universally accepted as valid, then moral certainty must be found somewhere apart from the transitory and diverse world of everyday experience; for Kant, it is found in the **structure of reason** itself. The ultimate basis for morality must for him be **purely rational** or a priori, not in any way empirical or **a posteriori** (i.e., derived from experience). On this note, Kant writes:

> Is it not of the utmost necessity to construct a pure moral philosophy which is completely freed from everything which may be only empirical and thus belong to anthropology? That there must be such a philosophy is self-evident from the common idea of duty and moral laws. Everyone must admit that a law, if it is to hold morally, i.e., as a ground of obligation, must imply absolute necessity; he must admit that the command, "Thou shalt not lie" does not apply to men only, as if other rational beings had no need to observe it. The same is true for all other moral laws properly so called. He must concede that the ground of obligation here must not be sought in the nature of man or in the circumstances in which he is placed, but sought *a priori* solely in the concepts of pure reason, and that every other precept which rests on principles of mere existence, even a precept which is in certain respects universal, so far as it leans in the least on empirical grounds (perhaps only in regard to the motive involved), be called a practical rule but never a moral law.[2]

6.3 THE CONCEPT OF THE GOOD WILL

In the "First Section" of the *Foundations of the Metaphysics of Morals,* Kant picks up on the idea that moral goodness is not something external or psychological. Though he admits that things like riches, power, intelligence, honor, wit, judgment, and other talents of the mind are desirable, he refuses to accept that they are unconditionally good in themselves. Intelligence, for example, may be put to bad use by the bank robber. As Kant puts it, qualities like "power, riches, honor, even health, general well-being, and the contentment with one's condition which is called happiness, make for pride and even arrogance if there is not a good will to correct their influence on the mind and on its principles of action."[3] Kant concludes that, "Nothing in the world—indeed nothing even beyond the world—can possibly be conceived which could be called good without qualification except a good will."[4]

The **good will** to which Kant makes reference is not good because of what it is able to accomplish or because of its ability to achieve some sought-after end. It is also not an attitude of good **intention** or grim determination involving a holier-than-thou **psychological posture.**[5] Rather, good will entails bringing forward all the means in one's power to do that which is one's **duty.** A person is morally good if he or she performs an act motivated by the desire to do one's duty, simply for the sake of duty alone.[6] The morally virtuous person is not concerned with maximizing people's happiness or cultivating moderation in one's lifestyle, but with doing what is required by principles of morality.

6.4   THE NOTION OF DUTY

Kant believes it is important to distinguish between acts done "for the sake of duty" and acts done "in accordance with duty."[7] Although actions performed for the sake of duty are performed in accordance with duty, if they are carried out correctly, not all actions done in accordance with duty are done for duty's sake. Kant offers us an illustration to support his contention that not all actions in accordance with duty possess moral worth:

> . . . it is in fact in accordance with duty that a dealer should not overcharge an inexperienced customer, and wherever there is much business the prudent merchant does not do so, having a fixed price for everyone, so that a child may buy of him as cheaply as any other. Thus the customer is honestly served. But this is far from sufficient to justify the belief that the merchant has behaved in this way from duty and principles of honesty. His own advantage required this behavior; but it cannot be assumed that over and above that he had a direct inclination to the purchaser and that, out of love, as it were, he gave none an advantage in price over another. Therefore, the action was done neither from duty nor from direct inclination but only for a selfish purpose.[8]

6.5   INCLINATION VERSUS DUTY

Kant also distinguishes between actions performed out of **inclination** and those performed out of a **recognition of duty,** arguing that only the latter type is genuinely moral.[9] If, for example, one is so predisposed by temperament to act benevolently toward others, then according to Kant, one is just doing "what comes naturally" and there can be no **moral worth** in this instance. How can there reasonably be moral praise for someone who is benevolently inclined toward his or her neighbors by temperament. If the person's temperament were different, then he or she would not be benevolent. Kant writes:

> To be kind where one can is duty, and there are, moreover, many persons so sympathetically constituted that without any motive of vanity or selfishness they find an inner satisfaction in spreading joy, and rejoice in the contentment of others which they have made possible. But I say that, however dutiful and amiable it may be, that kind of action has no true moral worth.[10]

Kant's skepticism about inclination having moral worth is supported partly by the fact that genuinely moral actions characteristically involve a conflict between inclination and duty. As an illustration of what is meant here, Kant asks us to imagine a person whose life has been entirely clouded by sorrow.[11] This individual has had all his sympathies toward others extinguished. Though the individual is still capable of improving the lot of others, his deadened sensibility leaves him untouched by their unfortunate plight. He simply has no inclination to help as he is totally preoccupied with his own needs. Now if this individual, who has no desire to help others, tears himself away from his own preoccupations to assist a particular distressed individual, say, because of a recognition of duty, then his action assumes moral worth. The individual is benevolent from duty, not from inclination. A test of moral character, then, is whether one is strong enough to follow duty in spite of one's strong inclination not to do so.[12]

Given that for Kant an action must be performed for the sake of duty and in accordance with duty if it is to have moral worth, the question arises as to how duty is to be conceived. In Kant's **formalistic, nonconsequentialist** account, duty has nothing to do with the effects or results of actions. One's moral duty is not to promote happiness or to achieve given purposes. Kant writes, "the purposes we may have for our actions and their effects as ends and incentives of the will cannot give the actions any unconditional and moral worth."[13]

6.6 The Kantian conception of duty is inextricably bound up with **reason.** Kant regards man as rational by nature and argues that a good man acts in accordance with moral law which is universally binding on all rational beings. While everything, for Kant, works according to laws, only rational beings such as man have the capacity of acting according to the conception of laws, that is, according to principles. The capacity to do this reflects will. In this vein, Kant states that, "Duty is the necessity of an action executed from respect for law."[14]

6.6 THE CATEGORICAL IMPERATIVE

6.7

6.8 According to Kant, everytime one acts on one's own volition, the individual operates under a **maxim,** that is, a rule or directive. For instance, if in situation A, one chooses to do act B, one is acting on the maxim, "In situation A, do B."[15] In order for a maxim or rule of conduct to be morally acceptable, it must be consistent with or derived from the ultimate principle of morality, which Kant labels the **categorical imperative.**[16] Kant has given the categorical imperative a number of different interrelated definitions. His first formulation states: "Act only according to that maxim by which you can at the same time will that it should become a universal law."[17] In this definition, a moral maxim is one which can without contradiction be willed to be a rule of conduct for everyone. The categorical imperative implies that the essence of morality lies in acting on the basis of an **impersonal principle** which is **valid for every person,** including oneself.[18] As morality has a rational foundation for Kant, one must be able to **universalize**

maxims of conduct in a **logically consistent** fashion if they are to be binding on all rational creatures. Maxims which cannot be universalized consistently are not moral or morally justified. For example the maxim, "Never help others, but always be helped by them," could not be accepted as a valid moral rule to follow because of its logical implications. It would be illogical even to talk about accepting help from others if the maxim were universalized and acted upon, since nobody would ever try to help others and there would be no help to be accepted. The maxim's logical inconsistency makes it morally unacceptable. From this illustration, we see how the categorical imperative's formal requirement of universal consistency allows us to evaluate morally specific concrete rules of conduct. The categorical imperative acts as the ultimate standard of moral judgment.

6.7   A second formulation of the categorical imperative draws attention more to its social implications. It states: "Act so that you treat humanity, whether in your own person or in that of another, always as an end and never as means only."[19] According to this statement of the categorical imperative, we should show respect for all human beings and avoid exploiting anyone. When we exploit others and disrespect them in this way, we treat them merely as objects or **means** to our own ends. We fail to see others as beings whose existence has absolute worth in itself. In Kant's view, the dignity and worth of any human being are not conditional on any empirical factors. Just as you would not wish to be used and exploited by others, simply so that their ends could be attained, so too is it wrong for you to use and exploit people or treat them merely as means to gain your own ends.

6.8   We see in this second formulation of the categorical imperative the requirement of **reversibility.** This concept holds that a maxim or rule of conduct is morally unacceptable if the individual acting on it would not wish to be the person most disadvantaged or most adversely affected by its applications. If one approves of a maxim, one must approve of it both from the perspective of the one who benefits and from that of the one most negatively affected. An act must be acceptable to an individual regardless of whether the individual is at the giving or receiving end of an action. If, for example, one chooses to approve of stealing in his or her own case, then the person must be willing to become victimized by theft as well if the corresponding maxim is to be considered acceptable. Presumably, nobody wishes to be robbed and therefore no rational, moral thinker would accept such a maxim.

The formal criteria of universality, consistency, and reversibility lead to the idea that moral maxims are also **impartial.** That is, the rightness or wrongness of actions and the moral adequacy of their underlying maxims have nothing to do with **who** happens to be in a favored or disadvantaged position with respect to the actions. Certain acts are either right or wrong in themselves regardless of whose interests are served and regardless of the favorable or unfavorable consequences to oneself. The categorical imperative is an abstract principle which requires that empirical content be removed from moral maxims in the process of their ethical appraisal and justification. Since morality must have a purely rational a priori basis, particulars of content referring to specific persons, places, times, interests, desires, inclinations, and so forth, must be removed when determining the moral adequacy of maxims. Recall that morality cannot have for Kant an empirical or anthropological basis, for this would in his view not provide for a solid and secure foundation for ethics. Empirical, anthropological, and scientific studies of man based on observation and induction cannot produce absolute necessity. Only reason provides the **certainty** which is required for a universal and binding morality.

6.8 Another element contained in the categorical imperative is that of **prescriptivity.** One cannot simply opt out of morality if one chooses. Moral requirements are binding on all rational beings **unconditionally.** One cannot justifiably or consistently argue that morality applies to everyone else but "not me"; or that everyone should always tell the truth "but me," and so on. Furthermore, one is not freed from moral obligation just because one does not feel like acting in respect of the moral law or because acting in such a fashion does not further one's own interests or happiness. Moral principles apply to everyone unconditionally whether they like them or not.

CATEGORICAL VERSUS HYPOTHETICAL IMPERATIVES

Finally, it should be mentioned that Kant's formalistic criteria of moral acceptability (i.e., rationality, prescriptivity, universality, consistency, impartiality, reversibility, and unconditionality) lead him to make a distinction between **categorical moral imperatives** and **hypothetical imperatives.** In contrast to moral imperatives which display all of the formalistic characteristics listed, hypothetical imperatives are always **qualified** in some fashion. A hypothetical imperative takes on the form, "One ought to such and such *if...*" A **condition** is therefore attached. Not everyone is bound by the imperative. For instance, the imperative, "One ought to practice the piano daily" is only binding if one plays the piano and/or if one wishes to become a virtuoso. Not everyone plays and not everyone wishes to become a great musician. Similarly, the imperative, "One ought to go to church on Sunday" is only conditionally binding. If one is a Christian, the duty may be in force. However, if one is Jewish, Muslim, Buddhist, or atheist, then there is no unconditional duty in this regard. One must attend church only if one is Christian, and nobody has a moral duty to become one. Faith cannot be legislated.

A benefit of Kant's distinction between hypothetical and categorical imperatives is that we now have an objective method of determining which commands and duties are morally relevant and acceptable and which pertain to prudential, religious, or economic considerations, for example. Kant's categorical imperative provides us with a rational basis for establishing which actions are right and which are wrong. His theory poses a serious challenge to the view that morality is purely personal, subjective, relative, and not amenable to any kind of objective discussion and evaluation. According to Kant, morality is universal and absolute.

PROGRESS CHECK 6.1

Instructions: *Fill in the blanks with the appropriate responses listed below.*

hypothetical	categorical
prescriptive	consistency
a priori	good will
duty	inclination
reason	maxim
categorical imperative	reversibility
means	consequences
relative	

1. Immanuel Kant does not base his concept of morality on faith or utility, but rather on _____.
2. Principles of morality do not have an empirical basis for Kant, as they are _____, that is, independent of experience.
3. A directive or rule of conduct is called a _____.
4. Imperatives which are conditional are labeled _____ by Kant.
5. The second formulation of the categorical imperative dictates that we always respect persons and treat them as ends in themselves, never only as _____ to our own ends.
6. Morality is certainly not _____ according to Kant.
7. While teleologists such as Bentham and Aristotle stress things like happiness and pleasure as the end of morality, Kant stresses _____. For this reason, his theory is labeled deontological.
8. Benevolent actions performed by _____ have no moral worth.
9. The basis of morality from which all moral maxims are derived is called the _____.
10. To say that moral principles are binding on everyone and that all of us are obliged by them is to suggest that they are _____.
11. Genuinely moral maxims or principles contain no "if's," "and's," or "but's." They are _____.
12. In Kant's formalist account, neither riches, power, wit, nor intelligence are necessarily good. The only thing which is intrinsically good is the _____.
13. Moral maxims must be display logical _____, if they are to be considered acceptable.
14. The _____ test requires that one be prepared to exchange places with the person(s) most adversely affected by the application of a particular principle.
15. For Kant, _____ are irrelevant to the morality of an action.

SUMMARY

1. The Basis of Morality

   Kant rejects consequences, transcendent realms, and happiness as the basis of morality.

   Pure reason is accepted as the basis of morality.

2. The Good Will

   It is the only thing valuable in itself.

   It is not an attitude of good intention or grim determination.

   It involves a desire to do one's duty for duty's sake alone.

3. Distinction between "for the sake of duty" and "in accordance with duty"

   Not all actions done in accordance with duty are done for the sake of duty.

   Moral actions are done for the sake of duty.

4. Inclination versus Duty

   "Good" actions performed by inclination lack moral worth.

   Moral actions typically involve overcoming inclination.

5. Duty's Relation to Reason

   Duty is acting in accordance with moral law out of respect for and recognition of the law which derives from pure reason.

6. The Categorical Imperative

   It is the ultimate basis for all moral duties.

   It is impersonal, binding, impartial, unconditional, universal, a priori, rational, logically consistent, and reversible.

7. Two (of Five) Formulations of the Categorical Imperative

   "Act only according to that maxim by which you can at the same time will that it should become a universal law."

   "Act so that you treat humanity, whether in your own person or in that of another, always as an end and never as a means only."

8. Hypothetical versus Categorical Imperative

   Hypothetical imperatives are conditional or qualified.

   Categorical imperatives are unconditional and unqualified.

   Moral imperatives are categorical.

REFERENCES

Albert, Ethel, Theodore Denise, and Sheldon Peterfreund (eds.). *Great Traditions in Ethics.* Belmont, CA: Wadsworth, 1984.

Hospers, John. *Human Conduct: Problems of Ethics.* New York: Harcourt Brace Jovanovich, 1972.

Kant, Immanuel. *Foundations of the Metaphysics of Morals.* Indianapolis, IN: Bobbs-Merrill, 1959.

———. *Lectures on Ethics.* Indianapolis, IN: Hackett Publishing, 1963.

Ross, Sir William David. *Kant's Ethical Theory.* New York: Oxford University Press, 1954.

Singer, Marcus G. "The Categorical Imperative," in *Moral Philosophy: An Introduction,* ed. Jack Glickman. New York: St. Martin's Press, 1976.

NOTES

1. Immanuel Kant, *Lectures on Ethics*, trans. Louis Infield (Indianapolis: Hackett Publishing, 1963), pp. 148–154.
2. Immanuel Kant, *Foundations of the Metaphysics of Morals* (Indianapolis: Bobbs-Merrill, 1959), p. 5.
3. Kant, *Foundations*, p. 9.
4. Ibid.
5. John Hospers, *Human Conduct: Problems of Ethics* (New York: Harcourt Brace Jovanovich, 1972), pp. 264–296. See Hospers for an excellent explication of Kant's moral theory.
6. Kant, *Foundations*, p. 10.
7. Ibid., p. 13.
8. Ibid., pp. 13–14.
9. Ibid., p. 14.
10. Ibid.
11. Ibid.
12. John Hospers, *Human Conduct*, pp. 265–266.
13. Kant, *Foundations*, p. 16.
14. Ibid.
15. Hospers, *Human Conduct*, p. 276.
16. Kant, *Foundations*, p. 34.
17. Ibid.
18. Ethel Albert, Theodore Denise, and Sheldon Peterfreund, *Great Traditions in Ethics* (Belmont, CA: Wadsworth, 1984), p. 211.
19. Kant, *Foundations*, p. 47.

7

JOHN RAWLS: MORALITY AND SOCIAL JUSTICE

EDUCATIONAL OBJECTIVES: After reading this chapter the student will be able to:

7.1 Explain what is meant by saying John Rawls is a social contractarian.

7.2 Define what Rawls means by "society."

7.3   State what, if any, advantages there are to adopting Rawls' concept of social justice.

7.4   Describe the design of the original position.

7.5   Define "veil of ignorance."

7.6   Elucidate the concept of justice as fairness.

7.7   Paraphrase the reasons why Rawls rejects the utilitarian concept of justice.

7.8   Define the principle of equal liberty.

7.9   Explain the primacy of justice over happiness and goodness.

7.10 State the basic liberties of all citizens in the just society.

7.11 Define the difference principle.

7.12 Explain how the difference principle contrasts to the principle of utility.

7.13 Define and explain the "maximin" principle of justice.

FOCUS QUESTIONS

1. In what ways are social institutions and their practices not immune from moral evaluation?

2. How does Rawls conceptualize society? How else could it be conceived? What would this alternative view mean for Rawls' notion of social justice?

3. Is there anything "unrealistic" about the original position? If so, what? Are there any reasons for abandoning this concept?

4. How do the Rawlsian and utilitarian conceptions of justice differ?

5. What concept of justice emerges out of the original position?

6. Does Rawls assign different weights to moral concepts such as "goodness" and "rightness"? Explain.

7. Can you provide any social applications of the equal-liberty principle and the difference principle?

8. What is Rawls' "maximin" solution to the problem of social justice?

JOHN RAWLS (1921-)

John Rawls was born in Baltimore in 1921. He studied at Cornell University and at Princeton, where he earned his doctorate in 1950. His social contract theory of society serves to illustrate how classical philosophy continues to exert an influence on contemporary thought. Rawls openly admits his debt to contractarian philosophers like Locke and Rousseau. He also states that his theory is highly Kantian in nature and, as such, is not entirely original. Rawls' important contribution to ethical and sociopolitical philosophy comes from the fact that he has taken Kantian and social contractarian ideas to a higher level of abstraction; he has synthesized and organized these ideas by means of a simplifying framework that allows them to be more fully appreciated. Rawls' updated version of Kantianism/social contractarianism constitutes, for him, the most appropriate moral basis for a democratic society. He argues that it is better than utilitarian alternatives. The late Lawrence Kohlberg, another Harvard professor and psychological researcher, has argued that the highest stage of moral development in the individual, as evidenced by the most adequate ethical-reasoning abilities, is reflected in the principles of justice articulated by Rawls and extracted from his theoretical device known as "the original position." John Rawls' most important work is entitled, *A Theory of Justice.* In it, we find an explanation of his socioethical position and a defense of his views on the moral life of individuals within society.

JUSTICE AND THE SOCIAL CONTRACT TRADITION

7.1   The philosopher John Rawls has developed a theory of justice designed to be a viable, more satisfactory alternative to those concepts of justice provided by **utilitarianism** and **intuitionism**.[1] In his classic work, *A Theory of Justice*, Rawls underscores the idea that sociopolitical institutions are proper targets of moral evaluation. His theory is constructed to offer a workable method for solving problems related to social morality. Belonging to the **social contract** tradition of Locke, Rousseau, and Kant, Rawls presents the view that the ultimate basis of society rests on a set of **tacit agreements** among its members. He sees a major theoretical problem of his as one of defining the basic principles entailed in these agreements which a well-ordered society must espouse if it is to be based on a solid moral foundation.

For Rawls, the tacit agreements upon which people would naturally base society primarily involve principles of **justice**. Pointing to the importance of justice, he writes, "Justice is the first virtue of social institutions, as truth is of systems of thought. A theory however elegant and economical must be rejected or revised if it is untrue; likewise laws and institutions no matter how efficient and well-arranged must be reformed or abolished if they are unjust."[2] In the Rawlsian account, every individual possesses an **inviolability** founded on justice, and nothing, not even the welfare of society as a whole, can override it. In a just and moral society, the liberties of equal citizenship are established and the **rights** which are secured by the individual cannot be made subject to political bargaining. Whether or not we ascribe fundamental rights to persons cannot properly be determined by some kind of calculation of social interests. Rawls claims that the only occasion when a particular injustice is tolerable is when it is required to circumvent an even greater injustice.[3]

7.2   In order to appreciate better Rawls' notion of justice and how it operates, it is helpful to get a clearer picture of how he conceptualizes **society.** Rawls regards society as a self-sufficient association of individuals. In their interpersonal relations, people acknowledge that certain rules of conduct are binding on them and, in most cases, they act upon them. These binding rules of society constitute a system of cooperation designed to further the good and improve the welfare of those who participate. Society, then, is a type of cooperative venture for purposes of mutual advantage. Within society, we find an **identity of interests** as social cooperation allows for a better life for everyone than would be possible for any single person to enjoy if left to live solely by his or her own efforts.[4]

Rawls recognizes, of course, that even within a cooperative system, **conflicts of interest** will inevitably arise. Persons will tend to disagree, for instance, about how the greater benefits secured by their collaborative efforts should be distributed. In pursuit of their life goals, persons typically perceive things differently and generally prefer a larger share of benefits to a smaller one. Obviously, not everyone can have a larger share; nor is it always feasible to give everyone access to the same resources. In view of this, Rawls believes that:

> [a] set of principles is required for choosing among the various social arrangements which determine this division of advantages and for underwriting an agreement on the proper distributive shares. These principles are the principles of social justice: they provide a way of assigning rights and duties in the basic institutions of society and they define the appropriate distribution of the benefits and burdens of social cooperation.[5]

7.3   Rawls' conception of social justice enables one to become the **ideal observer** in the resolution of social conflict. His notion of justice is intended to serve as a **common point of view** from which the conflicting claims of opposing parties may be **fairly adjudicated.** A shared understanding of justice allows for individuals with disparate aims and purposes to establish the bonds of **civic friendship.**[6] This shared understanding can be regarded as constituting the basic charter of a well-ordered human association. In such an association or society, each person accepts, and knows that other persons accept, the same fundamental principles of justice. It should be added here that when referring to **persons,** Rawls means not only particular individuals but also groups or collective agencies. When he speaks of the justness or injustice of any **practice,** he means whatever *activity* is specified by a system of rules (for example, rights, roles, duties, and offices).

7.4   THE ORIGINAL POSITION AND THE "VEIL OF IGNORANCE"
7.5

In order to arrive at the specific principles of social justice, Rawls uses a theoretical device called the **original position.**[7] The original position is a purely **hypothetical situation** in the sense that it has never actually existed in reality. It is not a historical event or empirical set of circumstances. In the original position, persons are placed behind a **veil of ignorance.** They are ignorant of their place, class position, or social status within society. They do not know what their fortune is in the distribution of natural assets, abilities, intelligence, strength, and so on. They are unaware as well of their peculiar psychological inclinations and what definition they and others have given to the good life. What is specified about the parties in the original position is that they are **rational,** free and equal moral beings, each having similar needs, interests, and capacities. Furthermore, parties in the original position have their own goals and are **mutually disinterested.** This is not to suggest that the parties are egoists, only concerned with their own worth, prestige, and power, but that the parties are generally concerned with furthering their own interests and not with furthering someone else's goals.[8] In this situation of mutual disinterest, it is understandable that parties will sometimes come into conflict over the distribution of social advantages.

7.6
Assuming that conflicts among the opposing parties are to be settled rationally, not through violence or war, Rawls works out his theory by determining which rational principles of justice would likely be chosen by individuals in the original position, when placed behind the veil of ignorance. Ignorance of one's particular fortune or inclinations ensures that nobody is advantaged or disadvantaged in the initial selection of principles by the outcome of natural chance or by the **contingencies** of social circumstances. Principles of justice arising out of the original position are freely and mutually agreed upon in an initial situation that is **fair** from everyone's perspective. As Rawls puts it, "Since all are similarly situated and no one is able to design principles to favor his particular condition, the principles of justice are the result of a fair agreement or bargain."[10] The principles agreed to in the original position define what Rawls calls **justice as fairness.**[11]

The concept of justice as fairness which emerges out of the original position serves to regulate criticism and reform of all social institutions. With mutually agreed-upon principles of justice, people can prepare a constitution and set up a legislature to enact laws which are consistent with these principles. Of course, Rawls realizes that people cannot literally contract from the hypothetical original position, since at birth they already find themselves with some particular status and psychological endowment, in some particular society, and given some particular life prospects. Nonetheless, Rawls believes that, to the extent a society satisfies the principle of justice as fairness, it conforms to the principles which free and equal individuals would accept for their mutual advantage under circumstances that are fair. Choosing these principles, people can decide **in advance** how they will regulate their claims against one another and what rights, duties, and freedoms will form the constitutional foundation of their society.

7.7
In his elaboration of the two specific principles which are to be included

under his notion of justice as fairness, Rawls first explains why he rejects the utilitarian conception of justice. Refusing to accept "utility" as a standard of justice, Rawls writes:

> Offhand it hardly seems likely that persons who view themselves as equals, entitled to press their claims upon one another, would agree to a principle which may require lesser life prospects for some simply for the sake of a greater sum of advantages enjoyed by others. . . . [A] rational man would not accept a basic structure merely because it maximized the algebraic sum of advantages irrespective of its permanent effects on his own rights and interests. Thus it seems that the principle of utility is incompatible with the conception of social cooperation among equals for mutual advantage.[12]

7.8 THE PRINCIPLE OF EQUAL LIBERTY
7.9

Having rejected the principle of utility, Rawls contends that persons in the original position would likely choose two fundamental principles. The first is the **principle of equal liberty.** It states, ". . . each person is to have an equal right to the most extensive basic liberty compatible with a similar liberty for others."[13] Note that such a principle would be accepted without a knowledge of anyone's particular ends and without knowledge of what it is to anyone's advantage. The implicit agreement, therefore, would be to have everyone's pursuits and interests fall within the boundaries of what the principles of justice require. People would be expected to refrain from choosing ends which would violate the liberties of others and were liberties that they would expect for themselves. The advantage of some could not be purchased justifiably at the expense of others' freedoms—certainly not in a situation of equality and cooperation for mutual advantage. Furthermore, whereas utilitarians such as Bentham do not distinguish among pleasures and see all pleasures as equally valuable and worth pursuing, Rawls maintains that "the principles of right, and so of justice, put limits on which satisfactions have value; they impose restrictions on what are reasonable conceptions of one's good."[14] From the Rawlsian **deontological,** social-contract perspective, the concept of **rightness** overrides and is prior to the concept of **goodness.**[15] The liberty to pursue ends must be limited by considerations of justice. In this vein, Rawls says:

> A just social system defines the scope within which individuals must develop their aims, and it provides a framework of rights and opportunities and the means of satisfaction within and by the use of which these ends may be equitably pursued. The priority of justice is accounted for, in part, by holding that the interests requiring the violation of justice have no value. Having no merit in the first place, they cannot override its claims.[16]

7.10 The basic liberties of all citizens required by the first principle include (1) political liberty, that is, the right to vote and run for public office; (2) freedom of speech and assembly; (3) freedom of thought and liberty of conscience; (4) personal freedom; (5) the right to own property; and finally, (6) freedom from arbitrary arrest and seizure. The liberties listed here represent the basic rights of every person within society and ideally none of them is to be violated. These basic rights define the boundaries within which social practices must fall if they are to be considered acceptable, right, or just.

The statement of the first principle clearly tells us that people are to be regarded as free and equal. Systems of rules defining practices of various social institutions must therefore be administered equitably. There should be a spirit of **impartiality** and **disinterestedness** characterizing the distribution of advantages. No individual should arbitrarily receive preferred treatment. For example, if a firm offers a position of employment and draws up job specifications, the equal liberty principle requires that all applicants be judged by the established criteria. If it were the case that someone without the specified and required credentials were offered the position, the principle would not be upheld because an exception was made, presumably on the basis of irrelevant considerations (for example, appearance). In addition, the principle would not be equitable or fairly administered if particular individuals were excluded on criteria not related to the job (such as sex or race). We can see, then, how considerations of rightness and justness can become involved even in social hiring practices, a point which underscores Rawls' claim that social institutions are proper objects of moral evaluation.

7.11   THE DIFFERENCE PRINCIPLE
7.12

The difference principle is the second principle falling under Rawls' conception of justice as fairness. It states: "Social and economic inequalities, for example inequalities of wealth and authority, are just only if they result in compensating benefits for everyone, and in particular for the least advantaged members of society."[17] The difference principle should not be misunderstood here as equivalent to the utilitarian greatest-happiness principle which seeks to promote the greatest happiness for the greatest number. The difference principle does not permit inequalities in institutional practices on the grounds that the hardships or burdens of some are offset by a greater good of the majority. In Rawls' view, "it is not just that some should have less in order that others may prosper."[18] Rawls does not suggest by this that everyone must be treated precisely the same. He believes that citizens of a country do not object to people having different positions within society (for example, prime minister, president, or judge), each with its own special rights and duties. What they object to is the pattern of honors and rewards set up by a practice (for example, the privileges and salaries of government officials).[19] They may also object to the distribution of power and wealth which comes about by the different ways in which people avail themselves of the opportunities allowed by a particular practice (for example, the concentration of wealth that may develop in a free market environment and allow for large entrepreneurial and speculative rewards). In order to justify inequalities, there must be reason to believe that the practice involving the inequality, or resulting in it, will ultimately work for the advantage of *every* person engaging in it—not just the majority. Thus individuals must find their conditions and prospects under a situation of inequality preferable to what they would be without it. In short, every person must gain from the inequality, if that inequality is to be permissible.

In order to make acceptable the difference principle, which allows for differences of treatment, an important condition must be met. It is necessary that the offices to which special benefits are attached are open to all who meet the necessary requirements. Such offices must be won in a fair competition wherein contestants are judged on their merits. The fact that an excluded individual nevertheless benefits from the efforts put forward by those allowed to compete does not legitimize this unjust treatment, according to Rawls.[21] There are intrinsic goods involved in the skillful and devoted exercise of various offices and practices. If one is prevented from functioning in those particular offices or practices, then one is deprived of one of the most important ways in which individuals realize their **human potential.** One is robbed of one's humanity, so to speak.

The suggestion that societal positions should be won by fair competition does not mean that absolutely everyone has a right to compete and be seriously considered for every job. Remember, the difference principle allows for the possibility of inequality if it works to the advantage of every individual and especially to the advantage of the least well off. Suppose, for instance, that an airline establishes a minimum level of corrected vision for all of its pilots. Now, such a regulation does in fact work against those who cannot reach the minimum. Some people will, in effect, be excluded from consideration for a pilot's job. Nonetheless, this vision requirement should not be regarded as unjust. A pilot with limited vision is a danger to the airline's passengers, as well as to himself or herself. Everyone, including the candidate pilot, benefits by the application of the vision requirement, albeit through a form of "unequal" treatment.[22] The difference principle may also be at work in some government economic policies. One frequently hears how unjust it is that huge corporations are given tax breaks, whereas the average taxpayer is "unduly" saddled with an ever-increasing share of the tax burden. It could be argued, however, that by this apparent unequal treatment, corporations will have more available capital to invest in new business ventures; in turn, this will create new or better jobs and certainly benefit those worst off in society, namely, the unemployed. Were the tax burden proportionately equal, perhaps no new job opportunities would be created and the unemployed would remain that way, thus worse rather than better off.

7.13 THE MAXIMIN SOLUTION TO THE PROBLEM OF SOCIAL JUSTICE

In closing, it is worth noting that Rawls' combination of the two principles arising out of the original position is called "the **maximin solution** to the problem of social justice."[23] When the equal liberty principle and the difference principle are combined under the maximin solution, the general rule is to rank alternatives by their worst possible outcomes: thus we adopt "the alternative the worst outcome of which is superior to the worst outcomes of the others."[25] This guideline helps **maximize** the lot of those **minimally** advantaged, a fundamental goal of the Rawlsian just society.[26] The maximin rule focuses our attention on the worst that can happen under each alternative course of action, and it instructs us to make a decision in light of that. Rawls' notion of justice, then, is a **reciprocity** concept. Rightness is not ultimately determined by consequences. Rather the reciprocity element inherent in Rawls' theory of justice "requires that a practice be such that all members who fall under it could and would accept it and be bound by it."[27] Rawlsian justice requires the mutual acknowledgment of principles by free people. No person has authority over another. Each is willing to accept the worst position as it might be assigned by one's enemy or opponent in a situation of conflict. This makes the element of reciprocity essential to justice and fairness.

PROGRESS CHECK 7.1

Instructions: *Fill in the blanks with the appropriate responses listed below.*

original position	equal liberty principle
difference principle	veil of ignorance
rightness	utilitarianism
impartiality	society
social contract	maximin principle

1. The theory of justice presented by John Rawls is in direct contrast with the one offered by _____.
2. A theory which interprets morality and justice in terms of a set of tacit agreements among societal members is a type of _____ theory.
3. An association of self-sufficient individuals who cooperate for purposes of mutual advantage is called a _____.
4. If social conflicts are to be fairly adjudicated, they must be handled with _____.
5. The _____ is a theoretical device used by Rawls to draw out the principles of justice as fairness.
6. According to the _____, one should in a situation of social conflict adopt the alternative course of action whose worst outcome is superior to the worst outcomes of the other alternatives.
7. The fairest principles of social justice can be obtained in advance of social conflicts when contracting members are placed behind the _____ and thereby made unaware of what is to their advantage or disadvantage.
8. Rawls' theory is a deontological position which stresses the importance of _____ over goodness.

9. The _____ states that every individual should have an equal right to the most extensive basic liberty compatible with a similar liberty for others.

10. The _____ states that social and economic inequalities are just only if they result in compensating benefits for everyone, and in particular the least advantaged in society.

SUMMARY

1. Rawls' Theory
   It is an alternative to utilitarianism and intuitionism.
   It is a further development of social contract theory.
   It is a treatment of the moral and sociopolitical basis of society.

2. Rawls' Concept of Society
   Societies are self-sufficient associations of individuals.
   Societal rules of conduct are binding on all members.
   Society is a cooperative venture for purposes of mutual advantage.
   Entails both identity of interests and conflicts of interests.

3. Principles of Social Justice
   They provide a common moral viewpoint.
   They fairly adjudicate conflicts.
   They serve as a basis of civic friendship.
   They are impartial, binding, unbiased, and freely chosen by rational agents.

4. The Original Position
   A theoretical device.
   A hypothetical situation.
   It places parties behind a veil of ignorance.
   It can draw out principles of justice as fairness.
   Serves as the basis of Rawlsian contractarianism.

5. Justice as Fairness
   Emerges out of establishment of principles in the original position.
   Can be used to criticize and reform social institutions.
   Can be used for legislative purposes.
   It is what free and equal individuals would contract to accept for their mutual advantage under fair circumstances.

6. Rawls' Rejection of Utilitarianism
   Rational persons who view themselves as equals would not accept lesser life prospects for a greater sum of advantages.

7. Principle of Equal Liberty
   Each person is to have an equal right to the most extensive basic liberty compatible with a similar liberty for others.

Guarantees all citizens political liberty, the right to vote and run for public office, freedom of speech and assembly, freedom of thought and liberty of conscience, personal freedom, the right to own property, and freedom from arbitrary arrest and seizure.

8. The Difference Principle

Social and economic inequalities are just only if they result in compensating benefits for everyone—especially for the least advantaged in society.

Differs from the greatest happiness principle.

Offices having special rights and privileges must be won in fair competitions.

9. The Maximin Solution

One should adopt the alternative the worst outcome of which is superior to the worst outcomes of the others.

Requires one to maximize the lot of those minimally advantaged in society.

Falling under it are Rawls' first two principles.

REFERENCES

Barry, B. M. *The Liberal Theory of Justice*. Oxford: Clarendon Press, 1973.

Daniels, N. (ed.), *Reading Rawls*. New York: Basic Books, 1975.

Rawls, John. *A Theory of Justice*. Cambridge, MA: Harvard University Press, 1971.

———. "Ethics and Social Justice." In *Great Traditions in Ethics*, ed. Albert, Denise, and Peterfreund. pp. 364–381.

———. "Justice as Fairness." In *Ethics: Selections from Classical and Contemporary Writers*, ed. Oliver A. Johnson. 5th ed. Toronto: Holt, Rinehart and Winston, 1984, pp. 434–443.

Wolff, R. P. *Understanding Rawls*. Princeton, NJ: Princeton University Press, 1976.

NOTES

1. John Rawls, *A Theory of Justice* (Cambridge: Harvard University Press, 1971). For his rejection of utilitarianism and intuitionism, see pp. 22–40. Rawls rejects utilitarianism because it makes equality and liberty contingent on such things as efficiency calculations. He rejects intuitionism because it allows for a plurality of first principles which sometimes conflict and it gives no method of weighing principles against one another. Presumably these first principles are self-evident and necessary. However, when two or more self-evident and necessary principles conflict, intuitionism has no way of resolving the conflict. Rawls believes his theory of justice can help in this instance.
2. Rawls, *Justice*, p. 3.
3. Ibid., p. 4.
4. Ibid.
5. Ibid.
6. Ibid., p. 5.
7. Ibid., p. 12.
8. Ibid., p. 13.
9. Ibid., p. 12. A contingency can be seen as something conditional, a particular, or something factually or empirically true, but not necessarily true.
10. Ibid., p. 12.
11. Ibid.

12. Ibid., p. 14.
13. Ibid., p. 60.
14. Ibid., p. 31.
15. A deontological ethic stresses duties and rights over happiness and pleasurable consequences.
16. Rawls, *Justice*, p. 31.
17. Ibid., pp. 14–15.
18. Ibid., p. 15.
19. John Rawls, "Ethics and Social Justice," in *Great Traditions in Ethics*, ed. Ethel Albert, Theodore Denise, and Sheldon Peterfreund. (Belmont, CA: Wadsworth, 1984), p. 370.
20. Ibid., p. 371.
21. Ibid.
22. This example of the "pilot" is an adaptation of the "bus driver" example found in Vincent Barry, *Applying Ethics: A Text with Readings* (Belmont, CA: Wadsworth, 1982), pp. 52–53.
23. Rawls, *Justice*, p. 152.
24. This point is highlighted by Vincent Barry, *Applying Ethics*, p. 51.
25. Rawls, *Justice*, pp. 152–153.
26. See ibid., pp. 153–154, for an illustration of the maximin principle at work.
27. See Barry, *Applying Ethics*, p. 53.

Self-Test

Social Morality

_____ 1. Jeremy Bentham's name is most closely associated with the moral theory called:

(a) social contract
(b) deontology
(c) utilitarianism
(d) egoism

_____ 2. Immanuel Kant agrees with the idea that the morality of actions can be determined by reference to consequences.

(a) true
(b) false

_____ 3. To which concept does John Rawls attribute primary importance in matters of morality?

(a) virtue
(b) character
(c) goodness
(d) rightness

_____ 4. The concept of utility can be equated with:

(a) duty, rights, and liberty
(b) virtues, ideals, and beliefs
(c) benefit, advantage, pleasure, and happiness
(d) altruism, obligation, and self-sacrifice

_____ 5. According to Jeremy Bentham, nature has placed mankind under the governance of two sovereign masters:

(a) Apollo and Dionysus
(b) Mars and Zeus
(c) Pain and Pleasure
(d) Ignorance and Wisdom
(e) Light and Darkness

_____ 6. Jeremy Bentham was in favor of punishment in only limited cases. He opposed punishment whenever it was:

(a) groundless, inefficacious, unprofitable, expensive, and needless
(b) universal, prescriptive, normative, and moral
(c) useful, beneficial, and pleasure-producing
(d) retributive, vindictive, and obligatory

_____ 7. Where does J. S. Mill recommend we look for happiness?

(a) in the pursuit of riches and wealth
(b) in developing a noble reputation
(c) in satisfying our curiosity and pursuing higher intellectual interests or in working for the common good
(d) in developing self-mastery and in the cultivation of virtue

_____ 8. On which of the following does Kant base his conception of morality?

(a) pleasure
(b) happiness
(c) self-mastery
(d) reason
(e) tradition and authority

_____ 9. A truth claim which is purely rational and necessarily the case is:

(a) normative
(b) a posteriori
(c) a priori
(d) probabilistic

_____ 10. The Kantian categorical imperative states that:

(a) we should live a life of moderation
(b) we should act in our rational self-interest
(c) we should love our neighbors and be prepared to sacrifice
(d) we should act only on those moral rules of conduct which could be made universally prescriptive

_____ 11. According to John Rawls, the principles governing society should be based on:

(a) love
(b) tradition
(c) justice
(d) authority
(e) utility

_____ 12. The "maximin solution" to the problem of social justice recommends that:
   (a) we minimize the lot of the best-off in society
   (b) we maximize the lot of the worst-off in society
   (c) we maximize social utility by minimizing government control
   (d) none of the above

_____ 13. The "original position" is:
   (a) a state of nature wherein individual is opposed to individual
   (b) a hypothetical situation wherein individuals freely select principles of justice to be used in the adjudication of social conflict
   (c) the only acceptable mode of having sex
   (d) none of the above

_____ 14. According to the principle of equal liberty:
   (a) people must refrain from choosing ends that violate the liberties of others if they would expect those liberties for themselves
   (b) the advantage of some cannot be purchased at the expense of others' freedoms
   (c) limits must be placed on which satisfactions have value
   (d) none of the above
   (e) a, b, and c

_____ 15. Who said, "It is better to be a human being dissatisfied than a pig satisfied; better to be a Socrates dissatisfied than a fool satisfied."
   (a) Plato
   (b) Kant
   (c) Mill
   (d) Bentham
   (e) Rawls
   (f) John Candy

16. What is the purpose of Bentham's hedonistic calculus? How is it used? Explain.

17. How does the utilitarianism of John Stuart Mill differ from that of Jeremy Bentham?

18. Explain Kant's distinction between things which are conditionally good and things which are unconditionally good.

19. Comment on the morality of actions in the context of Kant's distinction between inclination and duty.

20. Explain Kant's "formalism." What does it mean to describe his theory as formalistic?

8

PHILOSOPHICAL VERSUS SCIENTIFIC APPROACHES TO THE STUDY OF MORALITY

OVERVIEW

1. Scientific Approach to the Study of Morality
2. Philosophical Approach to the Study of Morality
3. Types of Moral Claims and Inquiries
4. Progress Check
5. Learning Exercises
6. Summary
7. References
8. Notes

EDUCATIONAL OBJECTIVES: After reading this chapter the student will be able to:

8.1 State the basic aims and methods of science.
8.2 State the basic aims and methods of philosophy.
8.3 Distinguish between scientific and philosophical approaches to the study of morality.

8.4 Explain the "is–ought" distinction.

8.5 Name and explain the two types of moral–philosophical inquiry.

8.6 Express greater confidence in understanding the nature and scope of moral philosophy.

8.7 Explain the differences among empirical, normative, and a priori statements.

FOCUS QUESTIONS

1. What is meant by saying that scientists approach the study of morality empirically?
2. What kinds of questions about morality are relevant to scientists?
3. What is the difference between normative and nonnormative statements?
4. How is normative ethics different from metaethics?
5. Why is it important to be cognizant of the types of moral claims being made in the context of moral controversy?
6. Are value judgments verified or are they justified? Explain.

In Part I (chapters 1–7) of this work, the ideas of several different ethical thinkers were discussed in terms of the distinction between individual and social morality. A major goal of Part I was to help newcomers to philosophical ethics identify the boundaries of the moral domain. It should be noted at this point that there exist differences between philosophy and other disciplines of inquiry with respect to the methods used in studying morality. We start this chapter, therefore, by briefly clarifying the basic differences between philosophy and the scientific forms of inquiry as they relate to moral study.

8.1 SCIENTIFIC APPROACH

Sciences such as psychology, sociology, and anthropology make morality an object of **empirical** study. To say that morality is studied empirically means that methods of **observation** and **controlled experiment** are typically used. Scientific researchers attempt to **measure** and **describe** what is **true,** or at least highly **probable,** about moral conduct and experience. In their investigations, researchers strive to achieve the ideal of scientific **objectivity.** They are not in the business of making value judgments about the moral phenomena which are studied. Instead, scientists are interested in providing **correlational findings, causal** and/or **functional explanations.** Given the methods and goals of scientists, we find psychologists, for instance, interested in tracing the development of moral-reasoning abilities in children and adolescents. Sociologists may be concerned with examining the function of morality in group organization. Anthropologists, by contrast, might be inclined to uncover the origins and development of morality in social-human evolution. Whatever their particular concerns, the causal, functional, and descriptive preoccupations of scientists steer them in the direction of answering empirical questions about the "how," "why," "when," "where," and "what" of morality and moral experience. Methods of statistical analysis are frequently employed to **verify** findings or to support factual claims which are made about moral experience. If possible, **predictions** about future moral events are also offered. Although scientists study morality, they do not wish to be **moralistic.** They do not wish to **prescribe** what ought to be done; nor do they wish to judge what values are good or bad. Desiring to be neutral and objective, scientists try to express their claims as **nonnormative** statements. Empirical findings are not designed to be **evaluative** or somehow laden with normative **value judgments.**

8.2 PHILOSOPHICAL APPROACH TO THE STUDY
8.3 OF MORALITY
8.4

The philosophical approach to the study of morality may be either **normative** or **metaethical.** Normative philosophical inquiry involves going beyond empirical investigation. In contrast to scientific researchers who make empirical claims about what is factually true or likely the case, philosophers sometimes make **normative** statements about how humans **should** behave or what **ought** to be the case. Normative inquiry frequently leads philosophers to **prescribe** courses of action and to make **evaluative judgments** about what is **right** or **wrong, good** or **bad, praiseworthy** or **blameworthy.** Thus, while empirical scientific investigation (or everyday experience) may yield evidence that human beings often act in their own self-interest, the moral philosopher engaged in normative inquiry asks whether humans should or should not act in this fashion. The "fact" that they do does not necessarily mean that morally speaking they "should." Most philosophers question the idea that one can derive a moral normative "ought" from an empirical "is" of experience. Just because it is true that some people kill, steal, cheat, and rape, does not mean one can justifiably conclude on that basis that they should. Philosophers are thus not interested in verifying nonnormative empirical findings (the job of science), but rather they are concerned to **justify** evaluative judgments about what ought or ought not to be the case, what is good or bad, or what is praiseworthy or blameworthy.

Some normative moral inquiry attempts to establish what ought to be done in specific moral situations or in particular moral controversies like abortion and capital punishment. Other normative inquiry is more general in nature. As was learned in Part I, philosophers have articulated over the ages a number of different normative moral theories that outline systems of basic ethical principles which they claim are applicable to everyone. These theories can be regarded as blueprints for moral life. They give direction and guidance in moral decision making and action. By appealing to these general moral principles in situations of specific moral dilemma, one can determine what ought or ought not to be done. Some normative theories (for example, utilitarianism) stress the effects or results of actions in evaluating their rightness, while others (for example, Kantian deontology) focus on such things as logical consistency and universalization.

8.5
8.6 A second philosophical approach to morality is **metaethics.** It has two basic aspects and the first is analytical. Metaethics concerns itself with the meanings of ethical terms. While the philosopher preoccupied with normative issues might ask whether or not the country's laws on abortion are right, the metaethicist might ask what is meant by the term "right" itself. Does right mean that which is consistent with the will of the majority? Does right mean that which an individual approves of? Or, does right mean that which expresses divine will? In asking such questions, metaethicists involve themselves in nonnormative inquiry, yet of a type which is neither empirical nor scientific. Rather than describing moral conduct or stating moral prescriptions, metaethicists ask for clarifications and elucidations of moral concepts.

A second aim of metaethicists is to examine critically the ultimate foundations of particular ethical systems. For instance, they may study the rationale or justification provided for any system's adoption of its fundamental principles. Metaethical inquiry is thus theoretically one step removed from normative deliberation. In contrast to the utilitarian philosopher who may wish to prescribe a particular course of action on the basis that it will likely maximize pleasure or happiness, the metaethicist questions why pleasure or happiness should serve as the ultimate ethical foundation of action and decision making in the first place.

8.7 TYPES OF MORAL CLAIMS AND INQUIRIES

Some claims about morality, or in support of moral arguments, are relevant to science and empirical investigation, while others are pertinent to theoretical philosophy and rational inquiry. Thus, when moral disputes arise, efforts should be made to determine what kinds of claims are in conflict so that proper steps may be taken to resolve the conflict. Perhaps the dispute can be resolved simply by obtaining relevant facts. For example, some people may be in favor of capital punishment because they believe it acts as a deterrent, while others may be opposed to it because they believe it is ineffectual. The conflict here stems from opposing opinions based on differing beliefs of what is true. If it could be proven conclusively in an empirical fashion that capital punishment does in fact deter, or that it does not in fact deter, then the dispute in this case could be easily resolved, for it hinges on the truth or falsity of this factual–empirical premise. If, however, one were not questioning the effectiveness of capital punishment, but objecting morally to the principle of using any type of corporal punishment as a proper way of dealing with wrongdoing in the first place, the basis of disagreement would not be factual in nature. At issue here would be such considerations as the wrongdoer's rights, respect for persons, the value of life, rehabilitation versus retribution, and so on. A plausible argument could be put forward that even murderers do not lose their human dignity and right to life as a result of killing others. Such an argument could be based on appeals to ultimate principles, say, or on the recognition of the absolute value of life. In this case, the argument's validity could not be established simply by appeals to facts. Scientific evidence cannot tell us whether or not murderers have rights. The argument that they do or do not must be supported and evaluated on rational grounds.

To determine whether a particular dispute about morality can be settled by scientific or philosophical procedures, then, it is first necessary to establish what kinds of claims, statements, or theses are being advanced by the conflicting parties. Once this is established, it can be determined how the dispute should be resolved, rationally or by appeals to empirical evidence.

8.7   **Empirical Claims about Morality**

If a moral thesis advanced by someone can be verified or falsified by facts derived from observation or by using methods of scientific experimentation, then it is empirical. Let us suppose, for example, the thesis is advanced that children from highly industrialized nations develop more quickly in their moral-reasoning abilities than do children from third-world, developing countries. In this case, the truth or falsity of this claim can be determined by conducting a comparative study. Using an objective standard of adequate moral reasoning, we might test subjects from industrialized nations and those from third-world countries longitudinally and/or by cross-section; we would control for contaminating variables which might distort the findings, compare findings from both groups, and use proper methods of statistical analysis in interpreting the data. By appealing to what is found in experience, we would set out to determine the truth or falsity of our empirical claim. Of course, any findings obtained would be **contingent.** What is empirically true today could be false tomorrow. Conditions in the world could change in such a way that those from third-world countries might develop more quickly in their moral reasoning. There is nothing in principle preventing this. Scientific claims expressed as empirical conclusions must therefore be regarded as **probabilistic,** not **necessary.**

A Priori Claims   In contrast to empirical claims which are contingent and **a posteriori,** or derived from experience, other types of claims are **a priori** or independent of experience. The truth or falsity of a priori claims cannot be determined by experience or sensory observation. A priori claims are recognized to be true or false by reason alone or by what might be called **intellectual intuition.**[1] Such claims are noncontingent. They express what must be absolutely and necessarily true. Such claims are not dependent on space–time considerations. They are true for all people, in all places, at all times. Though experience may have to awaken in us an awareness of the truth of a priori statements, once discovered their truth is recognized independently of experience. For example, children need experience to learn that three plus two equals five. However, once this truth is appreciated, no experience could falsify it. No rational thinker can doubt this statement, and nothing in experience could call into question its **veracity.**

In *A Preface to Philosophy*, Mark Woodhouse outlines several different kinds of a priori claims. The first kind is the definitional statement, such as, "Triangles have three sides" or "All bachelors are unmarried males." In both cases the meanings of the terms are explicitly stated. The second kind of a priori claim includes statements whose necessary truth follows directly from the meanings of the key terms. Woodhouse gives the following example: "John cannot be an atheistic Baptist." This statement is "necessarily" true given the meanings of atheist and Baptist. Being a Baptist presupposes in part that one believes in God. Hence, it is self-contradictory to claim that one is an atheistic Baptist. One cannot logically apply both key terms to the same person. One need not appeal to experience to verify this statement, nor could experience falsify it. We know its truth a priori.

A third kind of a priori statement is a **tautology.** The necessary truth of a tautology stems from its logical form or from particular principles of logical inference. For example, God either exists or He does not exist (either P or not-P). God cannot be and not be at the same time. To suggest that this is possible is illogical. We know this a priori, that is, by pure rational intuition.

The first three types of a priori statements can be described as "analytic." The denial of any analytic a priori proposition leads to self-contradiction. One cannot logically have atheistic Baptists, square triangles, or a God who both exists and does not exist at the same time. In the history of philosophical inquiry there has also arisen some controversy over whether or not there is a fourth kind of a priori claim, one which can be recognized intuitively as true or valid but which does not lead to self-contradiction when denied. Philosophers call this disputed type of claim **synthetic a priori.**

Some like Immanuel Kant argue that synthetic a priori statements are possible. They point out that the necessary truth of them is not dependent upon the meanings of key ethical terms or on any logical form. Although analytic a priori statements are empty of content, synthetic a priori statements provide us with information about the world. The analytic statement "All bachelors are unmarried men" does not tell us anything about reality. The claim is true by definition. Nothing in the world could change its truth; nothing in the world is required to prove its truth. Examples of so-called synthetic a priori statements include: "Moral responsibility presupposes freedom of action," and "Every event has a cause." In the former case, "moral responsibility" can be defined independently of "freedom of action." Thus one can discuss whether actions are free or determined without having to consider the notion of moral responsibility. In the latter statement, the idea of "event" need not be defined in terms of "cause." Some would also argue that this proposition is true necessarily. If someone claimed to have discovered an event such as a flood, war, or famine for which there was no cause, then those arguing for the possibility of a synthetic a priori would answer that the person has not searched hard enough or has overlooked the cause. It could be argued that we know a priori that everything is caused. The basis of such a claim is **reason,** not experience.

The philosopher Immanuel Kant has argued that there exist synthetic a priori claims in the realm of morality.[2] His formulation of the categorical imperative is one example. Recall that the categorical imperative states: "Act only according to that maxim by which you can at the same time will that it should become a universal law." The second part of this imperative dictates that we never use people solely as means to our ends, but rather that we treat them as ends in themselves. For Kant, the truth and validity of synthetic a priori propositions are self-evident. They are recognized as such by rational intuition.

Normative Claims   Normative claims differ from empirical and analytical statements. Empirical statements assert what is factually true or false. Analytic (a priori) statements tell us what must logically be the case given our rational intuitions. Normative statements, on the other hand, either **evaluate** what is the case or **prescribe** what *ought* to be or *should* be done. Individuals making normative claims assert **value judgments** about what is right or wrong, good or bad, praiseworthy or blameworthy, obligatory or prohibited. They recommend what views should be adopted and what courses of action should be taken. Examples of normative claims include "Mother Teresa is a good person," "One ought always to act in one's own self-interest," and "Fornication is wrong."

Assuming for the moment the validity of synthetic a priori statements, it should be noted that they somewhat overlap with normative statements. Thus some synthetic a priori statements are normative, but not all normative statements are synthetic a priori. The claim "Every event has a cause" is synthetic a priori but not normative. "You should go to church" is a normative statement which is not necessary in any a priori sense. The principle that we should not use people solely as means to our ends could be argued as both normative and synthetic a priori.

For purposes of this text, the controversy surrounding synthetic a priori judgments will be avoided. The basic distinctions thus to keep in mind are those among empirical, normative, and analytic (a priori) statements.

Normative claims may be particular or general. "I ought to repay my debt to John" is an example of a "particular" normative statement. "People should never lie" is an example of a general normative statement. As we know, empirical claims are validated by relevant facts, observation, and experimentation, whereas analytic claims are based on rational intuition. By contrast, particular normative claims are supported by appeals to defensible general moral principles. For example, the particular normative claim "John's throwing the rock through the neighbor's window is wrong" could be based on the general moral principle that "Whatever actions damage other people's property are wrong." Since John's rock throwing damages others' property, the rock throwing is therefore wrong.

Of course, general moral principles used to support particular normative assertions must be justified as well. The various ways in which they can be supported and tested will be examined in more detail in the next chapter, which discusses patterns of reasoning. For now, it is sufficient to say that some general principles are based on, or defended by, appeals to even more general principles. If someone asked, for example, "Why are actions which damage other people's property wrong?" the defense might be, "Whatever costs people money and makes them work unnecessarily is wrong; and since actions which damage others' property cost them money and require unnecessary work, such actions are therefore wrong." Such a line of reasoning could continue until fundamental principles like justice or happiness were appealed to. Since few would question why happiness and justice are considered good in themselves, they require no further justification. Basic principles like justice and happiness serve as ultimate justifications for particular normative claims.

PROGRESS CHECK 8.1

Instructions: *Fill in the blanks with the appropriate responses listed below.*

justify	fact–value
metaethics	verify
science	is
objective	ought
philosophy	nonnormative
psychologists	utilitarianism
normative	

1. Morality is a subject which can be studied from the perspective of _____ or _____.
2. Scientists do not wish to make value judgments about the morality they are studying. They wish to remain _____.
3. _____ would be most likely to study the development of moral-reasoning abilities in children and adolescents.
4. Statements which express factual conclusions are _____.
5. Statements which express value judgments are _____.
6. The _____ distinction helps us to understand how we cannot derive a moral _____ from an _____ of experience.
7. Scientists _____ their empirical findings by experiment and observation.
8. Moral philosophers _____ their conclusions by reason, argument, and debate.
9. _____ determines the rightness or wrongness of actions by referring to their consequences.
10. _____ is a philosophical approach to the study of morality which concerns itself primarily with meaning and conceptual analysis.

LEARNING EXERCISE 8.2

Instructions: *Describe the statements below as either empirical (E), normative (N), or analytic a priori (A).*

_____ 1. More men than women study ethics at college.

_____ 2. Seven plus five equals twelve.

_____ 3. All college students should study ethics.

_____ 4. A square is a figure comprised of four equal sides and four right angles.

_____ 5. Women should have access to abortion.

_____ 6. A widow is a married woman whose husband has died.

_____ 7. One should obey the law.

_____ 8. It is my opinion that people should not cheat on their tax forms.

_____ 9. Many people cheat on their income tax forms.

_____ 10. The earth either is flat or it is not flat.

_____ 11. The majority of citizens is in favor of capital punishment.

_____ 12. Philosophy is the best general education course in which college students can enroll.

_____ 13. It is good to help famine victims.

_____ 14. The pope says premarital sex is wrong.

_____ 15. John believes that all further immigration should be stopped.

_____ 16. You ought not to lie to your parents.

_____ 17. One should not treat others unfairly.

_____ 18. Socrates was a good citizen.

_____ 19. Firstborn individuals tend to be more successful in life.

_____ 20. So far, I find ethics difficult to understand.

LEARNING EXERCISE 8.3

Instructions: *Follow the directions below.*

1. Construct five empirical statements.

2. Construct five normative statements.

3. Construct five a priori statements.

LEARNING EXERCISE 8.4

Instructions: *Fill in the blanks with the appropriate answers.*

1. Professor Scardamalia is doing research on the relationship between cognitive development and moral behavior. Her topic is a subject of _____. (empirical investigation, philosophical inquiry, logical analysis)
2. On the basis of his clinical observations of people, Sigmund Freud has concluded that moral conflicts arise when sexual libidinal impulses are inconsistent with or suppressed by the demands of social reality. His conclusion is intended to be _____. (analytical, scientific, normative, metaethical)
3. Scientists do not wish to make value judgments about the morality they are studying. They wish to remain _____. (objective, noncommittal, flexible)
4. "You should donate some of your earnings to charity." This statement is _____. (descriptive, prescriptive, nonnormative)
5. One moral theory which stresses results in evaluating the moral rightness or wrongness of action is _____. (nonconsequentialism, ethical egoism, divine command theory)
6. _____ concerns itself with the meanings of ethical terms and the rational foundations of normative theories. (empirical inquiry, metaethics, scientific investigation)
7. Psychologists, sociologists, and anthropologists are examples of _____. (philosophers, scientists, metaethicists)
8. _____ would be the ones interested in studying the development of moral-reasoning abilities in children and adolescents. (philosophers, scientists, metaethicists)
9. If we accept that all men are mortal, that Socrates is a man, and conclude therefore that Socrates is mortal, our conclusion is a _____. (logical fact, deductive prescription, normative statement)
10. "I find this exercise difficult." This statement is _____. (logical, empirical, metaethical)
11. "A square is an enclosed figure having four equal sides and four right angles." This statement is _____. (empirical, a priori, normative)
12. Particular normative claims are justified by appeals to _____. (facts, commands, general principles)
13. "People should always keep their promises." This is an example of a _____ statement. (particular normative, general normative, descriptive empirical)
14. Knowledge which is derived from experience is _____. (a priori, a posteriori, intuitive)

15. "Most North Americans condone premarital sex." This represents a _____ statement. (prescriptive, a priori, empirical)

SUMMARY

1. There are two basic approaches to the study of morality:
   Scientific
   Philosophical
2. The Scientific Approach
   Is used by psychologists, sociologists, and anthropologists
   Is empirical in nature
   Uses methods of controlled observation and experiment
   Asks the how, why, when, what, and where questions about morality
   Is objective
   Words its conclusions as nonnormative statements
3. Two Types of Philosophical Approach
   Normative approach: prescribes action and makes value judgments; distinguishes between "is" and "ought," "facts" and "values"
   Metaethics: questions the rational foundations of moral systems and theories as well as the basis of moral justification
4. Types of Claims Relevant to Moral Inquiry
   Empirical claims: verified by observation and experiment
   A priori claims: either analytic or synthetic; recognized as true by intellectual intuition; are necessary, not contingent
5. Normative Claims
   Evaluate, judge, and prescribe
   Refer to what is good or bad, right or wrong, praiseworthy or blameworthy, obligatory or prohibited
   Are particular or general
   Are justified rationally, not verified empirically

REFERENCES

Barry, Vincent. *Applying Ethics: A Text with Readings.* Belmont, CA: Wadsworth, 1982.
Facione, Peter, Donald Scherer, and Thomas Attig. *Values and Society: An Introduction to Ethics and Social Philosophy.* Englewood Cliffs, NJ: Prentice Hall, 1978.
Solomon, Robert C. *Ethics: A Brief Introduction.* Toronto: McGraw-Hill, 1984.
Woodhouse, Mark B. *A Preface to Philosophy.* Belmont, CA: Wadsworth, 1984.

NOTES

1. Mark Woodhouse, *A Preface to Philosophy*, 3rd ed. (Belmont, CA: Wadsworth, 1984).
2. Immanuel Kant, *Foundations of the Metaphysics of Morals*, trans. Lewis White Beck (Indianapolis, IN: Bobbs-Merrill, 1959), p. 38.

9

MORAL REASONING SKILLS FOR ARGUMENT AND DEBATE

EDUCATIONAL OBJECTIVES: After reading this chapter the student will be able to:

9.1 Characterize the nature of opinions.

9.2 Characterize the nature of arguments.

9.3 Distinguish between arguments and opinions.

9.4 Understand and appreciate the importance of "Socratic humility" in philosophical discussion and debate.

9.5 Explain inductive logic.

9.6 Explain how random selection and other sampling procedures are important to induction.

9.7 Contrast deductive arguments with opinions.

9.8 List the parts of a logical syllogism.

9.9 Explain the procedure of deductive logic.

9.10 Point out the differences between "validity," "truth," and "soundness" in logical syllogisms.

9.11 List the parts of a practical syllogism.

9.12 Compare practical and logical syllogisms.

9.13 Explain the use of practical syllogisms.

9.14 Test the validity of practical syllogisms at the level of conclusion, factual premise, and value premise.

9.15 Define and use the role-exchange test in evaluating principles and value premises.

9.16 Explain and use the new-cases test.

9.17 Explain and use the consistency and universalizability test.

9.18 Explain and use the higher-order principle test.

FOCUS QUESTIONS

1. How can you tell whether an individual is presenting an argument or stating an opinion?

2. What can be said about opinions? Do they have any value or are they worthless?

3. Are there any dangers in merely stating opinions? If so, what are they?

4. How should the term "argument" be understood in a philosophical context? How is this term generally understood?

5. What is meant by rational disinterest? What indicates to you that someone is arguing with rational disinterest? How do you know someone is not rationally disinterested?

6. What are some of the advantages of adopting the psychological stance of "Socratic humility"?

7. How are inductive and deductive logic dissimilar?

8. Can you give one or two examples of inductive reasoning by analogy?

9. Can you identify any scientific, empirical studies where false conclusions were drawn because of unfair sampling procedures? If so, what caused the unfairness?

10. How is the logical syllogism different from the practical syllogism?

11. Can you distinguish between validity, truth, and soundness in the context of philosophical argumentation?
12. How can one evaluate a practical syllogism?
13. Can you identify one moral value principle by which you live? Evaluate it using the four tests mentioned in the text. Does your principle hold up under close examination? If not, how should you modify the principle? Or, should you reject the principle entirely?

9.1   PERSONAL OPINIONS

There are different kinds of opinions, some more acceptable than others. Judges and lawyers, for instance, may issue opinions on the legality of particular public policies. Such stated opinions are usually based on extensive research and careful thought. By contrast, the expressions of personal opinion we hear on a daily basis are typically less well thought out. In one respect these everyday, thoughtless opinions are "cheap." We can all afford to have them on any topic, even if we know very little or nothing about the topic. Opinions are especially abundant when the topic is a controversial moral one. A characteristic about these everyday opinions is that they are often not accompanied by reasons.[1] No **grounds** are stated for espousing them. Frequently, personal opinions are simply blurted out in a spontaneous fashion. They may be intended either to fill space in idle conversation, express emotions, or elicit reactions from others. This last function is certainly true of newspaper editorialists who express opinions all the time. By their opinionating, they often try to make people think about, or reconsider, their viewpoints on some contemporary social issue.

To the extent that personally stated opinions initiate discussion and cause us to stop and think, they are worthwhile. In many cases, they serve as the first step to genuine philosophical argument and debate. They can act as a type of springboard for further indepth ethical analysis and deliberation. The problem, however, is that all too often discussions begin and end with statements of unreasoned opinion. Emotions are vented and viewpoints are stridently expressed, but little is accomplished by way of insight, further understanding, or clarification of the issues concerned. Unfortunately, many people take great pleasure in forcing their opinions upon others, winning shouting matches, name-calling, and making others look foolish or stupid. The problem is that screaming and one-upmanship do not take us very far down the road of sober thought and rational moral understanding.

9.2   MORAL ARGUMENT
9.3
9.4

In moral and philosophical discussions, arguments are not intended to be violent fights. They do not represent confrontations of egos filled with hostility and mutual resentment.[2] The **argument** in a philosophical context is positive. Philosophers make a livelihood out of constructing and analyzing arguments. Arguments are ideally conducted in a friendly, level-headed way. They serve as a vehicle to further human understanding on whatever moral issue is being disputed. If one adopts a proper philosophical attitude of **rational disinterestedness,** and if one is firmly committed to the pursuit of knowledge and truth, one is not concerned with winning or losing debates. The objective of argument is increased insight and greater enlightenment achieved by all. If one develops the philosophical humility of Socrates, one is actually aware of one's own ignorance and the distinct possibility that one may frequently be wrong. If we can learn only one thing from Socrates, perhaps it should be that we ought not to be presumptuous with respect to what we know and believe unquestioningly that we are right in our philosophical viewpoints. It would be better if we entered into ethical discussions and debates with **Socratic humility** and with the hope of learning, not with the aim of winning, furthering our reputations, or massaging our own egos. Adopting this **psychological stance** of Socratic humility will, interestingly enough, remove defensiveness and help one to focus on the issue at hand in a more rational and impartial fashion. This stance will also influence one to express viewpoints in a cautious and tentative way, not stridently or arrogantly.

The beginning student of ethics wishing to master the skills of philosophical argumentation and critical analysis must become acquainted with at least two basic types of reasoning: (1) **inductive logic** and (2) **deductive logic.** Inductive logic is a rational process of thought used to support empirical claims, statements, or propositions. In an ethical context, it can be used to support factual premises which are contained within broader moral arguments. If one wishes to question the validity of a moral argument on the grounds that its factual premise is false, one should appreciate the mechanics of the reasoning process which led to that factual premise. One should also be able to pinpoint flaws in the application of that process in any particular moral argument.

With respect to deductive logic, a distinction needs to be made between two of its variations. Deductive logic can be used in both moral and nonmoral contexts. Perhaps the most commonly used and recognized deductive argument is the **syllogism.** Used in a nonmoral context, it can be referred to simply as a **logical syllogism.** When employed in a moral or normative context, it will be referred to here as a **practical syllogism.** The descriptive adjective "practical" is appropriate as moral value making affects all of our lives in real and concrete ways. Moral value decisions have practical consequences for us. The differences and similarities between logical and practical syllogisms will soon become apparent. First, let us examine the pattern of reasoning known as inductive logic.

9.5   INDUCTIVE LOGIC

Inductive logic is a form of reasoning that leads to **probable conclusions,** not necessary ones. Suppose, for instance, that we are informed that John has lied on his job application, on his income tax return, and to his wife. We might then conclude that he will probably lie about information provided on his medical history required to purchase a life insurance policy. Given the fact that he has lied in other contexts, he will *likely* lie in this one as well. However, since our inductive conclusion is based on facts of experience, because these facts are never complete, and because new facts tomorrow or the day after may have the effect of weakening or changing or contradicting today's assumptions, we can never be absolutely sure about our conclusion.[3] Perhaps John has experienced some kind of religious or moral conversion which has led to a complete character transformation. Maybe John was a liar in his wayward youth but now he is a wise old man committed to the value of truth. Many empirical variables could weaken the soundness of the inductive inference made in this case.

Inductive arguments supporting empirical claims sometimes proceed by **analogy.** For example, arguments for the probable existence of life on other planets are analogical.[4] They are based upon the presumed similarities between conditions found on earth and those on other planets. Mark Woodhouse provides for us a formal mode of analogical inductive argumentation.[5]

Items A, B, and C have characteristics X and Y.
A and B have characteristic Z.

Therefore, C probably has characteristic Z also.

A feature of analogical arguments (and inductive arguments more generally) is that they are stronger or weaker by degree. They are not usually rejected or accepted in an all-or-nothing fashion. The soundness of analogical inductive reasoning in particular depends on such things as the number and variety of characteristics which appear to be similar in the samples, the number of samples used, and the strength of the conclusions relative to the premises.[6]

Still another form of induction is the **inductive generalization.**[7] When we make an inductive generalization, we make a statement about all, some, or none of a class based on our examination of only a part of that class. Inductive generalizations are not simply **generalized descriptions.**[8] Let us suppose, for example, that we surveyed the members of a neo-Nazi youth group organization in a particular county and discovered that 99 percent of the members hated blacks, Catholics, and Jews. In stating this fact, one is not going beyond the facts; one is only presenting a generalized description of what is the case. However, if one were to conclude that 99 percent of the members of all youth group organizations in North America hated blacks, Catholics, and Jews, one would be making an inductive generalization.

9.6   As can be readily appreciated in the example above, inductive generalizations can easily be prone to error unless certain precautions are taken while arriving at them. If one wishes to make a generalization about a class of people or things based on samples taken from that class, one must take care to ensure that the sample is sufficiently **large.** If one had surveyed the feelings and attitudes of members belonging to one hundred youth group organizations in many counties and in many provinces and states, instead of in just one county, state, or province, then any generalization about the percentage of members hating blacks, Catholics, and Jews across North America would be placed on firmer ground.

Inductive generalizations must be based on **fair samples.** One must ask whether the sampling is truly representative of the whole class (for example, youth groups). As has already been intimated, if the sample is large enough, it is likely to be more rather than less representative of the class. But if a large sample is unfair or distorted, then its size is irrelevant to the soundness of the generalization. Let us suppose, for instance, that only neo-Nazi youth groups were surveyed in our sampling of one hundred. Surely, these organizations are not representative of other major youth groups like the Boy Scouts and Girl Guides. It is important in the interests of fairness and objectivity, then, that our samples be **randomly selected.** Every segment of the class (for example, youth groups) about which we are generalizing must have an equal chance of being selected. If we wish to make inductive generalizations concerning youth group attitudes based on a limited sample, we must ensure that our sampling procedures allow for all youth groups being randomly selected. This includes not only neo-Nazi youth groups but athletic clubs and volunteer associations like the Candy Stripers, the Boy Scouts, and so on. Random sampling may be ensured by studying different geographic locations and by taking such things as socioeconomic factors, age, and education into account.

9.7 DEDUCTIVE LOGIC
9.8

The process of deduction is a pattern of reasoning essential to philosophical inquiry. Stating deductive arguments is not like stating opinions. Since opinions are groundless and unsupported, they seem to go nowhere. When one states an opinion, there is typically no indication of movement or progress in rational thought. By contrast, deductive logical argument is comprised of a series of statements which fit together as a **syllogism.** Deductive arguments begin with premises and end with conclusions. Conclusions obtained from deductive arguments can be said to follow, or be derived from, preceding premises. Below are two examples of deductive logical syllogisms.

Example 1: Major Premise: *All men are mortal.*
Minor Premise: *Socrates is a man.*
Conclusion: *Socrates is mortal.*

Example 2: Major Premise: *If a person has an XX genotype, the person is female.*
Minor Premise: *Dale has an XX genotype.*
Conclusion: *Therefore, Dale is female.*

The content and particulars of the syllogisms above may be removed so that the syllogism may be expressed in a purely formal way.

> Major Premise: *All Ps are Qs.*
> Minor Premise: *S is a P.*
> Conclusion: *Therefore, S is a Q.*

9.9   In the process of deductive reasoning, one attempts to argue for the truth of a conclusion by deducing a statement from a number of others which are assumed to be true. A problem arises, however, because arguments are not always expressed in a logical step-by-step fashion. Conclusions may sometimes be preceded and followed by supporting premises in a garbled or jumbled way.[9] While some premises may be explicitly stated, others may be implied. When analyzing arguments, it is helpful therefore to extract from detailed discussions those relevant premises and conclusions which fit together to form logical syllogisms. The analysis and evaluation of the argument can thereby be facilitated.

9.10   In the context of appraising and evaluating deductive arguments, a distinction needs to be made between **validity** and **truth.** Validity and truth are not the same thing when referring to logical syllogisms. If a deductive argument proceeds correctly to form, it is **deductively valid.**[10] If an argument does not proceed correctly, then it is invalid. However, an argument can be valid even if its premises and conclusions are false. For example,

> Major Premise: *All birds are black.*
> Minor Premise: *Prince Philip is a bird.*
> Conclusion: *Prince Philip is black.*

In the example above, it is clear that not all birds are black. Some are red and others are blue. It is also clear that Prince Philip is a man, not a bird. Yet the conclusion follows necessarily from the two preceding premises. In short, valid arguments may sometimes lead to false conclusions. If an argument is valid in form and if its premises are true, then we have a good argument, one which can be described as **sound.**[11] On the other hand, an argument can be described as **unsound** if its premises are false or if it is invalid in form. Thus, premises are true or false, while arguments are valid or invalid. Valid arguments based on true premises are sound, while invalid arguments or valid arguments based on false premises are unsound.

PRACTICAL SYLLOGISMS

9.11   A practical syllogism is essentially the same in form as a logical syllogism, and its conclusions are derived from preceding premises. In this case, however, the major premise of the argument is a normative statement or some sort of value judgment. Hence, the major premise of a practical syllogism is not self-evidently or analytically true, that is, true by definition. Also, it cannot be verified—as can empirical or factual premises—by experiment and observation. The major premise of a practical syllogism, called the **value premise,** is not proven scientifically or empirically but rather justified by appeals to standards and principles. The process of justifying value premises is therefore a rational one. Since principles of right conduct and standards of goodness cannot be based on what "is" the case, for what is may frequently be evil and immoral, the ultimate basis of justification is reason, not experience. Using reason we can determine what "ought" to be or what is good regardless of what is.

9.12
9.13
The equivalent of the logical syllogism's minor premise is the practical syllogism's **factual premise.** As the term implies, the factual premise makes some empirical claim about the world. The factual premise is either true or false. Though one may be unable at present to prove the truth or falsity of a particular factual premise, given our limited knowledge and technology, it must be possible in principle to do so. If someone made the factual claim, for example that there is gold on Pluto, we would likely have no way at this point to determine whether or not Pluto does in fact contain gold. The point is that factual premises contained within practical syllogisms are empirically verifiable in principle.

If one accepts the value premise of a practical syllogism and if the corresponding factual premise is true, then it is possible to derive a conclusion about what is good or bad, right or wrong, or a conclusion about what ought or ought not to be done. Below are three examples of practical syllogisms.

Example 1

Value Premise: *That which undermines the safety of individuals is wrong.*
Factual Premise: *Placing toxic waste dumps near populated areas undermines the safety of individuals.*
Conclusion: *Placing toxic waste dumps near populated areas is wrong.*

Example 2

Value Premise: *Anyone who kills and steals to earn a living is evil.*
Factual Premise: *Bonnie and Clyde kill and steal to earn a living.*
Conclusion: *Bonnie and Clyde are evil.*

Example 3

Value Premise: *We should not commit acts which break the law.*
Factual Premise: *Acts of civil disobedience break the law.*
Conclusion: *We should not commit acts of civil disobedience.*

9.14
The practical syllogism can be evaluated at three levels. First, one may examine the conclusion to see whether it follows logically from preceding premises. If the wording of the conclusion is inaccurate or if the premises of the argument do not lead us to the stated conclusion, then the argument is invalid. The following example illustrates an incorrect conclusion.

Value Premise: *We should not promote that which produces violence in the world.*
Factual Premise: *Rock music produces violence in the world.*
Conclusion: *Therefore, I should not let my son buy record albums.*

The correct conclusion, of course, is: *Therefore, we should not promote rock music.* If we were to accept the value and factual premises stated above, we might be sympathetic to the son not being allowed to purchase rock-and-roll records, but this conclusion does not follow logically in the syllogism given the wording of the premises.

Let us assume for a moment that the wording of the conclusion in the rock-and-roll syllogism is correct. The question then arises as to whether or not we would be forced to accept the argument as stated. This brings us to the second level of evaluation. Even if the practical syllogism is valid in form and even if the conclusion follows logically from the preceding claims, we may still be able to reject it if the factual premise is incorrect, that is, false. Empirical studies could be conducted to determine whether rock music, in this instance, causes aggression or promotes violent conduct. Behavior at rock concerts could be observed and the behavior of rock-music listeners could be compared with the conduct of those who do not listen to such music. A number of observational and experimental techniques could be used to determine the truth or falsity of the factual premise. If the factual premise were discovered to be false, then the argument would have to be rejected. Though valid in form, its false premise would make it unsound.

Lastly, practical syllogisms may be evaluated at the level of the value premise. An argument may be valid in form and the factual premise may also be true, yet it is still possible that the argument may have to be rejected. The value premises of practical syllogisms act as general rules or principles justifying the particular value judgments found in the conclusions of those syllogisms. If the value premise of the syllogism is itself unjustifiable, then so too must be the conclusion which follows from it. It is essential, therefore, that students learning to reason deductively in moral matters learn to evaluate and justify the value premises of moral arguments.

TESTING VALUE PREMISES

9.14
9.15   **Role-Exchange Test**

Value premises can be tested in a variety of ways. One way of determining the acceptability of a value premise is by using the **role-exchange test.**[12] This test requires us to ask whether we would be willing to exchange places with the person or persons most disadvantaged by the application of a moral rule or principle in a particular set of circumstances. If one is not prepared to be the most disadvantaged in the application of the rule or principle, then it is probably unjustified or inadequate in some fashion. Let us suppose, for instance, that a number of trustees proposed that Vladimir Gorky and Fred Runningbear should not be allowed to enroll at an exclusive private boarding school. Further, let us assume that the only reason given is that these students are not white, Anglo-Saxon, and/or Protestant. If such were the case, the argument would run something like this.

Value Premise: *Students who are not white, Anglo-Saxon, and Protestant should be prevented from attending this private school.*
Factual Premise: *Vladimir and Fred are not white, Anglo-Saxon, and Protestant.*
Conclusion: *Vladimir and Fred should be prevented from attending this private school.*

Applying the role-exchange test forces us to ask whether we would like to exchange places with Vladimir and Fred and still accept the principle which has been posited. Presumably, the school trustees would not like their options reduced or their freedom restricted simply because of their racial, ethnic, or religious background. The trustees would, no doubt, dislike being discriminated against, as would anyone else. If the school trustees could not accept being discriminated against themselves, or if they could not tolerate being treated unfairly if the principle proposed were applied to them, then the principle acting as the value premise of their argument would fail the role-exchange test. It would have to be rejected on this basis.

9.16   New Cases Test

If a general moral rule or principle is deemed acceptable and used as a premise to justify one value judgment in a particular set of circumstances, then it should be equally applicable to other similar sets of circumstances.[13] If it is not, then there is something likely wrong with the rule or principle. For example, let us suppose that the general normative rule from which we are justifying a particular moral judgment is, "People should never lie." To test this principle, we examine not only the case in which it was applied, but also other cases where it should apply.

Case Number 1: Maria tells her mother that she has not seen her mother's wallet when, in reality, she stole it to use the money inside to buy a new dress. In this case, Maria is lying only to satisfy her personal wants. She is using deception to further her own self-interests. Intuitively, most of us would recognize such action as wrong. The general rule stated is thus upheld and strengthened. Suppose, however, that it is 1942 and Maria is harboring dissident Polish priests and Jewish refugees in her basement. Let us also imagine SS officers are knocking at Maria's door, asking her if she knows the whereabouts of those same dissidents and refugees. If Maria tells the truth, the refugees and dissidents are likely to be killed. If she lies, then they are likely to be saved. No doubt most moral thinkers would argue that Maria should lie in order to preserve and protect life. But if this is the case, then it is not true that "people should *never* lie." It could be strongly argued that people *should* lie if lying spares life.

Let us take yet another new case. Suppose, for instance, that one of our country's spies is being interrogated by the enemy. This spy has information on the Star Wars technology designed as a defense system against missile attack. The enemy wants this information so that it may successfully undertake a first-strike offensive without hindrance. Our prisoner spy must make a choice, that is, to lie and say that he or she has no Star Wars information, or to tell the truth and give the enemy a military advantage which, in turn, would jeopardize the safety and security of our nation. Surely, most people would consider lying acceptable in this case.

Thus we find that the more cases wherein the principle "People should never lie" can be shown not to apply, the less adequate or justifiable is this moral judgment. If many new cases can be presented which call into question the principle under consideration, then it must either be modified in some acceptable fashion or totally rejected. In this case, the general rule about lying could be modified to read, "People should never lie except when life and national security are at stake." Though this modification is likely still not to be perfect, it transforms the original principle in such a way that it is now more adequate and justifiable. Further new cases might necessitate further modifications, however.

9.17 **Consistency and Universalizability Test**

In order for rules and principles acting as value premises to be justifiable, they must be logically consistent and universalizable. Inconsistent principles and rules are those that are self-contradictory. Since they are irrational, they cannot serve as a sound and coherent basis for the justification of moral conduct and particular moral judgments. The following principle is inconsistent: "People should make promises with the intention of breaking them." Some might claim that politicians actually live by this principle in their efforts to be elected. To the extent that they do, they are guilty of an inconsistency. The concept of promise keeping necessarily entails the intention of keeping one's word. Making a promise with no intention of keeping it is self-contradictory. Promises designed to be broken are not promises at all but rather deceptions or lies.

Apart from failing the consistency test, the principle about promise making and breaking fails the closely related **universalizability test** as well. If the principle were universalized and if it were deemed right that all people should make promises with the full intention of breaking them, then the institution of promise keeping would become self-defeating. Promises would become unbelievable. Nobody would ever trust someone making a promise. When applying the universalizability test, we ask, "What if everyone acted according to this principle?" or, "Could I will that everyone should live by this principle?" If one cannot will that a particular value premise be acted upon or accepted by all or if it is inconsistent and self-defeating, then the value premise is inadequate and unjustified.

9.18 **Higher-Order Principle Test**

A fourth way to test value premises is by applying the higher-order principle test. We alluded briefly to this concept earlier when discussing "normative claims." The point was made then that particular moral judgments—the sort found in conclusions of practical syllogisms—are justified by value premises, which represent more general moral judgments. I also indicated that these general value premises must themselves be justified by appeals to even higher-order principles if they are to be considered adequate and sound. If the higher-order principles used to justify value premises are inconsistent themselves or if they fail the role-exchange test, for example, then the value premises derived from these higher-order principles are unacceptable. Quite simply, the higher-order principle test is based on the notion that value principles (premises) we use in drawing particular moral conclusions are acceptable only if they can be derived or deduced from even more general principles which are acceptable. We frequently use the higher-order principle test in daily conversation or during informal arguments on controversial issues. An illustration of how we do this might be helpful.

JEANETTE: You shouldn't butt your cigarettes on the college's carpet.
MARK: What's wrong with doing that?
JEANETTE: Well, you're obviously going to destroy public property.
MARK: So what?
JEANETTE: So what? Didn't anyone ever teach you that actions which destroy public property are wrong?

At this point, Jeanette's claim about what Mark should not do can be expressed in syllogistic form.

Value Premise: *Actions which destroy public property are wrong.*
Factual Premise: *Butting a cigarette on the college's carpet is an action destroying public property.*
Conclusion: *Butting a cigarette on the college's carpet is wrong.*

Mark is not satisfied with Jeanette's argument for why he should not butt his cigarette on the college carpet.

MARK: So what? I'm destroying public property. What's wrong with that?

In asking the question, Mark is demanding a further justification. In order to provide it, Jeanette appeals to a higher-order principle.

JEANETTE: In destroying public property, you're making people work unnecessarily and ultimately forcing them to pay higher taxes.
MARK: So, what's the big deal about that?
JEANETTE: I'll tell you what the big deal is. Paying higher taxes and making people work unnecessarily makes people unhappy.
MARK: So?
JEANETTE: So? I think anything which makes people unhappy is wrong.

Again, Jeanette's position can be worded in a valid syllogism.

Value Premise: *Actions which make people unhappy are wrong.*

Factual Premise: *Actions like butting cigarettes on carpets destroy public property and make people unhappy by forcing them to pay higher taxes and work unnecessarily.*

Conclusion: *Actions like butting cigarettes on carpets which destroy public property are wrong.*

We see above that the conclusion is the same as the value premise of the first syllogism which began Jeanette's argument. The value premise of the second syllogism could in turn act as the conclusion of yet another higher-order syllogism, if required. The process of justification involving higher-order principles can be illustrated.

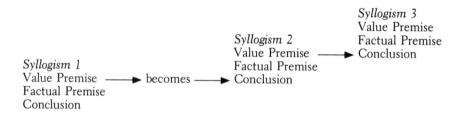

PROGRESS CHECK 9.1

Instructions: Insert the proper responses in the blanks below.

opinion	argument
grounds	one-upmanship
Socratic humility	rational disinterest
deductive logic	inductive logic
practical syllogism	syllogism
probable	necessary
analogy	inductive generalization
random selection	valid
sound	value premise
role-exchange test	new-cases test
universalizability test	consistency test

1. At best, inductive logic can only lead to _____ conclusions.
2. The basic form of deductive logic is captured by the _____.
3. A goal of the moral philosopher is to develop a psychological posture of _____.

4. Rather than being biased or self-serving, philosophers try to conduct their inquiries objectively and dispassionately, that is, with _____.

5. If the premises of a logical syllogism are true and if the conclusion follows from them, then the conclusion is _____.

6. In merely stating an opinion, one fails to give _____ for holding it.

7. An _____ shows evidence of movement or progress in rational thought.

8. If one wishes to make an _____ about a population based on an empirical study of only a fraction of its members, one must be careful in the interests of fairness and objectivity to use procedures of _____.

9. A logical syllogism begins with a major premise, while a _____ begins with a value premise.

10. An expressed _____ may be little more than an emotional outburst having no basis of justification.

11. A _____ argument has true premises and is _____ in form.

12. Moral arguments should result in greater insight, clarification, and understanding. Persons arguing should not be concerned with winning or _____.

13. The major premise of a practical syllogism is called the _____.

14. In _____, the necessary conclusion is derived from preceding premises.

15. When one uses the _____, a principle found acceptable in one set of circumstances is applied to other similar sets of circumstances to see whether or not it holds up.

16. In advocating a particular moral principle, one should evaluate it by using the _____. Here, one asks whether or not one would be willing to be the person most disadvantaged by the application of the principle.

17. "Earth and Mars both have hydrogen and oxygen. Earth has life and thus so must Mars in all likelihood." This reasoning by _____ is characteristic of one form of _____.

18. "People should never prescribe for others what they ought to do." This principle fails the _____. In order to recommend it, one must do what is being proscribed.

19. When one asks, "Would I want everyone to live by this principle?" one employs the _____.

LEARNING EXERCISE 9.2   Inductive Logic

Instructions: *Below are several illustrations of inductive reasoning. State why you agree or disagree with the conclusions.*

1. John is very interested in the nature and development of genius. After reading the biographies of Albert Einstein, Nicholas Kopernik (Copernicus), and

Chopin the composer, John discovered that they all ate hearty breakfasts. He concluded that eating a hearty breakfast contributes to genius and intelligence.

2. Recently, we met Joe, Bill, and Gaylord, who are Indian men from the local reserve. They have all broken the law and spent time in jail. Fred is also an Indian from the local reserve. We can conclude, therefore, that he has broken the law and spent time in jail.

3. Every time I have visited my mother-in-law, I have ended up leaving in a bad mood. If I go to her place next Sunday, I'll leave in this same bad mood again.

LEARNING EXERCISE 9.3   Completing Logical Syllogisms

Instructions: Fill in the blanks with the appropriate premises and conclusions.

1. **Major Premise:**   If a person is a freshman, the person is a college or university student.

   Minor Premise:

   Conclusion: Susan is a college or university student.

2. **Major Premise:**

   Minor Premise: Jean-Marc is a bachelor.

   Conclusion: Jean-Marc is an unmarried man.

3. **Major Premise:**   Triangles are three-sided figures.

   Minor Premise: That is a triangle.

   Conclusion:

4. **Major Premise:**   Philosophers are lovers of wisdom.

   Minor Premise: Mario is a philosopher.

   Conclusion:

5. **Major Premise:**   Environmental contaminants cause cancer.

   Minor Premise:

   Conclusion: DDT causes cancer.

LEARNING EXERCISE 9.4   Constructing Logical Syllogisms

Instructions: Construct five of your own logical syllogisms below.

1. **Major Premise:**

   Minor Premise:

   Conclusion:

2. **Major Premise:**

   Minor Premise:

   Conclusion:

3. **Major Premise:**

   Minor Premise:

   Conclusion:

4. **Major Premise:**

   Minor Premise:

   Conclusion:

5. **Major Premise:**

   Minor Premise:

   Conclusion:

LEARNING EXERCISE 9.5   Practical Syllogisms

Instructions: *Fill in correctly the missing premises and conclusions.*

1. **Value Premise:**   Actions which violate the will of the majority are wrong.

   Factual Premise: Smoking in public places is an action which violates the will of the majority.

   Conclusion:

2. **Value Premise:**   You should not do that which will endanger your health.

   Factual Premise:

   Conclusion: Therefore, you should not drink to excess.

3. **Value Premise:**

   Factual Premise: Policies to increase taxes will reduce corporate profits.

   Conclusion: Therefore, you should not accept policies to increase taxes.

4. **Value Premise:**

   Factual Premise: Laws prohibiting kissing in public are outdated.

   Conclusion: Therefore, laws prohibiting kissing should be erased.

5. **Value Premise:**   Things which arouse our base animal instincts are evil.

   Factual Premise: Rock music arouses our base animal instincts.

   Conclusion:

LEARNING EXERCISE 9.6 Creating Your Own Practical Syllogisms

Instructions: Construct your own practical syllogisms.

1. Value Premise:

   Factual Premise:

   Conclusion:

2. Value Premise:

   Factual Premise:

   Conclusion:

3. Value Premise:

   Factual Premise:

   Conclusion:

4. Value Premise:

   Factual Premise:

   Conclusion:

5. Value Premise:

   Factual Premise:

   Conclusion:

LEARNING EXERCISE 9.7 Testing Value Principles

Instructions: Evaluate the value premises/principles stated below using (a) the role-exchange test, (b) the new cases test, (c) the consistency and universalizability test, and (d) the higher-order principle test.

1. One should lie to others when it is in one's self-interest to do so.
2. Stealing is always wrong.
3. You should take short-cuts to school even if this involves trespassing on other people's property.
4. You should always respect people and treat them as ends in themselves; don't use them solely as means to your personal ends.
5. Visible racial and ethnic minorities should not be allowed into this country.
6. Everyone but me should fill out his or her income tax forms honestly.

SUMMARY

1. Opinions

    Are not accompanied by reasons

    Are groundless

    Are spontaneously blurted out

    May sometimes initiate philosophical discussion and debate

    Are sometimes mere expressions of emotion

2. Arguments

    Are desired, not avoided by philosophers

    Are friendly, not filled with hostility and resentment

    Are conducted in a spirit of rational disinterest

    Aim to increase insight and understanding

    Are not designed to make others look silly or stupid

    Should be presented with Socratic humility

    Have movement or progression, that is, they lead somewhere

3. Inductive Logic

    Leads to probable conclusions

    Is based on the facts of experience

    Can proceed by analogy

    Could involve inductive generalizations

    Sometimes necessitates fair procedures of random sampling when making generalizations

4. Deductive Logic

    Begins with a major and minor premise and ends with a conclusion

    States "necessary," not "probable" conclusions

    Distinguishes between validity, truth, and soundness

    Has as its basic pattern of reasoning the syllogism

5. Practical Syllogisms

    Have the same basic structure as logical syllogisms, only the major premise is a value judgment or normative statement

    Ultimately must be justified by reason and appeals to standards and principles

    Are not verified empirically, though the factual premise must be true if the syllogism is to be sound

    Can be evaluated at three levels: the conclusion, the factual premise, and the value premise

6. Testing Value Premises and Principles

    Role-Exchange Test: requires one to exchange places with the person or group most disadvantaged by the application of a value principle

New-Cases Test: takes a principle deemed acceptable and used as a premise to justify one value judgment in a particular set of circumstances and applies the principle to other relevant, similar sets of circumstances to see if it stands up

Consistency and Universalizability Test: involves asking, "Could I will that everyone should live by this principle?"; rejects inconsistent and self-contradictory principles

Higher-Order Principle Test: evaluates the value premises of syllogisms by appeals to more general and ultimate principles

REFERENCES

AVER (Association for Values Education and Research), University of British Columbia. *Prejudice* (teacher's manual). Toronto: Ontario Institute for Studies in Education, 1978.

Barry, Vincent. *Applying Ethics: A Text with Readings.* Belmont, CA: Wadsworth, 1982.

Johnson, R. H., and J. A. Blair. *Logical Self-Defense.* 2nd ed. Toronto: McGraw-Hill Ryerson, 1983.

Runkle, Gerald. *Theory and Practice: An Introduction to Philosophy.* New York: Holt, Rinehart and Winston, 1985.

Solomon, Robert. *The Big Questions—A Short Introduction to Philosophy.* New York: Harcourt Brace Jovanovich, 1982.

Woodhouse, Mark B. *A Preface to Philosophy* 3rd ed. Belmont, CA: Wadsworth, 1984.

NOTES

1. The content for this part of the discussion is largely derived from R. H. Johnson and J. A. Blair, *Logical Self-Defense,* 2nd ed. (Toronto: McGraw-Hill Ryerson, 1983).
2. Ibid.
3. Vincent Barry, *Philosophy: A Text with Readings,* 2nd ed. (Belmont, CA: Wadsworth, 1983), p. 334.
4. Mark Woodhouse, *A Preface to Philosophy* (Belmont, CA: Wadsworth, 1984), p. 46.
5. Ibid., p. 47.
6. For a further discussion of this and other points relating to analogical reasoning, see Woodhouse, *A Preface to Philosophy,* pp. 46–48.
7. Runkle, *Theory and Practice: An Introduction to Philosophy,* pp. 463–465.
8. Ibid., p. 463.
9. Woodhouse, *A Preface to Philosophy,* pp. 45–46.
10. For a discussion of this, see Robert C. Solomon, *The Big Questions: A Short Introduction to Philosophy* (Toronto: Harcourt Brace Jovanovich), p. 12.
11. Ibid., p. 12.
12. Teacher's Manual to *Prejudice,* by the Association for Values Education and Research, University of British Columbia (Toronto: The Ontario Institute for Studies in Education, 1978), p. 10.
13. Ibid., p. 11.

10

LOGICAL FALLACIES: ERRORS IN REASONING

EDUCATIONAL OBJECTIVES: After reading this chapter the student will be able to:

10.1   Explain how fallacies differ from other types of logical errors in moral and philosophical reasoning.
10.2   Define and identify instances of ad hominem arguments.
10.3   Explain why ad hominem arguments are attractive.
10.4   Give illustrations of when it is proper to question personality and character in moral argumentation.
10.5   Define and identify instances of the "straw-man" fallacy.
10.6   Explain the fallacy of begging the question.
10.7   Identify and give examples of circular reasoning.
10.8   State what is meant by the "fallacy of two wrongs."
10.9   Give an illustration of reasoning characteristic of the fallacy of two wrongs.
10.10   Define and identify instances of the "slippery-slope" fallacy.
10.11   Explain the fallacy of appealing to authority.
10.12   Provide different kinds of improper authoritative appeals.
10.13   Know when proper authoritative appeals can be made.
10.14   Define and identify examples of the "red-herring" fallacy.
10.15   Define and identify examples of the guilt-by-association fallacy.

FOCUS QUESTIONS

1. Why is it important to be able to define and identify types of fallacious reasoning?
2. How are diversion and intimidation used in fallacious reasoning? Give examples.
3. How should one deal with logical fallacies once recognized?
4. In a society where traditional values are crumbling, what is wrong with appealing to authority in moral matters? Can we ever call upon authorities justifiably to support our viewpoints?
5. What is the problem with "ego investment" in moral argumentation?

Rationality in moral argument requires that a number of skills be mastered. So far, processes of inductive and deductive reasoning have been covered, and an opportunity has been provided to practice them. These two processes of logical thinking are essential to the proper articulation of factual premises and for the formulation of valid moral arguments. Procedures for testing and evaluating the soundness of arguments, the truth of premises, and the acceptability of value principles have also been discussed and practiced.

10.1   Errors in moral reasoning do not always arise simply from incorrect factual premises, unjustifiable value principles, or from unintended faulty usages of inductive or deductive logic. Sometimes they occur as a result of **fallacious reasoning.** Fallacies or forms of fallacious reasoning are used in attempts to persuade us emotionally or psychologically, not rationally. Since this work is not a course in logic, it would be inappropriate to discuss all of the fallacies here. What will be discussed are those logical fallacies which are most commonly used in everyday moral argument and which serve to cloud clear thinking on moral matters.

10.2   AD HOMINEM FALLACY

When morality is being discussed, people invariably will disagree among themselves about different positions on particular issues. When voicing one's disagreement, the most logical response is to criticize the contrary positions taken by one's opponents, not the opponents themselves. Attacking the person or group instead of the person's or group's argument, is labeled the **ad hominem fallacy.**

Fallacious ad hominem reasoning is abundant in everyday conversation, in business, politics, and in the press. For example, shortly after a 1984 national election, a newly elected government leader was criticized for his patronage appointments. Rather than deny that these appointments were made, or argue for the justifiable role of patronage in the political system, or instead of trying to justify his actions by pointing out the competence of those appointed, he chose to attack personally the politician who alleged that patronage had occurred. The government leader charged that the politician making the accusation was a hypocrite. He alleged that the politician and his party were guilty of patronage themselves while in office and that they consequently had no moral right to criticize the current government. Of course, the rightness or wrongness of patronage does not depend on who is criticizing it. If it did, then using the same logic we might be forced to condone murder just because a convicted murderer now condemns killing. By attacking the politician personally, the government leader tried to divert attention away from the real issue of his patronage appointments. He attempted to have the voters focus on the accusing politician's own guilt and past actions. This diversionary tactic does not logically justify the government leader's own actions though, unfortunately, it might be effective in getting him "off the hook" in the eyes of noncritical, unthinking spectators of the national political scene.

10.3   Though ad hominem arguments exemplify a type of fallacious reasoning, some people continue to be persuaded by them. These arguments can be **emotionally satisfying,** insofar as they belittle or disparage the person(s) with whom we disagree. We find it unsettling to be forced to concede that an individual we dislike has made a valid point.[1] Also, there is sometimes a lot of ego investment in the viewpoints we espouse. Hence, when people attack our viewpoints, we may perceive such attacks as attacks on ourselves. In a reflexive fashion, we may counterattack with a personal challenge of our own. Personal attacks and ego assertions are, however, contrary to the spirit of **rational disinterest** and **Socratic humility,** which were discussed earlier. Personal attacks and counterattacks may serve to vent emotions and display dominance or aggressiveness, but they should be avoided in philosophical discussion.

The ad hominem fallacy has been expressed in formal terms by Ralph Johnson and Anthony Blair.

1. M responds to Q, a position N has taken, by attacking N rather than by attacking Q.
2. The attack on N is not relevant to the assessment of Q.[2]

There are different variations of the ad hominem argument. The most common involves a criticism of someone's **personality** or **character.** In arguing against another, disparaging remarks could be made about the person's ethnic heritage or racial background. Insinuations might also be made about the **underlying motives** and **special interests** of the other. In short, whenever one attempts to divert our focus away from the substantive issues of the debate and toward the person espousing the contrary viewpoint, one is attacking the advocate of the contrary viewpoint and not the viewpoint itself.

10.4   Though attacks of the person usually reflect ad hominem fallacies and erroneous thinking, they are not always inappropriate.[3] For instance, if an advocate of a position appeals to authority or expert opinion to support a particular claim, one may properly question the background and motives of the authority.[4] For example, if someone tells you that a particular brand of blue-jeans is the best and uses an athlete's endorsement of it as an authoritative basis of judgment, one may question the athlete's expertise on the matter or the person's special interests. Given that the athlete has advertised for this brand of jeans, it is conceivable that he or she earns a percentage on the gross sales of the blue-jeans. It is also possible that the athlete dislikes blue-jeans and never wears them, and hence, knows nothing about them. In view of these possibilities, it is only fair to challenge his interests and credentials if we are asked to accept the individual's authoritative judgment.

Shifting the focus from what is said to who is speaking may also be justified sometimes if **credibility** is seriously in question. Imagine that someone has developed a reputation for being a chronic liar and that this person has been asked to testify in a murder case. The adversarial lawyer in the case may wish to discredit the testimony of the person by attacking his personality and by illustrating how the person has lied repeatedly in the past. There may be just cause for being skeptical about a person's statements or positions, simply because it is *that* person who holds them.

10.5   STRAW-MAN FALLACY

Another form of fallacious reasoning involves the construction and burning of a "straw man." One is guilty of this fallacy when one deliberately **misrepresents** an opponent's position, offers it in such a way that it is unacceptable, and then proceeds to argue against the implausible, set-up version of the argument that was never the opponent's in the first place. A criticism of the set-up version is regarded as a rejection of the opponent's real argument. The straw-man fallacy can be summarized formally in the following fashion.

1. A attributes to G the view or position X.
2. G's position or view is not X but rather Z.
3. A criticizes X as if it were the position taken or view held by G, when this is not the case.
4. A concludes that, therefore, G's true position Z is no good.[5]

For the purposes of illustration, let us suppose that G is a computer management consultant and that he has been hired to improve the efficiency of an office. Let us imagine that he recommends that typewriters in the office be replaced by word processors and that secretaries be trained to use them. The use of word processors will presumably decrease duplication of work and increase the speed at which assignments can be completed. Let us also suppose that in this case, A, a secretary, is adverse to change and likes things to remain just as they are. Suppose she replies to the consultant's recommendation by saying, "Oh this computer expert, he believes he can change the whole world for the better. He thinks that all of humanity's problems have a technological solution. But I'll tell you something, he's wrong. High technology is not going to eradicate evil and suffering in the world, nor will it reduce the problems of stress, boredom and meaninglessness in this office. This so-called computer expert really can't help us. High technology as a matter of fact has contributed to boredom and meaninglessness. I don't think we should accept his recommendation."

In this hypothetical example, the secretary attributes to the computer consultant a viewpoint which is not his. He believes that he can improve the efficiency of the office. The secretary, however, criticizes claims never made by the consultant, that is, that he can solve all of humanity's problems and that he can alleviate the problems of stress, boredom, and meaninglessness with high technology. She then rejects that suggestion about using word processors on the basis that high technology has caused problems, not alleviated them. Thus, the claim made by the consultant is rejected. Note that criticisms are directed at claims never made by the consultant as a means of rejecting the consultant's *actual* claim. The straw-man fallacy diverts attention from the real claim while at the same time rejecting it.

10.6 BEGGING THE QUESTION
10.7

The fallacy of begging the question involves using as a premise of one's argument the conclusion one is trying to establish. Reasoning which begs the question is therefore *circular*. It quite literally takes one around and around. Suppose, for example, that someone asks you how you know that God exists. Then let us suppose that your answer is, "Because it says so in the Bible." Your questioner might ask a follow-up question: "How do you know the Bible provides the truth?" If you answer, "Because it is the inspired word of God," you have begged the question. The existence of God is proved by the Bible whose inspired truth must presuppose the existence of God in the first place. One cannot presuppose as a premise of one's argument what one sets out to prove as conclusion. This is fallacious reasoning. Below, this type of fallacious reasoning is expressed formally:

1. *B* is presented in an argument as a premise in support of conclusion *X*.
2. *B* asserts the same proposition as *X*; or, in the context of the argument, *B* is acceptable only if *X* has already been accepted.[6]

10.8 FALLACY OF TWO WRONGS
10.9

When committing this fallacy, one defends a particular wrongdoing by drawing attention to another instance of similar behavior. Suppose, for example, that after a college football game, an individual rushed on to the field and proceeded to tear down the goalposts at one end of the field. Let us also imagine that this individual was apprehended by security guards and later charged with malicious vandalism. The individual makes in his defense the point that many people were tearing down the goalposts at the other end of the field and that this action must be all right since the others were not charged. The fact that others were also tearing down goalposts and causing damage does not justify the individual's action; he just happened to get caught while the others did not. One wrongdoing cannot be justified by pointing to another wrongdoing. Speeding on the highway is another example. When stopped for this traffic violation, a person might argue that he or she was speeding simply to keep up with traffic. Most police officers will not accept this line of reasoning; another's speeding cannot justify one's own. Formally stated, the fallacy of "two wrongs" can be expressed in the following fashion:

1. *A*'s conduct or action, *W*, has come under criticism.
2. *A* tries to defend *W* by citing *Y*, *Z*, or *S*—allegedly similar actions the wrongness of which is accepted or at least not challenged.
3. *Y*, *Z*, *or S* are not relevant to or sufficient for the defenses of *W*, or of *A* for having done *W*.[7]

10.10 SLIPPERY-SLOPE FALLACY

The slippery-slope fallacy involves objecting to something because one incorrectly assumes that it will surely lead to other undesirable consequences. For example, one may object to legalized abortion on the grounds that it will inevitably lead to infanticide and eventually to genocide. Notice here that the objection is not against abortion but to the infanticide and genocide to which one assumes it will necessarily lead. However, the conclusion drawn here is not inevitable. Legalizing and accepting abortion does not necessitate that we will countenance infanticide or genocide. Such practices are separate and distinct. Each must be considered independently and evaluated on its own terms. While the practice of abortion may or may not desensitize us to certain forms of life, there is no guarantee that it will make us callous to the point that we will kill babies or exterminate whole peoples whom we find objectionable. There is no **necessary causal connection** between abortion and genocide and/or infanticide. The slippery-slope fallacy may be presented in the following fashion.

1. A claims that if M is permitted, it will lead to X; X will then lead to Y, and so on to Z.
2. A maintains that Z is not desired; therefore, M should not be permitted.
3. A minimum of one step in the causal chain is unsupported and thus open to challenge.[8]

10.11 FALLACY OF APPEALING TO AUTHORITY
10.12

Moral positions are sometimes argued for by appeals to authority. Some types of appeals to authority are proper, while others are not. Let us first consider improper appeals.

One improper appeal to authority involves the notions of **popularity** and **democracy**.[9] In this instance, an argument is supported by an appeal to numbers alone. One could say for example that, "Abortion should be available on demand since a majority of citizens in this country are in favor of it." Though some might be tempted to accept this line of reasoning, it is no different in form from saying, "Slavery was good and should have been accepted in the southern United States simply because a majority of those southerners were in favor of it." Put simply, the majority can be wrong. The viewpoints held by the majority and their actions may violate sound principles of ethical conduct and morality. We should not, therefore, be morally swayed by the authority of majority opinion or majority rule.

Another type of improper appeal to authority can be found in television advertising. As was pointed out earlier, celebrities are frequently used to endorse products and further causes. Athletes may try to persuade us to drink milk or use particular hygiene products though they are not nutritionists and know very little or nothing about health care. When advertisers attempt to persuade us to buy their products simply because people like Wayne Gretzky, Joe Namath, or Larry Bird say we should, the persuasion attempt is not properly rational but psychological. Presumably we have respect for these sports celebrities and want to be like them. It is hoped we will be inclined to take their word about a product. If we accept the persuasive appeals of likeable but unqualified authorities, then we have fallen prey to a form of fallacy.

The fallacy of appealing to authority may also involve **traditional wisdom**.[10] Actions which are justified by relying exclusively on past **conventions** are not necessarily justified at all. An authoritative appeal based on traditional wisdom typically might be expressed so: "X is right because this is how it's always been," or "No woman should be prime minister or president because we have never had one before." Surely, no fair-minded and reasonable person would want to deny someone the position of president or prime minister simply because of gender. Furthermore, denying women their rightful place in the workworld is discriminatory. If traditional wisdom has led to past unfairness and discrimination, then that traditional wisdom should be reevaluated, modified and, if necessary, rejected. Though traditional wisdom may have important moral insights to offer, it is not in itself unquestionably valid.

10.13   If one wishes to appeal to authority in a proper fashion, then one must be sure that the authority has made **recognized contributions** to a specific field of inquiry. The authority's scholarship and research must be presented to the proper group of inquirers for **evaluation** and **appraisal**.[12] This group must deem the person's work significant and valid if that person is to be considered an authority. Public scrutiny and the collective judgment of one's peers and colleagues thus serve to confer authority on any individual.

It should be noted here that appeals to authority are usually best restricted to the empirical sciences or to fields of inquiry whose task it is to pursue and arrive at objective knowledge and truth. Authoritative appeals can be made in subject areas such as physics, chemistry, and history. Statements made in these disciplines can usually be verified in principle and hypotheses can be tested. There are clear public standards which can be used to test the validity of empirical and scientific claims.

Authoritative appeals are much more open to question in such fields of value inquiry as morality and aesthetics. Though philosophers agree to a large extent on the norms of rational thought and on what constitutes errors in reasoning, they often begin with differing and sometimes conflicting assumptions. Since different normative assumptions and principles cannot be proven true or false by empirical observation and experiment, the possibility that moral authorities will disagree among themselves becomes virtually inevitable. In moral philosophy and in other areas of value inquiry, where interpretation and personal preference play a role, where the boundaries of the subject matter are in dispute, and where authorities have no empirical means or scientific procedures to settle disputes, authoritative appeals cannot be made legitimately. Moral conflicts must be settled rationally, not by reference to authoritative opinions. Even if appeals to God's authority in moral matters are made, they are not free of problems. Does God condemn an action like fornication because it is immoral, or is fornication immoral simply because God says it is wrong? This is a metaethical question to which no answer can be found using objective scientific procedures. In any event, if God condemns fornication because of its inherent immorality, then one need not worry about the problem of authority in this case. If it is claimed, however, that fornication is wrong only because God condemns it, then the question arises as to whether or not God is good and just, given the evil in the world. One must ask why God's will should be obeyed. Why should we not be self-willed? Answers to questions like these are not clear-cut. Methods of dealing with these questions are not firmly preestablished and accepted by all. Appeals even to God's authority demand rational inquiry, argument, and evaluation. In short, appeals to authority in moral argument can as a general rule be regarded as incorrect procedure. Improper appeals to authority can be summed up formally:

1. A appeals to the authority of B in supporting claim X (which belongs to a field of inquiry Z).
2. Z is not a field in which authoritative knowledge can or does exist.
3. Or, A is not an authority about matters in field Z; or Z is a field of inquiry where knowledge is obtainable but there is among the authorities in field Z a lack of consensus that such claims as X are true; or A has a special interest in X's being accepted.

10.14   RED-HERRING FALLACY

The name of this fallacy comes from the sport of foxhunting.[13] In this sport, hunters on horseback follow a pack of hounds tracking a fox's scent. In order to divert the hounds from the hunt in order to save the fox, dried and salted red herring was drawn across the fox's track ahead of the pack. The dogs would be diverted by the fresher and stronger scent and the fox would be left alone.

In the red-herring fallacy, a contentious claim or position is defended by taking the offensive. This is done by setting up a new issue which has only a very weak or tenuous connection with the original old one. The defender then proceeds to argue for the new issue or position which is likely to be more supportable and probably less open to debate and questioning. The red-herring maneuver is thus a procedure of counterattack. The intention of the person introducing the red herring is to divert the opponent from his or her original line of attack. The red-herring fallacy can be formally expressed:

1. In an adversarial context, A has made a claim, X, that is or implies a criticism of a position that M holds or identifies with.
2. M responds to A by asserting Z, which introduces an issue irrelevant to the acceptability of X, and thereby instigates in the debate a shift of focus away from the question of X's acceptability.[14]

A good example of a red-herring argument is found in the 1972 Canadian federal election. Someone asked then prime minister Pierre Elliot Trudeau what had happened to the "Just Society" he had promised in 1968. Trudeau took the offensive suggesting that the questioner ask Jesus Christ what had happened to the just society Christ had promised two thousand years ago.[15] Implicitly, Trudeau was suggesting that he could not be expected to keep his promise if Christ had failed to keep His. Of course, the analogy between making political campaign promises and the Christian hope of peace and goodwill is very questionable. Nonetheless, Trudeau was successful in diverting attention and leaving behind the issue of his promise of social justice given four years earlier.

10.15   FALLACY OF GUILT BY ASSOCIATION

When guilty of this form of fallacious reasoning, one is usually in an adversarial situation. An attempt is made to discredit an opponent or that opponent's policies, claims, or positions by drawing attention to an alleged association which the opponent has with some already discreditable individual or group. The attempt to discredit is not direct, as in typical ad hominem arguments, but rather indirect. The "guilt" of the discreditable individual or group is transferred to the opponent. Let us suppose, for example, that during an election campaign, an Italian-American member of Congress spoke in favor of deregulating the trucking industry. Let us imagine that the member's opponent in the election argued against deregulation and despite knowing the clean legal record and proven integrity of the congressman, he drew the public's attention to the member's uncle—a notable underworld leader with connections in the trucking industry. The point of doing this was to imply, or indirectly suggest, that the congressman also has ties to the underworld and supports deregulation only to further the interests of organized crime. Without directly charging the member with crime and never having or showing proof of underworld activities, suspicison is nonetheless raised about the congressman's innocence. The political opponent tries to undermine the member's credibility, integrity, and justifiability of his position on deregulation through guilt by association. However, the member barely even knows his uncle or anything about that uncle's underworld crime activities. To assume guilt by familial association is in this case "dirty politics." The fallacy of guilt by association can be expressed formally:

1. An individual attacks W (or W's position, claim, or thesis, etc.) on the basis of some alleged connection or association between W and another person or group.
2. The alleged association does not exist, or else the alleged association does not provide relevant or sufficient support for the individual's criticism of W.[16]

PROGRESS CHECK 10.1

Instructions: *Fill in the blanks with the appropriate responses listed below.*

ad hominem fallacy
fallacy of two wrongs
slippery-slope fallacy
fallacy of appealing to authority
fallacy of guilt by association

fallacious reasoning
straw-man fallacy
begging the question
red-herring fallacy
diversionary or intimidating tactics

1. Reasoning which is circular illustrates _____.
2. If, in an argument, one attacks one's opponent and not that opponent's claim or position, then one is guilty of the _____.
3. If one tries to justify a particular wrongdoing by pointing to the fact that others are committing the same wrongdoing, then one is guilty of the _____.
4. If one intentionally misrepresents an opponent's argument and then proceeds to criticize and reject a position not held by one's opponent, then one is guilty of committing the _____.
5. Processes of argumentation which are designed to persuade us by emotional or psychological appeals, and not by reason, are reflective of _____.
6. Attempts at discrediting an opponent's claim or position by drawing attention to an alleged relationship between the opponent and some already discredited person, group, or body are indicative of the _____.
7. Attempts to justify one's moral viewpoint by making reference to so-called expert opinion indicate _____.
8. If one erroneously concludes that action M will necessarily lead to actions X, Y, and eventually Z (which is undesirable), then one has committed the _____.
9. A philosophical counterattack which diverts attention to an irrelevant point reflects the _____.
10. In general, fallacies are examples of _____.

LEARNING EXERCISE 10.2

Instructions: *Below you will find examples of fallacious reasoning. Identify which fallacies are committed by placing the appropriate letter next to the example.*

(a) ad hominem fallacy
(b) straw-man fallacy
(c) begging the question
(d) fallacy of two wrongs

(e) slippery-slope fallacy
(f) fallacy of appealing to authority
(g) red-herring fallacy
(h) fallacy of guilt by association

_____ 1. I don't think we should accept the councilman's arguments in favor of Sunday shopping in our town—he's a Godless communist afterall.

_____ 2. As a Christian, I am opposed to abortion in all cases since my church prohibits this practice. In my view, abortion is wrong because my church leaders tell us that it is a violation of God's law.

_____ 3. Two students were having a disagreement about cars. Student A said, "I can prove to you that Toyota Celicas are faster than Ford Mustangs. John owns a Celica and he told me that he has beaten every Mustang he has ever raced." Student B asked, "How do you know John is telling the truth?" Student A replied by saying, "Someone who drives the fastest car wouldn't have to lie."

_____ 4. We should not let any central American country be ruled by communist leaders. If we do, then sooner or later Mexico will become communist, along with the islands in the Caribbean and no doubt Canada.

_____ 5. I think it's perfectly all right to speed along the Lakeshore highway. Everyone I've seen drives at ten to fifteen kilometers over the limit.

_____ 6. The governor supports tax increases for middle-income earners. This doesn't surprise me. He's always been against unions and this is just another measure designed to undermine them. If we allow for these tax increases and the undermining of unions, democracy in this country will be threatened.

_____ 7. One evening in a Detroit bar, the Canadian tourist said to the bartender, "You know, the USA is not as democratic and free as your fellow Americans allege. Women and minorities are discriminated against; lobby groups exercise inordinate power; and the fear of being victimized by criminals in the streets frightens people from wandering outdoors in the evening. The bartender replied by saying, "What are you talking about, the USA is the greatest. We're the strongest nation in the world. We have the best universities and the most advanced space technology. Give me a break, O.K.?"

_____ 8. You can't seriously be considering voting for the Democratic candidate in the next election. Why democrats are no different from socialists these days. It would be disastrous if the Democrats ruled this country. The socialist party in France was so inefficient and corrupt it almost led the country into bankruptcy. Just think what the Democrats would do here with all their socialist policies. The Democrats would ruin this nation.

LEARNING EXERCISE 10.3

Instructions: *Provide examples of the fallacies indicated below.*

1. Ad Hominem Fallacy
2. Straw-Man Fallacy
3. Begging the Question
4. Fallacy of Two Wrongs
5. Slippery-Slope Fallacy
6. Fallacy of Appealing to Authority
7. Red-Herring Fallacy
8. Fallacy of Guilt by Association

SUMMARY

1. Ad Hominem Fallacy
    Logically incorrect response
    Involves a personal attack of the opponent (e.g., motives or interests)
    Present in everyday conversations, politics, and business
    Diversionary tactic
    Emotionally satisfying
2. Straw-Man Fallacy
    Deliberate misrepresentation and rejection of opponent's argument
    Diversionary tactic
3. Begging the Question
    Indicated by circular reasoning
    Involves presupposing as a premise of one's argument what one is setting out to conclude
4. Fallacy of Two Wrongs
    Involves justifying one wrongdoing by another
    Irrational and childish (that is, if doing wrong is O.K. for him, then it's O.K. for me too)
5. Slippery-Slope Fallacy
    Involves objecting to M because one erroneously believes that M will lead to X, Y, and Z, which are undesirable
    Based on false causal relationships or unwarranted assumptions about what will occur

6. Fallacy of Appealing to Authority

   Based on incorrect appeals to popularity, democracy, figures of importance or celebrities, and traditional wisdom

   Authorities may be unqualified

   Authorities may conflict

   Authorities may be self-interested

7. Red-Herring Fallacy

   Used in adversarial situations

   Contentious claims or positions defended by taking the offensive

   New issue set up having only tenuous relationship with the original point being made

8. Fallacy of Guilt by Association

   An attempt to discredit an opponent by drawing attention to an association which the opponent allegedly has with an already discredited individual or group

REFERENCES

Barry, Vincent. *Applying Ethics: A Text with Readings.* Belmont, CA: Wadsworth, 1982.

Ehninger, Douglas. *Influence, Belief, and Argument: An Introduction to Responsible Persuasion.* Glenview, IL: Scott, Foresman, 1974.

Engel, Morris. *With Good Reason: An Introduction to Informal Fallacies.* 2nd ed. New York: St. Martin's Press.

Johnson, R. H., and Blair, J. A. *Logical Self-Defense.* 2nd ed. Toronto: McGraw-Hill Ryerson, 1983.

McDonald. *The Language of Argument.* 4th ed. New York: Harper and Row, 1983.

Woods, John, and Douglas, Walton. *Argument: The Logic of Fallacies.* Toronto: McGraw-Hill Ryerson, 1982.

NOTES

1. R. H. Johnson and J. A. Blair, *Logical Self-Defense,* 2nd ed. (Toronto: McGraw-Hill Ryerson, 1983), p. 82.
2. Ibid., p. 79.
3. Ibid., p. 81.
4. Ibid.
5. Adapted from ibid., p. 74.
6. Adapted from ibid., p. 58.
7. Adapted from ibid., p. 107.
8. Adapted from ibid., p. 164.
9. Vincent Barry, *Applying Ethics: A Text with Readings* (Belmont, CA: Wadsworth, 1982), p. 20.
10. Ibid., p. 20.
11. Ibid.
12. Johnson and Blair, *Logical Self-Defense,* p. 146.
13. Ibid., p. 87.
14. Adapted from ibid., p. 89.
15. Ibid., p. 88
16. Adapted from ibid., p. 84.

Self-Test

Skills

_____ 1. Psychologists, sociologists and anthropologists study morality:
  (a) normatively
  (b) empirically
  (c) purely rationally
  (d) epistemologically

_____ 2. In conducting their studies, scientists try to uphold the scientific ideal of:
  (a) prescriptivity
  (b) objectivity
  (c) normativity
  (d) insanity
  (e) emotionality

_____ 3. A statement which is true or false in principle is:
  (a) nonnormative
  (b) normative
  (c) prescriptive
  (d) evaluative

_____ 4. Philosophers make a distinction between facts and values. This is because:
  (a) value judgments are ultimately justified by appeals to facts
  (b) one can easily confuse the two
  (c) value judgments cannot be justified solely by appeals to facts
  (d) philosophers believe that making conceptual distinctions is good in itself
  (e) none of the above

_____ 5. The philosophical study of morality may be either:
  (a) empirical or factual
  (b) normative or prescriptive
  (c) normative or metaethical
  (d) normative or metaphysical

_____ 6. "Women develop more quickly than men in their moral-reasoning abilities." This is:
  (a) a normative claim about morality
  (b) an empirical claim about morality
  (c) a value judgment about female superiority
  (d) an example of wishful thinking
  (e) a normative opinion which could, in principle, be justified

_____ 7. A factual claim whose truth depends on temporal or spatial factors is:
  (a) necessary
  (b) universal
  (c) unconditional
  (d) contingent
  (e) a disguised value judgment

_____ 8. Claims whose truth is recognized by rational or intellectual intuition are:
  (a) a posteriori
  (b) a priori
  (c) conditional
  (d) contingent

_____ 9. The statement "Michael cannot be an atheistic Christian" is an example of:
  (a) a conditional claim
  (b) a contingent claim
  (c) an a priori claim
  (d) a claim which is necessarily true
  (e) C and D
  (f) A and B

_____ 10. A normative claim:
  (a) simply states the facts
  (b) is an unfounded and unjustified opinion
  (c) is always emotionally based
  (d) makes a value judgment of some sort
  (e) none of the above

_____ 11. "Moral responsibility presupposes freedom of action." This claim is:
  (a) empirical
  (b) normative
  (c) a priori
  (d) none of the above

_____ 12. When one tests moral principles using the role-exchange test, one asks:
  (a) what if everybody acted on this principle?
  (b) so what?
  (c) how would you like to be the person most disadvantaged?
  (d) could you apply this principle to other similar cases?

Identifying Statements

Instructions: _Next to each statement below, place the appropriate letter. (F = factual statement; N = normative statement; A = a priori statement.)_

_____ 1. Proabortionists are terrible people.
_____ 2. Prolife supporters are idiots.
_____ 3. Legalized gambling will promote organized crime.
_____ 4. A triangle is a three-sided figure.
_____ 5. Everyone should study moral philosophy.
_____ 6. A bachelor is an unmarried man.
_____ 7. Cheating on exams is on the increase.
_____ 8. Capital punishment should be reinstated.
_____ 9. Children with AIDS should not be allowed to attend regular schools.
_____ 10. Seven plus five equals twelve.

Instructions: *Fill in the Blanks*

1. Opinions are distingished by the fact that they are not accompanied by _____; they are groundless.
2. In moral or philosophical argument, the proper attitude to adapt is one of _____.
3. There are two basic types of logic, (a) _____ and (b) _____.
4. What are the three parts of a practical syllogism?
   (a) _____
   (b) _____
   (c) _____
5. Inductive logic can provide us only with _____ conclusions.
6. Deductive logic can provide us with _____ conclusions.
7. When making an inductive generalization, it is important that our group of subjects be _____ selected.
8. In deductive logic, conclusions are _____ from preceding _____.
9. Give one example of a logical syllogism.
   Major Premise: _____.
   Minor Premise: _____.
   Conclusion: _____.
10. Valid logical arguments may not lead to correct or _____ conclusions.
11. When using the higher-order principle test to justify one's claim, the _____ of the tested syllogism becomes the _____ of another justifying syllogism.
12. If one argues against X because one wrongly presupposes that X will necessarily lead to other undesirable consequences, then one commits the _____ fallacy.
13. If one misrepresents another's argument and then rejects the misrepresentation, then one commits the _____ fallacy.

14. If one objects to abortion *solely* on the grounds that one's church is opposed to it, then one commits the fallacy of _____.

15. "I can't accept the Prime Minister's foreign policy because he's such a hypocrite." This reasoning commits the _____ fallacy.

16. If in defence of one's own position, one counterattacks and shifts the focus of the argument to something more acceptable, then one is guilty of committing the _____ fallacy.

17. Fallacies of logical reasoning are used either as _____ tactics or _____ tactics.

18. Fallacies are designed to persuade us _____ not logically.

Abortion

11

"A FEMINIST VIEW OF ABORTION"

Jean MacRae

EDUCATIONAL OBJECTIVES: After reading this chapter the student will be able to:

11.1 Identify the "myths" surrounding the abortion issue.

11.2 Give reasons for rejecting these so-called myths.

11.3 Describe the experience of women with unwanted pregnancies.

11.4 Explain the concept of "compulsory pregnancy."

11.5 Discuss how sexism plays a role in mattters of contraception and unwanted pregnancy.

11.6 State the biological argument opposing abortion.

11.7 Give MacRae's reasons for rejecting the biological argument.

11.8 List other elements constitutive of human life beyond physical existence.

11.9 Articulate the problem of "ensoulment" as it relates to the abortion issue.

11.10 Provide reasons for rejecting the legal contention that "abortion is murder."

11.11 Explain MacRae's reasons for not accepting the value of human physical life as absolute.

11.12 Explain why a belief in a transcendent God can give us no concrete guidelines for the solution of moral problems such as abortion.

Jean E. MacRae M.T.S. Harvard Divinity School, Founder, New Words, a feminist bookstore, Cambridge, Mass. Administrator, Massachusetts Coalition of Battered Women Service Groups.

11.13 Comment on the new light shed on the abortion issue by the women's movement.

11.14 Explain how masculine theology and a sexist, male-dominated social philosophy pressure women in situations of unwanted pregnancies.

11.15 Provide ways in which the abortion problem can be diminished.

FOCUS QUESTIONS

1. How do women's emotional reactions and psychological symptoms get tied up with the abortion issue?
2. What empirical evidence does MacRae provide in her attempts to explode "myths" surrounding the abortion issue? Is it sufficient to persuade us? Why or why not?
3. How is unwanted pregnancy a form of physical violence? Is MacRae justifiably or unjustifiably drawing a parallel between the two notions?
4. How does a sexist society set the stage for unwanted pregnancies?
5. What can be said about the biological status of the fetus?
6. Can one favor abortion even from a religious perspective? How so?
7. In what way are the mother and fetus involved in a struggle?
8. Is the value of "physical" human life absolute?
9. What problems can arise when attempting to apply religious belief to moral problems such as abortion?
10. How can the abortion problem be minimized?

SYNOPSIS

MacRae's article published in the early 1970s presents a proabortion argument stated from a feminist's perspective. It begins by exploding several so-called myths surrounding the issue of intentionally and prematurely terminating pregnancies. Specifically, the belief is questioned that abortion is a renunciation of motherhood and that it is some kind of rare traumatic occurrence which necessarily breeds guilt and anxiety in women. MacRae makes reference to European studies which suggest that emotional trauma resulting from abortion is far less than commonly thought. She suggests that any trauma which does occur is probably due to the clandestine and anxiety-ridden task of procuring an abortion, not the abortion itself. MacRae rejects the contention, therefore, that abortion is morally and naturally wrong as supposedly evidenced by the guilt reactions of women who choose it. The psychological trauma is simply not present to the degree many assume. MacRae also points to estimates suggesting that in France abortions are more numerous than live births and how certain cultural groups accept abortion as commonplace in cases of desertion, for example, and in situations where pregnancy occurs in the first year of marriage. MacRae focuses the reader's attention on the Mataco, a South American Indian tribe which accepts abortion of the first fetus as a matter of course in order to make subsequent childbearing easier.

MacRae also discusses in this work the experience of women during the gestational period preceding childbirth and then goes on to explain what she means by the concept of "compulsory pregnancy." Where pregnancy is unwanted yet forced upon a woman, it is compulsory and akin to physical violence according to MacRae. As for the argument that women must accept responsibility for their sexual conduct, she regards it as naive, especially in view of the fact that no method of birth control is perfect and that there is an element of sexism in our male-dominated society which militates against women taking proper and adequate precautions to prevent pregnancy.

MacRae also rejects the biological argument against abortion which depicts the fetus as an independent organism, having an individual genetic identity and initiating development on its own. She suggests that in making such an argument there is often a biased, selective process in the presentation of the data. However the fetus is conceptualized, there can be no doubt she says that it depends on the mother for its nourishment and growth. The fetus is parasitic as evidenced by the decline in health in many prospective mothers. Given this, MacRae concludes that the fetus is part of the mother, that is, a part of her body. Moreover, MacRae alludes to the fact that when human life is generally discussed, outside the emotionally laden context of abortion, biology takes on less importance. What becomes more salient in discussions of human life are things like language, creativity, values, and morality, none of which a developing fetus possesses. MacRae makes passing mention as well of the possibility that even if a person is a being in relation to God and possessing an everlasting soul, it is not necessarily true that "ensoulment" occurs at conception. Citing Gordon Kaufman for support, she intimates that a soul could develop within the individual along with a sense of selfhood and a capacity for love and trust. Her point seems to be that religious belief need not necessarily lead to the conclusion that abortion is wrong. If ensoulment is something which occurs or develops at birth, then abortion might be acceptable even from a religious perspective.

After arguing in favor of abortion from social, biological, and religious vantage points, MacRae then moves on to legal issues surrounding the controversy. Rejecting the "abortion is murder" assertion on the grounds that it is a frequent, culturally universal experience that does not leave women feeling like murderers, she asks the rhetorical question "whether the well-being of the more actual than potential human life of the mother is not in fact more important than the physical existence of the more potential than actual fetus." MacRae underscores here the fact that there is a type of struggle present in an unwanted pregnancy. The body and well-being of a person (that is, the mother) are controlled by the fetus. Compulsory pregnancy demands an excessive sacrifice on the part of the mother for the welfare of another being. In attempting to humanize the fetus, the mother is dehumanized.

Jean MacRae also argues in favor of abortion by making reference to religious thinkers in a context outside of the issue of ensoulment. She points out that several Christian thinkers (for example, Fletcher, Gustafson, and Barth) call into question the value of human "physical" life as absolute. They believe that human life is many-valued and that physical existence is not necessarily ultimate or overriding. Furthermore, a belief that God is love or God is just does not lead logically to the idea that physical life should be preserved in all cases. Circumstances may dictate otherwise (for example, the just war).

In closing, MacRae argues that abortion is not a negation of human life but an affirmation of women's lives and significant others around them who stand to be adversely affected by the birth of an unwanted child. In seeking abortions, women are concerned to affirm values of life outside of motherhood. They are placed in a position of having to resist a history of masculine theology and secular philosophy which praise the virtue of selflessness as it applies to women in the abortion problem. MacRae rejects the idea that women should place their own welfare in a subordinate position to a life which has barely begun. She advocates that the abortion issue be reconceptualized in terms of women's autonomy and right to self-determination. MacRae believes that if women develop a sense of autonomy and self-esteem, much of the abortion problem will be eliminated: "Only when women are raised to care enough for themselves to deal with their relations to men, their futures, and their personhood, will they be able to avoid self-destructive situations such as unwanted pregnancy."

[11.1, 11.2] Before describing women's experience of unwanted pregnancy as I have observed it in my counselling work, an analysis of some of the mythology which has grown up around abortion might be helpful. A taboo topic in our society until relatively recently, abortion was thought to be anathema, a dark, unusual happening. It has also been a long-held belief that any woman who undergoes abortion will suffer trauma and deep-seated guilt for years after, presumably because what she has done is inherently wrong and unnatural. Abortion is murder and the renunciation of maternity. Undoubtedly there has been some truth to this assertion, as a result of the dutiful internalization on the part of women of this very construction. It must also be taken into account that in a society in which abortion is proscribed by law, women must go underground to terminate pregnancies. As a re-

sult, many women may well be traumatized by abortion, but it is the clandestine and anxiety-ridden task of obtaining the abortion rather than the event itself that induces trauma and guilt. The same might be said of the procedure of obtaining a legal so-called "therapeutic" abortion involving a demonstration of mental instability or illness. It is inevitable that many women come out of such an experience thinking of themselves as mentally unstable or sick by virtue of having wanted an abortion.

With the advent of more liberal laws on abortion in some European countries, abortion has been experienced in a more neutral environment, and the psychological and moral sequelae of abortion have been researched. Several studies conducted in Europe have exploded the myth of guilt and traumatic reaction to abortion. A study done by Dr. Martin Ekblad in Sweden of

479 women interviewed at least twenty-two to thirty months after abortion showed that 75% had no self-reproach, 14% had mild self-reproach and 11% reported serious self-repoach. Many of these women had suffered deep anxiety prior to the abortion; in a "normal" group only 6% suffered from serious self-reproach. Other studies have corroborated these results or show that an even smaller percentage of women suffer from guilt or trauma following hospital abortion.[1] This is not to say that decisions about abortion are easy. Unwanted pregnancy and abortion are usually difficult and unhappy experiences and the decision to abort is made with serious consideration. This research material only calls into question the assertion that abortion is morally and naturally wrong as evidenced by the inevitable guilt reaction of most women who choose it.

In addition to myth-breaking research, cross-cultural studies have raised doubts about the "nature" of abortion. Lawrence Lader gives several examples of societies in which abortion is considered a matter of course:

> The Mataco, for example, a South American Indian tribe supposedly abort the first fetus to make subsequent child-bearing easier. Among American Indians the Crow and the Assiniboni favor abortion in cases of desertion. In New Britain, it is considered essential for a pregnancy in the first year of marriage.[2]

Abortion has been widely practiced not only in societies where it is accepted, but also in countries where it is illegal. In spite of the illegality of abortion, it is estimated that there are more abortions than live births every year in France. If, as John Noonan entitle an article on the subject, the anti-abortion position has been "an Almost Absolute Value in History," it must also be remembered that not only was he talking about the history of Western Christian, male-dominated society alone, but also that in the unofficial history of women everywhere abortion has been universally and frequently experienced.

[11.3] What is the experience of women with unwanted pregnancies? First, we must take seriously the fact that they are aware that their bodies are transformed against their wills. For all, this means a new bodily feeling and eventually a new shape. For many, it means nausea, dizziness, and inability to work and be normally active. For some, it means illness, exacerbation of other medical problems, and perhaps even threat of death. Experienced as a result of choice, pregnancy, like sex, can be a happy event or at least one happily taken on in the desire of children. Unwanted pregnancy is experienced as a form of physical violence. It has been observed that oppressed groups suffer from unequal access to goods and services and also from physical violence and intimidation. Kate Millet observes that an example of such physical violence in the case of women is the death of a number of women each year as a result of illegal abortion.[3] She might well add the incidence of unwanted pregnancy.

[11.4] Any discussion of unwanted pregnancy is incomplete without an investigation of how such pregnancies occur. Some ethicists have been puzzled at the meaning of the phrase "compulsory pregnancy." They argue that women know very well that they're risking pregnancy when they engage in sexual intercourse and that they are free to practice contraception or refuse sexual intercourse. Hence any pregnancy that accrues was freely risked, if not chosen, and there is no such thing as a compulsory pregnancy. Such a view is not surprisingly naive but also overlooks the technological inadequacy of birth control and the affects of sexism in connection with the use of birth control and psychological pressures on women.

[11.5] The fact that we have no "ideal" method of birth control has often been forgotten. Harriet Pilpel has noted that if all married women used the IUD (which not all women can accommodate) there would be from 350,000 to 700,000 unwanted pregnancies every year.[4] Added to the unequal distribution of contraceptive information and devices among different age and class groups of women, such facts demonstrate that contraception is not an adequate solution at this time. Not only has technology and the social system been inadequate, but the sexist structure of our society has set the stage for numbers of unwanted pregnancies. With regard to birth control, Pam Lowry, co-ordinator of Pregnancy Counseling Service, has pointed out that traditional female taboos have discouraged women from using contraceptives which entail touching their own genitals (foam and diaphragm) and have kept them away from doctors who give pelvic examinations. The double standard, still a reality in our society, and the lack of sex education, militate against women, who are primarily responsible for contraception, given the extant methods, consciously taking responsibility for birth control. To do this would mean consciously admitting they were going to enter into a sexual relationship. Rather, they will subconsciously wait to be "swept off their feet." Furthermore, both partners could take responsibility for seeing that birth control is used, but often the responsibility is foisted only on the woman. In a society in which women's social status and security are largely dependent on their associations with males, our idea of rape may be extended to include not only forced physical assault, but intercourse forced by social and psychological pressures. Many women who are about to become engaged conceive unwanted pregnancies in an effort to insure marriage, which they were conditioned to

regard as of paramount importance. When this desperate act fails or promises to endanger a young relationship, the pregnancy is finally approached more realistically.

[11.6] What of the woman's relationship to the fetus? With the development of embryology and fetology, we have learned that the genetic code determining individual biological identity is set at conception and that rapid growth of the fetus gives it a recognizable form very early in pregnancy. In addition, the circulatory and other physiological systems of the fetus are independent, and the placenta and umbilical connection are outgrowths of the fetus, not the mother. Ramsay says "The blastocyst now devotes some of its foreordained cellular powers to throwing out a lifeline by which it can be attached to the life of the mother."[5] Although Ramsay admits that the placenta takes from the mother what it needs, he concludes that ". . . the navel, which is supposed to be an external mark of the dependence of everyone since Adam and Eve, is actually a sign of independent and entitatively distinct activity of the germinating cells."[6]

[11.7] Much of the biological argument against abortion is presented in this way. It seems probable that there is often a selective process in presenting biological data, and that in the material of Ramsay's, the parasitic character of the relationship of mother and fetus is obscured by fetus-oriented biology. No matter how true it is that the fetus' system is independent, it cannot be overlooked that the nourishment for its growth comes from the mother's nutritive resources. Rachel Conrad Wahlberg states in her article "The Woman and the Fetus 'One Flesh,' " "There is a cannibalistic element here; the fetus actually feeds on the mother's body. . . . The parasitical aspect is reflected in the fact that a mother's health can be dragged down during pregnancy if she is not getting the proper nourishment."[7] What of the mother's experience of the fetus? Whether the fetus is an independent organism, it is inside the body of the mother and is constituted of her nourishment. Experientially it is one flesh with the mother. **[11.8]** Women who abort do not perceive themselves as murderers. Nor is this perception an incidental or purely subjective reaction on the part of an aberrant few acting in their own interests. Those who consider the fetus to be inviolable base its humanity on its biological nature. In contrast, however, some theologians have considered other dimensions more centrally constitutive of life as human. Gordon Kaufman has pointed out:

> If anyone were to ask us in a context not so loaded with emotion and misconception what characterizes human life as distinct from other forms of life? We would be likely to suggest that such features as the use of language, concern for value, ideals, morality, religiousness, a power of imagination and creativity which makes possible production of magnificent works of art, the capacity to decide and act and the like.[8]

[11.9] In addition to these general characteristics of humanity, Professor Kaufman discusses those which are reflected in the religious category "ensouled," a term often applied to the fetus in traditional theological anti-abortion arguments.

> God's gift of the "soul" . . . is not the special implantation of a distinct substance at conception; it is rather the evoking of selfhood and responsibility and the capacities for love and trust, through the loving care of parents in the first years of life.[9]

[11.10] The "abortion is murder" assertion may seem so extreme that we need not concern ourselves with it, but it is just this definition that forms the basis of anti-abortion legislation, according to which the state protects the life of the fetus, and therefore it does have to be dealt with. The fact that the overwhelming majority of women who freely choose abortion do not experience themselves as murderers, and the fact that abortion is not an aberrant or strange, but a frequent and culturally universal experience, forces us to question the validity of a material description of abortion. We must ask whether the well-being of the more actual than potential human life of the mother is not in fact more important than the physical existence of the more potential than actual fetus. Perhaps no bell tolls for the fetus because the reality of the fetus is significantly different than that of a more actualized human being.

Another important observation can be made. The question of abortion has to do with the *unique* struggle between two living beings. It is only in the case of unwanted pregnancy that the *body* and the whole well-being of a person is controlled by another human being. This observation helps us cut through the "wedge arguments" such as: if the fetus does not possess human characteristics such as language, neither does the one-month-old child—will infanticide be next? It is only in the case of the fetus that only one person can take responsibility for its nurture, the biological mother. The state or society can intervene in the case of the unwanted child, but must force a woman to endure an unwanted bodily and social identity in the case of the fetus. In the last analysis, we are not dealing with the problem of the nature of the fetus, but with the problem of what kind of sacrifice is excessive to demand of one person for the welfare of another being. Women are simply saying, in their demand for access to abortion, that compulsory pregnancy is too much. The humanization of the fetus cannot take place at the cost of the dehumanization of another human being. This is especially true given the nature of the parent-child relationship and the effects of maternal deprivation of unwanted children on the children themselves.

[11.11, 11.12] The refusal to treat the values of women with unwanted pregnancies seriously has been part of our history of not taking women seriously in general, but it has also resulted from a tradition of regarding the value of human physical life as absolute. Keeping in mind theories of just war and other situations in which killing has been justified, it seems that the fetus has been a symbol used to bolster up this tradition. Several Christian ethicists, however, have criticized this tradition, which is the absolutization of a finite value. Joseph Fletcher has called it a kind of vitalism and even Barth, in his discussion of abortion, has questioned whether God's will might not indicate the termination of pregnancy in some cases. In fact, as James Gustafson has pointed out, both Christian theology and human experience point to the fact that human life is many-valued, and the value of human life is not absolute. A belief in a transcendent God leaves us with no concrete guidelines for the solution of moral problems:

> Insofar as the transcendent God is the One beyond many (H. R. Niebuhr) or the unspeakable ground of being (Tillich) he is particularly devoid of meaningful content, and thus man is left almost no substantial theological resources in the determination of the values and purposes which ought to govern his participation in the created order including his use of physical life.[10]

Even if we can attribute some character to God in our theological affirmations, they are non-concrete. We may say God is just, or God is love, but have no more of a guideline as to what love might dictate in a concrete situation. "Although God is loving and wills that men shall be loving, love is not *prima facie* consistent with the preservation of human life under all circumstances."[11] It is impossible to erect a rigid valuational structure, and it is untenable to establish any one value as absolute. We can't rest on the security of the absolute value of physical life, but may find ourselves acting arbitrarily and without meaning if we cannot give expression to the other legitimate values which motivate our action.

Gustafson observes that " . . . men have learned that circumstances of human experience often require them to alter things they professed to be of absolute value."[12] In the case of abortion, men will have to learn from women that unwanted pregnancy brings other values into play which are of relatively greater importance than the physical life of the nascent fetus.

[11.13] What values does the movement for the liberation of women and the new self-understanding of women bring to the discussion of abortion? While the traditional moral arguments against abortion have focused their thinking on the nature of the life of the fetus, the women I have encountered seeking abortion have focused their thinking on the social and emotional problems involved. They consider the desirability of making or prolonging a bad marriage, interrupting their education or work, having more children than they feel they can cope with, traumatizing or burdening their parents, or suffering rejection and the stigma of extramarital pregnancy. Some of these concerns center around the welfare of the pregnant woman and others the welfare of other persons involved.

The demand for abortion-law repeal has undeniably come about in a time when women are beginning to break away from concepts of themselves as both virgins and mothers. Sexual freedom unmatched by an adequate response from the society in terms of sex education and availability of contraceptive devices has led to many unwanted pregnancies. Unwanted pregnancy is less and less something to which women unquestioningly surrender themselves. In seeking abortion, they are not negating the value of human life but are affirming other values of their own lives and the lives of significant others who would be adversely affected by their pregnancy and the birth of an unwanted child. They are affirming the value of their own personhood as more multi-dimensional than child-bearer. It is not simply a matter of convenience on the part of women, but a matter of taking into their own hands the definition of their selves. It is not only women but also families, friends, and society which stand to benefit from the contribution of mature, responsible persons, who as such have an active and creative capacity to give to others rather than simply a passive and non-personal surrender of their bodies and "maternal instincts." If an absolutizing affirmation of the value of the life of the fetus results in the manipulation of the bodily and mental integrity of women, the value of life as a whole is neglected and many individuals are done a serious wrong.

[11.14] A balanced construction of our concept of abortion would be one which would not manipulate women into seeing themselves as guilty or as passive servants of procreation. Valerie Goldstein's analysis of the danger for women at this point in history of masculine theology which emphasizes the virtues of selflessness is applicable to the abortion problem.[13] The pressure of theological and secular anti-abortion arguments on women to be selfless and regard their own welfare as secondary to that of a barely beginning life which will become determinative of their identity, reinforces women in their sins of failing to become whole selves and failure to establish their own understanding of the reality they experience. If women can resist these pressures, abortion will be reconceptualized and renamed.

[11.15] This process is as important as changing legislation on abortion. Many see abortion as a temporary problem with the hope that better methods and distribution of birth-control devices will make the need for abortion obsolete. In the meantime, they argue that abortion laws should remain restrictive as an affirmation of the value of life will stand society in good stead in the long run of dealing with the larger issues of life and death. Whether pro or con the repeal of abortion laws, I think every sensitive person hopes the need for abortion will diminish. Obviously it is not the ultimate answer to unwanted pregnancy. However, it is unlikely that technical advances in birth control or sex education will in themselves solve the problem. For women the issue of abortion must be a larger issue in that the concern with the right to control one's bodily existence must be expanded to comprehend a more basic sense of autonomy on the part of women. The right to abortion is more than a necessary stop-gap. While relatively safe, any medical procedure should be avoided if possible. But more important, unwanted pregnancy is by definition a situation in which women find themselves against their better judgement. With the exception of rape and contraceptive failure, unwanted pregnancy is the result of a lack of intentionality and self-love (caring) in women. In saying this, I do not intend to "blame the victim" as I think is clear from the above, but to point out that a thorough-going sense of autonomy and self-esteem in women will be one of the most significant ways in which abortion will be eliminated. Only when women are raised to care enough for themselves to deal with their relations to men, their futures, and their personhood, will they be able to avoid self-destructive situations such as unwanted pregnancy. While the drive for autonomy which is embodied in the women's liberation movement seems to propound an ethic which is individualistic to the point of selfishness, I feel the real importance of an authentic sense of self is that one gives to others best from a position of strength rather than of weakness.

Postscript: July, 1982

In the ten years that have passed since this article was written, the struggle to establish and maintain the right to choose abortion has become an integral part of gaining that ability to be autonomous, referred to in the last paragraph, that will eventually lessen the need for abortion. In the early 1970s, feminists were beginning to fathom the power of men in patriarchal society to trap women in roles that serve men's interests. Since then, an understanding of the range of that power has unfolded as we have learned more about the pervasiveness of sexual harassment in the workplace, the frequency of rape and incest, and the extent and severity of wife-beating. Not only has the last decade not brought major improvements in contraception, but the safety of the most widely used methods has been called into question.

In light of these developments, I would no longer speak of "women's sins of failing to become whole selves" or unwanted pregnancy as the result of a "lack of intentionality and self-caring in women." My hope for the possibility of such individual control over women's destinies was informed by the central role of consciousness-raising in the early women's movement.

While still affirming the power of women to take control of their own lives, I now believe that this must happen in the context of concerted action to win and protect women's rights. Many abortion-rights groups have expanded their concerns to include working against sterilization abuse, another abridgement of reproductive freedom. These struggles in themselves will be part of the process of transforming society. Only in a society that recognizes women's basic right to self-determination in formal ways such as equal rights and access to abortion for all women, rich and poor, will women and men, girls and boys, be able to respect women's and girls' rights not to risk unwanted pregnancy as well as to terminate it.

NOTES

1. Lawrence Lader, *Abortion* (Indianapolis: The Bobbs-Merrill Company, Inc., 1966), pp. 21–22.
2. Ibid., p. 22.
3. Kate Millet, *Sexual Politics* (New York: Avon, 1969), p. 44.
4. Harriet Pilpel, "The Right to Abortion," *Atlantic Monthly*, June 1969.
5. Paul Ramsay, "Points in Deciding about Abortion," in *The Morality of Abortion*, John T. Noonan Jr., Ed. (Cambridge, MA: Harvard University Press, 1970), p. 70.
6. Ibid., p. 72.
7. Rachel Conrad Wahlberg, "The Woman and the Fetus 'One Flesh'," *The Christian Century*, Sept. 8, 1971, p. 1046.
8. Gordon Kaufman, "An Unexamined Question," *The Unauthorized Version*, Harvard Divinity School, Vol. II, no. 6, 1971, p. 2.
9. Ibid.
10. James Gustafson, "God's Transcendence and the Value of Human Life," *Christian Ethics and the Community* (Philadelphia: Pilgrim Press Book, 1971), p. 143.
11. Ibid., p. 146.
12. Ibid., p. 142.
13. Valerie Saiving Goldstein, "The Human Situation: A Feminine Point of View," pp. 10–12.

PROGRESS CHECK 11.1

Instructions: *Fill in the blanks with the appropriate responses listed below.*

motherhood	absolute
rape	trauma
parasitic	physical violence
self-reproach	Mataco
selfless	autonomy

1. Forcing women to endure unwanted pregnancies is a form of _____.
2. Masculine theology and sexist secular antiabortion arguments demand that women be _____ and place their own welfare below that of the developing fetus.
3. Insofar as the fetus depends on the mother for survival and growth, it is _____.
4. In a society where women's social status and security largely depend on associations with males, intercourse forced by social and psychological pressures may be regarded as a form of _____.
5. Some see abortion as a renunciation of _____.
6. European studies indicate that _____ results far less from abortion than is usually thought.
7. Proabortionists like MacRae reject the idea that the value of physical life is _____ and that it overrides other psychological and social values.
8. One "myth" MacRae attempts to explode is the one about abortion necessarily resulting in emotional or psychological _____.
9. Abortion can be regarded not as a rejection of life but an affirmation of women's _____.
10. The _____ supposedly abort the first fetus to make later child-bearing easier.

LEARNING EXERCISE 11.2

Instructions: *Identify the following statements as either factual claims (F) or value judgments (V).*

_____ 1. Abortion is murder and the renunciation of maternity.

_____ 2. Several studies conducted in Europe have exploded the myth of guilt and traumatic reaction to abortion.

_____ 3. Abortion has been widely practiced not only in societies where it is accepted but also in countries where it is illegal.

_____ 4. Experienced as a result of choice, pregnancy, like sex, can be a happy event or at least one happily taken on in the desire for children.

_____ 5. Women who abort do not perceive themselves as murderers.

_____ 6. The well-being of the mother is more important than the physical survival of the fetus.

_____ 7. Infanticide will inevitably follow after legalized abortion.

_____ 8. Women should be selfless and sacrifice their personal goals and interests for the developing fetus, soon to become a newborn child.

_____ 9. Human physical life is an absolute value which cannot in any way be overridden.

_____ 10. Those belonging to the women's movement are selfish.

LEARNING EXERCISE 11.3   Completing Syllogisms

Instructions: _Complete the following syllogisms by filling in the missing premises and conclusions._

1. **Value Premise:**   We should not accept that which rejects maternity.

   Factual Premise:

   Conclusion: Therefore, we should not accept abortion.

2. **Value Premise:**   We should legalize that which is widely accepted in society.

   Factual Premise: Abortion is widely accepted in society.

   Conclusion:

3. **Value Premise:**

   Factual Premise: Legalizing abortion promotes women's autonomy.

   Conclusion: Therefore, we should be in favor of legalizing abortion.

4. **Value Premise:**   That which leads to the dehumanization of women is wrong.

   Factual Premise:

   Conclusion: Therefore, compulsory pregnancy is wrong.

5. **Value Premise:**   That which reduces the need for abortion is good.

Factual Premise: A change from the sexist attitudes of society will reduce the need for abortion.

Conclusion:

LEARNING EXERCISE 11.4 Testing Principles

Instructions: *Test the adequacy of the following principles using the role-exchange test, the new-cases test, the higher-order principle test, and the universalizability and consistency test.*

1. Widely practiced activities not resulting in guilt or anxiety are morally acceptable.
2. Women who feel psychologically pressured to have sexual intercourse should not be forced to endure "compulsory pregnancies" and childbirth.
3. Women should not be subjected to physical violence.
4. Women should no longer be expected to accept greater and unequal responsibility for contraception.
5. Women should have the unconditional right to make choices which involve the elimination of obstacles to personal and career development.

12

"THE UNBORN CHILD IN CIVIL AND CRIMINAL LAW"

Ian Gentles

EDUCATIONAL OBJECTIVES: After reading this chapter the student will be able to:

12.1   Explain the contradiction between civil and criminal law as it applies to the issue of abortion.

12.2   Outline Western historical views on the status of the unborn child.

12.3   State briefly the current legal positions on abortion adopted in Canada and the United States.

12.4   Cite a case study illustrating the unborn child's right of inheritance.

12.5   Cite case studies illustrating the unborn child's right to compensation for injuries suffered in the womb.

12.6   State the legal status of the fetus during "out-of-womb" surgery.

12.7   Give possible options for the resolution of the legal contradiction involved in the abortion issue.

12.8   Explain the argument from pluralism supporting abortion.

12.9   Give reasons for Gentles' rejection of the proabortion argument from pluralism.

12.10   Explain the "pragmatic argument" favoring abortion.

12.11   Give reasons why Gentles rejects the pragmatic argument.

12.12   State Gentles' conclusion on the abortion issue.

This chapter appeared in an earlier version in *The Right to Birth*, eds. Eugene Fairweather and Ian Gentles (Anglican Book Centre, Toronto, 1976). Reprinted by permission of the author, Ian Gentles.

FOCUS QUESTIONS

1. Are matters of abortion and protection of the unborn unique to North American society in the twentieth century?
2. What is meant by "quickening"? What historical significance does it have for the abortion issue?
3. Does the unborn child possess any legal rights? Provide evidence.
4. What argument can be given to support the notion that the mother should have the right to dispose of the fetus as she deems fit?
5. How can the contradiction regarding abortion as it involves criminal and civil law be resolved?
6. What is the argument from pluralism and why is it rejected?
7. What is the pragmatic argument and why is it rejected as well?
8. What recommendations on abortion are made by Gentles?

SYNOPSIS

This 1976 essay draws attention to the contradiction between civil and criminal law on the issue of abortion. Court cases are cited which indicate that the unborn child has the legally recognized right to inherit property, the right to sue for injuries while in the womb, and the right to be protected from abuse or neglect by the mother. The point is also stressed, however, that under existing laws the unborn child has no right not to be killed by the mother through intentional and premature termination of pregnancy, better known as abortion. In view of the fact that the right to life is indispensable for the exercise of these other rights and that it is not protected or guaranteed vis-à-vis the mother, who can kill the fetus with impunity, Gentles concludes that current civil and criminal laws pertaining to the unborn child are contradictory. By law, a mother may not abuse her unborn child, though she may kill it at will.

Gentles begins with a brief review of the status of the unborn child in the legal traditions of Western civilization. After providing historical examples of how the rights of the unborn have been recognized and upheld throughout the centuries, he draws attention to the fact that a liberalization of abortion laws has occurred in North America and that this trend is continuing throughout the rest of the world. The movement toward eliminating hindrances against abortion is regarded as a striking contrast to the growing recognition of the civil rights of the unborn child as evidenced by numerous court decisions which are cited and described. For example, Gentles discusses the case of a woman who, during her pregnancy, refused on religious grounds a blood transfusion necessary to the fetus for its survival. The New Jersey Supreme Court ordered that the transfusion be given, arguing that the unborn child is entitled to the protection of the law, notwithstanding the mother's wishes.

Gentles maintains that the contradiction at the root of our legal system must be removed. Two options are possible. The civil rights of the unborn child must either be eliminated or the fundamental right of the unborn not to be killed must be upheld and protected. A single consistent moral position must be taken by society through the law.

The "argument from pluralism" which is discussed demands that abortion be accepted and removed from legal consideration on the grounds that nobody has a right to impose one's own personal moral views on others, especially not in a tolerant, liberal democratic society. Gentles rejects this argument on several counts. First, he contends that the policy to remove abortion from law is not neutral or value free. A moral decision is made to ignore the child in the womb, who is the silent victim of abortion. Second, he argues that the elimination of abortion from legal codes will create a climate that will exert pressure on women to procure abortions simply for sake of convenience or for the alleviation of stress. Abortion may also become a quick-fix solution for social problems such as housing shortages. Third, Gentles disputes the claim that there is disagreement about the humanity of the fetus. He contends that virtually all medical authorities agree that human life begins at conception and he advocates that if any uncertainty still remains, the benefit of the doubt should go to the fetus.

Gentles also rejects the "pragmatic argument" in favor of abortion. It is based on the assumption that women who are prevented from legally procuring an abortion will obtain one by illegal means. Gentles argues that the fact that a law is frequently broken does not justify the abolition of the law. If it did, then laws prohibiting theft and tax evasion would have to be likewise eliminated. Besides, according to Gentles, studies show that only a small fraction of women denied legal abortions resort to illegal means of obtaining them though threats are often made. Gentles cites a Danish study as well which indicates that four-fifths of the women denied abortions were later satisfied to have borne children. A Czech study is also presented which suggests that children born to reluctant mothers fared just as well as children born to mothers who did not initially seek abortions. Finally, Gentles concludes his article by advocating legislation to provide solid protection for the unborn child. He favors abortion only in those cases when pregnancy threatens the physical life of the mother. Adopting this position is to accept the duty to protect innocent human life. For Gentles, this is a duty any civilized society should accept.

[12.1] There exists today a grotesque contradiction at the heart of our legal system as it touches the unborn child. On the one hand, the unborn child enjoys the right to inherit property; she* can sue for injuries inflicted while in the womb; and she has the right to be protected from abuse or neglect by her mother. On the other hand, she no longer enjoys that right which is the indispensable precondition of the exercise of all her other rights—the right not to be killed. How has this contradiction come about? Is there any way it can be resolved?

[12.2] To begin answering these questions we shall review briefly the status of the unborn child in the legal traditions of Western civilization. An interesting fact is that from the earliest times, protection of the unborn has never been a merely Judeo-Christian idiosyncrasy. Many centuries before Christ, the Sumerians, the Assyrians, and the Hittites protected prenatal human life in their legal codes.[1] The oath framed for physicians by the Greek doctor Hippocrates in the fourth century BC was well-known for its pledge "not to give a deadly drug to anyone if asked for it, nor to suggest it. Similarly, I will not give to a woman an abortifacient pessary. In purity and holiness I will guard my life and my art." The authorities on the English common law, from Bracton in the thirteenth century through Coke in the seventeenth century to Blackstone in the eighteenth, all treated abortion as a crime.[2] Blackstone summed up the law's position in the second half of the eighteenth century in the following words:

> Life is the immediate gift of God, a right inherent by nature in every individual; and it begins in contemplation of law as soon as an infant is able to stir in the mother's womb. For if a woman is quick with the child, and by a potion or otherwise killeth it in her womb; or if any one beat her, whereby the child dieth in her body and she is delivered of a dead child, this, though not murder, was by the ancient law homicide or manslaughter. But the modern law doth not look upon this offense in quite so atrocious a light, but merely as heinous misdemeanor.[3]

There is a vivid illustration of the law's concern for the unborn child in the Salem witch trials. In the summer of 1692 six people were found guilty of witchcraft and promptly sentenced to death. On August 19 of that year all but one—a certain Elizabeth Proctor—were hanged. Taking refuge in a custom honored by the common law, goodwife Proctor pleaded pregnancy. Her execution was accordingly stayed until such time as her child should have been born, on the ground, as the historian of these events has put it, "that the child she was carrying was

an innocent person." Happily, even after her child was born, the sentence against Elizabeth Proctor was allowed to lapse and she lived out her natural life.[4]

[12.3] With their primitive medical knowledge, the jurists of the pre-modern period did not believe that it was possible to speak of an abortion before the time of quickening (i.e., the time when the mother feels the child move in her womb). Since human life did not evidently come into existence before quickening, there could not be a law against destroying it before that time. However, this anomaly was abruptly eliminated in 1803, when a law was passed making abortion a felony at any time during pregnancy.[5] This law was inherited by Canada and remained unaltered until 1969. In that year the law was amended to make an abortion permissible in cases when a three-member hospital abortion committee deemed that continuation of the pregnancy would endanger the life or health of the mother. Four years later, the United States Supreme Court swept away all criminal legislation against abortion in that country in the historical decision in *Roe* v. *Wade* (January 22, 1973).

The trend throughout the world in the past fifteen years toward eliminating legal hindrances against abortion is in striking contrast to the growing recognition of the civil rights of the unborn child. As recently as the end of the last century, Chief Justice Holmes in the United States had declared that the unborn child had no rights in a court of law, since he was merely a part of his mother, and not, legally speaking, a person.

[12.4] This statement disregarded the fact that the unborn child's right to inherit had already been established in English common law as early as 1798, at which time it was declared that whenever it would be for his benefit, the child in the womb "shall be considered as absolutely born."[6] The first Canadian case to overturn the prevalent view expressed by Holmes was *In Re Charlton Estate* (1919). A certain Charlton had left a sum of money to be divided among "all the living children" of his brother. A child who was born three and a half months after Charlton died subsequently sued for a share of the estate, asserting that he was living at the time of his uncle's death. The Manitoba Court of King's Bench upheld the suit on the ground that a gift to "all living children" included the child who was in his mother's womb ("en ventre sa mère") at the time.[7]

The same principle was upheld in another case the following year. A certain Mrs. Giddings successfully sued the Canadian Northern Railway for negligence in the death of her husband, a locomotive fireman. In addition to the damages she won for herself, the court also awarded her child $6,000, even though he was unborn at the time of his father's death. The fact that he was unborn was judged to be "immaterial so long as the action is for the benefit of the child."[8]

These two cases influenced many other decisions, with the result that the unborn child's right to inherit and own property is now clearly recognized.

[12.5] The much more difficult question of the unborn child's right to compensation for injuries suffered in the womb has also been decisively settled in this century in the child's favor. The Supreme Court of Canada seems to have set the standard for the rest of the English-speaking world by its momentous decision in the case of *Montreal Tramways* v. *Léveillé* (1933).[9] The court recognized that in 1933, "the great weight of judicial opinion in the common-law courts denies the right of a child when born to maintain an action for prenatal injuries." Nevertheless, it boldly reversed judicial precedent by declaring that a child who suffers injury while in its mother's womb as the

result of a wrongful act or default of another has the right, after birth, to maintain an action for damages for its prenatal injury. Judge Lamont justified the rejection of precedent in this case on the basis of the following principle:

> If a child after birth has no right of action for prenatal injuries, we have a wrong inflicted for which there is no remedy. . . . If a right of action be denied to the child it will be compelled, without any fault on its part, to go through life carrying the seal of another's fault and bearing a very heavy burden of infirmity and inconvenience without any compensation therefor.

The principle laid down by Judge Lamont was confirmed in 1972 in *Duval et al.* v. *Séguin et al.*[10] The child of Thérèse Duval was permanently handicapped both physically and mentally, as a direct result of a car accident which occurred while she was *en ventre sa mère*. In deciding in favor of the child, the judge quoted Lord Atkin's dictum: "The rule that you are to love your neighbour becomes, in law, you must not injure your neighbour." Although the unborn child was to be regarded as the "neighbour" of the negligent driver, the judge declined to state whether the child was a person in law, or at which stage she became a person.

[12.5] In the case of *Watt* v. *Rama* in the Supreme Court of Victoria in the same year, there was no such reluctance to recognize the unborn child as a legal person.[11] The plaintiff, Sylvia Watt, had suffered brain damage and epilepsy as a result of a car accident involving her mother when the mother was two months pregnant. The defense argued that a two-month-old fetus was merely part of her mother and therefore not entitled to legal protection. The judge rejected the plea, observing that there was no essential difference between a newborn child and a child not yet born.

As its property, real or personal, is protected, so should its physical substance be similarly protected by deeming it to be a person in being and imposing a duty of care on any other person not to commit any act of carelessness which as a reasonable man he should anticipate would injure the physical substance of the unborn child.

The judge concluded by affirming that, for the purpose of protecting her interests, Sylvia Watt was deemed to be a person at the time of the collision—two months after conception—and was thus entitled to compensation for the injuries she had suffered at that time.

The progress of the civil law in recognizing the personhood of the unborn child is trenchantly summarized by William L. Prosser, the dean of American tort law. Before 1946, he points out, most American authorities were agreed that the child could not sue for prenatal injuries. However, the situation was transformed so rapidly in the next quarter of a century that "it is now apparently literally true that there is no authority left still supporting the older rule." Furthermore, "all writers who have discussed the problem have joined in condemning the old rule, in maintaining that *the unborn child in the path of an automobile is as much a person in the street as the mother,* and in urging that recovery should be allowed upon proper proof" (emphasis added).[12]

One problem has not yet been resolved: whether the child has to be born alive in order for a suit to be entered on her behalf. Prosser believes that the trend is in the direction of holding that the child does not have to be born alive.[13] This would seem to be a logical conclusion, since it is hard to see why one should be less liable for destroying a child's life than for merely causing her to be injured. Indeed, a large number of recent cases in American courts have ruled not only that the unborn child is a person, but

that an action for the wrongful death of an unborn child is maintainable even when she is stillborn.[14]

In North America, then, it is clear that no one has the right to kill the unborn child, or injure her, or deprive her of her property. No one, that is, except her mother. And after the decision in *Roe* v. *Wade,* the mother has, in the United States, the unrestricted right to take the child's life. Moreover, given the abortion-on-demand situation that prevails in most large Canadian cities, the mother has practically the same right in this country. This has created a profound conflict between the civil and the criminal law. Take the hypothetical example of a woman who is pregnant with her first child at the time of her husband's death. In his will he has divided his estate between his wife and all his living children. The law has established that the child in the womb can rightfully inherit a share of his father's estate. Canadian criminal law, as it is interpreted in many parts of the country, also permits the woman to destroy her child at will, right up to the moment before it is born. Legally speaking therefore, the woman would be at liberty to have an abortion in order to keep all of her husband's estate to herself.

We can think of another instance where the interest of the unborn child may clash with those of the mother or father. Since 1963, thanks to the work of the New Zealand fetologist Dr. Albert Liley, it has been possible to make life-saving transfusions of blood to fetuses that have developed acute anemia in the womb. In one such instance where a blood transfusion had been diagnosed as medically necessary to save the unborn child's life, the mother refused the transfusion for religious reasons. Nonetheless, the New Jersey Supreme Court ordered the transfusion to be administered, stating that

We are satisfied that the unborn child is entitled to the law's protection and that an appropriate order should be made to insure such transfusions to the mother in the event that they are necessary in the opinion of the physician in charge at the time.[15]

[12.6] In 1981 the first reported successful out-of-the-womb surgery was carried out on a five-month-old unborn baby. Performed in San Francisco, the critical thirty-minute operation now points the way to the correction of a whole series of birth defects in the future.[16] The irony of this particular medical breakthrough is that, during the half hour she spends outside the womb during the operation, the child enjoys the status of a legal person, with her life fully protected. Once back in the womb, however, she resumes the status of a non-person, having, in effect, re-entered a free-fire zone where she could be killed with impunity.

The contradiction between the unborn child's status under the civil law and her status under the criminal law has led to schizophrenic behavior in the courts. In 1972, for example, an Ottawa woman was approved for a legal abortion by a hospital therapeutic-abortion committee, but her husband objected to the abortion, was able to have himself recognized as the guardian of the unborn child, and secured a temporary injunction against the abortion. Before his application for a permanent injunction could be heard, he and his wife were reconciled and she abandoned her attempts to abort the child.[17]

In 1981, the boyfriend of a girl in Thunder Bay who had been pressured into having an abortion by her parents won an injunction against the abortion on behalf of himself and the unborn child. This injunction, the first to be granted involving an unmarried couple, confirmed that an unborn child can, in effect, act as co-plaintiff to defend her own life.[18] More interesting

still was the decision of a Halifax Family Court judge not only to stop an abortion at the request of the woman's estranged husband, but to appoint a private citizen, unrelated to the family, as the unborn child's legal guardian. While the court may have exceeded its jurisdiction, it seems to have established the first instance where a child in the womb has had a guardian appointed on her behalf.[19]

To compound the confusion further, two recent cases, one Canadian, one British, have recognized the personhood of the unborn child in criminal suits. The British judge ruled that a Belfast child wounded by a bullet fired into her mother's abdomen was a legal person, with the right to sue for damages for criminal injury, and awarded her $8,800.[20] In the Canadian case, which involved a charge of criminal negligence, a British Columbia judge ruled that a fetus in the process of birth is a person under the Criminal Code. The baby in question was stillborn, allegedly because of the criminal negligence of the midwife in attendance. The defense lawyer had argued that there could be no charge of criminal negligence, since the fetus was not a person. Prior to the judge's decision, a child was not, in fact, considered to be a person under the Criminal Code until she had emerged in a living state from the body of her mother.[21]

So far, we can see that the unborn child's rights have been won vis-à-vis the outside world. It could be maintained that there is nothing inconsistent or irrational in allowing the child's mother to kill her through abortion, while at the same time denying to everyone else the right to injure her or deprive her of her property. The mother, after all, is the only one who has to surrender her body for the nine months of possible discomfort, embarrassment, or even physical hazard that a pregnancy can entail. Her relationship with her unborn child is clearly unique, and qualitatively different from anyone else's relationship with the child. Given that her body is being occupied by a fetus who may not be welcome in her eyes, should the mother not at least have the right to dispose of it as she pleases?

Just recently, this argument, which is condensed in the popular phrase "a woman's right to control her own body," has had to face an unexpected and awkward challenge. Since about 1970, in Canada and elsewhere, there has been much concern about child abuse, together with a determination to reduce its prevalence. In addition, there is now a much sharper awareness of how crucial are the nine months before birth in shaping the individual's whole future physical and psychological well-being. Many proponents of child welfare therefore urge that protection against abuse should extend into the prenatal period, and that mothers should be accountable for the welfare of their unborn children, Furthermore, they should, like anyone else, be liable for prosecution if they are guilty through negligence or abuse, of causing injury to their unborn child.

In 1981 the Ontario Family Court in Kenora recognized a fetus as "a child in need of protection" under the terms of the Child Welfare Act because of the physical abuse she suffered through her mother's excessive consumption of alcohol and the mother's failure to obtain proper treatment. The implication was clear that the fetus is protected from abuse by her mother during the full nine months of pregnancy, starting from conception. In fact, it was noted that fetal damage from alcohol is most likely to occur during the first three months of pregnancy.[22]

The Supreme Court of British Columbia came to a similar conclusion in 1982, in the case of a heroin-addicted mother whose newborn baby suffered violent symptoms of withdrawal and possible long-term damage to her health. After about seven weeks, when the baby was taken off opium, she

> demonstrated the effects of withdrawal with the following severe physical symptoms: Incessant, inconsolable crying, vomiting, inability to sleep, twitching, reluctance to feed, poor sucking performance, irritability, resistance to being held, explosive diarrhea, profuse sweating, jittery limbs, barking cough, physical tension and squirming. The diarrhea was of special concern, because if not corrected the resultant water loss could lead to shock and death. In addition the baby developed severe anemia which continues to be a danger.

At four months of age the baby was still withdrawing from addiction, according to the attending physician.

> ... The infant goes through the same withdrawal syndrome as an adult and experiences extreme spasms in the stomach, excruciating pain, and vomiting.

Moreover, the baby required very careful attention to her nutrition, since drug-addicted babies need twice the calories of a normal child for brain and organ growth.

In light of this harrowing description of the consequences of the mother's heroin addiction, the court ruled that the fetus whose mother is drug-addicted is "a child in need of protection," and that such a child "is born *having been abused*" (emphasis added). There was therefore no need to wait until the mother abused the child after birth before requiring that she submit to involuntary supervision.[23]

The Ontario and British Columbia decisions find support in David M. Steinberg's *Family Law in Family Courts*, where it is stated that a child in the womb may be considered a child in order to secure protection from abuse by her mother.[24]

So a mother may not neglect or abuse her unborn child. But she may still legally kill her. Aware of the pressing need to remedy this state of affairs, the director of the Canadian Law Reform Commission advocates that the unborn child's rights already established by judicial decision should be enshrined in a statute. According to Edward Keyserlingk, "there should be no contest at all between a mother's desire to smoke or consume drugs excessively and the unborn's right to be legally protected against the serious risk of resulting disability." The provision of adequate nutrition, adequate prenatal checkups, the avoidance of excessive smoking, drinking, or drug-taking should be made into a legal obligation involving potential liability for parents, doctors, and others. " . . . The law must conclude more coherently and explicitly than it has to date that the unborn has its own juridical [legal] personality and rights."[25] Yet he goes on to say that the unborn's rights would end when the mother decides to have an abortion.

Does this make sense? Would *you* rather have the right to "adequate prenatal checkups" than the right not to be killed through abortion? The stark absurdity of this position grows out of the irreducible reality that all the rights the unborn has won in the course of this century depend, as their indispensable precondition, on the right to live. Since I possess the right to inherit, to own property, and not to be injured, neglected or abused before I am born, then logically I must also possess the right to life, since without it none of my other rights can be exercised.[26]

[12.7, 12.8, 12.9] This terrible contradiction at the heart of our legal system cannot endure. Either we shall have to eliminate the civil rights that have been so painfully won for the unborn child, or we shall have to recognize her most fundamental right, the right not to be killed, even by her par-

ents. We cannot have it both ways. Moreover, whatever we do, a morality will have been imposed. To think that the neutral, liberal, and value-free policy is to remove abortion from the law is to be misled. To accept the argument from pluralism is to turn a blind eye to the silent victim of every abortion—the child in the womb. It would be hardly less logical to advocate removing murder from the criminal code on the ground that, in a pluralistic society, we do not have any right to impose our moral views upon those who wish to murder.

The argument from pluralism also ignores the fact that societies that do eliminate abortion from their legal codes do not thereby give people a free choice in the matter. Instead, an "abortion climate" takes over, and overwhelming pressure is exerted on women to resort to abortion as the way out of any distressful or inconvenient pregnancy. This pressure is exerted by husbands, boyfriends, parents, peers, social workers, doctors, and governments. Governments find abortion an easy way of avoiding hard social problems like the shortage of reasonably priced family housing.

There is yet another defect in the argument from pluralism. It is said that, since there is disagreement about whether the fetus is a human being, we should allow those who believe that abortion is morally permissible to act on their beliefs. Some people certainly *wish* that there were disagreement about the humanity of the fetus. Virtually all medical authorities, however, agree that the life of the human individual begins at the moment of conception.[27] But even if there were disagreement, would it not be both prudent and humane to give the fetus the benefit of the doubt, to accept its humanity and therefore its right to legal protection? What would we say if people were arguing that blacks instead of fetuses were not human, and that people should have the right to kill them? This, after all, is the position that some people took in the United States of America just more than a century ago. Would we not argue that blacks should have the benefit of the doubt and be included within the human family, with appropriate legal protection? Is not the best rule of thumb to frame our definition of who is human broadly enough to avoid excluding particular classes of people who may happen to be out of public favor at a given moment?

[12.10] At this point some people will raise a pragmatic argument. It is all very well to talk of protecting the unborn child, they say, but women have always had abortions, and they always will. No law can stop them. The only question is whether they should have abortions that are legal and safe, or should be condemned to seek back-alley "butchers," criminal abortionists who endanger their life and health.

[12.11] This argument has a particle of truth to it, but only a particle. There are some women in every society and in every age who will seek abortions no matter what the law says. But the number is far smaller than is usually alleged by advocates of legalized abortion.[28] But there is little doubt that a strong law protecting the unborn child, especially if it is combined with life-promoting social policies, will reduce the incidence of abortion. This conclusion is borne out by studies, conducted in several countries, of women who were refused legal abortions. In every study it was found that only a small proportion of the women resorted to criminal abortions, although many of them had threatened to do so. Even more surprising, it was discovered in a Danish study that four-fifths of the women later said they were satisfied to have borne their children. Moreover, a Czech study revealed that these children fared just as well as children whose mothers had not tried to abort

them.[29] No law is ever completely effective, but laws do have an educative function. They express the commonly accepted standards of behavior of a society, and many people consciously model their behavior according to what the law informs them is acceptable. The fact that a law is frequently broken is no reason in itself for doing away with that law. The laws against child abuse, theft, tax evasion, and assault are broken far more often than the laws against abortion. But they are still useful, both because they express our public moral standards, and because they undoubtedly prevent an even greater incidence of the offenses they prohibit.

[12.12] If the argument of this essay is correct, the most enlightened social policy would be to legislate solid protection of the unborn child. Such protection means that abortion would only be permissible when continuation of the pregnancy would result in the death of the mother. To adhere to this position is not to adopt a censorious moralism. It is simply to recognize that the protection of innocent human life is the most basic duty of any civilized community. Our community will be neither healthy nor civilized so long as we fail in that duty.

NOTES

*I have referred to the unborn child as "she" and "her" throughout this essay, as a reminder that at least half the victims of abortion are female.

1. James B. Pritchard, *Ancient Near Eastern Texts Relating to the Old Testament*, 2nd ed. (Princeton: 1955), pp. 175, 181, 184 ff., 190.
2. Dennis J. Horan, et al., "The Legal Case for the Unborn Child," in T. W. Hilgers and D. J. Horan, eds., *Abortion and Social Justice* (New York: 1972), pp. 122–24.
3. *Blackstone's Commentaries*, 15th ed., vol. I, p. 129.
4. Edward Synan, "Law and the Sin of the Mothers," in E. A. Synan and E. J. Kremer, eds., *Death Before Birth: Canadian Essays on Abortion* (Toronto, 1974), pp. 146f.

5. Proclaimed by George III in 1803.
6. *Thellusson* v. *Woodford* (1798-9), *English Reports*, vol. 3, p. 163.
7. *Western Weekly Reports* (1919), vol. I, p. 134.
8. *Giddings* v. *Canadian Northern Railway Company*, *Dominion Law Reports* (1920), vol. 53.
9. *Supreme Court Reports* (1933), p. 456.
10. *Ontario Reports* (1972), vol. II.
11. *Victoria Reports* (Australia), 1972, p. 353.
12. William L. Prosser, *Handbook of the Law of Torts*, 4th ed. (St. Paul, 1974), pp. 335-6. The other eminent authority on tort law, the Australian, John G. Fleming, agrees that courts in Britain and the Commonwealth are now willing to entertain suits for prenatal injuries. *The Law of Torts*, 5th ed. (Sydney, 1977), p. 159.
13. Prosser, p. 338. Fleming, on the other hand, holds that the child must still be born alive in order to be a plaintiff (p. 161).
14. Horan et al., art. cit., p. 113 and references cited in n. 35.
15. Ibid, p. 115.
16. *Globe and Mail*, 16 November 1981.
17. Ibid., 28 January 1972.
18. Ibid., 6 February 1981.
19. Ibid, 25 September 1979.
20. Ibid., 3 November 1979.
21. Ibid, 8 November 1979.
22. *Re Children's Aid Society of Kenora and Janis L.*, 14 September 1981, Ontario Provincial Court of the District of Kenora. (Not reported) See the Judgment of Madam Justice Proudfoot in this chapter.
23. *Re In the matter of judicial review of a decision of Judge P. d'A. Collings respecting female infant born Dec. 11th, 1981*. Supreme Court of British Columbia, 13 April 1982.
24. Carswell, 1981, vol. 1, 2nd ed. p. 112.
25. *Globe and Mail*, 2 April 1982.
26. E.-H. W. Kluge, "The Right to Life of Potential Persons," *Dalhousie Law Journal*, vol. 3, 1977, pp. 846-7.
27. See for example, a standard textbook, Leslie B. Arey, *Developmental Anatomy*, revised 7th edition (Philadelphia, 1974), p. 55.
28. See the *Report of the Committee on the Operation of the Abortion Law* [The Badgley Report] (Ottawa, 1977), pp. 71-2, and C. B. Goodhart, "On the Incidence of Illegal Abortion," *Population Studies*, vol. xxvii (1973), pp. 207-33.
29. Cf. Hans Forssman and Inga Thuwe, "One Hundred and Twenty Children Born after Application for Therapeutic Abortion Refused," *Acta Psychiatrica Scandinavica*, 42 (1966), 71-74; Henrik Hoffmeyer, "Medical Aspects of the Danish Legislation on Abortion," in David T. Smith, ed., *Abortion and the Law* (Cleveland, 1967), p. 201; V. Schuller and E. Stupkova, "The Unwanted Child in the Family," *International Mental Health Research Newsletter*, 14/3 (Fall, 1972), 7f.

PROGRESS CHECK 12.1

Instructions: *Fill in the blanks below with the appropriate responses.*

censorious moralism

pluralism

contradiction

abortifacient pessary

Montreal Tramways v. *Léveille*

pragmatic

quickening

indispensable precondition

Roe v. *Wade*

unique relationship

1. While proabortionists would generally oppose others besides the mother deciding if pregnancies can or should be terminated, they believe the mother should have the right to choose whether or not a pregnancy will be continued because of her _____ to the fetus.

2. The Greek doctor Hippocrates pledged never to give women an _____ as a way of preventing pregnancy and childbirth.

3. The right to life is a(n) _____ for the exercise of the rights to inherit property and to be protected from injury and abuse.

4. The _____ argument assumes that women will obtain illegal abortions from backstreet butchers if they are prevented from procuring them by legal means.

5. The _____ decision in the United States swept abortion away from all criminal legislation.

6. Jurists in the premodern period believed that _____ marked the point at which human life begins.

7. The argument from _____ states that in a liberal democratic society, individual women should have the right of personal choice in private matters of abortion and that, in a spirit of tolerance and freedom, no one else should have the right to impose his or her own will upon the mother.

8. The case of _____ reversed judicial precedent by deciding that a child who suffers injury while in the womb as the result of a wrongful act has the right, after birth, to sue for damages.

9. According to Ian Gentles, there exists a _____ between current civil and criminal laws as they relate to matters of abortion.

10. Gentles does not believe his antiabortion position reflects a _____ , but rather a recognition that we all have a basic duty to protect innocent human life.

LEARNING EXERCISE 12.2

Instructions: *The following statements are either taken or derived from the article by Gentles. Identify them as either normative (N) or empirical (E).*

_____ 1. Under current law, the unborn child enjoys the right to inherit property.

_____ 2. Pregnant women convicted of witchcraft should not be sentenced to death.

_____ 3. The unborn child should be entitled to the law's protection.

_____ 4. In 1981 the Ontario Family Court in Kenora recognized a fetus as a child in need of protection under the terms of the child welfare act.

_____ 5. Abortion should be removed from any legal code in the interests of neutrality and in the recognition of women's personal freedom of choice.

_____ 6. Virtually all medical doctors agree that the life of the human individual begins at the moment of conception.

_____ 7. The fetus deserves the benefit of the doubt if there remains any disagreement about its humanity.

_____ 8. Women prevented from having legal abortions will seek criminal abortionists to provide the services they need.

_____ 9. A law should not be done away with simply because many people choose to break it.

_____ 10. Abortion is permissible only when the physical life of the mother is in danger.

LEARNING EXERCISE   12.3

Instructions: _Fill in the blank spaces to complete the following practical syllogisms relating to the abortion question._

1. **Value Premise:**   Contradictory laws should be revised.

   Factual Premise: Civil and criminal laws on abortion are contradictory.

   Conclusion:

2. **Value Premise:**   Legal persons should have their lives protected by law.

   Factual Premise:

   Conclusion: The unborn child should have its life protected by law.

3. **Value Premise:**   We should not accept that which pressures women to have unsafe abortions.

   Factual Premise: The elimination of abortion from legal codes pressures women to have unsafe abortions.

   Conclusion:

4. **Value Premise:**

   Factual Premise: The continuation or termination of pregnancy is a matter which affects women's physical and emotional health.

   Conclusion: Women should therefore have the right to make personal choices on the continuation or termination of pregnancy.

5. **Value Premise:**

   Factual Premise: Abortion laws are frequently broken.

   Conclusion: Therefore, abortion laws should be abandoned.

LEARNING EXERCISE   12.4

Instructions: _Test the adequacy of the following value premises. Give reasons for their acceptability or unacceptability using the new cases test, the role-exchange test, the higher-order principle test, and the universalizability and consistency test._

1. Laws which are frequently broken should be abandoned.
2. Abortions are morally justifiable since they are permitted by law.
3. Women who will be inconvenienced by pregnancy and childbirth should opt to have an abortion.
4. No women, excepting myself, should be allowed to have an abortion.
5. Laws which restrict an individual's freedom of choice are wrong.

Capital Punishment

13

"DEFENDING THE DEATH PENALTY"

Walter Berns

EDUCATIONAL OBJECTIVES: After reading this chapter the student will be able to:

13.1 State the position taken by classical political philosophers on the subject of the death penalty.

13.2 Give a possible explanation for why we are reluctant to punish and put someone to death.

13.3. Identify the source of moral ambivalence.

13.4 Provide rationales for why criminals are punished.

13.5 Explain objections to viewing punishment as retribution.

13.6 Discuss the relevance of human dignity to considerations of punishment.

13.7 Explain how punishment serves a positive function.

13.8 Illustrate how anger can contribute to developing moral community.

13.9 Elucidate how the concept of "awe" has relevance for the issue of capital punishment.

Reprinted by permission, Walter Berns, "Defending the Death Penalty," *Crime & Delinquency*, October 1980, pp. 503–527.

FOCUS QUESTIONS

1. Historically speaking, has capital punishment been generally accepted or rejected?
2. Why are people reluctant to punish?
3. Does the Bible clearly tell us whether or not capital punishment should be accepted?
4. What reasons can be given to justify punishment?
5. Does Berns believe that all people possess human dignity unconditionally? Why or why not?
6. Must punishment concern itself only with fear and deterrence? Does it have any positive function?
7. Is the emotion of anger wrong in itself? Are there situations where anger is desirable? How should it be dealt with?
8. What is meant by the concept of moral community?
9. In what sense should the law be awful according to Berns?

SYNOPSIS

The next essay presents an argument in defense of the death penalty. Its author, Walter Berns, begins by relating some personal experiences which serve to illustrate how capital punishment is an emotionally loaded subject of discussion. He recognizes that liberal thinkers generally believe that no rational person can possibly defend the death penalty. Although he admits that the history of the death penalty is filled with ruthlessness and fanaticism, Berns draws attention to the fact that opposition to it is a relatively recent phenomenon. Citing Jeremy Bentham as the exception, he states that historically speaking almost all political philosophers discussing capital punishment before the current debate were in favor of it. In view of this Berns asks the rhetorical question, whether we are truly morally superior, more concerned with human rights, more concerned with crime and punishment, or more humane than great thinkers such as John Locke and John Stuart Mill. By means of another rhetorical question, he intimates that it is not our moral superiority or heightened sensitivity but rather our guilt and moral ambivalence which do not permit us to put criminals to death. Although some try to use biblical text to support opposition to capital punishment, Berns claims that the Bible cannot serve as a basis for its abolition. If anything, the thinking and practices of people during more religious times would suggest that the Bible supports the death penalty. When governments and people's lives were more closely connected to and directed by scripture, death was a customary penalty. Berns thus concludes that no cogent opposing argument to capital punishment can be derived either from biblical sources or from political philosophy. He does admit, however, that legitimate objections to the death penalty may still remain on grounds of fairness and discriminatory practices regarding its application.

Berns attributes the abolition movement to Cesare Beccaria, whose book in 1764, *On Crimes and Punishments,* attempted to effect changes in the criminal codes of western European nations by creating a modern liberal state. According to Berns, the liberal state is the source of the moral ambivalence that makes us hesitant and guilty about punishing. Some people try to ease their consciences by viewing punishment as a form of rehabilitation. There are some who punish in hopes of deterring innocent people from becoming criminals. Still others wish to punish criminals in order to incapacitate them and to prevent further crimes outside the prison. Berns offers reasons for rejecting all of these rationales for punishing. He claims that we find it difficult to admit that, in part, we punish, for purposes of retribution. Berns disagrees with Justices Brennan and Marshall who contend that exacting retribution deprives individuals of human dignity. He argues that if everyone possesses human dignity no matter what he does, and if human dignity is the standard used to determine who deserves what, then unless everyone deserves to be punished, nobody deserves to be punished as everyone is the same and should be treated alike. Berns' point is that criminals lose their dignity in choosing to commit vile crimes. By punishing them we give criminals what they deserve in view of their diminished dignity. Not everyone deserves identical and equal treatment simply by virtue of being human. For him, human dignity and the rights which follow therefrom are not unconditional. Building a world on the idea of unconditional human dignity represents one in which all confidence has been lost with respect to opinions of right and wrong, and of good and evil.

Berns underscores in his essay the positive dimension of punishment. While punishment may deter crime through fear, it can serve more importantly to inculcate law-abiding habits. The mechanism involved in this inculcation of law-abiding habits revolves around the satisfaction of the law-abiding person's anger. For Berns, anger is a condition of a decent community. He suggests we should be seriously concerned if indifference and cowardice result at the sight of crime. People ought to feel angry when wrongdoings have been committed. The job of the law is to control or calm that anger by punishing the criminal. In so doing, the anger of the law-abiding person is satisfied and his law-abidingness is rewarded. Punishment indirectly praises proper conduct and teaches law-abidingness. Punishment is therefore not purely negative, relying on fear, but positive in its satisfaction of anger. Anger, then, is not in itself reprehensible. When it results at the sight of crime, it can be an expression of our care for others. Anger need not be selfish like greed or jealousy. When tamed and educated, it can be generous and socially constructive. Also, when aroused for the right reasons, anger deserves to be rewarded.

In closing, Berns advocates that the law be made "awful," or awe-inspiring. He provides reasons for rejecting banishment and incarceration as appropriate forms of punishment for making the law awful. He contends that only the death penalty can be effective to achieve this end.

For Capital Punishment is, so far as I know, the first book-length defense of the death penalty written by someone other than a professional law-enforcement officer.[1] As its author, I expected to be denounced in the liberal press, and I was. The best I could have hoped for was that the book would not be reviewed in certain journals. Unfortunately, the *New York Review of Books* did review it,[2] in a manner of speaking (the reviewer suggested that its author ought to be psychoanalyzed). Surprisingly, the *New York Times,* at least in its daily edition, gave it a good review, one I could have written myself;[3] Garry Wills, on the other hand, devoted an entire column to the book, during the course of which he told several outright lies about me and the book.[4] Then when I appeared on a live television show in Washington debating the death penalty with a man who has devoted his entire professional life to the effort to abolish it, my wife, at home, began to receive threatening telephone calls, many of them saying that her husband was the only person who deserved to be executed (or, as one persistent caller put it, "to sizzle"); these calls continued until we were forced to change our telephone number, which is now unlisted.

I recite these events only to make the point that capital punishment is a subject that arouses the angriest of passions. I suspect that opponents of the death penalty also receive threatening telephone calls, but somehow I doubt that theirs could match mine in nastiness. To the opponents of the death penalty, nothing can be said in its favor, and anyone who tries is a scoundrel or a fool. "Hang-hards" (Arthur Koestler's term) might defend it, the Ayatollah Khomeini might defend it, and police officers might be forgiven for defending it, but no rational person can defend it. That was Garry Wills's opinion, and that appears to be the opinion of the liberal world in general.

[13.1] In one respect, at least, I have no quarrel with my hostile critics. The history of capital punishment is surely one that should give everyone pause: too many fanatics, too much ruthlessness, and too many disgusting public spectacles. On the other hand, there is also a history of the argument concerning capital punishment, and that history reveals something that ought to give pause to its opponents and arouse some doubts regarding the opinion prevailing in today's intellectual circles. Long before the current debate, political philosophers addressed themselves to the question of justice and, therefore, of crime and punishment; none of them, with the qualified exception of Jeremy Bentham, opposed the death penalty.[5] Opposition to capital punishment is in fact a modern phenomenon, a product of modern sentiment and modern thought. Except to unreconstructed progressives—I mean persons who believe that every area of thought is characterized by progress—this fact is one that ought to cause us at least to hesitate before, so to speak, picking up the telephone.

Do we really know more about crime and punishment than did the ancients? Are we better qualified to speak on these subjects than Sir Thomas More? Are we more concerned with human rights than were the founders of the school of human rights —say, John Locke? Than the founders of the first country—our own—established specifically to secure these rights? In matters of morality are we the superiors of Kant? Are we more humane than Tocqueville? Than John Stuart Mill? Thomas Jefferson? George Washington? Abraham Lincoln?

[13.2] Or, alternatively, have we become so morally ambivalent, and in some cases, so guilt ridden, that we cannot in good conscience punish anyone and certainly not to the extent of putting him to death? In this connection, it is relevant to point out that, contrary to the public statements of some modern churchmen, the Bible cannot be read to support the cause of abolition of capital punishment—not when its texts are read fairly.[6] Furthermore, it is not insignificant that in the past, when the souls of men and women were shaped by the Bible and the regimes that ruled in the West were those that derived their principles from the Bible, death was a customary penalty. Some of these regimes were the most sanguinary known to history, which suggests that piety and harsh punishment go together.

[13.3] I am not contending that there might not be moral objections to capital punishment (there certainly are when it cannot be imposed fairly, or in a non-discriminatory fashion), but only that neither political philosophy nor the Bible lends support to these objections. The abolition movement stems, instead, from what can fairly be described as an amoral, and surely an anti-religious, work: Cesare Beccaria's unusually influential *On Crimes and Punishments*, first published in 1764.[7] Beccaria, whose teacher was Thomas Hobbes, set out to accomplish more than a few changes in the criminal codes of Western European countries: His revisions required the establishment of the modern liberal state, a state from which the Church's influence would be excluded. Like Hobbes, Beccaria argued that there is no morality outside the positive law.[8] Here is the source of that moral ambivalence to which I referred and which has gradually come to characterize the so-called enlightened opinion respecting punishment; the public opinion lags behind somewhat. A Norwegian judge (quoted by the well-known criminologist Johannes An-

denaes) remarked this when he said that "our grandfathers punished, and they did so with a clear conscience [and] we punish too, but we do it with a bad conscience."[9]

[13.4] Why, indeed, do we punish criminals? Some of us try to ease our uneasy consciences by saying that the purpose of punishment is the rehabilitation of the criminal. But we ought to know by now that we cannot in fact rehabilitate criminals. An occasional criminal, yes, but not criminals as a class or in significant numbers. We cannot rehabilitate them any more successfully than our penitentiaries can cause them to repent, or to become penitent. One reason for this is that too many of us, and especially those of us in the rehabilitation business, are of the opinion that criminals are not wicked. Who are we to ask them to repent when, essentially, we think they have nothing to repent of? How can we in good conscience ask them to be rehabilitated when, in effect, we deny that there is a moral order to which they should be restored? We look upon the criminal as disturbed, yes; sick, perhaps; underprivileged, surely; but wicked, no. Karl Menninger, a leading criminal psychologist, accuses us in *The Crime of Punishment* of being criminals because we damn "some of our fellow citizens with the label 'criminal.'"[10] We who do this are, he says, the only criminals. The others are sick and deserve to be treated, not punished. The immorality of this position, whose premise is that no one is responsible for his acts, requires no elaboration.

Or we punish criminals in order to deter others from becoming criminals. Punishment for this purpose is utilitarian, and, like Beccaria, we can justify something if it is truly useful. But again, to inflict pain on one person merely to affect the behavior of others is surely immoral, as our criminology texts have not hesitated to tell us.

Perhaps we can be persuaded of the necessity to punish criminals in order to incapacitate them, thereby preventing them from committing their crimes among us (but not, of course, against their fellow prisoners). I must point out, however, that unless we concede, as I do, that even incarcerated criminals are no less worthy of our concern than are law-abiding persons, this policy is also immoral.

[13.5, 13.6]   What we have not been able to do (although there are signs here and there that this is changing[11]) is to admit that we punish, in part at least, to pay back the criminal for what he had done to us, not as individuals but as a moral community. We exact retribution, and we do not like to admit this. Retribution smacks of harshness and moral indignation, and our Hobbesian-Beccarian principles forbid the public expression of moral indignation. In the 1972 death penalty cases, Justice Marshall went so far as to say that the eighth amendment forbidding cruel and unusual punishment, forbids "punishment for the sake of retribution."[12] In the words of Marshall's closest colleague, Justice Brennan, to execute a person in order to exact retribution is to deprive him of his human dignity, and "even the vilest criminal [is] possessed of common human dignity."[13]

In the past, when men reflected seriously on the differences between human and other beings, human dignity was understood to consist of the capacity to be a moral being, a being capable of choosing between right and wrong and, with this freedom, capable of governing himself.[14] Unlike other animals, a human being was understood to be a responsible moral creature. The "vilest criminal" was not being deprived of his human dignity when he was punished, not even when he was punished by being put to death; he had lost his dignity when he freely chose to commit his vile crimes. Retribution means to pay back, or to give people what they deserve to get, and it implies that different people deserve to get different things. But if human dignity is the standard according to which we determine who deserves to get what, and if everyone, no matter what he does, possesses human dignity, as Brennan would have it, then no one deserves to be treated differently and, unless everyone deserves to be punished, no one deserves to be punished.

I agree that a world built on Brennan's idea of human dignity may not exact retribution. It has lost all confidence in its opinions of right and wrong, good and evil, righteous and wicked, deserving and undeserving, and human and inhuman. It is, as the most eloquent opponent of the death penalty put it—I refer to the late Albert Camus—a world without God. As he said so well in his brilliant novel, *L'Etranger,* this is a world of hypocrites affecting the language of justice and moral outrage. Of course it is entitled to execute no one; such a world may punish no one. And that, he said, is our world. He did not act as if he believed it—he was a very brave enemy of both Hitler and Stalin —but he did most emphatically say it.[15]

The issue of capital punishment can be said to turn on the kind of world we live in (or the world we want to live in); a moral world or a morally indifferent world.

Contrary to Justices Marshall and Brennan, we in the United States have always recognized the legitimacy of retribution. We have schedules of punishment in every criminal code according to which punishments are designed to fit the crime, and not simply to fit what social science tells us about deterrence and rehabilitation: the worse the crime, the more severe the punishment. Justice requires criminals (as well as the rest of us) to get what they (and we) deserve, and what criminals deserve depends on what they have done to us.

[13.7] To pay back criminals is not only just but, as Andenaes allows us to see, useful as well. For years he has been speaking of what he calls "general prevention," by which he means the capacity of the criminal law to promise obedience to law, not by instilling fear of punishment (the way of deterrence), but by inculcating law-abiding habits. I think the criminal law has this capacity, although Andenaes has never been able to explain the mechanism by which it works. To do so requires me to adopt an old and by now familiar manner of speaking of the law.

The law, and especially the criminal law, works by praising as well as by blaming. It attaches blame to the act of murder, for example, by making it a crime and threatening to punish anyone convicted of having committed it. This function of the law is familiar to us. What is unfamiliar is the way in which the law, by punishing the guilty and thereby blaming them for deeds they commit, also praises those persons who do not commit those deeds. The mechanism involved here is the satisfaction of the law-abiding person's anger, the anger that person ought to feel at the sight of crime. This anger has to be controlled, of course, and we rightly condemn persons who, at the sight of crime, take it upon themselves to punish its perpetrators. But we ought not condemn the anger such persons feel; indeed, that anger is a condition of a decent community. When no one, whether out of indifference or out of cowardice, responds to a Kitty Genovese's screams and plaintive calls for help, we have reason really to be concerned. A *citizen* ought to be angry when witnessing a crime, and, of course, that anger takes the form of wanting to hurt the cause of the anger—for example, whoever it was who mugged and murdered Kitty Genovese. The law must control or calm that anger, and one way it can do that is by promising to punish the criminal. When it punishes the criminal it satisfies that anger, and by doing so, it rewards the law-abiding persons who feel it. This is one purpose of punishment: to reward the law-abiding by satisfying the anger that they feel, or ought to feel, at the sight of crime. It rewards, and by rewarding praises, and therefore teaches, law-abidingness.

[13.8] Anger, Aristotle teaches us,[16] is the pain caused by him who is the object of anger. It is also the pleasure arising from the hope of revenge. It has to be controlled or tamed, but it is not in itself reprehensible; it can be selfish, but, contrary to Freud, it need not be selfish. In fact, it is one of the passions that reaches out to other persons —unlike greed, for example, which is purely selfish—and, in doing so, can serve to unite us with others, or strengthen the bonds that tie us to others. It can be an expression of our caring for others, and society needs people who care for each other, people who, as Aristotle puts it, share their pleasures and their pains, and do so for the sake of others. Anger, again unlike greed or jealousy, is a passion that can cause us to act for reasons having nothing to do with selfish or mean calculation; indeed, when tamed and educated, it can become a most generous passion, the passion that protects the community by demanding punishment for its enemies (and criminals are enemies). It is the stuff from which both heroes and law-abiding citizens are made; and when it is aroused for the right reasons (and it is the job of the law to define those reasons), it deserves to be rewarded.

Criminals are properly the object of anger, and the perpetrators of great crimes (James Earl Ray and Richard Speck, for example) are properly the objects of great anger. They have done more than inflict injury on isolated individuals (and this is especially evident in the case of Ray). They have violated the foundations of trust and friendship, the necessary elements of a moral community. A moral community, unlike a hive of bees or hill of ants, is one whose members (responsible moral creatures) are expected *freely* to obey the laws; and, unlike a tyranny, are *trusted* to obey the laws. The criminal has violated that trust, and in doing so, has injured not merely his immediate victim but also the community as such. It was for this reason that God said to the Jewish community, "Ye shall take no satisfaction [or ransom] for the life of a murderer, which is guilty of death: but he shall be surely put to death."[17] The criminal has called into question the very possibility of that community by suggesting that human beings cannot be trusted freely to respect the property, the person, and the dignity of those with whom they are associated. Crime is an offense against the public, which is why the public prosecutes it.

If, then, persons are not angry when someone else is robbed, raped, or murdered, the implication is that there is no moral community because these persons do not care for anyone other than themselves. When they are angry, that is a sign of their caring; and that anger, that caring, should be rewarded. We reward it when we satisfy it, and we satisfy it when we punish its objects, criminals.

So the question becomes, how do we pay back those who are the objects of great anger because they have committed terrible crimes against us? We can derive some instruction in this subject from the book of Genesis, where we find an account of the first murder and of the first disagreement as to the appropriate punishment of a murderer. Cain killed Abel, and, we are told, God forbade anyone to kill Cain in turn: Vengeance, said the Lord, is mine, and he exacted that vengeance by banishing Cain "from the presence of the Lord."[18] The appropriate punishment would appear to be death or banishment; in either case, the murderer is deprived of life in the community of moral persons. As Justice Frankfurter put it in a dissent in one of the expatriation cases, certain criminals are "unfit to remain in the communion of our citizens."[19]

To elaborate this point, in my book I discussed two famous literary works dealing with murders: Shakespeare's *Macbeth* and Camus' *L'Etranger* (variously translated as *The Stranger* or *The Outsider*).[20] I pointed out that in *Macbeth* the murderer was killed, and I argued that the dramatic necessity of that death derived from its moral necessity. That is how Shakespeare saw it.

As I indicated above, Camus' novel treats murder in an entirely different context. A moral community is not possible without anger and the moral indignation that accompanies it; and it is for this reason that in this novel Camus shows us a world without anger. He denies the legitimacy of it, and specifically of an anger that is aimed at the criminal. Such an anger, he says, is nothing but hypocrisy. The hero—or antihero—of this novel is a stranger or outsider not because he is a murderer, not because he refuses to cry at his mother's funeral, not because he shows and feels no remorse for having murdered (and murdered for no reason whatever); he is a stranger because, in his unwillingness to express what he does not feel—remorse, sadness, regret—he alone is not a hypocrite. The universe, he says at the end of the novel, is "benignly indifferent" to how we live. Such a universe, or such a world, cannot justify the taking of a life—even the life of a murderer. Only a moral community may do that, and a moral community is impossible in our time; which means there is no basis for friendship or for the ties that bind us and make us responsible for each other and to each other. The only thing we share, Camus says in his essay on the death penalty, is our "solidarity against death," and an execution "unsets" that solidarity.[21]

Strangely, when some of the abolitionists speak of the death penalty as a denial of human dignity, this is what they mean. Abe Fortas, writing after he left the supreme court, said that the "essential value," the value that constitutes the "basis of our civilization," is the "pervasive, *unqualified* respect for life."[22] This is what passes for a moral argument for him (and I have no doubt that he speaks for many others). In contrast, Lincoln (who, incidentally, greatly admired Shakespeare's *MacBeth*[23]), who respected life and grieved when it was taken, authorized the execution of 267 men. His respect for life was not "unqualified." He believed, as did the founders of our country, that there were some things for which people should be expected to give up their lives. For example, as he said at Gettysburg, Americans should be expected to give up their lives in order that this nation "shall have a new birth of freedom."

There are vast differences between Camus, a man of deep perception and elegance of expression, and Fortas, but they shared a single vision of our world. Camus, however, gave it a label appropriate to the vision: a world without dignity, without morality, and indifferent to how we treat each other. There are statutes in this world forbidding crimes, but there is no basis in the order of things for those statutes. It is a world that may not rightly impose the sentence of death on anyone — or for that matter punish anyone in any manner — or ask any patriot to risk his or her life for it.

[13.9] Shakespeare's dramatic poetry serves to remind us of another world, of the majesty of the moral order and of the terrible consequences of breaching it through the act of murder (the worst offense against that order). Capital punishment, like banishment in other times and places, serves a similar purpose: It reminds us, or can remind us, of the reign of the moral order, and enhances, or can enhance, its dignity. The law must not be understood to be merely statute that we enact or repeal at our pleasure and obey or disobey at our convenience, especially not the criminal law. Whenever law is regarded as *merely* statutory, by which I mean arbitrary or enacted out of no moral necessity or reflecting no law beyond itself, people will soon enough disobey it, and the clever ones will learn to do so with impunity. The purpose of the criminal law is not merely to control behavior — a tyrant can do that — but also to promote respect for that which should be respected, especially the lives, the moral integrity, and even the property of others. In a country whose principles forbid it to preach, the criminal law is one of the few available institutions through which it can make a moral statement and, thereby, hope to promote this respect. To be successful, what it says — and it makes this moral statement when it punishes — must be appropriate to the offense and, therefore, to what has been offended. If human life is to be held in awe, the law forbidding the taking of it must be held in awe; and the only way it can be made to be awful or awe-inspiring is to entitle it to inflict the penalty of death.

Death is the most awful punishment available to the law of our time and place. Banishment (even if it were still a legal punishment under the constitution[24]) is not dreaded, not in our time; in fact, to judge by some of the expatriated Vietnam war resisters I used to see in Toronto, it is not always regarded as a punishment. And, despite the example of Gary Gilmore, the typical offender does not prefer death to imprisonment, even life imprisonment. In prison the offender still enjoys some of the pleasures available outside and some of the rights of citizens, and is not utterly outside the protection of the laws. Most of all, a prisoner has not been deprived of hope—hope of escape, of pardon, or of being able to do some of the things that can be done even by someone who has lost freedom of movement. A convicted murderer in prison (Ray) has retained more of life than has the victim (Martin Luther King). A maximum-security prison may be a brutal place, and the prospect of spending one's life there is surely dreadful, but the prospect of being executed is more dreadful. And for the worst of crimes, the punishment must be most dreadful and awful—not most painful (for the purpose of punishment is not simply to inflict pain on the guilty offender), but awful in the sense of "commanding profound respect or reverential fear."

Whether the United States, or any of them, should be permitted to carry out executions is a question that is not answered simply by what I have written here. The answer depends on our ability to restrict its use to the worst of our criminals and to impose it in a nondiscriminatory fashion. We do not yet know whether that can be done.

NOTES

1. Walter Berns *For Capital Punishment: Crime and the Morality of the Death Penalty* (New York: Basic Books, 1979).
2. June 28, 1979, pp. 22–25.
3. July 16, 1979, III, p. 14.
4. Garry Wills, "Capital Punishment and a Non Sequitur," *Washington Star*, Apr. 16, 1979, A-11. Wills's column was actually devoted to an excerpt from the book which was published in *Harper's* (April 1979). My reply To Wills was published in the *Washington Star*, Apr. 21, 1979, A-9.
5. See Berns, *For Capital Punishment*, pp. 21–22.
6. Ibid., pp. 11–18.
7. Cesare Beccaria, *On Crimes and Punishments*, trans. Henry Paolucci (Indianapolis: Bobbs-Merrill, Library of Liberal Arts, 1963).
8. Ibid., p. 41.
9. Joannes Andenaes, *Punishment and Deterrence*, with a foreword by Norval Morris (Ann Arbor, Mich.: University of Michigan Press, 1984), p. 133.
10. Karl Menninger, *The Crime of Punishment* (New York: Viking Press, 1969), p. 9. At the twenty-second National Institute on Crime and Delinquency, Menninger was given the Roscoe Pound Award for his outstanding work in "the field of criminal justice"; see *American Journal of Corrections*, July–August 1975, p. 32.
11. See, for example, Norval Morris, "The Future of Imprisonment: Toward a Punitive Philosophy," *Michigan Law Review*, May 1974, pp. 1161–1180; and Andrew von Hirsch, *Doing Justice; The Choice of Punishments*, Report of the Committee for the Study of Incarceration (New York: Hill & Wang, 1976).
12. *Furman v. Georgia*, 408 U.S. 238, 343–1244 (1972).
13. Ibid., pp. 272–273.
14. Pico Della Mirandola, *Oration on the Dignity of Man*, trans. A Robert Caponigri (Chicago: Henry Regnery, Gateway Editions, 1956).
15. See comments below.
16. Aristotle, *Rhetoric* 1378b1–5.
17. Numbers 35:31.
18. Genesis 4:15–16.
19. *Trop v. Dulles*, 356 U.S. 86, 122 (1958). Dissenting opinion.
20. Camus was the most powerful and eloquent opponent of capital punishment. See Albert Camus, "Reflections on the Guillotine," in *Resistance, Rebellion and Death*, trans. Justin O'Brien (New York: Knopf, 1961).
21. Ibid., p. 222.
22. Abe Fortas, "The Case against Capital Punishment," *New York Times Magazine*, Jan. 23, 1977, p. 29. Italics added.
23. In a letter from Lincoln to James H. Hackett written on August 17, 1863, Lincoln says, "Some of Shakespeare's plays I have never read, whilst others I have gone over perhaps as frequently as any unprofessional reader. Among the latter are *Lear, Richard Third, Henry Eighth, Hamlet*, and especially *Macbeth*. I think nothing equals *Macbeth*. It is wonderful." *The Collected Works of Abraham Lincoln*, vol. 6, Roy P. Basler, Ed. (New Brunswick, NJ: Rutgers University Press, 1953), p. 393.
24. Banishment, insofar as it would be comprehended by expatriation, has been declared an unconstitutionally cruel and unusual punishment. *Affroyim v. Rusk*, 387 U.S. 253 (1967).

PROGRESS CHECK 13.1

Instructions: *Fill in the blanks with the appropriate responses listed below.*

awful
Cesare Beccaria
rehabilitation
retribution
anger

community
ambivalent
Jeremy Bentham
deterrence
dignity

1. The fear of punishment acts as a _____ to crime.
2. Many people have become hesitant and guilt-ridden about punishment because they have become morally _____.
3. *On Crimes and Punishments* was written by _____. It advocates the establishment of a modern liberal state.
4. One political philosopher opposed to the death penalty is _____.
5. Punishment, seen as giving a person what he or she deserves, is a form of _____ .
6. _____ need not be selfish like jealousy or greed. It can serve to unite people and consolidate bonds of trust.
7. The law must be made _____ in the sense that it must evoke reverential respect.
8. In order to assuage their guilt, some people regard punishment as a form of _____ for the criminal.
9. Indifference and cowardice in the face of crime undermines the bonds of _____.
10. Berns argues that criminals lose their _____ when they commit vile crimes.

LEARNING EXERCISE 13.2

Instructions: *Identify the following statements as either value judgments (V) or nonnormative claims (N).*

_____ 1. Capital punishment arouses the angriest of passions.
_____ 2. Opposition to capital punishment is a modern phenomenon.
_____ 3. No liberal thinker should favor capital punishment.
_____ 4. We cannot rehabilitate criminals.
_____ 5. To inflict pain on one person merely to affect the behavior of others is immoral.
_____ 6. Criminals are no less worthy of our concern than are law-abiding persons.

_____ 7. We do not like to admit that we exact retribution from criminals.

_____ 8. The vilest criminal possesses common human dignity.

_____ 9. Society has lost all confidence in its opinions of right and wrong.

_____ 10. The criminal law inculcates law-abiding habits.

_____ 11. The law-abiding person's anger deserves to be satisfied.

_____ 12. Anger can be an expression of our caring for others.

_____ 13. Anger aroused for the right reason is good.

_____ 14. If people are not angered by the sight of crime, then there is no evidence that a moral community exists.

_____ 15. Capital punishment makes the law awful.

LEARNING EXERCISE 13.3

Instructions: _Complete the following syllogisms._

1. **Value Premise:** Forms of punishment leading to disgusting public spectacles should be abolished.

   Factual Premise:

   Conclusion: Capital punishment should be abolished.

2. **Value Premise:** We should accept forms of punishment which develop respect for the law.

   Factual Premise:

   Conclusion: We should accept the death penalty.

3. **Value Premise:**

   Factual Premise: Anger is an emotion which strengthens the bonds of moral community.

   Conclusion: Anger is not reprehensible.

4. **Value Premise:** The greatest crimes against humanity should be punished by the death penalty.

   Factual Premise: Murder is one of the greatest crimes against humanity.

   Conclusion:

5. **Value Premise:**

   Factual Premise: Capital punishment satisfies the law-abiding person's anger.

   Conclusion: We should accept capital punishment.

LEARNING EXERCISE 13.4

Instructions: *Test the adequacy of the following statements and arguments. Use the role-exchange test, the new cases test, the higher-order principle test, and the universalizability and consistency test. Look for any fallacies.*

1. We should be inclined to accept capital punishment since virtually all political philosophers in the past have supported it. Opposition is relatively recent.
2. Since we in Canada and the United States have always recognized the legitimacy of retribution, we should continue to accept capital punishment as a form of "getting back" or giving criminals what they deserve.
3. We should reject the views of those opposing capital punishment since their objections stem from moral uncertainty and ambivalence.
4. If a person does not become angered at the sight of crime, then the individual is morally ambivalent.
5. We should favor capital punishment since it promotes reverential respect for the law.

14

"THE FOLLY OF CAPITAL PUNISHMENT"

Arthur Koestler

EDUCATIONAL OBJECTIVES: After reading this chapter the student will be able to:

14.1 State Arthur Koestler's position on the issue of using capital punishment as a deterrent.

14.2 List the groups of people who apparently are not deterred by the death penalty.

14.3 Explain the alleged deterrent value of capital punishment with respect to the professional criminal class.

14.4 Give Koestler's reasons for rejecting the claim that the death penalty is effective with professional criminals.

14.5 Comment on what possible effects the death penalty may have on juries determining the guilt of criminals charged with murder.

14.6 Summarize the effects which historically speaking have stemmed from the abolition of capital punishment.

14.7 Respond to the claim that public executions would make capital punishment more effective as a deterrent.

14.8 Explain how advocates of the death penalty deal with evidence which is counter to their position.

14.9 Provide Koestler's response to those refusing to accept statistical evidence which is contrary to their pro-capital punishment views.

Reprinted by permission of Sterling Lord Literistic, Inc. Copyright © 1957.

FOCUS QUESTIONS

1. On what basis does Koestler object to capital punishment?
2. What exactly is meant by deterrence? How is it different from retribution? Are retribution and deterrence necessarily related?
3. Would capital punishment be effective if it were more frequently and publicly administered? Why or why not?
4. What support, if any, can be mustered for using the death penalty as a deterrent?

SYNOPSIS

In this article, Arthur Koestler addresses himself to the "deterrence argument" that is frequently used in support of capital punishment. He recognizes that there are ethical objections to using capital punishment as a deterrent, but chooses in this instance to reject deterrence on a purely utilitarian basis. He contends that capital punishment is not effective as a deterrent and, consequently, the deterrence argument used in its favor should be rejected.

Early in the article Koestler asks who, in fact, is deterred by capital punishment. Certainly those who have murdered already are not deterred in countries or states where executions follow murder convictions. The one-third of all murderers who commit suicide are likely not deterred. Those murderers who are insane and mentally deranged probably do not understand deterrence and the consequences of their actions. In 80 to 90 percent of all murders, where people kill in anger, drunkenness, or passion, there is likely no thought given to deterrence. For self-destructive individuals who for perverse reasons wish to be executed, capital punishment may even act as an incentive. Finally, Koestler points out that for those who think they have discovered the perfect method of murder (for example, poison), the belief is held that they will never be caught, so deterrence has little impact. Koestler concludes that the only ones left for whom capital punishment could act as a deterrent are those belonging to the professional criminal class. Yet murder, he states, is not typically a crime of professionals; it is a crime committed by amateurs.

Koestler recognizes that opponents to his position could argue that the reason professional criminals rarely commit murder is precisely because of the threat of the gallows. Abolish the gallows, and the murder rate would increase. In response to this objection, Koestler underscores the fact that his objector's claim is based on an unproven assumption. He also proceeds in the remainder of the essay to present statistical, historical, and international evidence which calls into question the deterrence value of capital punishment. The facts repeatedly suggest that the absence of capital punishment or its abolition has no appreciable effect on the murder and crime rates. Koestler quotes the British Parliamentary Select Committee, which, after studying results in states that had completely or partially abolished capital punishment, concluded, "capital punishment may be abolished in this country [Britain] without endangering life or property, or impairing the security of society."

Koestler also rejects capital punishment because it has more of a deterrent effect on legal juries than on criminals. He draws attention to how jurors typically find reasons for not invoking capital punishment in cases of murder and that for this reason, the death sentence is rarely administered, even when in effect.

Koestler recognizes that if capital punishment had, in fact, a deterrent effect, it would be most evident in cases of public executions. Yet, public executions conducted in the past served as a prime opportunity for pickpockets to commit crimes, due to the enthusiastic attention of most spectators on the proceedings and not their purses. Koestler mentions a prison chaplain who found that out of 167 persons awaiting execution, 164 had previously witnessed executions. In view of such evidence, the British Parliament decided in 1868 to make all executions private. Koestler concludes that if public hanging does not deter, it is even less likely that private hangings or executions will deter.

In view of the overwhelming evidence which rejects the deterrence value of capital punishment. Koestler addresses the issue of how it is that advocates of the death penalty still use deterrence as part of their platform. He claims that those favoring capital punishment often choose to ignore statistics. Advocates also casually dismiss the evidence, if they notice it at all, saying that statistics lie, that they do not prove anything, or that they can be used dishonestly. Such advocates in countries such as Britain argue that findings from other nations have no bearing on one's own. In rebuttal, Koestler points out that advocates of capital punishment offer no counterevidence to support their case, while ignoring the evidence which does exist. Koestler asks why scientists and insurance companies use statistics if they do not prove anything, and he suggests that in statistical analyses of large samples of countries, individual national differences are canceled out. Koestler concludes by expressing his astonishment at how people still continue today to use deterrence as an argument in support of capital punishment when, indeed, there are no reasonable grounds for doing so.

The arguments in defense of capital punishment have remained essentially the same since Lord Ellenborough's days. In the recent Parliamentary debates the Home Secretary, Major Lloyd George, again patiently trotted out the three customary reasons why the Government opposed abolition: that the death penalty carried a unique deterrent value; that no satisfactory alternative punishment could be designed; and that public opinion was in favor of it.

[14.1] The second and third points will be discussed in later chapters. At present I am only concerned with the first and main argument. To give it a fair hearing, we must set all humanitarian considerations and charitable feelings aside, and examine the effectiveness of the gallows as a deterrent to potential murderers from a coldly practical, purely utilitarian point of view. This is, of course, a somewhat artificial view, for in reality "effectiveness" can never be the only consideration; even if it were proved that death preceded by torture, or on the wheel, were more effective, we would refuse to act accordingly. However, it will be seen that the theory of hanging as the best deterrent can be refuted on its own purely utilitarian grounds, without calling ethics and charity to aid.

A deterrent must logically refer to a "deterree," if the reader will forgive me for adding a verbal barbarity to the barbarous subject. So the first question is: who are the hypothetical deterrees, who will be prevented from committing murder by the threat of hanging, but not by the threat of long-term imprisonment? The fear of death is no doubt a powerful deterrent; but just how much more powerful is it than the fear of a life sentence?

[14.2] The gallows obviously failed as a deterrent in all cases where a murder has actually been committed. It is certainly not a deterrent to murderers who commit suicide—and one-third of all murderers do. It is not a deterrent to the insane and mentally deranged; nor to those who have killed in a quarrel, in drunkenness, in a sudden surge of passion—and this type of murder amounts to 80 percent to 90 percent of all murders that are committed. It is not a deterrent to the type of person who commits murder because he desires to be hanged; and these cases are not infrequent. It is not a deterrent to the person who firmly believes in his own perfect method—by poison, acid bath, and so on—which, he thinks, will never be found out. Thus the range of hypothetical deterrees who can only be kept under control by the threat of death and nothing short of death, is narrowed down to the professional criminal class. But both the abolitionists and their opponents agree that "murder is not a crime of the criminal classes"; it is a crime of amateurs, not of professionals. None of the points I have mentioned so far is controversial; they are agreed on by both sides. . . .

[14.3] Who, then, are the deterrees for whose sake this country must preserve capital punishment, as the only European democracy except Eire and France—which, from the judicial point of view, is not very enviable company? What type of criminal, to repeat the question in its precise form, can only be ruled by the threat of hanging, and nothing short of hanging? It is at this point that the issue between abolitionists and their opponents is really joined. The opponents' argument may be summed up as follows. As things stand, the professional criminal rarely commits murder; but if the threat of the gallows were abolished, he would take to murder, and the crime rate would go up.

[14.4] This, of course, is an unproved assumption; a hypothesis whose truth could only be tested either (a) by experiment, or (b) by drawing on analogies from past experiences in Britain and abroad. The House of Commons in 1948 voted for the experiment. It said: let us suspend executions for five years, and see what happens. The House of Lords rejected it after it was informed by the Lord Chief Justice that the twenty Judges of the King's Bench were unanimous in opposing the measure. His main argument against the five-year suspension was that the experiment would be too dangerous; his second argument, that if the dangerous experiment were tried, abolition would come to stay. He used both arguments in the same speech. So much for the experimental method.

Now for the second method: by analogy or precedent. Perhaps the oddest thing about this whole controversy is that the

Judges, who live on bread and precedent, never quote a precedent in support of their thesis that abolition leads to an increase in crime. After all, the burden of proof for this assumption lies on them; and since there is a gold mine of precedent at their disposal of what happened after the abolition of capital punishment for some two hundred and twenty different categories of crime, why do they never, never treat us to a single case? Why do we never hear: you want to repeal the capital statute for murder; look what happened after the repeal of statute 14 Geo. 2, c.6, s.1 (174) (burglary), 7 Will. 4 & 1 Vic.; c.89, s.2 (arson), 9 Geo. 4, c.31, s.16 (rape), 8 Geo. 1, c.22 (1921) (forgery)? Why is it that the reformers, these reckless destroyers of the bulwarks of tradition, always rely on history for support, whereas on this particular issue the keepers of tradition act as if the past did not exist?

Yet the present situation is fraught with precedents and echoes of the past. In the ten years 1940–49 the number of murders known to the Police in England and Wales amounted to 1,666 cases; the number of executions in the same period was 127. Expressed in annual averages, we have 170 murders but only 13 executions. That means that the law as it stands is only found applicable in practice in 7 percent of all cases; in Scotland even less: only 1 in 35, that is, under 3 percent of all murderers are actually executed. The law says that murder shall be punished by death; but in about 95 out of 100 cases the law cannot be applied for a variety of reasons which will be discussed in detail later on. And that again means, as in all cases in the past when such glaring discrepancies occurred, that the law has outlived its time and has become an anachronism.

There are, as we saw before, two methods of remedying such a situation. The first is to bring the law up to date; the second, to put the clock of history back. The latter solution was advocated by the Lord Chief Justice in his evidence before the Royal Commission of 1948, when he suggested that fewer people ought to be reprieved and that it was perfectly proper to hang a person who is certified insane, but is not insane according to the M'Naghten Rules of 1843. We have discussed in sufficient detail the disastrous results to which such attempts to put the clock back have led in the course of the eighteenth and early nineteenth centuries.

The opposite method was tried from approximately 1920 onward. The basic reason why it was tried was the same which underlies the present inquiry: the law had become outdated, and therefore largely inapplicable and ineffective. In November, 1830, the Jurors of London presented their remarkable petition to the Commons. It ran:

> That in present state of the law, jurors feel extremely reluctant to convict where the penal consequences of the offense excite a conscientious horror in their minds, lest the rigorous performance of their duties as jurors should make them accessory to judicial murder. Hence, in Courts of Justice, a most necessary and painful struggle is occasioned by the conflict of the feelings of a just humanity with the sense of the obligation of an oath.

[14.5] The deterrent of the gallows affected the jury more than the criminal; the juries went on strike, as it were. They made it a rule, when a theft of goods worth forty shillings was a capital offense, to assess the value of the goods at thirty-nine shillings; and when, in 1827, the capital offense was raised to five pounds, the juries raised their assessment to four pounds nineteen shillings. Present-day juries, as we shall see, bring in verdicts of "guilty, but insane" in cases where, according to medical evidence and the Judge's direction, the accused must be regarded as sane before the law. "It would be following strict precedent," says Mr. Gardiner in the *Law Quarterly*, "for the perversity of jurors to be the prelude to reform."

The perversity of the jurors reached such an extent that it led, in 1830, to the famous "Petition of Bankers from 214 cities and towns," urging Parliament to abolish the death penalty for forgery—not for any sentimental, humanitarian motives, but to protect themselves against the forgers to whom the gallows proved no deterrent. Here is the full text of the petition:

> That your petitioners, as bankers, are deeply interested in the protection of property, from forgery, and in the infliction of punishment on persons guilty of that crime.
> That your petitioners find, by experience, that the infliction of death, or even the possibility of the infliction of death, prevents the prosecution, conviction and punishment of the criminal and thus endangers the property which it is intended to protect.
> That your petitioners, therefore, earnestly pray that your honorable House will not withhold from them that protection to their property which they would derive from a more lenient law.

[14.6] Few of the bankers may have read Beccaria or Jeremy Bentham, and few would probably have subscribed to their philosophy. Yet for reasons of hard-headed expediency, they subscribed to the theory of the "minimum effective penalty. It took Parliament another six years to abolish capital punishment for forgery. The usual warnings were uttered that this measure would lead to the "destruction of trade and commerce" and in Chief Justice Lord Mansfield's opinion the answer to the predicament was that capital sentences for forgery ought always to be carried out. Yet when death for forgery was abolished, the number of commitments for that crime fell from 213

in the three years before repeal to 180 in the three subsequent years.

If the death penalty were a more effective deterrent than lesser penalties, then its abolition for a given category of crime should be followed by a noticeable increase in the volume of that crime, precisely as the hanging party says. But the fact tells a different story. After the great reform, the crime rate did not rise; it fell—as everybody except the oracles had expected. And yet the era of reform coincided with one of the most difficult periods in English social history. As if History herself had wanted to make the task of the abolitionists more difficult, the repeal of the death penalty for offenses against property during the 1830's was immediately followed by the "hungry forties." The great experiment of mitigating the rigor of the law could not have been carried out under more unfavorable circumstances. Yet half-way through the experiment, when the number of capital offenses had been reduced to fifteen, His Majesty's Commissioners on Criminal Law, 1836, summed up their report as follows:

> It has not, in effect, been found that the repeal of Capital Punishment with regard to any particular class of offenses has been attended with an increase of the offenders. On the contrary, the evidence and statements to be found in our appendix go far to demonstrate that ... the absolute number of the offenders has diminished.

And at the conclusion of the most dangerous experiment in the history of English criminal law, Sir Joseph Pease was able to state in the House of Commons that "the continual mitigation of law and of sentences has been accomplished with property quite as secure, and human life quite as sacred."

[14.7] "Deterrence" is an ugly and abstract word. It means, according to the *Oxford Dictionary*, "discouragement by fear." If the arguments in favor of the gallows as the supreme deterrent were true, then public executions would have the maximum discouraging effect on the criminal. Yet these public exhibitions, intended to prove that "crime does not pay," were known to be the occasion when pickpockets gathered their richest harvest among the crowd. A contemporary author explains why: "The thieves selected the moment when the strangled man was swinging above them as the happiest opportunity, because they knew that everybody's eyes were on that person and all were looking up."

Public executions not only failed to diminish the volume of crime; they often caused an immediate rise in their wake. The hanging of a criminal served, less as a warning, than as an incitement to imitate him. Fauntleroy confessed that the idea of committing forgery came to him while he watched a forger being hanged. A juryman, who found Dr. Dodd guilty of forgery, committed soon afterwards the same crime and was hanged from the same gallows. Cumming was hanged in Edinburgh in 1854 for sexual assault, which immediately led to a wave of similar assaults in the region. In 1855, Heywood was hanged in Liverpool for cutting the throat of a woman; three weeks later, Ferguson was arrested in the same town for the same crime. The list could be continued indefinitely. The evidence was so overwhelming that a Select Committee of the House of Lords was appointed in 1856; it recommended that public executions should be abolished because they did not deter from crime. The Lords would not believe it, and did nothing. Ten years later, the Royal Commission of 1866 inquired into the same question, and came to the same result as the Select Committee. One of the most striking pieces of evidence before the Commissioners was a statement by the prison chaplain in Bristol, the Reverend W.

Roberts, that out of 167 persons awaiting execution in that prison, 164 had previously witnessed at least one execution. What would the British Medical Association say of the value of a patent medicine for the prevention of polio, if it were found in 167 polio cases that 164 had been treated with that medicine?

Two years after the Royal Commission's reports, Parliament decided that executions should henceforth be private. However, if watching with one's own eyes the agony of a person being strangled on the gallows does not deter, it seems logical to assume that an unseen execution in a more gentlemanly manner would deter even less. One may further argue that if the penalty of hanging does not frighten even a pickpocket, it would not frighten a potential murderer, who acts either in momentary passion, or for incomparably higher stakes. Yet these were not the conclusions reached by the lawgivers. They assumed that while watching an execution from a few yards' distance did not act as a deterrent, reading a Home Office communique about it did.

The results of the abolition of the death penalty for crimes against property provide a powerful argument for abolishing it altogether. But in itself, the argument is not conclusive. The fact that abolition of the death penalty did not increase the volume of cattle-stealing strongly suggests, but does not prove, that abolition of the death penalty would not increase the volume of murder. That proof can only be initiated by analogy with other crimes; it must be completed by actual precedents for the crime of murder itself.

Fortunately, these precedents are available through the experience of the thirty-six states which have abolished capital punishment in the course of the last hundred years.

The evidence has been studied by criminologists and Departments of Justice all over the world, and summarized with previously unequalled thoroughness by the British Parliamentary Select Committee of 1929–30 and the Royal Commission on Capital Punishment of 1948–53. The report and evidence of the first fills some eight hundred closely printed pages; the report of the second, plus its Minutes of Evidence, nearly fourteen hundred pages of quarto and folio. The conclusion of the Select Committee is summed up as follows:

> Our prolonged examination of the situation in foreign countries has increasingly confirmed us in the assurance that capital punishment may be abolished in this country without endangering life or property, or impairing the security of society.

The conclusions of the Royal Commission were essentially the same, although more cautiously expressed. Their terms of reference prevented them from considering the question whether capital punishment should be abolished or not; they were only allowed to make recommendations concerning changes in the existing capital law. Moreover, their report was unanimous, whereas the Select Committee report of 1930, as the previous Royal Commission report of 1866, was a majority report. The Commission's final conclusion regarding the expected consequences of abolition (which they managed to smuggle in, though the terms of reference excluded this question) was formulated thus:

> There is no clear evidence of any lasting increase [in the murder rate following abolition] and there are many offenders on whom the deterrent effect is limited and may often be negligible. It is therefore important to view the question in a just perspective and not to base a penal policy in relation to murder on exaggerated estimates of the uniquely deterrent force of the death-penalty.

They reached this conclusion by taking two types of evidence into account: on the one hand, the crime statistics of foreign countries; on the other, the opinion of the British Police Force, the prison services, and the judges. It is to this second, or local evidence that the expression "exaggerated estimates" refers; and in their conclusions the Commissioners make some allowances for it. But in the text of their report, as distinct from their cautious "conclusions," they make their findings unmistakably clear. They dismiss the police's and the judges' contention that abolition would entice burglars to wear firearms: "We received no evidence that the abolition of capital punishment in other countries had in fact led to the consequences apprehended by our witnesses in this country." Their opinion on the general effect of abolition on the crime rate in foreign countries is equally unambiguous. They analyzed the staggeringly extensive material which they had assembled under three headings:

(a) by comparing the homicide statistics of a given country before and after abolition of the death-penalty:

(b) by comparing the homicide statistics of neighboring countries of a similar social structure, some of which have abolished the death-penalty and some not, over the same period of time;

(c) by analyzing the possible influence of the number of executions in a given country in a particular year on the homicide rate in the immediately following period.

Concerning (a), they state: "The general conclusion which we have reached is that there is no clear evidence in any of the figures we have examined that the abolition of capital punishment has led to an increase in the homicide rate, or that its reintroduction has led to a fall."

Concerning (b), their findings are mainly

based on comparisons between the homicide curves in closely related states in the U.S.A.; and between New Zealand and the Australian states:

> If we take any of these groups we find that the fluctuations in the homicide rate of each of its component members exhibit a striking similarity. We agree with Professor Sellin that the only conclusion which can be drawn from the figures is that there is no clear evidence of any influence of the death-penalty on the homicide rates of these States, and that, "whether the death-penalty is used or not, and whether executions are frequent or not, both death-penalty States and abolition States show rates which suggest that these rates are conditioned by other factors than the death-penalty."

Concerning (c), they state: " . . . about the possible relation between the number of executions in particular years and the incidence of murder in succeeding years . . . we are satisfied that no such relationship can be established."

[14.6] Once more the mountains labored and a mouse was born. The mountainous statistical survey of the Royal Commission of 1948 merely confirmed the findings of the Select Committee of 1930, which confirmed the findings of all abolitionist countries in the course of the last century for crimes against property: to wit, that abolition has not caused an increase in murder nor stopped the fall of the murder rate in any European country; and that in the non-European countries, the U.S.A., Australia, and New Zealand, the ups and downs of the murder rate show a striking similarity in states of similar social structure whether the death penalty is used or not.

[14.8] The defenders of capital punishment are well aware that the statistical evidence is unanswerable. They do not contest it: they ignore it. When pressed in debate, they invariably fall back on one of two answers: (a) "statistics lie" or "do not prove anything"; (b) that the experience of foreign countries has no bearing on conditions in Britain. Let us examine both answers.

[14.9] That "statistics don't prove anything" is, of course, nonsense; if it were true, all insurances companies, physicists, and engineers would have to go out of business, and the Chancellor of the Exchequer could never present a Budget. Statistics are indispensable in every human activity; and like every tool they can be put to careless and dishonest use. Statistics cannot prove or disprove that smoking "causes" lung cancer; it can prove that the average Englishman is taller than the average Italian. In the first example, the observational range is too small in relation to the number of causative factors involved. In the second example, the statistician merely states a fact which can be interpreted in various ways; by race, nourishment, climate, and so on.

In discussing the statistics of abolitionist Europe, we have to distinguish with great care between fact and interpretation. The facts are beyond dispute; throughout the twentieth century, abolition was in no European country followed by an increase in the murder rate, and was in nearly all countries followed by a decrease. These facts can be interpreted in the following manners:

(1) Abolition causes a fall in the murder rate.
(2) Abolition causes an increase in the murder rate, but this increase is too small to stop the general downward trend of the murder rate, which is due to different causes.
(3) Abolition does not perceptibly influence the murder rate one way or another.

All three interpretations are possible, although the examples of post-war Germany and post-war Italy . . . seem to contradict the second hypothesis; but that, of course, is not conclusive. It is at this point that the comparisons between similar states with different legislation come in. They prove that "both death-penalty states and abolition states show rates which suggest that they are conditioned by other factors than the death penalty. . . . The general picture is the same—a rise in the rates of the early twenties and a downward trend since then."

This eliminates interpretations (1) and (2) and leaves us with (3): that the death penalty cannot be proved to influence the murder rate one way or another.

Let us make the point clearer by a familiar example. If the medical profession wants to test the efficiency of a new serum there are, by and large, two methods of doing this. The first is to administer the serum to a number of patients and see how the results compare with the use of older medicines. The substitution of prison sentences in lieu of capital punishment was an experiment of this kind. It showed that it was followed nearly everywhere in Europe by a fall in the fever chart of crime. This in itself did not prove that the new treatment was the direct *cause* of the improvement, because perhaps the epidemic was on the wane anyway; but it did prove that the new treatment could at least not be sufficiently harmful to impede the fall on the fever chart, whatever the cause of that fall. The second method is used as a check on the first. The new serum is administered to patients in one hospital ward, and the rate of recovery is then compared to that in a second or "control" ward, where treatment is continued on the old lines. If the rate of recovery remains substantially the same in both wards, the British Medical Association will conclude that the new treatment is just as good or bad as the old one, as far as its deterrent effect on the disease goes. The choice will then be decided by other considerations. If the new treatment is less painful or repellent, then only the oldest fogeys of the profession will,

just for the hell of it, stick to their ancient method.

To sum up: the experience of the civilized world proves as conclusively as the most rigorously sifted evidence can ever prove, that the gallows is no more effective than other non-lethal deterrents.

But statistics don't bleed; let us always remember the individual sample falling through the trap.

So much for the contention that "statistics don't prove anything." The second stock answer of the hang-hards runs: "Foreign experience doesn't prove anything, because foreigners are different." It was said in defense of death for shoplifting when all the rest of Europe had abandoned it; it is repeated today with the same unction. The grain of truth in it is that no nation is like any other nation; thus the example of, say, Switzerland *alone* would be of little value because Switzerland is a more "peaceful" country than England. But the whole point of the statistical approach is that, over a large number of samples, individual differences cancel out, and the general trend common to all is revealed.

Now the evidence concerning abolition embraces thirty-six countries with vastly different populations, and in different periods of development; agricultural and industrial nations, old and new civilizations, countries rich and countries poor, Latin, Anglo-Saxon, and Germanic races, hot-tempered and placid people, countries which became abolitionist after a long period of peace and security, and others, like Germany and Italy, which have only just emerged from war, demoralized by defeat, brutalized by years of totalitarian terror. The convincingness of the proof rests precisely in the fact that, however different the countries and conditions, abolition was nowhere followed by an increase in the crime-rate, or any other noticeable ill effect.

The general reader who is new to this

controversy would naturally assume that the opponents of abolition have their own arguments, figures, and evidence on the same reasoned and factual level as the abolitionists, and that it would require a good deal of expert knowledge to decide which party is right. This is not the case. The defenders of capital punishment have produced no evidence of their own; nor contested the correctness of the documentary material assembled by Royal Commissions, Select Committees, etc.; nor even tried to put a different interpretation on it. They simply ignore it; as they ignore the experience gained from mitigations of the law in this country's own past. When challenged, they invariably and uniformly trot out the same answers: there is no alternative to capital punishment; statistics don't prove anything; other nations can afford to abolish hanging, but not Britain, because the criminal Englishman (or Welshman or Scotsman) is different from any other criminal in the world; for foreigners prison may be a sufficient deterrent, the English criminal needs the gallows.

Since the Select Committee's report, the Royal Commission has vastly extended the scope of the former's inquiry, and arrived at the same results. The answer of the hanghards remained the same. It seems hardly believable that in a nation-wide controversy which has now been going on for some twenty-five years, one side should produce, with ant-like diligence, facts, figures, and historic precedent, mobilize the whole array of psychiatry and social science, borne out by impartial Royal Commissions—and the other side should content themselves with evasions, stonewalling, and the ever repeated nonsense about the unique and indispensable deterrent value of the death penalty. The legend about the hangman as the protector of society has been refuted and exposed to ridicule on every single past occasion, and yet it popped up again on the next.

This is perhaps the saddest aspect in this whole heart- and neck-breaking business. For it shows that an officially sponsored lie has a thousand lives and takes a thousand lives. It resembles one of the monster squids of deep-sea lore; it spurts ink into your face, while its tentacles strangle the victim in the interest of public welfare.

PROGRESS CHECK 14.1

Instructions: Fill in the blanks with the appropriate responses listed below.

anachronism
burden of proof
precedent
capital punishment
professional criminal class

deterrence
utilitarian
public executions
fact
deterree

1. Koestler's objection to using capital punishment as a deterrent is not moral in this essay, but rather _____ .
2. Judges and others in favor of capital punishment as a deterrent never quote _____ to support their claim that abolition of the death penalty leads to an increase in crime.

3. The _____ falls on those advocating capital punishment to show that it does in fact deter.

4. An outdated law is an _____.

5. _____ means "discouragement by fear."

6. _____ have failed to diminish the amount of crime.

7. The conclusion of the British Parliamentary Select Committee (1929–1930) stated that _____ could be abolished without risking property and the security of society.

8. When discussing the statistics surrounding capital punishment, it is important to distinguish between _____ and interpretation.

9. One who is deterred is a _____.

10. The _____ rarely commits murder.

LEARNING EXERCISE 14.2

Instructions: Complete the following syllogisms.

1. **Value Premise:** We should accept forms of punishment which the majority favors.

   Factual Premise:

   Conclusion: Therefore, we should accept capital punishment.

2. **Value Premise:**

   Factual Premise: The death penalty is a punishment which does not deter.

   Conclusion: Therefore, the death penalty should be abolished.

3. **Value Premise:** Individuals who refuse to acknowledge evidence contrary to their own position are unreasonable.

   Factual Premise: Advocates of capital punishment are individuals who refuse to acknowledge evidence contrary to their own position.

   Conclusion:

4. **Value Premise:**

   Factual Premise: The claim that capital punishment deters is a myth.

   Conclusion: The claim that capital punishment deters should be rejected.

5. **Value Premise:** Cruel and inhumane punishments should be eliminated.

   Factual Premise:

   Conclusion: Capital punishment should be eliminated.

Sexuality

15

"THE JUSTIFICATION OF SEX WITHOUT LOVE"

Albert Ellis

EDUCATIONAL OBJECTIVES: After reading this chapter the student will be able to:

15.1 State Albert Ellis' position on nonaffectional sex.
15.2 Distinguish between affectional love as desirable and affectional love as necessary.
15.3 Explain how matters of conformity and hypocrisy become involved in arguments opposed to nonaffectional sex.
15.4 State four objections to Ellis' position.
15.5 Provide Ellis' criticisms of possible objections to his position.

FOCUS QUESTIONS

1. To what kind of "necessity" is Ellis making reference when he argues that affectional sex is desirable but not necessary.
2. What seems to be the moral and philosophical basis of Ellis' argument that nonaffectional sex is acceptable in many cases?

Albert Ellis, "The Justification of Sex without Love," in *Sex without Guilt* (New York: Lyle Stuart, 1958) pp. 66–75. Published by arrangement with Lyle Stuart.

3. Is Ellis guilty of committing the "is–ought" fallacy? Explain.

4. What response do you have to Ellis' claim that, "We had better accept our biosocial tendencies or our fallible humanity—instead of constantly blaming certain of its relatively harmless, though still somewhat tragic, aspects"?

5. Does Ellis adequately take into account the rights and feelings of those with whom one has nonaffectional sex? Do they matter? Does moral responsibility enter into the situation of nonaffectional sex? If so, how? If not, why not?

SYNOPSIS

Albert Ellis presents and defends the thesis that sexual relations based on love are desirable but not necessary. He admits that he prefers sex to be love-based or affectional, but he supports the position that nonaffectional sex (that is, sex without love) is also acceptable. In this article, Ellis offers seven arguments in support of his thesis; he considers several objections to his position and concludes by criticizing the objections.

Ellis' first supporting argument points out that many individuals actually do find pleasure in sexual relations without love. If, in the interests of fairness, we are to recognize the rights to sexual satisfaction of literally millions of people, then according to Ellis it would be wrong to label individuals engaging in nonaffectional sex as criminals. The rights of these individuals should be acknowledged and protected. Second, since people can find sex without love satisfying and since sometimes they can even prefer it to affectional sex, we should not condemn them. Third, Ellis argues that people, particularly females, are unthinkingly conformist and hypocritical in their rejection of nonaffectional sex. Ellis' fourth supporting argument is biological in nature. He argues that sex is a biological drive in part and that, as such, it is basically nonaffectional. Consequently, it is wrong to make those who experience sexual desire guilty. Fifth, the claim is made by Ellis that there are many people in society who have little or no capacity for love. Denying these unfortunate people sexual release would just add to their misery and this would not be good. Sixth, Ellis emphasizes that situations exist in which people find more satisfaction in nonloving coitus than in having sex within a love affair. One may enjoy sex with a love partner, but this does not preclude experiencing immense satisfaction in having nonloving sex with another. Finally, two people may get along well as sex partners in the same way that two individuals might get along well as business partners or scientific associates. Ellis does not see the necessity of involving love in this case.

After presenting his seven supporting arguments, Ellis summarizes his position by stating that we should accept our biosocial tendencies and stop blaming ourselves for drives and desires which are a normal expression of our humanness. If we insist that love is a prerequisite to acceptable sex, then we unnecessarily condemn millions of people to self-blame and atonement.

In the second part of his article, Ellis acknowledges and criticizes several objections to his position. The first objection is based on the notion that nonloving sex is self-defeating insofar as in the pursuit of immediate sexual gratification, one will miss out on even greater enjoyment. Although Ellis admits this could be true if sex were never loving, if it were sometimes loving and sometimes not, then he maintains that the individual having both affectional and nonaffectional love would miss very little, if anything.

Another objection to Ellis is based on the idea that if one sacrifices sex without love in the present, greater pleasure will be had with love-based sex later. Ellis criticizes this objection on a factual basis, pointing out that no empirical evidence exists to support this claim.

A third objection to Ellis' position stems from the belief that if nonaffectional and affectional sex are permitted, then nonaffectional sex will drive out affectional sex. Ellis criticizes this objection on the grounds that his clinical experience suggests the contrary. For example, males wishing to have stable, loving relationships are frequently those who have had multiple casual affairs.

Related to the last objection is the notion that sex without love is easier to find than sex with love. Consequently the first option would allegedly be preferred by most. Ellis shows no concern over this possibility. If the total happiness of individuals' lives is increased, what does it matter? Ellis refers to his clinical experience, citing again the fact that individuals capable of having sex with love usually seek and find it. Those who remain nonaffectional in sexual affairs typically need psychotherapeutic help before they can become capable of affectional affairs. One exception to this rule is the effectively functioning individual who is so dedicated to ideas or things (someone like Immanuel Kant) that he or she rarely, if ever, becomes lovingly involved with other people. Such dedicated individuals usually have normal sex drives, and Ellis concludes that it is entirely acceptable for them to have nonaffectional sex to conserve energy and time for nonamative (nonloving) pursuits.

A scientific colleague of mine, who holds a professorial post in the department of sociology and anthropology at one of our leading universities, recently asked me about my stand on the question of human beings having sex relations without love. Although I have taken something of a position on this issue in my book, *The American Sexual Tragedy*, I have never quite considered the problem in sufficient detail. So here goes.
[15.1, 15.2] In general, I feel that affectional, as against nonaffectional, sex relations are *desirable* but not *necessary*. It is usually desirable that an association between coitus and affection exist — particularly in marriage, because it is often dif-

ficult for two individuals to keep finely tuned to each other over a period of years, and if there is not a good deal of love between them, one may tend to feel sexually imposed upon by the other.

The fact, however, that the coexistence of sex and love may be desirable does not, to my mind, make it necessary. My reasons for this view are several:
[15.3] 1. Many individuals—including, even, many married couples—*do* find great satisfaction in having sex relations without love. I do not consider it fair to label these individuals as criminal just because they may be in the minority.

Moreover, even if they are in the minority (as may well *not* be the case), I am sure that they number literally millions of men and women. If so, they constitute a sizable subgroup of humans whose rights to sex satisfaction should be fully acknowledged and protected.

[15.3] 2. Even if we consider the supposed majority of individuals who find greater satisfaction in sex-love than in sex-sans-love relations, it is doubtful if all or most of them do so for *all* their lives. During much of their existence, especially their younger years, these people tend to find sex-without-love quite satisfying, and even to prefer it to affectional sex.

When they become older, and their sex drives tend to wane, they may well emphasize coitus with rather than without affection. But why should we condemn them *while* they still prefer sex to sex-love affairs?

[15.3, 15.4] 3. Many individuals, especially females in our culture, who say that they only enjoy sex when it is accompanied by affection are actually being unthinkingly conformist and unconsciously hypocritical. If they were able to contemplate themselves objectively, and had the courage of their inner convictions, they would find sex without love eminently gratifying.

This is not to say that they would *only* enjoy nonaffectional coitus, nor that they would always find it *more* satisfying than affectional sex. But, in the depths of their psyche and soma, they would deem sex without love pleasurable *too*.

And why should they not? And why should we, by our puritanical know-nothing-ness, force these individuals to drive a considerable portion of their sex feelings and potential satisfactions underground?

If, in other words, we view sexuoamative relations as desirable rather than necessary, we sanction the innermost thoughts and drives of many of our fellowmen and fellow-women to have sex *and* sex-love relations. If we take the opposing view, we hardly de-

stroy these innermost thoughts and drives, but frequently tend to intensify them while denying them open and honest outlet. This, as Freud (1924–50, 1938) pointed out, is one of the main (though by no means the only) source of rampant neurosis.

[15.3] 4. I firmly believe that sex is a biological, as well as a social, drive, and that in its biological phases it is essentially non-affectional. If this is so, then we can expect that, however we try to civilize the sex drives—and civilize them to *some* degree we certainly must—there will always be an underlying tendency for them to escape from our society-inculcated shackles and to be still partly felt in the raw.

When so felt, when our biosocial sex urges lead us to desire and enjoy sex without (as well as with) love, I do not see why we should make their experiencers feel needlessly guilty.

[15.3] 5. Many individuals—many millions in our society, I am afraid—have little or no capacity for affection or love. The majority of these individuals, perhaps, are emotionally disturbed, and should preferably be helped to increase their affectional propensities. But a large number are not particularly disturbed, and instead are neurologically or cerebrally deficient.

Mentally deficient persons, for example, as well as many dull normals (who, together, include several million citizens of our nation) are notoriously shallow in their feelings, and probably intrinsically so. Since these kinds of individuals—like the neurotic and the organically deficient—are for the most part, in our day and age, *not* going to be properly treated and *not* going to overcome their deficiencies, and since most of them definitely *do* have sex desires, I again see no point in making them guilty when they have nonloving sex relations.

Surely these unfortunate individuals are sufficiently handicapped by their disturbances or impairments without our adding to their woes by anathematizing them when they manage to achieve some nonamative sexual release.

[15.3] 6. Under some circumstances— though these, I admit, may be rare—some people find more satisfaction in nonloving coitus even though, under other circumstances, these *same* people may find more satisfaction in sex-love affairs. Thus, the man who *normally* enjoys being with his girlfriend because he loves as well as is sexually attracted to her, may occasionally find immense satisfaction in being with another girl with whom he has distinctly nonloving relations.

Granting that this may be (or is it?) unusual, I do not see why it should be condemnable.

[15.3] 7. If many people get along excellently and most cooperatively with business partners, employees, professors, laboratory associates, acquaintances, and even spouses for whom they have little or no love or affection, but with whom they have certain specific things in common, I do not see why there cannot be individuals who get along excellently and most cooperatively with sex mates with whom they may have little else in common.

I personally can easily see the tragic plight of a man who spends much time with a girl with whom he has nothing in common but sex: since I believe that life is too short to be well consumed in relatively one-track or intellectually low-level pursuits. I would also think it rather unrewarding for a girl to spend much time with a male with whom she had mutually satisfying sex, friendship, and cultural interests but no love involvement. This is because I would like to see people, in their 70-odd years of life, have maximum rather than minimum satisfactions with individuals of the other sex with whom they spend considerable time.

I can easily see, however, even the most intelligent and highly cultured individuals spending a *little* time with members of the other sex with whom they have common sex and cultural but no real love interests. And I feel that, for the time expended in this manner, their lives may be immeasurably enriched.

Moreover, when I encounter friends or psychotherapy clients who become enamored and spend considerable time and effort thinking about and being with a member of the other sex with whom they are largely sexually obsessed, and for whom they have little or no love, I mainly view these sexual infatuations as one of the penalties of their being human. For humans are the kind of animals who are easily disposed to this type of behavior (Grant, 1957).

I believe that one of the distinct inconveniences or tragedies of human sexuality is that it endows us, and perhaps particularly the males among us, with a propensity to become exceptionally involved and infatuated with members of the other sex whom, had we no sex urges, we would hardly notice. That is too bad; and it might well be a better world if it were otherwise. But it is *not* otherwise, and I think it is silly and pernicious for us to condemn ourselves because we are the way that we are in this respect.

We had better *accept* our biosocial tendencies, or our fallible humanity—instead of constantly blaming ourselves and futilely trying to change certain of its relatively harmless, though still somewhat tragic, aspects.

For reasons such as these, I feel that although it is usually—if not always—*desirable* for human beings to have sex relations with those they love rather than with those they do not love, it is by no means *necessary* that they do so. When we teach that it *is* necessary, we only needlessly condemn millions of our citizens to self-blame and atonement.

The position which I take—that there

are several good reasons why affectional, as against nonaffectional, sex relations are desirable but not necessary—can be assailed on several counts. I shall now consider some of the objections to this position to see if they cannot be effectively answered.

[15.5] It may be said that an individual who has nonloving instead of loving sex relations is not necessarily wicked but that he is self-defeating because, while going for immediate gratification, he will miss out on even greater enjoyments. But this would only be true if such an individual (whom we shall assume, for the sake of discussion, *would* get greater enjoyment from affectional sex relations than from nonaffectional ones) were *usually* or *always* having nonaffectionate coitus. If he were *occasionally* or *sometimes* having love with sex, and the rest of the time having sex without love, he would be missing out on very little, if any, enjoyment.

Under these circumstances, in fact, he would normally get *more* pleasure from *sometimes* having sex without love. For the fact remains,and must not be realistically ignored, that in our present-day society sex without love is *much more frequently* available than sex with love.

Consequently, to ignore nonaffectional coitus when affectional coitus is not available would, from the standpoint of enlightened self-interest, be sheer folly. In relation both to immediate *and* greater enjoyment, the individual would thereby be losing out.

[15.5] The claim can be made of course that if an individual sacrifices sex without love *now* he will experience more pleasure by having sex with love in the future. This is an interesting claim; but I find no empirical evidence to sustain it. In fact, on theoretical grounds it seems most unlikely that it will be sustained. It is akin to the claim that if an individual starves himself for several days in a row he will greatly enjoy eating a meal at the end of a week or a month. I am sure he will—provided that he is then not too sick or debilitated to enjoy anything! But, even assuming that such an individual derives enormous satisfaction from his one meal a week or a month, is his *total* satisfaction greater than it would have been had he enjoyed three good meals a day for that same period of time? I doubt it.

[15.5] It may be held that if both sex with and without love are permitted in any society, the nonaffectional sex will drive out affectional sex, somewhat in accordance with Gresham's laws of currency. On the contrary, however, there is much reason to believe that just because an individual has sex relations, for quite a period, on a nonaffectional basis, he will be more than eager to replace it, eventually, with sex with love.

From my clinical experience, I have often found that males who most want to settle down to having a single mistress or wife are those who have tried numerous lighter affairs and found them wanting. The view that sex without love eradicates the need for affectional sex relationships is somewhat akin to the ignorance is bliss theory. For it virtually says that if people never experienced sex with love they would never realize how good it was and therefore would never strive for it.

[15.5] Or else the proponents of this theory seem to be saying that sex without love is so greatly satisfying, and sex with love so intrinsically difficult and disadvantageous to attain, that given the choice between the two, most people would pick the former. If this is so, then by all means let them pick the former—with which, in terms of their greater and total happiness, they would presumably be better off.

I doubt, however, that this hypothesis *is* factually sustainable. From clinical experience, again, I can say that individuals who are capable of sex with love usually seek and find it; while those who remain nonaffec-tional in their sex affairs generally are not particularly capable of sex with love and need psychotherapeutic help before they can become thus capable.

Although, as a therapist, I frequently work with individuals who are only able to achieve nonaffectional sex affairs and, through helping them eliminate their irra-tional fears and blockings, make it possible for them to achieve sex-love relationships, I still would doubt that *all* persons who take no great pleasure in sex with love are emo-tionally deficient. Some quite effective indi-viduals—such as Immanuel Kant, for in-stance—seem to be so wholeheartedly dedicated to *things* or *ideas* that they rarely or never become amatively involved with people.

As long as such individuals have vital, creative interests and are intensely absorbed or involved with *something,* I would hesitate to diagnose them as being necessarily neu-rotic merely because they do not ordinarily become intensely absorbed with *people.* *Some* of these nonlovers of human beings are, of course, emotionally disturbed. But *all?* I wonder.

Disturbed or not, I see no reason why individuals who are dedicated to things or ideas should not have, in many or most in-stances, perfectly normal sex drives. And, if they do, I fail to see why they should not consummate their sex urges in nonaffec-tional ways in order to have more time and energy for their nonamative pursuits.

PROGRESS CHECK 15.1

Instructions: *Fill in the blanks with the appropriate responses listed below.*

affection
unthinkingly conformist
biosocial tendencies
clinical experience
nonaffectional sex

guilty
necessary
biological
ideas
sex-without-love

1. Albert Ellis believes that affectional sex relations are desirable, but not
   _____ .
2. Many individuals in society have no capacity for _____ .
3. Sex is a _____ drive.
4. People who claim that sex is enjoyable only when accompanied by affection are being _____ .
5. We should not feel _____ when our sex urges lead us to desire and enjoy coitus without love.
6. Rather than continually blaming ourselves and trying to change, we should accept our _____ .

7. According to Ellis, it is wrong to believe that _____, if permitted, will eventually drive out affectional sex.

8. _____ informs Ellis that those who desire stable loving relationships have frequently had lighter affairs and found them lacking in many important respects.

9. People dedicated to _____ have normal sex drives usually and should not be prevented from satisfying their biosocial needs.

10. Younger people often find _____ quite satisfying.

LEARNING EXERCISE 15.2   **Identifying Statements**

Instructions: *Albert Ellis considers a number of claims in supporting his position. Some of them are factual or empirical in nature, while others are value judgments or normative. Place an "F" next to the factual claims and "V" next to the value judgments.*

_____ 1. Affectional sex relations are desirable.

_____ 2. Many individuals find great satisfaction in having sexual relations without love.

_____ 3. The rights of those who engage in nonaffectional sex should be protected.

_____ 4. In their early years, people tend to find sex without love quite satisfying.

_____ 5. Women, who condemn nonaffectional sex, are hypocritical.

_____ 6. I firmly believe that sex is a biosocial drive.

_____ 7. We shouldn't make people feel guilty about having sex.

_____ 8. Many people in society have little or no capacity for affection or love.

_____ 9. Some people find more satisfaction in nonloving coitus than in loving coitus.

_____ 10. A relationship based on nothing else but sex is tragic.

_____ 11. When we teach that affectional love is necessary, we needlessly condemn millions of our citizens to self-blame and atonement.

_____ 12. Nonloving sex relations are wicked.

_____ 13. If an individual sacrifices sex without love now, he will experience more pleasure by having sex with love in the future.

_____ 14. People who become involved in multiple nonloving affairs find them wanting.

_____ 15. People who are dedicated to ideas should be allowed to consummate their sex urges in nonaffectional ways.

LEARNING EXERCISE 15.3   Completing Syllogisms

Instructions: Complete the following syllogisms.

1. **Value Premise:**   We should not accept activities which make people sexually imposed upon by others.

   Factual Premise:

   Conclusion: We should not accept nonaffectional sex.

2. **Value Premise:**

   Factual Premise: Nonaffectional sex produces great satisfaction in people's lives.

   Conclusion: Therefore, we should condone nonaffectional sex.

3. **Value Premise:**   Satisfying our natural, biological drives is good.

   Factual Premise: Nonaffectional sex satisfies our natural biological drives.

   Conclusion:

4. **Value Premise:**

   Factual Premise: Condemning nonaffectional sex makes people feel guilty about natural urges.

   Conclusion: Therefore, condemning nonaffectional sex is wrong.

5. **Value Premise:**   The rights of minority groups should be protected.

   Factual Premise: Those advocating sex without love constitute a minority group.

   Conclusion:

LEARNING EXERCISE 15.4   Testing Value Principles

Instructions: Test the principles below for their justifiability, looking for logical fallacies and using the role-exchange test, the higher-order principle test, the new-cases test, and the universalizability and consistency test.

1. Pleasure-producing activities are morally acceptable.
2. Biological drives should be satisfied.
3. Making people feel guilty is always wrong.
4. Using people for your own sexual satisfaction is wrong.
5. We should accept nonaffectional sex since a majority are in favor of it.

16

"CHRISTIAN SEXUAL ETHICS"

Lewis B. Smedes

EDUCATIONAL OBJECTIVES: After reading this chapter the student will be able to:

16.1 Outline four moral perspectives from which sexual intercourse outside of marriage can be evaluated.

16.2 State the risks of having sexual intercourse outside of marriage.

16.3 Explain why considerations of caution leave us with no clear-cut decisions about the morality of sexual intercourse.

16.4 Distinguish between moralities based on caution and those based on concern.

16.5 Elucidate how the "morality of personal relationships" separates itself from other moralities of caution and concern.

16.6 Explain how sexual interactions stemming from relationships of functional association differ from those based on mutual regard and respect.

16.7 Paraphrase Smedes' criticisms of alternative moralities to the morality of law.

16.8 Present the Christian, morality-of-law position on sexual intercourse.

Lewis B. Smedes, "Christian Sexual Ethics," in *Sex for Christians* (Grand Rapids: Eerdmans, 1978), 115–130. Used by permission.

SYNOPSIS

In his essay, Lewis Smedes addresses the issue of sexual morality. More specifically, he examines the acceptability of sexual intercourse outside of marriage from four moral perspectives: (1) the morality of caution, (2) the morality of concern, (3) the morality of personal relationships, and (4) the morality of law. Smedes explains in his work how different considerations become salient or more important when sexual intercourse is evaluated from each one of the four alternative viewpoints. For example, although the morality of caution instructs us to go ahead with intercourse only if we are reasonably sure we will not get hurt, the morality of concern draws attention to the risk of causing hurt to someone else. In the morality of personal relationships the primary focus is on how intercourse will affect the relationship between the involved parties. The emphasis of the morality of law is placed on the act of sexual intercourse itself. Finally, Smedes asks a fundamental question regarding Saint Paul's prohibition against sex outside of marriage: "What is there about sexual intercourse that makes it morally improper for unmarried people?"

After an appraisal and evaluation of the various moral perspectives, Smedes endorses the morality of law, which in effect reflects Christian New Testament morality on the matter of sexual intercourse. Smedes rejects the morality of caution because it leaves the moral agent without a clear-cut choice. The decision about whether or not to have sexual intercourse is reduced to some kind of imprecise cost-benefit analysis whereby the act under consideration is regarded as something as innocent as a gentle kiss. Smedes contends that sexual intercourse is an action which cannot be dealt with so lightly or in isolation from other important considerations involving other people. In this respect, the morality of concern goes one step further. Possible hurt to others (for example, friends, family, and community) counts against having sexual intercourse more heavily than possible hurt to oneself, calculated in relation to the amount of pleasure produced. According to Smedes, despite its preoccupation with others, the morality of concern regards sexual intercourse as morally neutral. Questions about its rightness or wrongness can be answered only in relation to its consequences. The morality of intercourse is therefore circumstantial. Sexual intercourse is neither right nor wrong in itself. If the risks of harmful consequences for others are small enough, unmarried people are at liberty to go ahead with the act.

In contrast to the moralities of caution and concern, the morality of personal relationships draws attention away from external circumstances and risk-benefit analyses and toward the emotional and psychological bond of the individuals involved. The question is whether or not intercourse will strengthen the relationship between persons. Acceptable sex can only be had in a relationship of mutual respect where the parties regard each other as human beings worthy of respect, not objects to be used for physical delight. Smedes questions the morality of personal relationships, asking how two unmarried people can know ahead of time whether or not intercourse will enrich and strengthen their relationship. Trying it to find out robs the act of sexual intercourse of its moral significance. The decision whether to engage in sex must be made in this case based on very uncertain personal insights and intuitions. The ground for moral decision making on this matter becomes very shaky.

Smedes argues that the three moralities discussed above either trivialize the morality of sexual intercourse or else they make decision making contingent on questionable factors such as circumstances and personal insights. No clear-cut decisions about the morality of sexual intercourse can therefore be based on such factors. By contrast, Smedes believes the morality of law provides a concrete and solid basis for evaluating the morality of sexual intercourse. The morality of law assumes that sexual intercourse has a built-in factor that disqualifies it for unmarried people. This morality leads to the conclusion that even if nobody gets hurt by it and even if personal relationships could be enriched by it, sexual intercourse is wrong for everybody except married people. The act of sexual intercourse must be evaluated in a context of who people really are, how they are expected to fulfill their lives in sexual love, and how they are to live in a community of persons extending beyond private personal relationships. Smedes underscores the fact that men and women were created by God to live out their closest personal relationship in a permanent, exclusive union. The Christian morality of law sees sexual intercourse as an act which involves two people in a life-union. This union is total and unbreakable. Thus, Smedes argues that, "There is no such thing as casual sex, no matter how casual people are about it." In the case of sex outside marriage, unmarried people engage in a life-uniting act without life-uniting intent. According to the Christian view, when two individuals have sex without a commitment to life-union, they commit sin. The wrongdoing goes beyond practical considerations, concern for people, or the desire to promote personal relationships. The wrongness of sexual intercourse outside marriage is rooted in its contradiction of reality.

[16.1] 1. THE MORALITY OF CAUTION

Any reasonable single person trying to make a rational decision about his sexual activity will "count the cost." The first thing they may ask is: "Am I likely to get hurt?" Sexual intercourse has some risk along with certain possible rewards for unmarried people, and the cautious person will weigh the risks. The question of "getting hurt" has two parts: (1) how seriously can I get hurt, and (2) how great is the risk of getting hurt? If the odds are not good and the possible hurt pretty serious, the cautious person may decide to wait until marriage, when the risk will be mostly eliminated.

[16.2] The hurts that sexual intercourse could cause unmarried people are obvious enough. Getting pregnant, even in a permissive society, is a painful experience for an unmarried woman. Once pregnant, she has no way of escaping a painful decision: she can abort the fetus, she can give the baby up for adoption, or she can rear the child herself. Or, of course, she can get married — but this may not be an option for her. The route of abortion has been paved by liberalized laws. But no matter how easy it may be to get, and no matter what her intellectual view of abortion may be, she is likely to find out afterwards that it is a devastating experience for herself, especially if she is sensitive to the value of human life. Adoption is another route. Every child given up for adoption may be God's gift to some adoptive parents. This is a compensation. But giving up children nourished to birth inside their own bodies is something few young women can do without deep pain. Keeping the baby and rearing it may be easier than it used to be. Many communities no longer lash the unwed mother with their silent judgment: this may be only be-

cause the community does not care, but it still makes life easier for the mother. But rearing the baby alone is still heavy with problems for the unmarried mother in the most tolerant society. Some may have a chance at marriage; but marriage forced on two people is an invitation to pain. In short, pregnancy can cause considerable hurt.

While pregnancy still hurts, the risk of it is not threatening to many unmarried people. However, any notion that the risk has been eliminated is careless thinking. The contraceptive pill has cut the chances, but it has not removed the possibility. Unwanted children, both in marriage and out of it, testify that no birth control device known up to this point is fail-proof. And, of course, there is the risk of that accidental time when precautions were neglected. As a matter of fact, the majority of young people having intercourse for the first time do not use any preventive means at all. Many young women refuse to take precautions because they do not want to think of themselves as planning for intercourse; it must happen only as they are swept into it in a romantic frenzy. Still, all things considered, the risk of pregnancy may have become small enough so that the cautious person may decide it is worth taking.

The threat of disease is a real one, especially for the promiscuous person. Antibiotics, once heralded as a sure cure, have stimulated virus strains more potent than ever. And venereal disease is currently in a virtual epidemic stage. Still, for prudent and selective people the odds seem comfortably against infection.

The risk of threatening an eventual marriage by premarital sex is hard to calculate. A deeply disappointing sexual experience before marriage could, one supposes, condition a person against happy sex in marriage. But, of course, unmarried people considering intercourse do not plan on having a bad experience. Guilt feelings about a premarital experience can inhibit one's freedom of self-giving in marriage sex: for example, a woman's inability to experience orgasm in marriage is sometimes traceable to guilt about premarital sex. And promiscuity before marriage could possibly make extramarital sex easier to fall into should marriage sex be unrewarding. But all these threats depend too much on how individual people feel; they are not useful as blanket judgments. The question of threat to marriage has to be answered in terms of the individuals involved.

[16.7] Jane, who believes religiously that sexual intercourse before marriage is a sin, runs a fairly strong chance of making marriage harder for herself by premarital intercourse, especially if she has sex with someone besides the man she marries. But Joan, who was reared in a moral no man's land, may not risk marriage happiness at all by having premarital sex, though she may risk it for much deeper reasons. All in all, the argument that sexual intercourse by unmarried people threatens their future marriage is a flimsy one; too much depends on the moral attitudes of the persons involved. This implies, of course, that one does not have to be one hundred percent moral to have a happy marriage, though it may help.

[16.3] The morality of caution leaves us with no clear-cut decision. Christian morality cannot support a blanket veto of sexual intercourse for unmarried people on this basis. It all depends on how the risks are calculated in each person's situation. The morality of caution will lead prudent people to ask with whom, why, and when they are having intercourse. But it is not enough to tell them that they ought not do it. Following the morality of caution alone, sexual morality comes down to this: if you are reasonably sure you won't get hurt, go ahead.

The point to notice is that the morality of caution is concerned only with possible hurt to the person involved. It does not bother with questions about the kind of act sexual intercourse is; it does not ask whether unmarried people are morally qualified for it on the basis of either their relationship or the nature of the act. I do not suppose that many people, in their best moments, will decide on the basis of caution alone. But wherever it is snipped away from the other considerations, it works on the assumption that sexual intercourse as such has no more *moral* significance than a gentle kiss.

[16.1, 16.4] 2. THE MORALITY OF CONCERN

Here we move beyond caution to a personal concern about the risk of causing hurt to others. The morality of caution asks: am I likely to get hurt? The morality of concern asks: am I likely to hurt someone else? The calculations of both moralities are roughly the same. The difference is that here concern is directed toward the other person. The crucial questions here will be how far one's concern reaches and how sensitive one is to the kinds of hurt he could cause. It may be that the concerned person will interpret the risks differently than the merely cautious person will.

For instance, a girl may be willing to take the risk of pregnancy as far as she is concerned. But if she considers the hurt that pregnancy may involve for the unwanted child, she may weigh the odds quite differently: the risk of pregnancy will be the same, but the possible hurt to others may count against having intercourse more heavily than if its pleasure is matched only against possible hurt to herself. If she gets pregnant, the girl may decide to abort or give the child up for adoption. The fetus has no choice. Here she is dealing with a potential person's right to exist. If she gives the child up for adoption, she is determining that the child will not be reared by its natural parents. And if she decides to keep the child, she may be forcing a situation of permanent disadvantage on another human being. This may sound as though only the woman is making the decision; but the same considerations must go into the thinking of her partner. By his act he may be risking severe disadvantages for another human being—or at least a potential human being—and giving that human being no choice in the matter. The unmarried couple may be able to opt for the risk; but the unwanted offspring is not given a chance to weigh the odds.

But again, the risk may seem small enough to take for the sophisticated person. And for some couples there is always a back-up emergency plan—marriage. But here again the element of concern is brought in: are the people involved reasonably sure that they won't hurt each other by getting married? The person with concern will ask the question and seek advice in answering it: but only he or she can give the answer for himself.

No person who makes decisions out of concern for others will run much risk of infecting another person with venereal disease. And a person who is truly concerned will be least likely to be a threat: he would not likely be a person who goes in for casual bed-hopping. The risk is not great for two people who are serious about sexual intercourse as an expression of deeply involved affection because the probability of promiscuity is not great. At any rate, the morality of concern would tell a person to be very careful, but it would probably not tell him to abstain from sexual intercourse entirely.

Personal concern looks a lot deeper than the risk of getting someone pregnant or spreading a disease. A concerned person will wonder how sexual intercourse will affect his partner as a whole person, because each person's sexual experiences are a major theme in the symphony he is creating with his life. No one can take sex out at night and put it away until he wants to play with it again. What we do with sex shapes what we are; it is woven into the plot of a drama we are writing about ourselves. The person with whom we have sexual relations cannot let his sexual passions dance on stage, take a curtain call, and go back to some backstage corner to let the rest of the play go on. So a concerned person will ask how a sexual experience can fit into the total life—the whole future—of that other person. Where will it fit in his memories? How will it be digested in his conscience? What will it do to his attitude toward himself? How will it help create the symphony that he can make of his life? The morality of concern reaches out into the tender tissues of the other person's whole life; and it refuses to endorse any act that will stunt that person's movement into a creative, self-esteeming, and freely conscious life.

However, it also goes beyond the other person. It asks about the people around them—their friends, their families, and their community. A single, discreet, and very secret affair may not bring down the moral walls of Jericho. But a Christian person of concern will think beyond his own affair: he must universalize his action and ask what the effects would be if unmarried people generally followed his example.

Much depends, naturally, on the kind of sex he is thinking about. If he is thinking about casual sex, on the assumption that all two people need for good sex is to like each other, we have one set of problems. If he is thinking about sleeping only with the person he is planning to marry, we have another. If he is thinking of casual sex, he will have to ask about the burdens on society created by a considerable number of unwanted children, a formidable increase in venereal disease, and a general devaluation of sexual intercourse as an expression of committed love. But if he is thinking only of sex between two responsible people who are profoundly in love—though not legally married—the question is limited to what the effect on public morals would be if everyone in *his* position felt free to have sexual intercourse. He might respond by saying that if it *were* moral from him, it would be moral for others. Thus public morality would not be damaged if everyone did it; habits and customs might change, and moral *opinions* would change, but morality itself would be unscathed. And he would be right—on this basis.

[16.7] Concern for the other person and his community sets the question within the perimeter of Christian love. It comes within the single blanket law that all of our decisions are to be made in responsible love. In the terms of this morality, sexual intercourse is morally neutral, and the question of its rightness or wrongness is answered only in relation to its consequences for other people. If the risk of harmful consequences is small enough, single people are free to go ahead. The morality of concern forces people to judge according to circumstances; for example, the answer to the question whether two mature retirees should refrain from sexual intercourse may be very different from that concerning two youngsters on a sexual high. Acting only out of loving concern, one puts aside the possibility that there may be something special about sexual intercourse that disqualifies everyone but married persons. It demands only that each person weigh the risks carefully and then make a responsible decision for his particular case.

3. THE MORALITY OF PERSONAL RELATIONSHIPS

[16.1, 16.5] Two things set off the morality of personal relationships from the first two: first, its focus is on how intercourse will affect the *relationship* between the two persons; second, its concern is more positive. The clinching question is whether sexual intercourse will strengthen and deepen the relationship. If it can be a creative factor in the relationship, it is good—provided, of course, neither person gets hurt individually. Behind this way of deciding the right and wrong of intercourse lies a whole new understanding of human beings as persons-in-relationship. The view is that the individual comes into his own in relationship: the "I" is a truly human "I" only as it exists in an "I-You" relationship. The tender spot in human morality, then, is always at the point of personal contact with another. And this is why the effect sexual intercourse has on the relationship is the pivotal question.

[16.6] The relationship can be creatively supported only when two people have regard for each other as ends to be served rather than as means to be used. When two people use each other in sexual intercourse, they hurt the relationship and corrupt the sexual act. They twist the relationship into a functional association. One has a functional relationship with a person whenever he concentrates on getting a service from him. What one wants from a plumber is to have his leaky faucet fixed, what he wants from a dentist is to have his toothache cured; what one may want from a sexual partner is to have his ego served or his sex drive satiated. In these cases one is after a functional association. But what someone wants in a personal relationship is to let the other person thrive as a person, to give him the regard and respect he merits as a friend, and to be privileged to grow into a relationship in which they will both desire no more from each other than mutual concern and enjoyment. In short, he wants the other person to be something along *with* him rather than merely to do something *for* him.

Now in most cases, two people in love treat each other in both functional and personal ways. There is constant tension between expecting one's friend to deliver the pleasures of friendship and respecting him only for what he is. In sexual love, the functional side often *tends* to shove the personal side into the background. The sex drive is so intense that it becomes a temptation to manipulate and even exploit the other person. To the extent that the functional is predominant in our sex lives, we treat the other person as a means and thus dehumanize him. When this happens sexual intercourse is immoral, not because it is sexual intercourse between two unmarried people but because it distorts and destroys a personal relationship.

Sexual intercourse can deepen and enrich a personal relationship only when it takes place within the reality of a personal relationship. This means that the preliminary questions two unmarried people must ask each other are: Do we already have a genuinely personal relationship that can be deepened and enriched? Do we have deep personal regard for each other? Do we treat each other now in integrity? Do we say no to any temptation to use each other? Did we accept each other as friends before sexual intercourse entered our heads? The possibility that sexual intercourse might be good for them travels with the answers to these preliminary considerations. Then they have to ask the clinching question: will sexual intercourse deepen and enrich or will it threaten and distort our relationship?

[16.7] But how can they possibly know what it will do? First of all, each person has to examine himself. He or she will have to probe his/her own feelings and ask personal questions about them: Is he being exploitative? Is he pressing the other person to do something he/she may not want to do? Is he minimizing the other person's freedom and dignity? But these questions are about negative factors that could hurt the relationship. How does he know that sexual intercourse will actually strengthen the relationship? This exposes the Achilles' heel of the morality of personal relationships.

Furthermore, how can this standard be applied? How can two unmarried people know ahead of time whether sexual intercourse will enrich their relationship? They could probably try it and find out. But that would summarily throw the moral question out of court. And perhaps this is the only way out for the morality of personal relationships. At best, the decision has to be made on very uncertain personal insights: the people involved can only guess beforehand what will happen to their relationship after they have got out of bed. They can probe their readiness with all honesty and still not know for sure how they will feel toward each other afterward.

If we were talking about two people's date for dinner or a concert, almost any risk might be worth taking. But sexual intercourse opens trap doors to the inner cells of our conscience, and legions of little angels (or demons) can fly out to haunt us. There is such abandon, such explosive self-giving, such personal exposure that few people can feel the same toward each other afterward. And if one thinks he is ready, he cannot be sure the other person is. The problem is not just that one of the two will feel sour toward the other; the problem is that one of the partners may unleash feelings of need for the other that he/she had no inkling existed. He/she may thus be catapulted into a commitment that the other is not ready to take. And so the relationship can be injured by one person's making demands on it that the other is not ready for. And the person who is least committed is likely to withdraw inwardly from a relationship that demands more than he can give.

If we could somehow segregate people according to maturity, and if only people over fifty used the morality of personal relationships, we might have a workable standard. If in addition to this, the decision were made with moral assistance from a community of friends and family, it might be a usable norm. And if the decision were made in the cool of the day, it would at least be manageable. But unmarried people moving toward sexual intercourse include many people whose experience in durable and creative relationships is almost nil. A decision concerning sex is often made alone in the passions of the night, when every untested lust may seem like the promptings of pure love. Perhaps there is a moral elite who could responsibly use a moral guideline with as many loose ends as this one; but there is no way of knowing for sure who they are.

So we are back where we started. Each of the three moralities for sexual intercourse focuses on factors outside of the act itself. None of them assumes that sexual intercourse has a built-in factor that in itself would disqualify unmarried people for it. But Christian morality has traditionally believed that there is such a factor. For it has maintained that, even if nobody gets hurt and even if a personal relationship could be enriched by it, it is wrong for all but married people. It has taught that there is more to sexual intercourse than meets the eye — or excites the genitals. Sexual intercourse takes place within a context of what persons really are, how they are expected to fulfill

their lives in sexual love, and how they are to live together in a community that is bigger than their private relationships. We now go on to ask about this special ingredient of sexual intercourse, for it stands behind the traditional Christian negative to unmarried people.

[16.1] 4. THE MORALITY OF LAW

New Testament morality on this point is a morality of law. Some things were morally indifferent; Paul insisted on this. For some things there was no law except the law of love; and love flourished in freedom. But when people, as in Corinth, applied Christian freedom to sex, Paul put up fences. One of the fences was marriage. He made no distinctions between casual sex, sex between engaged couples, or sex between mature widowed people. The no was unqualified. The question is: Why?

Before getting into Paul's sexual morality, we must concede that the Old Testament gives him shaky support. Female virginity had a high premium; but male virginity was not all that important. And female virginity was demanded not so much for virginity's sake as for social reasons: the family line had to be guarded at all costs. And the male in particular had a right to be absolutely certain that his children were his own. The society had no place in it for the unmarried woman, no place except the brothel. So the rules said that if a woman had sexual intercourse before marriage, then tried to fake virginity with her bridegroom and was exposed by failure to produce a bloodied sheet, she would be executed forthwith (Deut. 22:13–21). However, this was probably not likely to happen. If a man slept with a virgin who was not betrothed, he was obligated to pay a dowry to her father and marry her (Deut. 22:28, 29). And the prospects for an unmarried girl who had lost her virginity were so bad that no woman was likely to keep quiet about the affair. She would at least tell her father, who, threatened with loss of dowry, would put the fear of God into a reneging sex partner. A man was in real trouble, however, if he slept with a virgin betrothed to another man; he was in trouble with her fiancé and with her father, for it was especially their rights that he had abused. He would be stoned to death; and if their act was discovered in the city, the woman would also be stoned—on the assumption that she failed to cry for help (Deut. 22:23–27). But if a man slept with a prostitute, nothing was said because nothing was lost. Casual sex between young people, however, was probably nonexistent. Once a boy slept with a girl, he was expected to marry her; and the girl was not likely to be noble about it and let him off the hook.

The Old Testament as a whole did not read the seventh commandment as a no to sexual intercourse between unmarried people. The morality of sexual intercourse did not rest with the character of the act as much as with its possible consequences. What was wrong was for a man's rights to be violated. Unmarried sex violated the command against stealing as clearly as it did the command against adultery.

The New Testament looks at the question from a very different standpoint. It has a blanket word for sexual immorality: *porneia*, translated as fornication in the older versions and as immorality in the newer. Fornication includes more than sexual intercourse between people who are not married. It does refer to breaking one's oath of fidelity to a husband or wife (Matt. 5:32; 19:9); but it could include a lot of other practices, like homosexual relations. And Paul makes clear that it also means sexual

intercourse for unmarried people. In I Cor. 7 he concedes that to be both unmarried and a virgin is, under the circumstances, the best life. But "because of the temptation to immorality, each man should have his own wife and each woman her own husband" (I Cor. 7:2). Better to marry, he said, than to be ravished with unfulfilled desires. So he must have meant that "immorality" included sexual intercourse outside marriage. And if unmarried sexual intercourse was wrong, it was a serious wrong; it ought not even be talked about (Eph. 5:3). God's will is that we abstain from fornication, not giving way to "the passion of lust like heathen who do not know God" (I Thess. 4:6). Fornication is sin; intercourse by unmarried people is fornication; therefore, intercourse by unmarried people is sin.

[16.8] We must now ask the crucial question about Paul's blanket rule. What is there about sexual intercourse that makes it morally improper for unmarried people? Surely not every instance of coitus by unmarried people is simply a surrender to lust "like the heathen." And if it is not in lust, and it hurts no one, why is it wrong? Did Paul assume that it would always be in lust or would always be harmful? And if some unmarried people's sex was not lustful, would it then be morally proper? Divine law, though often expressed in negative rules, is rooted in a positive insight. The law against adultery, for example, reflects a positive view of marriage and fidelity. And this view of marriage rests on an insight that God created men and women to live out their closest personal relationship in a permanent, exclusive union. We may suppose that behind Paul's vigorous attack on fornication is a positive view of sexual intercourse.

Sexual intercourse involves two people in a life-union; it is a life-uniting act. This is the insight that explains Paul's fervent comment on a member of Christ's body sleeping with a prostitute (I Cor. 6:12–20): "Do you not know that he who joins himself to a prostitute *becomes one body* with her?" (v. 16—italics mine). Of course, Paul is horrified that a prostitute is involved: a Christian man is a moral clown in a brothel. But the character of the woman involved is not his basic point. Paul would just as likely have said: "Do you not know that he who joins himself to the prim housewife next door becomes one body with her?" And the incongruity would have been the same. Paul bases his remark on the statement in Genesis 2 that "the two shall become one." And he sees sexual intercourse as an act that signifies and seeks the intrinsic unity—the unbreakable, total, personal unity that we call marriage.

It does not matter what the two people have in mind. The whore sells her body with an unwritten understanding that nothing personal will be involved in the deal. She sells the service of a quick genital massage—nothing more. The buyer gets his sexual needs satisfied without having anything personally difficult to deal with afterward. He pays his dues, and they are done with each other. But none of this affects Paul's point. The *reality* of the act, unfelt and unnoticed by them, is this: it unites them- —body and soul—to each other. It unites them in that strange, impossible to pinpoint sense of "one flesh." There is no such thing as casual sex, no matter how casual people are about it. The Christian assaults reality in

his night out at the brothel. He uses a woman and puts her back in a closet where she can be forgotten; but the reality is that he has put away a person with whom he has done something that was meant to inseparably join them. This is what is at stake for Paul in the question of sexual intercourse between unmarried people.

And now we can see clearly why Paul thought sexual intercourse by unmarried people was wrong. It is wrong because it violates the inner reality of the act; it is wrong because unmarried people thereby engage in a life-uniting act without a life-uniting intent. Whenever two people copulate without a commitment to life-union, they commit fornication.

Thus Paul's reason for saying no to sexual intercourse for the unmarried goes a crucial step beyond all the common practical reasons. We can suppose that Paul would appreciate anyone's reluctance to risk getting hurt; we can be sure he would see a Christian impulse in a person's concern for the other person; and we may assume that he would endorse the notion that sexual intercourse ought to promote the personal relationship between the two partners. But his absolute no to sexual intercourse for unmarried people is rooted in his conviction that it is a contradiction of reality. Intercourse signs and seals—and maybe even delivers—a life-union; and life-union means marriage.

PROGRESS CHECK 16.1

Instructions: Fill in the blanks with the appropriate responses listed below.

the morality of concern	New Testament
the morality of caution	morally neutral
the morality of law	ends
the morality of personal relationships	functional association
casual sex	life-uniting

1. _____ involves a type of cost-benefit analysis of hurt with respect to oneself.

2. _____ considers sexual intercourse outside of marriage as contrary to nature or reality.

3. _____ differs from the morality of caution insofar as attention is directed toward the hurt likely to be caused to the other person.

4. _____ underscores the importance of establishing and maintaining an emotional bond between sex partners.

5. The morality of law is most closely related to the moral views expressed in the _____ .

6. According to Smedes, there is no such thing as _____, only people who engage in intercourse lightly.

7. Smedes argues that if the acceptability of sexual intercourse is made contingent on circumstances and consequences, then intercourse outside of marriage becomes _____.

8. The morality of personal relationships dictates that other people should be regarded as _____ to be served, not as means to be used.

9. In situations where people mutually and openly use each other in sexual intercourse (e.g., prostitution), their relationship is transformed into a _____ .

10. From the perspective of Christian morality of law, intercourse is a _____ act.

LEARNING EXERCISE 16.2

Instructions: *Complete the following syllogisms which are derived from arguments and ideas found in Smedes' article.*

1. **Value Premise:** People should not engage in activities which will cause personal hurt.

   Factual Premise:

   Conclusion: Therefore, people should not engage in sexual intercourse outside of marriage.

2. **Value Premise:**

   Factual Premise: Sexual intercourse outside marriage is an action which hurts others.

   Conclusion: Therefore, sexual intercourse outside of marriage is wrong.

3. **Value Premise:** Strengthening and deepening relationships is good.

Factual Premise: Sexual intercourse strengthens and deepens relationships.

Conclusion:

4. **Value Premise:**

   Factual Premise: Sexual intercourse outside marriage is acting in a way which violates God's plan.

   Conclusion: Therefore, sexual intercourse outside marriage is wrong.

5. **Value Premise:**   Life-uniting acts performed without life-uniting intent are wrong.

   Factual Premise:

   Conclusion: Therefore, sex with a prostitute is wrong.

LEARNING EXERCISE 16.3

Instructions: *Evaluate the following rules and principles. Look for logical fallacies and for failures to pass the tests of new cases, the higher-order principle, role-exchange, and universalizability and consistency.*

1. As long as I personally do not get hurt, then sexual intercourse is perfectly acceptable.
2. We should not satisfy our sexual appetites at the expense of others.
3. Sexual intercourse outside of marriage is wrong since the Bible says so.
4. Actions which hurt nobody are morally acceptable.
5. Doing what is natural is always right.

17

"PROFITS AND LIBERTY"

John Hospers

EDUCATIONAL OBJECTIVES: After completing this chapter the student will be able to:

17.1 State Hospers' position on the justifiability of profits in a capitalistic free-market economy.

17.2 Explain what from Hospers' perspective are the disadvantages of a state-controlled economy.

17.3 List the advantages of a profit-based, free-market economy.

17.4 Give Hospers' rationale for why millionaires and capitalistic entrepreneurs are not despicable "armed bandits."

17.5 Explain the conception of wealth which leads some individuals to despise rich and successful businesspeople.

FOCUS QUESTIONS

1. What constitutes a just wage? On what basis can it be said that someone (e.g., an entrepreneur) has earned too much?

From John Hospers, *Libertarianism*. Reprinted by permission of the author. First publication was by Nash Publishing Co., Los Angeles, 1971.

2. Are the products which consumers want always worth producing solely because of profit potential? Justify your answer.
3. Hospers explains how profits can benefit consumers and employees. Can the pursuit of profit harm them in any way? Elaborate.
4. Should the financial security of workers in this society rest solely on the employer's ability to earn a profit? Do employers have any responsibilities toward their workers? If so, what are they? If not, why not?
5. Is Hospers guilty of committing any fallacies in his position paper? If so, explain.
6. In a free economy, do some individuals gain an unfair advantage? If so, then how should their profits be viewed and dealt with?

SYNOPSIS

In this article, John Hospers defends profits and profit making in a capitalistic free-market economy. He begins by enumerating the advantages which profits and their allure bring to the marketplace. Hospers contends that profits and the prospect of increased wealth benefit not only the entrepreneur, but the consumer and worker as well. The consumer benefits in a competitive market where there is pressure to produce the best products at the lowest possible prices. In such a situation, the most efficient competitors will survive ensuring a healthy industry. A healthy industry, in turn, benefits the workers who take advantage of the creation of new jobs and the enhanced security of existing ones. Furthermore, enterprising individuals have their creativity, risk taking, hard work, and service to society rewarded. Given that profit-driven entrepreneurs translate their economic gains into such things as further plant expansions and research, one can say that society as a whole benefits by their efforts.

Hospers considers criticisms of profit to be groundless and absurd. He suggests that those criticizing profitmakers are ignorant of how a free economy works and that, to a large extent, their objections stem from envy and bitterness resulting from things like their own business failures and personal job losses. Hospers draws our attention to one objection directed at profitmaking, the notion that, "No one should have caviar until everyone has bread." This idea in essence holds that all people should have their basic needs met before we can allow individuals the luxuries made possible by large profits. Hospers refutes this objection by turning the logic upside down. He claims that if incentive of profit were removed then we probably would be worse off, not better off. He believes that "if no one were permitted to have caviar, finally not many people would have bread."

A second objection to profits rests on the notion that, "the riches of the rich are the cause of the poverty of the poor." Hospers rejects this objection because it is based on the allegedly false premise that there exists in society a certain "fixed" amount of wealth which can be divided and shared in a variety of ways. If this premise were true, then it would hold true that if some had more wealth then others would necessarily have less. Hospers, however, contends that wealth is not a fixed sum, or a static state. It grows and can continue to increase with ingenuity and hard work. The capitalist entrepreneur is not a bandit, according to Hospers. Such an individual does not steal from the poor or less well-off in order to obtain more and become rich. Products presented for sale in the marketplace are freely purchased without any coercion of the consumer. One can refuse to contribute to the wealth of an enterprising producer quite simply by choosing not to buy that producer's goods. Rather than seeing capitalistic entrepreneurs as armed bandits or avaricious individuals who prey on the less fortunate by taking so that others will have less, we should, according to Hospers, regard businesspeople as important and desirable contributors to society. Hospers believes their quest for profits benefits us all.

"He's earning too much—take it away from him!" "A hundred thousand a year while some people in the world are hungry? Nobody ought to be allowed to earn that much!" Such remarks are made, and they have a "humanitarian" sound. Yet, as I shall try to show, they result from ignorance of the function of profits in an economy: and to the extent that the suggestion is followed, the result is poverty for everyone.

[17.1, 17.2] In a free economy—one in which wages, costs, and prices are left to the competitive market—profits have a very important function: they help to decide what products shall be made, of what kinds, and in what amounts. It is the hope of profits that leads people to make the products (or provide the services): if little or nothing can be made from producing them, or not enough to justify the risk of investing the capital, the product will not be made; but the more one hopes to make from it, the more people will bend over backwards to produce it. The hope of profits channels the factors of production, causing products to be made in whatever quantities the public demands. In a state-controlled economy, controlled by bureaucrats, nothing at all may be made of a certain product much in demand, because the ruling decision-makers have decided simply not to make it;

and at the same time, millions of other things that nobody wants may be produced, again because of a bureaucratic decision. And the bureaucracy need not to respond to public demand. But in a free-enterprise economy, the producer who does not respond to public demand will soon find his warehouse full of unsalable products and his business bankrupt.

[17.1, 17.3] The hope of profits also makes for an enormous increase in the efficiency of production, for, other things being equal, the most efficient producer—the one who can cut out waste and motivate his workers to produce the most and best products —will earn the highest profits. And is there any reason why these profits should not be applauded? To the consumer, these profits mean that the industry producing the goods he wants is healthy and nicely functioning—one that can continue to deliver the goods, and probably for at least as low a price as its competitor, since otherwise more customers would have turned to the competitor. To the workers, profits of their employer mean that the employer is doing a good job for his customers—good enough so that they keep buying his product—and thus that they, the employees, are more secure in their jobs, and are more likely to receive higher wages in the future than are the employees of a company that is just barely making it. And as for the enterprisers, who can honestly say that they do not deserve the profits they received? First, they are risk-takers: they risked their capital to start the business, and had they lost no one would have helped them. Second, they spent not only their money (and borrowed money) on the enterprise, but, in most cases, years of their lives, involving planning, down to the last detail of production, the solution of intractable problems having to do with materials, supplies, and availability of trained help. Third, they anticipated the market, and did so more expertly than their competitors, for in order to make profits they had to have the right amount of merchandise at the right places for sale at the right time. Fourth, they provided the consumer a product or service (they could not *force* the consumer to buy from them; the consumer voluntarily elected to buy), in quantity—for a price, of course (after all his time and effort, should the enterpriser give it away, or sell it without receiving a return on it?), but nevertheless they provided it at a price which the consumer was willing to pay.

But the public, or a large segment of it, becomes envious and bitter, seeing that the man makes a profit. Perhaps the envious man has tried to start a business himself and lost it; or perhaps he just lost his job or can't pay some of his bills, and sees the employer living in a large luxurious house, in any case, he doesn't understand what side his bread is buttered on, for he doesn't realize that if the employer couldn't keep going, he himself would have no job. For whatever reason, he curses the employer because the man has a larger annual income than he does. Never mind that the employer took the risks, made the innumerable decisions (any one of which could have wrecked the business), and made *his* job possible in the first place:

he, the employer, must be brought down to the worker's level. So he curses him, envies him, and votes for higher taxes for his employer, which, if passed, will mean that the employer won't expand his business and hire extra employees, and in fact may even have to cut it down some, even including his (the worker's) job. Officially, his line is that the employer's profits are ill-got. And yet when one examines it carefully the complaint is groundless and absurd.

[17.3] Suppose that an enterprise can make a thousand dollars in profits by a certain amount of capital investment; let us call this amount of investment C. Suppose also there is a second enterprise, less efficiently run than the first, which can only make that same amount of profit by investing twice the capital—2C. People will then say that the first, the efficient, manager, is reaping an excessive profit. For on the same investment of capital he can make twice the profits as his sloppy competitor; and for this his profits are branded as "excessive." But this is absurd: the efficient producer who gets more profits has more money to convert into plant expansion, more reserve for research so that he can improve his product, more wherewithal to reduce consumer prices and still make a healthy profit, thus benefiting the consumer with lower costs. The consumer ought to be anxious to have the most efficient producer possible; for only in that way can he be sure of getting the best possible product at the lowest possible price. By producing efficiently, the producer can undercut his competitors and thus benefit the consumer, while at the same time earning larger profits by capturing a larger share of the market for himself. We should applaud, not condemn, efficient production.

Add to this the fact that our present insane tax laws penalize the producer for his profits, and thus penalize efficiency.

"Taxing profits is tantamount to taxing success in best serving the public. . . . The smaller the input (of money) required for the production of an article becomes, the more of the scarce factors of production is left for the production of other articles. But the better an entrepreneur succeeds in this regard, the more he is vilified, and the more he is soaked by taxation. Increasing costs per unit of output, that is, waste, is praised as a virtue."[1]

> There would not be any profits but for the eagerness of the public to acquire the merchandise offered for sale by the successful entrepreneur. But the same people who scramble for these articles vilify the businessman and call his profit ill-got.
>
> One of the main functions of profits is to shift the control of capital to those who know how to employ it in the best possible way for the satisfaction of the public. The more profits a man earns, the greater his wealth consequently becomes, the more influential does he become in the conduct of business affairs. Profit and loss are the instruments by means of which the consumers pass the direction of production activities into the hands of those who are best fit to serve them. Whatever is undertaken to curtail or to confiscate profits, impairs this function. The result of such measures is to loosen the grip the consumers hold over the course of production. The economic machine becomes, from the point of view of the people, less efficient and less responsive.[2]

Many people are so envious of, and bitter against, the man who earns a large salary or makes large profits, that they are unable to stand back impartially and try to understand what the role of profit is in an economy, and how it tends to increase everyone's income, not merely that of the man who receives it.

The man who receives a salary of $100,000 a year from his company—why does he get it? If he rendered no service, or if the company gained $10,000 as a consequence of hiring him, they would never pay him the $100,000. If they did, their costs of production overhead would be that much higher and they would have to charge more for their product (thus causing consumers to buy another brand instead) or absorb the cost somewhere else. Even if the man saved them just $100,000 a year, it would be no gain to them—they would just break even with him. But if his services save them $1,000,000 a year, then paying him the $100,000 is well worth it—and they would gladly pay him more in order to keep him. People who begrudge him the salary should ask, "Am *I* ingenious enough to save the company over $100,000 a year, if it hired me?"

[17.4] Now the man who does the employing: let us say that his business is successful and through the years he has become a millionaire. Special venom is reserved by the populace for such men, but this is entirely without justification. If he got a million a year as salary for some tax-supported office, or in graft from the taxpayers' money, then they would have a right to complain; for they would have to work that much harder to make up the difference. But if he gets a profit of a million a year *on the free market,* there is no cause for complaint. I may dislike the latest rock-and-roll singer who gets a million a year, but not one penny of his income comes out of my taxes; and on a free market I am in no way forced to buy (or listen to) his product. I can live in serene independence of his millions; I didn't pay a dime non-voluntarily to put this money into his coffers. I may think the public foolish for buying non-nutritional cereals, thus making the company receive large profits, but this only prompts in me a reflection on the foolishness of much public taste: I do not have to buy the cereal nor contribute to the cereal company in any way. (In fact the shoe is on the other foot: the company, because of its large profits, pays extremely high taxes.

Could it be that I pay less tax as a result?) Should I then support a campaign to force people by law *not* to buy the cereal, and thus decimate the company's profits? If I do this—and thus set a precedent against freedom of choice—the next year or the next decade, by the same token, by the same precedent I have set, someone may mount a successful campaign to force people by law not to buy whatever goods or service *I* produce. And if this happens, I shall deserve my fate, since I approved the principle of coercion in the first place. People should be free to make their own choices—which includes, of course, their own mistakes.

Instead of resenting it when individuals or companies make a million dollars, we should be happy. That million dollars means that there is a prosperous enterpriser who has created many jobs for people and bought equipment and so on (which in turn requires jobs to produce) to keep the product going. A million dollars made on the free market means that a great deal of money has filtered down to a very large number of people in the economy—and that a product is available at a competitive price, else the consumers would not have bought it in sufficient quantity to make our company its million. By contrast, a million dollars earned in government jobs means a million dollars milked from the taxpayer, which he could have spent in other ways.

> The future prosperity of everyone—including the needy—depends on *encouraging* persons to become millionaires; to build railroads, houses, and power plants; to develop television, plastics, and new uses for atomic power. The reason is simple: *No man in a free country can make a million dollars through the machinery of production without producing something that we common men want at prices we are willing to pay.* And no man will continue to produce something we want at a price we are willing to pay unless he has the *chance* to

make a profit, to become rich—yes, even to become a millionaire.[3]

[17.1, 17.4] There is an old saying, "No one should have caviar until everyone has bread." This is, when one examines it, one of the most confused statements ever made, though it is easily mouthed and chanted and is useful for political campaigns. If the enterpriser were not permitted to have his caviar, he would have far less incentive (perhaps no incentive at all) to produce anything, with the result that in the end fewer people would have even bread. The correct slogan would be, "If no one were permitted to have caviar, finally not many people would have bread."

[17.5] One of the prevailing impressions, which underlies many arguments in this area but seldom itself surfaces to the level of explicit argument, is that the riches of the rich are the cause of the poverty of the poor. The impression is one of a certain fixed quantity of wealth, and that if some persons have more, this must inevitably mean that others have less.

A little reflection is enough to refute this assertion. If there were only a fixed quantity of wealth, how is it that we have many hundreds of millionaires now, hundreds and even thousands of men with elaborate houses, cars, lands, and other possessions, whereas only a few kings and noblemen had anything like this in bygone ages? Where long ago only a comparative handful of people could live, at the borderline between existence and extinction, in a given area of land, today a thousand times that number live, and live so well that they need spend only 10 to 15 percent of their income on food and all the rest goes for other things, most of which were inconceivable to the population of centuries past.

What people do not comprehend is that wealth is not static, but *grows* as long as people are free to use their ingenuity to improve the quality of their life. Here are deposits of iron, lying in the ground century after century; they do no good to anyone as long as they are just lying there. Now someone devises an economical process for removing the iron from the ground; another devises a means for smelting it, and another for combining it with manganese and other metals to produce steel that can be used in buildings, railroad tracks, and countless other things. When all these factors of production are functioning and the steel is produced, the world's wealth has been increased. Consumers have something to use that they didn't have before, and workers have jobs that didn't exist before. Every party to the transaction is a gainer.

When ten men are adrift on a lifeboat and there is only a certain quantity of provisions, if one person takes more than his share it necessarily follows that others must have less. The example of the lifeboat, or something like it, seems to be the dominating image of those who think in this primitive way about wealth. They apparently believe that because some men are rich, others must therefore be poor, since the rich have taken it away from the poor. Now this *is* the case when a bandit takes away some of your possessions—he has more, and as a consequence you have less. Bandits do not create wealth, they only cause the same amount to change hands. The same happens when the tax-collector takes away by force some of what you have earned; the government too is not creative—it takes away from you to give to others. But the capitalist in a free society is *not* like that; he cannot force the money of you, the consumer, out of your hands; you pay him for a product or a service that did not exist, or did not exist as efficiently or in the same form, prior to his creative endeavor; his product (e.g, a car) or service (e.g., railroad transpor-

tation) is good enough in your eyes so that you voluntarily pay some of the money you have earned in exchange for it. The entrepreneur has brought something into being and offered it on the open market in exchange. He has created something new under the sun, which people may buy or not buy as they prefer.

No the world is not like a lifeboat. Wealth does increase, and it increases for all as a result of the efforts of a few creative men. The riches of the rich are not the cause of the poverty of the poor: the rich in a free enterprise society can become rich only (1) by hiring workers to produce something and (2) because these consumers on a free market choose to buy what the entrepreneur has offered. They are rich precisely *because* innumerable consumers have, through their purchases, voted for whatever product or service they have to offer. Not one penny of their income on the free market came from the taxed income of anyone else.

One would think that entrepreneurs were armed bandits robbing them by force, to hear the complainers talk, instead of the risk-takers who had the ideas, and, if things went right, benefited the public. But the fallacy persists; many well-meaning people, ignorant of how an economy functions, are trying their best to do them in. In a South American factory, agitated workers demanded a larger share of the profits, held meetings and finally burned down the factory. "That'll show the filthy profiteer!" they cried. And it is true that they had indeed done him in; his entire life's work and capital were burned to the ground in one night. But they too had lost: they were out of jobs—the jobs that the factory had provided no longer existed. Neither did the products that the factory had made, and consumers had that much less choice in deciding what to buy at the store.

NOTES

1. Ludwig von Mises, *Planning for Freedom* (South Holland, IL: Libertarian Press, 1952), p. 121.

2. Ibid., pp. 122, 123.
3. Dean Russell, *Cliches of Socialism* (Irving-on-Hudson, NY: Foundation for Economic Education, 1970), p. 186.

PROGRESS CHECK 17.1

Instructions: Fill in the blanks with the appropriate responses listed below.

efficiency   incentive
ignorance   bureaucrats
risk takers   wealth
choice   poverty
products   demand

1. There is no such thing as an absolute fixed sum of _____ which never increases and which leads us to the conclusion that "my having more" means "your having less."
2. Entrepreneurs are not bandits, but rather _____.
3. According to Hospers, objections to what are perceived as "excessive earnings" are based on _____ of how profits function in a free economy.
4. A state-controlled economy is not run by entrepreneurs but rather by _____.
5. The pursuit of profits increases the _____ of production.
6. Supporting campaigns to force people by law to refrain from buying a certain product reduces profits and violates a person's freedom of _____.
7. Profits are a necessary _____ in an efficient and productive free economy. Without them, fewer people would be wealthy and less money would be filtered down to a large number of people in society.
8. The riches of the rich are not the cause of the _____ of the poor.
9. Profits help decide which _____ will be made, of what kinds, and in what amounts.
10. State-controlled economies governed by bureaucrats are not likely to respond as often to public _____ for products.

LEARNING EXERCISE 17.2   Identifying Statements

Instructions: Next to the statements listed below, indicate whether they are factual (F) or value-laden (V)

_____ 1. Profits help to determine which products will be made.

_____ 2. A free-market economy is more efficient than a bureaucratic state-controlled economy.

_____ 3. People who are best able to motivate workers and reduce waste should earn more money.

_____ 4. Entrepreneurs deserve the profits they make.

_____ 5. A large segment of the public is envious and bitter toward the successful profiteer.

_____ 6. "No one should have caviar until everyone has bread."

_____ 7. "If no one were permitted to have caviar, finally not many people would have bread."

_____ 8. The riches of the rich are the cause of the poverty of the poor.

_____ 9. There is no such thing as a fixed quantity of wealth.

_____ 10. Competition in the marketplace is always good.

LEARNING EXERCISE 17.3

Instructions: _Complete the following syllogisms._

1. **Value Premise:**   People who earn extremely high profits are not despicable.

   Factual Premise:

   Conclusion: Therefore, millionaires are not despicable.

2. **Value Premise:**

   Factual Premise: Entrepreneurs are people who contribute to society.

   Conclusion: Entrepreneurs should be entitled to earn great sums of money.

3. **Value Premise:**   Whatever increases the wealth of a nation is good.

   Factual Premise: The activities of entrepreneurs increase the wealth of a nation.

   Conclusion:

4. **Value Premise:**

   Factual Premise: Profiteering increases efficiency.

   Conclusion: Profiteering is good.

5. **Value Premise:**   Threatening jobs is undesirable.

   Factual Premise:

   Conclusion: Restricting the activities of entrepreneurs is undesirable.

18

"BUSINESS ETHICS: PROFITS, UTILITIES, AND MORAL RIGHTS"

Alan H. Goldman

EDUCATIONAL OBJECTIVES: After reading the chapter the student will be able to:

18.1 Explain how "efficiency" and "utility" serve as justifications for the profit-maximization principle.

18.2 Outline the "rights" argument supporting the primacy of profit.

18.3 Understand the concept of "responsibility" as it pertains to the relationship between business manager and stockholder.

18.4 State the negative consequences which can and sometimes do result when managers base their business decisions on personal moral opinions and concerns to promote the public good.

18.5 Explain how market conditions can be subject to moral influence.

18.6 Paraphrase Goldman's reasons for rejecting the claims that profit maximization will be most efficient and that the application of this principle will maximize aggregate utility.

18.7 Illustrate how businesses can maximize profits at the expense of consumers and thereby contribute to disutility.

18.8 Show how, in the context of a society where wealth is not distributed evenly, profit maximization does not maximize aggregate utility.

18.9 Explain Goldman's argument about the role played by "rights" in setting limits upon profit maximization.

Alan H. Goldman, "Business Ethics: Profits," *Philosophy & Public Affairs*, vol. 9, no. 3 (Spring 1980). Copyright © 1980 by Princeton University Press. Reprinted by permission of Princeton University Press.

18.10 Give reasons why satisfying people's wants may not necessarily maximize aggregate utility or the public welfare.

18.11 List the moral constraints which must obtain if the primary pursuit of profit is to be maximally efficient.

FOCUS QUESTIONS

1. Is making a profit simply a matter of business, or, can it somehow relate to issues of morality? Explain.

2. How is the relationship between "utility" or "efficiency" and "rights" conceptualized in this article? Do you agree with Goldman's conceptualization? Why or why not?

3. What are some of the perceived disadvantages of allowing business managers to have their personal moral beliefs and values enter into decisions regarding profit maximization?

4. How can moral norms exert an influence on the marketplace even when business managers in no way try to impose their moral beliefs and values?

5. Can you give examples of how profit maximization may not always be most efficient? Illustrate.

6. What objection can be raised to the claim that the public's moral norms will operate on the marketplace? What factors could diminish the moral influence of consumers upon producers and price setters?

7. How is a society's distribution of wealth related to the ethical justifiability of profit maximization?

8. Does business simply satisfy consumer wants or does it create them? Are the wants satisfied or created always good and worth satisfying or creating? Explain.

9. Under what moral conditions is the pursuit of profit in business most efficient?

10. What objections could be raised to the position that satisfying the majority's wants justifies profit maximization?

SYNOPSIS

This essay by Alan Goldman addresses itself to the moral justifiability of the "profit-maximization principle" in business. He argues that the business manager's first priority—pursuing profits within legal limits—will not always be morally acceptable. While Goldman is not opposed to earning profits, his basic thesis seems to be that moral constraints involving "rights" create boundaries within which profit making must occur if it is to be deemed ethically acceptable.

The article begins by outlining a number of arguments in favor of giving primacy to the pursuit of business profits within legal limits. The first argument supporting profit maximization is utilitarian. It is based on the premise that public demands and wants are best satisfied in a situation where one is primarily working toward the maximization of profits. A second argument for profit maximization rests on the notion of "rights." Given the contractually based business arrangements of a free-market economy, primacy of profit will best serve to honor all parties' rights and extend alternatives to consumers, instead of restricting their freedoms, choices, and liberties. A third argument is based on the responsibility to stockholders. It can be argued that business managers are employees of stockholders, entrusted with money for the purpose of producing the highest returns possible on investments. They have no mandate or authority to sacrifice profits to aid what they perceive as worthy social and moral causes. The argument could be made that promoting the public good is the job of elected politicians, not businesspeople. To sacrifice profits for social benefit is tantamount to taxing stockholders without the authority to do so. Another objection to limiting profits deals with consumer choice. The argument is presented that managerial decisions which sacrifice profits end up limiting the range of choices available to the consuming public. Instead of allowing managers to impose their values and opinions and rather than allowing centralized political decision making to interfere with what is wanted, the market should be allowed to function freely as a mechanism for satisfying the preferences and values of people in society. This point ties into a fifth related moral argument supporting profit maximization: one could argue that moral norms do in fact operate in the marketplace. Public values are built into the market structure through consumer demand. Products and services which are considered morally objectionable will not be purchased. Businesses will therefore be pressured to operate within the moral constraints reflected by public demand. Managers, then, should subordinate their personal opinions of what has maximum value to the opinions of the public as expressed by consumer behavior in the marketplace. Finally, profit maximization can be justified on the basis of consequences. It is possible that well-intentioned sacrifices (for example, lowering profits to curb inflation) on the part of managers can have disastrous and unintended economic effects. These undesirable effects would result from a failure to conform to market forces. For example, lower prices could lead to overconsumption which could then in turn lead to long-term shortages.

In the second part of his paper, Goldman presents his objections to the arguments favoring profit maximization. Answering the utilitarian justification, Goldman claims that profit maximization is not necessarily most efficient, especially in a noncompetitive market. Under monopolistic conditions, profits might be maximized by lowering quality while at the same time raising prices. Profit maximization is most efficient only when the marketplace is purely competitive. No company or business can be overly influential. Tied into this is the issue of public knowledge. To the extent that businesses can hide behind the technical sophistication of many of their products and conceal from the public knowledge about product defects that would be expensive to remedy, managers can maximize profits at the expense of consumers. This would not be optimally efficient, certainly not for consumers. This is especially true if harm or personal injury result because of product defects. Goldman's point is that giving primacy to profit maximization is not compatible with the moral restraint needed to protect the consuming public.

Profit maximization is not maximally efficient for a third reason, according to Goldman. As he states, " . . . social costs or harm to the public does not always figure in producers' costs or in projected demand for products." For example, the waste and pollution resulting from a production process may not be recognized as being linked to specific products and, consequently, the disutility may not negatively influence demand for the products at all. Great social costs and harm to the public may arise from the production process, yet such costs and harm may not figure into the producers' costs, the consumers' choices and, in turn, the projected product demands. In such situations, production is not maximally efficient to the public.

A fourth objection to the efficiency argument is based on a consideration of one's ability to purchase. The distribution of goods to those most willing to pay for them does not necessarily mean that those who need or want them most will in fact get them. Dollar demand for products is largely a function of the current distribution of wealth. Unless it is the case that society's wealth is distributed equally or that inequality has little effect upon willingness to purchase, then the sale and distribution of goods in a free-market economy does not maximize collective satisfaction or aggregate utility. If prices are allowed to rise to what the market will bear, then basic needs and wants will go unsatisfied, since many do not possess the wealth or resources required to express their demands in the market. Thus, moral restraint over profit maximization is necessary again according to Goldman, in order to protect consumers' rights to necessities and to maximize utilities by distributing goods to those who need them most or would benefit from them most.

A fifth objection stems from the fact that businesses often "create" wants, which lead to greater wants and sometimes harmful side effects. Many of these wants are not fulfilling on a long-term basis and do not in any way contribute to a worthwhile life. These are artificially created wants and fundamentally irrational desires whose satisfaction is incompatible with utility maximization. In other words, the short-term happiness gained by satisfying artificially created needs masks a deeper utilitarian inefficiency.

Another assault on the efficiency justification of profit maximization is directed at the role played by advertising in the sale and promotion of products. According to Goldman, advertising glorifies the lifestyle of glamour and super-consumption. To the extent this is true, there probably results an overproduction of consumable products and an underutilization of resources for public goods which are less glamorous, less immediately enjoyed, not advertised, and less conspicuously consumed (for example, a clean environment or good education). Yet again, Goldman draws the conclusion that the primary pursuit of profit is efficient to the public only if it operates under certain moral constraints. By this idea he does not intend to suggest that if efficiency and profit maximization were achieved together, they would be necessarily ethically acceptable. Some business practices could be both maximally efficient (taking into account aggregate utility) and profit maximizing and still be morally objectionable. Public utility may be maximized by building nuclear power plants and glamorous but potentially dangerous cars; but Goldman asks rhetorically whether it is justified to allow considerations of aggregate utility to outweigh the shortened lives of a few factory workers or neighborhood residents. He goes on to give other examples of how profit maximization and aggregate social utility combined may not be morally decisive in coming to a conclusion about the ethical acceptability of certain products or business practices. After illustrating how profit maximization is less efficient in the "deeper" sense of utility maximization, and after considering the possible harmful effects profit maximization can have on people, Goldman concludes his critique by turning his attention to the notion of "rights" and its involvement in the argument under discussion. To the claim that business managers have no right to impose their moral opinions on consumers and stockholders, Goldman replies that the majority has no right to maximal utility and that the stockholders have no right to maximal profits if they result from a violation of the moral rights of even a small minority. As he says, "the business manager does not have the right to make decisions or retain products or processes that maim, poison, severely deprive, or contaminate even a few individuals unwilling to take such risks in the name of efficiency to the public or profits to stockholders." Whatever utility is generated by profit maximization cannot excuse violations of basic moral rights in the process. For Goldman, the basic point is that the profit maximization principle is only acceptable within the constraints imposed by moral rights.

I

[18.1] Arguments in favor of the primacy of pursuit of profit generally begin by appealing to classic analyses of the role of profit in a purely competitive free-market system. In this situation, given fluid resources and labor, knowledge of prices and product quality, the pursuit of profit results in the most efficient collective use and development of economic resources. Business people motivated by the prospect of profit, produce what has the greatest surplus of value to the public over cost. Public demand for a good or a service allows prices in that industry to rise. This attracts more producers to develop supplies or substitutes in order to satisfy that demand, until the marginal value of further production falls to that of other goods. At the same time goods or services are distributed to those whose demand, measured in terms of willingness to pay, is greatest. Thus pursuit of profit results in optimal allocation of resources, maximizing the value of economic output to society as a whole. Efficiency is achieved in satisfying demand at a given time, and increased productivity, through minimizing costs relative to output, is encouraged. This generates the economic progress necessary to social progress in satisfying needs and wants. Profits function in this system as incentives to investors or risk takers and as rewards to firms that use economic resources more efficiently than others.

Thus, it is argued, pursuit of profit in a competitive situation best promotes aggregate social good. Profits measure the surplus of the value to society of goods produced over the value of resources taken from the social pool. If the primary social function of business is to achieve the most efficient allocation and use of resources for satisfying the wants of the public, then degree of profit measures degree of fulfillment of social responsibility.[1] When competition reduces costs, reduces prices relative to costs, and attracts resources to satisfy demand, the market gives the public what it wants most efficiently. Aggregate created wealth is maximized and distributed to those with greatest dollar demand. Pursuit of goals other than maximizing profits will hinder the economic enterprise vital to self-defined aggregate social welfare. Profits of course benefit stockholders and executives, but if pursuit of profit is at the same time pursuit of maximum value to the public, then managers should be wary of the call to sacrifice self-interest to other values.

[18.2] This defense of placing profit first is thoroughly utilitarian: it provides maximum satisfaction of aggregate demand or wants. But it can also be argued that pursuit of profit in a free market honors rights of free producers and consumers. Fewer rights will be violated in this system than in alternative economies, since here goods will be produced and distributed through a series of voluntary transactions. Parties enter contractual relations only when they view the transactions as benefiting them. Selling an item for a profit extends alternatives to consumers rather than restricting freedoms or rights. In order to make a profit, a business must offer an alternative at least as attractive as others will offer to prospective buyers. Free agreements for mutual benefit will violate rights of neither party (assuming that no fraud is involved). But if the business person tries to place other values over the maximization of profit, he may in effect diminish alternatives and force consumers

to pay for products or features of products they might not want or be willing to pay for given the choice. Thus aiming at profits in a free competitive market maximizes satisfaction of wants as well as the possibilities for free transactions. If maximizing alternatives in order to satisfy the demands of consumers maximizes the range of their free choices, then this free economic system appears to be justified in terms of freedom and satisfaction of rights as well as in terms of greatest utility.

[18.3, 18.4] The substitution of the values of the business manager for those of the public, expressed through demand as this creates opportunities for profit, appears to limit the choices of consumers and stockholders. Consider, first, arguments on the relative authority of managers and stockholders. As Milton Friedman points out, managers are employees of stockholders; they are entrusted with their money for the express purpose of earning a return on it. But if they sacrifice profits in order to aid what they perceive to be moral or social causes—for example, by contributing to charity or by exceeding legal requirements for safety or anti-pollution devices not demanded by consumers—then they are in effect taxing stockholders without authority to do so.[2] A business manager whose direct application of personally held moral principles makes a difference to a decision is spending the money of other persons, money that is not his own, in a way that these other persons would not choose to spend it. The organization then operates as an extra-governmental institution for selective taxation and public spending. But these functions are better left to the real government. Restraints on private actions to promote the public good should be generated through the political process, embodying principles of majority rule and proper checks and balances. Public officials can be controlled by the electorate and endowed with the resources to determine properly the effects of taxation and public spending upon the general welfare. Business people lack the same restraints; they are not appointed on the basis of their ability to tax and spend for social welfare. The morally zealous manager assumes power without the accountability of the electoral process. He also is likely to lack the expertise to judge accurately the effects of his presumed moral sacrifice of profits.

Piecemeal decisions of individual managers cannot be based upon accurate prediction of cumulative effects on the economy or on consumer choice. Decisions that negatively affect profits will hurt stockholders, may hurt employees in terms of wages or jobs, may misallocate resources away from production with maximum public value, and may be cumulatively damaging to the economy. The point here is that the individual manager is not in a position, as the well advised government official presumably is, to assess these cumulative effects. Thus there are good reasons why corporate owners or stockholders do not trust executives to spend their money in accord with personal moral judgments, why they trust them only to maximize returns through most efficient allocation of resources. Other uses of corporate assets, which may be inconsistent with the values of those who own the assets, is a violation of that trust and exceeds the legitimate delegated authority of executives. Or so argues Friedman.

[18.5] Consider next the argument that claims that managerial decisions which sacrifice prospective profits limit consumer choice. When managers seek to maximize profits by maximally satisfying consumer demand, they allow the public to impose its own values upon business through the market mechanism. When competition exists, consumers need not buy from firms consid-

ered to violate the public interest or legitimate moral constraints. Certainly they will not buy products from which they expect harm to exceed benefit to themselves. The market, as reflected in potential profits, appears to be a more sensitive mechanism for satisfying a diverse set of values and preferences than either imposition of managerial values and moral opinions or centralized political decision, even if democratically determined.[3] The reason is that the values of any sizeable minority, even if very small relative to the entire population, can create a potential profit for some astute businessperson. But these values may not match those independently held by business managers, and the minority may not be sizeable or well organized enough to affect centralized decisions of government. An argument for deviating from the profit motive therefore must be an argument for imposing the independent judgments of business managers upon the consuming public, for substituting the values of the former small minority for those of all the various segments of the majority.

Turning more specifically to moral constraints, if a significant segment of the population considers a given moral norm important, the market should operate to impose that norm upon business, or at least to make it worthwhile for some business to accept or operate within its constraints.[4] The public's own values are built into the market structure via consumer demand. But if business managers seek to substitute their own moral judgments for the operation of the market — say by adding to a new line of automobiles safety features for which there is no demand rather than more lush interiors for which there is a demand — they either 'coerce the public into paying for what it would not want given the choice, or else lose out to the competition that provides what the public does want. Once again the managers will have exceeded the authority delegated to them by the public to use resources efficiently to satisfy expressed wants, and that delegated by stockholders to compete for returns on their funds.

The case is totally different when moral commitment contributes to long-range profit by according with the public's values as expressed through the market or as imposed by law. Safety or antipollution devices required by law or for which the public is willing to pay, contribution to programs that, improve the community environment and thereby improve employee morale or create effective public relations can all be justified in the name of long-run profit maximization. Here there is no limitation of public choice or taxation of stockholders. The businessperson stays within proper bounds as long as he accepts the public's values, as expressed through projected demand curves, rather than imposing his own. It is not a question of business managers having a license to be grossly immoral or harmful to consumers. Certainly no serious moral argument could support such license. It is a question only of whose opinion regarding satisfying wants and needs, realizing values, and honoring free choice should prevail—that of the business manager or that of the consuming public. The manager is under moral restraint to subordinate his opinion of what has maximum value to the opinion of the public as expressed through the market. But this restraint is equivalent to the demand to aim first at maximum long-range profits for his corporation. Harmful products or practices may increase short-term profits if they cut costs, but since they generate bad publicity, they are unlikely to be profitable in the long run. Given this moral constraint of the competitive market itself, the primary criterion for business decision must remain profitability, if business is to serve its vital social

function rather than usurp that of government or individual free choice.

[18.4] The argument on sacrificing profits by failing to set prices at maximal profit levels, say from the commendable desire not to contribute to inflation, is somewhat different from that on product features. In the case of prices, by failing to charge full value, the manager may fail to distribute his goods according to greatest demand, and, more importantly, he will encourage overconsumption in the present, create greater shortages of supplies in the future, and fail to encourage the development of more supplies or substitutes to meet real future demand. Thus, once again, well-intentioned sacrifices on the part of managers can have unintended and unfortunate economic effects, effects that derive from failure to conform to market forces.

In this set of arguments for the moral primacy of the profit principle in business, there is a final point suggested earlier that requires some expansion. A single firm or its managers that sacrifices profits to a moral norm is unlikely, in a competitive situation, to succeed in imposing the moral norm. Suppose, for example, that an executive in the automobile industry is convinced, and is objectively correct, that safety in cars is more important than glamour, comfort, or speed, but that cost-benefit market analysis clearly reveals that consumers are not (up to a certain degree—it is always a question of how much safety at what cost). The competition is ready to cater to the public's demand, even though consumer preference reflects only carelessness, ignorance, or failure to apply probabilities. If, under these circumstances, the executive strays too far from consumer preference or the pursuit of profit, he will not succeed in protecting the true public interest. First of all, it is always problematic to assume that interests of others vary from their preferences. In this case it might not be uncontroversially irrational for people to take risks by sacrificing some degree of safety for other values. But the thrust of the final consequentialist argument is independent of the validity of this assumption in particular cases. When consumers can buy from firms that give them what they freely choose to pay for, the firm that attempts to limit their choices by imposing its own values will simply lose out to the competition.

If opposed by consumer preference, a manager's personal moral norm may fail to take effect, and his attempt to impose it may well cause him to be replaced by the stockholders or cause his firm to become bankrupt. Then he will have sacrificed not only his own interest and that of his family without positive effect but also that of his employees and the segment of his community dependent on the position of his corporation. Actions that result in so much more harm than benefit are morally suspect even if well intentioned. The imposition of special norms, such as the pursuit of profit principle, that prevent such actions are then supported.

The converse of this argument also seems to follow. That is, the degree to which managers can afford to sacrifice profits to personal moral constraints indicates an unhealthy lack of competition in the industry in question. The luxury of abandoning the profit principle exists only for those who have somehow limited the entry of competitors who will aim to satisfy the public's values and demands.[5] Thus, to the degree that competition for profits exists, the attempt by business managers to impose their own moral principles at the expense of profits is unlikely to succeed in affecting what the public buys, but is likely to produce unintended harm to those dependent on their firms. To the degree that managers can succeed in making stockholders and consumers pay for the moral scruples of their firms, they will have exceeded their legitimate delegated authority to give the public what it wants efficiently, and this will indicate an economic fault in their industry. Business should then aim to satisfy the moral demands of the public as these are imposed by law and reflected in long-range profit potential. But their authority to act directly on personal values in managerial decisions should be limited by the profit principle itself.

This completes the initial case for strong role-differentiation in business according to the primacy of profit principle. Subsequent sections will attempt to expose its weaknesses.

II

[18.6] The arguments outlined above can be attacked initially by showing that profit maximization need not be efficient or maximize satisfaction of consumer wants. To the extent that maximum profits do not guarantee maximal aggregate utility to the public, the norm of profit maximization lacks even purely utilitarian justification. Counterarguments often begin by pointing out that the rider attached to the initial premise regarding market conditions is never perfectly satisfied in practice. Profit maximization is maximally efficient to the public only when conditions are purely competitive (when each firm is too small to influence prices in the industry single-handedly or to exclude other firms) and when consumers have perfect knowledge of product features, defects, prices, and alternative products. Lack of alternatives under more monopolistic conditions render business decisions inherently coercive in determining what the public must pay for features of products that may be more or less essential. Size generates power over consumers that must be countered by acceptance of moral restraints. To the degree that the market in a particular industry is noncompetitive, profits might be maximized by lowering quality while raising prices. Business managers in such industries must therefore recognize moral responsibility to the public as a reason for not doing so.

[18.6, 18.7] Second, as technological sophistication of products increases, public knowledge of their features decreases. To the degree that businesses can succeed in hiding from the public defects that would be costly to remedy, they can maximize profits at the expense of consumers. It is not always a matter of outright lying or fraud—few businesses would be expected to pay for publicizing every conceivable malfunction or accident involving their products. When relatively few consumers may be harmed by a defect, when consumption of the product is geographically widespread and knowledge of such harm is unlikely to influence consumption greatly, cost-benefit analysis might well call for ignoring the defect in order to maximize profit. If harm to the few is likely to be serious, then ignoring the defect is morally objectionable. In this case, the moral restraint necessary to protect the consuming public is not compatible with profit maximization.

[18.6] Third, social costs or harm to the public does not always figure in producers' costs or in projected demand for products. Direct harm from products themselves might be expected to influence demand for them (although, as argued in the previous paragraph, not always enough to make it profitable to prevent it); but harm from a production process that does not attach to the product may not influence demand at all. Pollution and waste disposal fall into this category. If such harms are imposed upon neighborhoods in which production is located and not internalized as costs to producers, then production is not maximally efficient to the public. Resources will be overused in relation to net value when full costs are not figured in potential profits. Some restraint, then, on the part of business on moral grounds in the way of refraining from polluting the environment or imposing other neighborhood costs will be a move toward more efficiency to the public. It might nevertheless not be profit maximizing, since consumers far removed from the neighborhood of production will be unlikely to choose products on the normal basis of whether or not neighborhood costs are imposed by the producer. Again we see a gap between profit maximization and public utility, a gap that could be filled by direct acceptance of responsibility for avoiding harm to the public, even at the expense of profits.

[18.6, 18.8, 18.9] Fourth, even creating maximum value in terms of satisfying net dollar demand when social costs are figured will not necessarily create maximum aggregate utility to the public. The reason is that dollar demand is as much a function of the existent distribution of wealth and income as it is a reflection of intensity of wants or needs for the goods in question. Distributing goods to those most willing to pay for them is not necessarily distributing them to those who want or need them most. Thus their distribution does not maximize aggregate utility or satisfaction, unless wealth is distributed equally or the effect of inequalities upon willingness to pay is negligible. For major necessities, unequal distribution will affect not only willingness, but ability to pay. If there is not enough decent housing or medical care to go around, for example, distributing them via a free market will not maximize satisfaction of want, need, or value—that is, it will not maximize aggregate utility. Those willing or able to pay most will not be those with greatest housing or medical needs. Rights aside, considerations of utility alone would not justify such a method of distribution. If prices are permitted to rise to what the market can bear, important needs and wants, indeed often those most vital and intensely felt, will go unsatisfied. There are many who cannot express their demands through the market. In areas of public decision-making we certainly would not consider it fair to allocate votes according to wealth. Why should we think it fair to allow production and distribution of economic goods to be determined by a system of voting with dollars? Once more, moral restraint in setting prices on the part of producers of necessities, and, in the case of services, on the part of professionals, seems necessary not only to protect rights to necessities, but to maximize utilities by distributing goods to those who need them most or would benefit most from them.

[18.6, 18.10] Fifth, there is the problem of the relation of consumer preferences to true interests and needs. In section 1, I argued that opposing preferences expressed through the market to a different conception of interests is often as problematic and objectionable as unwarranted paternalism. But, as Galbraith has argued, when honoring preferences does not seem to lead to long-rang satisfaction or happiness, they become suspect as being largely created by those who benefit from satisfying them.[6] The satisfaction of wants is utility-maximizing when the wants are given and represent disutilities when unsatisfied. But if the process in question includes creation of the wants themselves, and if their satisfaction results in greater wants or in other harmful side effects, then the whole process may be objectionable from a utilitarian point of view. As the ancient Greeks realized, contentment may be easier to achieve by eliminating superfluous desires than by creating and attempting to satisfy them.

Certainly for many businesses the goal of profit maximization requires the creation of demand as much as its satisfaction. Advertising and salesmanship are not merely informative. The fact that a certain set of desires is created by those who then attempt to satisfy them is not in itself grounds for condemning the desires or the process that creates them. Such cycles are as characteristic of desires for the most exalted aesthetic experience—appreciation of fine opera, for example—as they are of desires for electric gadgets or tobacco.[7] But this shows only that Galbraith's argument is incomplete, not that it is enthymemically unsound. When we have an independent criterion for wants worth fulfilling, then processes can be condemned which create those that fail to satisfy this criterion. One weak criterion that can be adopted from a want-regarding or utilitarian moral theory relates to whether satisfaction of the desires in question increases overall satisfaction in the long run, whether it contributes to a fulfilled or worthwhile life. Desires are irrational when their satisfaction is incompatible with more fundamental or long-range preferences, either because of harmful side-effects or because of the creation of more unsatisfied desires. Alcoholism is an example of such irrational desire, the satisfaction of which is harmful overall. Processes that create and feed such desires are not utility-maximizing, since even the satisfaction of these desires lowers the subject's general level of utility. The pursuit of profit might well encourage the creation of such wants, especially desires for quickly consumable products. When this occurs, the appearance of efficiency masks a deeper utilitarian inefficiency. The profit motive contributes more to negative than positive utility, creating more unsatisfied than satisfied wants.

[18.6, 18.10] It has been argued also against Galbraith that most people are not so influenced by advertisement. They learn to be distrustful of claims made in ads and take them with a grain of salt. But while it is true that consumers become resistant to specific product claims of advertisers, it is not at all so clear that they can easily resist the total life style that bombards them constantly in subtle and not so subtle ways in ads for beer, cars, perfume, clothes, and whatever else can be conspicuously consumed.[8] The desire for this life style may in turn influence particular desires for products or features of products that are irrational and would not arise without this continuous programming. Consumers may desire flashy and fast automobiles more strongly than safe ones; but this may be only because safety cannot be conspicuously consumed or because it does not provide the kind of dashing sexual allure that car advertisers attempt to project onto their products. If this preference is suspect in itself, it certainly appears more so when we recognize its source. In some industries there is a natural lack of rational restraint on the part of consumers of which those out for maximum profits can take advantage, for example in the funeral or health-care industries. In others, consumers can be influenced to view certain products as symbols of a glamorous life style and desire them on those grounds. Furthermore, the encouragement of a life style of super consumption by numerous advertisers probably results in overproduction of consumable products and underutilization of resources for public goods that are not advertised, not conspicuously consumed, and less immediately enjoyed—for example clean air, water, and soil, quality schools, and so on. The congruence between free-market outcome and aggregate utility or social good is once more suspect.

[18.11] Thus the pursuit of profit is efficient to the public only if it operates under certain moral constraints. It is not efficient or utility-maximizing if it results in elimination of competition and hence of alternatives for consumers, in deception regarding product defects, imposition of neighborhood social costs, the creation and exploitation of irrational desires, or the neglect of needs and wants of those unable to express demand from lack of wealth.[9] And it is likely to result in all of these if maximization of profits is accepted as the principal norm of business ethics. We have also countered the claim (suggested early in the first section) that immorality in business is never profit-maximizing in the long run. Certain immoral practices of a business will hurt its profits, since they will outrage the public, make consumers wary of the products of that business, and reduce demand for those products. Other objectionable practices, such as dishonesty toward suppliers or total callousness toward employees, will be damaging to the production process. The market does impose some moral constraints. But other practices—such as retaining defects in products while hiding them from the public (which is sometimes possible), inadequately servicing products, bribing officials or wholesale buyers, polluting and dumping wastes, or creating desires for harmful products—might maximize profits while being inefficient to the consuming public.

[18.10] Still other practices might be both profit-maximizing and efficient in relation to consumers and yet morally questionable. This would be the case if a product was desired (or desired at low cost) by many and yet extremely harmful to relatively few. Nuclear power plants or glamorous, yet potentially dangerous, automobiles might be examples. In the former case, aggregate utility might be maximized through cheap production of electricity, given enough customers who benefit, but is it justified to allow considerations of aggregate utility to outweigh the shortened lives of a few plant workers or neighborhood residents? Another example in this category relates to work and working conditions. Total exploitation of workers, even if possible, might not be profit-maximizing, since production suffers when employee morale is low. But, as Henry Ford discovered long ago, productivity does not vary always with the meaningfulness of work; in fact, in certain contexts it may vary inversely with the interest and possibility for self-realization in work. Nor is consumer demand linked to these variables in working conditions. Profit-maximization and efficiency may sometimes call for reducing work to series of simple menial tasks. But the quality of a people's lives depends substantially upon the type of work they do and their interest in it. Thus we may ask on moral grounds whether gains in efficiency or aggregate utility (up to a certain point), as signaled by increased profit potential, justify reducing work to a menial and dehumanizing level. Numerous other examples in this category involving workers or neighborhoods of production could be produced: questions such as the firing of longtime employees, or the relocation of businesses, in which profit-maximization and even aggregate social utility might not be morally decisive.

[18.9] This last category of immorality that is potentially profit-maximizing takes the argument to a new level. Prior paragraphs argued within a utilitarian moral framework: the point was to show how profit-maximization may not be efficient in the deeper sense of utility-maximization. But the cases just cited appeal to the notion of moral rights as opposed to aggregate utilities. For our purposes we may define a right as a moral claim to a good that over-

rides considerations of utility.[10] The fact that others might benefit more than I from my property does not justify transferring it to them against my wishes. In the first section, the proponent of profit-maximization argues that pursuit of profit in a free competitive market results in maximum efficiency—that is, in optimal allocation of resources for satisfying aggregate demand at least overall cost—and also honors rights and preserves freedoms by extending opportunities for free transactions. One who makes this claim might also argue against some of the initial utilitarian arguments in this section by appealing to rights. The argument that unsatisfied wants and low utility from distribution by demand are results of unequal wealth would be countered by appeal to an individual's right to keep or spend what he or she earns and to be rewarded in relation to productivity, which is more nearly approximated in a profit-oriented free market than in other economies.

[18.9, 18.11] But appeal to a plausible full theory of rights undoubtedly favors counterarguments to the profit-maximization principle. To the argument that business managers have no right to impose their moral opinions on the majority of consumers or upon stockholders, it can be replied that the majority has no right to maximal utility or the stockholders to maximal profits resulting from violation of the moral rights of even a small minority. Suppose the market reveals aggregate public preference for cheap electricity. Even if the majority of consumers are willing to take the risks involved in generating electricity by unsafe nuclear reactors, do they have a right to impose the risks and resulting severe harms on those who are unwilling to accept them? (The case is different if all are willing to take the risks and are equally exposed to them, or if those unwilling are able to avoid them without undue hardship.) The market reveals the preferences of consumers (sometimes based on ignorance or deception), as well as their willingness to pay for protection of rights of others. But whether rights ought to be honored does not depend upon the willingness of the majority to bear the sacrifices of honoring them. When buying goods, most consumers are not concerned with whether processes involved in their production impose severe harms or violate rights of others. But the effect of moral norms upon consumer demand is not a measure of the obligations they impose, nor even of their acknowledgment by individuals outside their roles as consumers. The business manager does not have the right to make decisions or retain products or processes that maim, poison, severely deprive, or contaminate even a few individuals unwilling to take such risks in the name of efficiency to the public or profits to stockholders. In general one cannot morally do for others what they would be morally unjustified in doing for themselves.

It is not sufficient that business internalize costs imposed upon the community or compensate victims harmed by their products or processes. This might be sufficient in cases like that of strip mining, where the costs of restoring land can be assigned to coal producers, but not when rights of persons against serious harm or risk are involved. The user of the asbestos-filled hair dryer or the driver of the Pinto that explodes or the infant deformed by chemical waste may not be willing to be harmed and then compensated. Rights are violated precisely when the harms imposed are so severe that we do not allow additions of lesser utilities to override. While rights cannot be overridden by aggregate utility, they can be and sometimes are overridden by other rights. Thus at certain stages of economic development, when scarcity is still the rule and the means for survival of many people

depends upon further growth, expansion of gross output spurred by the profit motive may be a reasonable social goal. But in such a case, rights to survival and satisfaction of basic needs are at stake, not utility or efficiency.[11] At later stages of relative abundance, as in our society, whatever efficiency is generated by maximization of profits cannot excuse violations of moral rights in the process. The rights and freedoms exemplified in free-market exchange are only a small subclass of those potentially at stake in economic transactions and decisions.[12] If there are, in addition to rights to earn and spend money as one chooses, negative rights not to be severely harmed and positive rights to have basic needs fulfilled, then the latter will not be adequately protected by free-market exchange when businessmen place profits first.

The profit-maximization principle, then, does not appear to be morally justifiable, except within ordinary moral constraints of honoring rights. It is not a question of business managers imposing purely subjective opinions upon a majority who hold contrary opinions. When moral rights of the kind I have mentioned are violated, the harms imposed are severe. Such cases are relatively easy to identify. When the profit-principle blinder is removed from the eyes of business executives, when consumers outside their roles as consumers are asked, they do not try to justify the imposition of such harms in the name of profit or efficiency. Indeed it is plausible to suppose that neither the public nor the majority of businesspersons approve of the maximization of profit principle, not because they are confused about the operation of a free market or ignorant of its virtues, but because a theory of moral rights of the type I am discussing captures significant aspects of common-sense moral consciousness. Rights against being harmed and to satisfaction of basic needs are seen to override considerations of efficiency or utility. When this theory is taken into account, the position of business manager does not appear to be strongly role-differentiated: profits cannot be placed above moral rights that impose constraints in all areas of non-professional behavior as well.

NOTES

1. Compare David Novick, "Cost-Benefit Analysis and Social Responsibility," *Social Issues in Business*, ed. F. Luthans and R. M. Hodgetts (New York, 1976), pp. 561–573.
2. See Milton Friedman, "The Social Responsibility of Business Is to Increase Its Profits," *Ethical Issues in Business*, ed. T. Donaldson and P. H. Werhane (Englewood Cliffs, NJ, 1979), pp. 191–197; see also his *Capitalism and Freedom* (Chicago, 1962), pp. 133–136.
3. Friedman, *Capitalism and Freedom*, p. 94.
4. Compare Joseph A. Pichler, " Capitalism in America," *Ethics, Free Enterprise, and Public Policy*, ed. R. T. De George and Joseph A. Pichler (New York, 1978), pp. 19–39.
5. See Charles F. Phillips, Jr., "What Is Wrong with Profit Maximization?" in *Issues in Business and Society*, ed. W. T. Greenwood (Boston, 1977), pp. 77–88.
6. See John Kenneth Galbraith, *The Affluent Society* (Boston, 1958), chap. 2.
7. For this reply to Galbraith, see F. A. von Hayek, "The Non Sequitur of the 'Dependence Effect,' " in *Ethical Theory and Business*, ed. Tom Beauchamp and Norman Bowie (Englewood Cliffs, NJ, 1979), pp. 508–512.
8. Compare John I. Coppett, "Consumerism from a Behavioral Perspective," in *Social Issues in Business*, pp. 444–454.
9. See also Thomas M. Garrett, *Business Ethics* (Englewood Cliffs, NJ, 1966), pp. 25, 144.
10. For expansion on this definition and defense of the claim that rights always override utilities, see Alan Goldman, "Rights, Utilities and Contracts," *Canadian Journal of Philosophy* 3 (sup. vol., 1977): 121–135.
11. Compare Robert Hay and Ed Gray, "Social Responsibilities of Business Managers," in *Social Issues in Business*, pp. 104–113.
12. See Peter Singer, " Rights and the Market," *Justice and Economic Distribution*, ed. John Arthur and W. H. Shaw (Englewood Cliffs, NJ, 1978), pp. 207–221; also Alan H. Goldman "The Entitlement Theory of Distributive Justice," *The Journal of Philosophy* 73 (1976): 823–835.

PROGRESS CHECK 18.1

Instructions: *Fill in the blanks with the possible responses listed below.*

utilitarian	opinions
rights	distribution
efficiency	responsibility
choice	competitive
constraints	unfortunate effects

1. Allowing the profit-maximization principle to operate in the marketplace will presumably extend consumer _____.
2. The _____ of wealth in a society where inequities exist will not facilitate maximum aggregate utility through profit-maximization in the marketplace.
3. We need moral restraint in setting prices not only to protect peoples' _____ to necessities, but also to maximize utilities by distributing goods to those who need them most or would benefit most from them.
4. Many business managers believe that stockholders are their primary _____.

5. Well-intentioned managers who allow their personal moral opinions to influence business decisions may find that as a product of their efforts, a number of _____ result.

6. Arguments which justify the application of the principle of profit maximization by referring to its efficient collective use and development of economic resources are _____.

7. According to Goldman, moral _____ involving rights override the profit-maximization principle.

8. It could be argued that business managers should not impose their personal moral _____ in business-related matters.

9. Where profit maximization rules, some would argue the marketplace is most _____.

10. Goldman rejects the claim that profit maximization will always lead to the most _____ use of resources.

LEARNING EXERCISE 18.2   Completing Syllogisms

Instructions: Complete the following syllogisms.

1. **Value Premise:** That which results in the most efficient collective use and development of economic resources is desirable.

   Factual Premise:

   Conclusion: Therefore, profit maximization is desirable.

2. **Value Premise:**

   Factual Premise: Profit maximization sometimes requires deceiving the consumer.

   Conclusion: Therefore, profit maximization is sometimes wrong.

3. **Value Premise:**   That which infringes upon people's rights to basic necessities is ethically unacceptable.

   Factual Premise: Giving primacy to profit maximization sometimes infringes upon people's rights to basic necessities.

   Conclusion:

4. **Value Premise:**

   Factual Premise: Advertising creates artificial needs to exploit people for profits.

   Conclusion: Advertising is objectionable.

5. **Value Premise:**   Harming the minority to benefit the majority is wrong.

Factual Premise: Acting on the profit-maximization principle sometimes harms the minority to benefit the majority.

Conclusion:

LEARNING EXERCISE 18.3   Evaluating Principles and Arguments

Instructions: *Evaluate the following principles and arguments for their acceptability. Look for fallacies and use the higher-order, and role-exchange tests, and the new-cases, universalizability, and consistency tests.*

1. Of course we should try to maximize the profits of the corporation. Anyone who would suggest otherwise is a communist pig in disguise.
2. I hate these "environmentalists" and "socialists." Why if they had their way, we'd be forced to stop almost completely our acid rain (sulfuric acid) emissions as early as tomorrow. Look what happened to England once the socialists took over power in government. The country almost went bankrupt. Surely we shouldn't allow socialists to cause the same economic disaster in this country. Let's reject their position on acid rain.
3. In a democratic, free-market economy we should always satisfy the desires of the majority by producing the products they want.
4. A business manager's first responsibility is always to produce the highest profit for his or her company's shareholders.
5. The pursuit of profits should not violate the basic rights of people.

World Hunger

19

"LIVING ON A LIFEBOAT"

Garrett Hardin

EDUCATIONAL OBJECTIVES: After reading this chapter the student will be able to:

19.1 Explain the use of metaphor and its risks in the understanding and resolution of human problems.

19.2 Briefly describe Hardin's use of the "lifeboat" as a metaphor.

19.3 State the dangers of adopting Christian-Marxist ideals when it comes to distributing the world's wealth and food resources.

19.4 Define what Hardin means by the "tragedy of the commons."

19.5 Outline briefly what is meant by the notion of a "world food bank" and explain how its operation does not in fact make it a bank, as such.

19.6 Illustrate how selfish special-interest groups benefit from humanitarian efforts to feed the world's hungry.

19.7 Explain what is meant by "the ratchet effect."

19.8 Provide reasons for why technological developments in food production which enable greater numbers of people to be fed are not necessarily beneficial but ecologically destructive.

Garrett Hardin, "Living in a Lifeboat," *BioScience* 24: 561–568. Copyright © 1974 by The American Institute of Biological Sciences.

FOCUS QUESTIONS

1. What is a metaphor? How does it operate in language? To which metaphors does Hardin make reference in his article? Can you think of other metaphors used as explanatory tools?
2. How might a spaceship act as a metaphor for life on the planet? For what reasons would it be inappropriate?
3. Why is living on the planet earth much like life on a lifeboat?
4. What moral or ethical problem arises out of the lifeboat metaphor?
5. How do Christianity and Marxism become involved in Garrett Hardin's discussion of lifeboat ethics?
6. What assumptions does Hardin make about human nature, or at least about some members of society? How do the assumptions relate to his concept of "the tragedy of the commons"?
7. Are only humanitarian interests served when food donations are made to starving peoples around the world? Explain.
8. Why are interventions by international food banks ultimately destined to failure according to Hardin?
9. What socioeconomic assumptions support food-aid donations?
10. What are the ecological ramifications of having adequately fed but overpopulated countries?

SYNOPSIS

The subject of Garrett Hardin's article is human survival as viewed from the perspective of world population and world food supply. In it, he addresses a number of crises dealing with reproduction, food shortages, limited resources, selfish exploitation of the environment, and threats to the quality of life for future generations. His major argument is that transferring wealth and food resources from richer to poorer nations in ways which conform to Christian–Marxist principles is, in fact, counterproductive and in the end suicidal for humankind. If we choose to live according to the Christian dictum prescribing that we be our "brother's keeper" and if we regulate society in a Marxist fashion to which Christianity is sympathetic, taking from each according to his abilities and giving to each only according to his needs, catastrophe will be the net result.

Hardin argues his point by making use of metaphor. After explaining why Kenneth Boulding's metaphor of the earth as a "spaceship" is unacceptable, he proceeds to design his own using the "lifeboat" as the model. Metaphorically speaking, each rich nation of the world can be conceptualized as a lifeboat filled with comparatively rich people. The world's poor, on the other hand, are in much more crowded lifeboats. Many of the poor fall out of their lifeboats, swim for a while, and hope to be admitted to a rich lifeboat or somehow benefit from the advantages aboard. The central moral problem arises: "What should the passengers on the rich lifeboat do?" This is the crux of lifeboat ethics. Of course, the lifeboat metaphor is intended to capture the harsh realities of the current world situation with all of its hunger, poverty, limited resources, and conflicts of interest.

Hardin underscores the fact that each lifeboat is limited in its capacity to take on passengers. While a margin of safety built into the lifeboat's construction may allow a few poor passengers aboard, there are far too many of them and violating the engineering safety factor could have disastrous results due to unfortunate future mishaps and accidents. In answering the question about what should the rich passengers do, Hardin offers three possible alternatives: (1) take on everybody whose needs are the same; (2) admit only enough to fill the unused excess capacity, and (3) admit no more to the boat and preserve the engineered safety factor. Opting for the first alternative would lead to complete catastrophe as the boat would be swamped and everyone would drown. There are simply too many people to take on. The second alternative would force the boat passengers to pay dearly in the end, since the safety factor would be gone and accidents would surely occur. In the meantime, the problem of passenger selection would confront the rich. Which ones should be let in? What should be the basis of selective discrimination? Most people would find the third alternative abhorrent. Their refusal to help would probably instill enormous guilt. Some self-sacrificing people might even prefer to jump out of the lifeboat and surrender their places to others, rather than watch their poorer counterparts struggle. As Hardin points out, however, the selfless actions of the guilt-ridden do not change the ethics of the lifeboat. Selfless people are simply replaced by needy people who must not themselves feel guilty about their sudden good fortune, evidenced by the fact that they have willingly replaced the rich occupants. The end result of selfless, conscience-stricken people surrendering their unjustly held positions is the elimination of such people from the lifeboat. All guilt is erased from the lifeboat, while lifeboat ethics continues to operate.

After illustrating how the metaphor of the lifeboat works, Hardin proceeds to apply it to the problem of human reproduction. He points out that the people inside the boats of wealthy countries are doubling in number every 87 years, and that on average those outside are doubling about every 35 years. Hardin then asks us to imagine that the number of poor people outside the lifeboat from the countries of Colombia, Venezuela, Ecuador, Morocco, Thailand, Pakistan, and the Philippines equal the number of rich people inside the "U.S. Lifeboat." He also asks us to suppose that all of these countries live by the Christian–Marxist ideal to give "to each according to his needs." Since everyone has a basic need to survive, all the poor would have to be brought aboard the U.S. boat. Every U.S. citizen would be responsible for looking after one poor person. If the boat were initially big enough, this would pose little problem. However, 87 years later the rich would only have doubled their population, whereas the poor of the above-mentioned nations would have multiplied so much that each rich person in the United States would have not one, but eight to support. Given this scenario, the lifeboat could not possibly keep afloat.

Moving on from this hypothetical example, Hardin then proceeds to discuss the notion of what he calls the "tragedy of the commons." He uses this notion to argue again that Christian–Marxist ideals are counterproductive. In a system which recognizes the rights of private property, people will accept their responsibility to care for it. If, however, resources, like a cattle pasture are operated as a commons, open to all, then the use of it will not be matched by individuals responsibly caring for it. In the case of a cattle pasture, the considerate herdsman who does not overload the commons with his grazing stock suffers more than a selfish one who dishonestly claims his needs are greater. Hardin's assumption is that one can never get entirely rid of selfish persons who will exploit the commons. He accepts human imperfection as given. He also contends that since Christian–Marxist societies cannot properly handle "errors" in the system (that is, selfish people), mutual ruin is inevitable in the commons. In support of his contention, he points to air and water pollution, to the management of western range lands, and to the overfishing in the oceans as examples of how the commons can be, and have been, exploited. The tragedy of the commons is that not all people can be trusted to restrain themselves in the use of communal resources.

The tragedy of the commons stemming from human selfishness and self-interest is what leads Hardin to oppose the proposal of a world food bank, put forward by Nobel laureate Norman Borlaug. Although the proposal initially appeals greatly to our humanitarian instincts, Hardin believes it lends itself to corruption, abuse, and selfish exploitation in actual practice. Hardin uses Public Law 480 in the United States to support his contention. This law allowed the transportation of billions of dollars worth of U.S. grain to the world's food-short, population-high countries over the past two decades. The net effect of this law, Hardin charges, is that the American taxpayer ended up losing while special-interest groups within the country gained handsomely. For example, farmers benefited because grain was bought from them by taxpayers; in effect, it was not donated by the farmers. Demand for grain increased and so did prices as a result. Of course increased demand led to increased food production, which in turn led to increased production in farm machinery, fertilizers, and pesticides. Owners of grain elevators profited, as did railroads because of transportation needs. In addition a gigantic bureaucracy was established which had a vested interest in continuing foreign aid, regardless of its merits. As Hardin puts it, "the combination of multiple and relatively silent selfish interest with highly vocal humanitarian apologists constitutes a powerful lobby for extracting money from taxpayers." Furthermore, Hardin contends that the establishment of a world food bank would allow slovenly national rulers to be irresponsible and not to plan and budget for emergencies. They would be tempted to have others come to their rescue in times of trouble. As the example of India's failure to repay a $3.2-billion food loan illustrates, the international food bank is not really a bank but, in actuality, a disguised one-way transfer mechanism for shifting wealth from rich countries to poor.

According to Hardin, such a transfer of wealth causes what he calls "the ratchet effect." This ratchet effect refers to population numbers and to how population growth results as a product of intervention from worldwide food donations. Food inputs from a world bank prevent population levels from lowering themselves as they are constantly pushed upward. When a society or nation reaches a state of "overpopulation" and when its safety factor is exhausted, an emergency such as a famine often results. If the emergency were just allowed to occur, the population size would correct itself naturally to proper levels. However, intervention by international food sources first rescues the stricken and then promptly creates a higher capacity for carrying the already too-high population. With unrestricted, irresponsible reproduction, another emergency eventually results, requiring yet another intervention. The situation is then stabilized, but now at even a higher level of population. Thus, continued interventions mean steadily growing populations and emergencies of increased magnitude. As Hardin states: "The process is brought to an end only by the total collapse of the whole system, producing a catastrophe of scarcely imaginable proportions." Food sharing leads to irresponsible reproduction. It motivates people to draw from rather than add to the store of food in the world. Rather than better or ameliorate the population–food shortage situation, food sharing makes it worse and, hence, the world food bank system is "pejoristic" (a term Hardin coins specifically to describe this situation). The pejoristic system is based on a number of questionable assumptions which relate GNP (gross national product) to population growth. These assumptions are spelled out and criticized in the essay.

Finally, Hardin concludes his article by addressing the ecodestruction caused by advances in the realm of plant genetics designed to increase food production. Producing more food to sustain more humans is not always or necessarily good. Every additional human being born means another demand on or depletion of all aspects of the environment, that is, food, air, water, unspoiled scenery, solitude, and so on. Growing populations necessarily decrease the supply of desirables like space and quiet. In already overpopulated countries like India, every saved life has the effect of diminishing the quality of life for subsequent generations. Transferring wealth and resources from richer countries to poorer ones may be well intentioned and humanitarian in purpose but, according to Hardin, it is misguided and potentially catastrophic in effect.

[19.1] Susanne Langer[1] has shown that it is probably impossible to approach an unsolved problem save through the door of metaphor. Later, attempting to meet the demands of rigor, we may achieve some success in cleansing theory of metaphor, though our success is limited if we are unable to avoid using common language, which is shot through and through with fossil metaphors. (I count no less than five in the preceding two sentences.)

Since metaphorical thinking is inescapable it is pointless merely to weep about our human limitations. We must learn to live with them, to understand them, and to control them. "All of us," said George Eliot in Middlemarch, "get our thoughts entangled in metaphors, and act fatally on the strength of them." To avoid unconscious suicide we are well advised to pit one metaphor against another. From the interplay of competitive metaphors, thoroughly developed, we may come closer to metaphor-free solutions to our problems.

No generation has viewed the problem of the survival of the human species as seriously as we have. Inevitably, we have entered this world of concern through the door of metaphor. Environmentalists have emphasized the image of the earth as a spaceship—Spaceship Earth. Kenneth Boulding[2] is the principal architect of this metaphor. It is time, he says, that we replace the wasteful "cowboy economy" of the past with the frugal "spaceship economy" required for continued survival in the limited world we now see ours to be. The metaphor is notably useful in justifying pollution control measures.

Unfortunately, the image of a spaceship is also used to promote measures that are suicidal. One of these is a generous immigration policy, which is only a particular instance of a class of policies that are in error because they lead to the tragedy of the commons.[3] These suicidal policies are attractive because they mesh with what we unthinkingly take to be the ideals of "the best people." What is missing in the idealistic view is an insistence that rights and responsibilities must go together. The "generous" attitude of all too many people results in asserting inalienable rights while ignoring or denying matching responsibilities.

For the metaphor of a spaceship to be correct the aggregate of people on board would have to be under unitary sovereign control.[4] A true ship always has a captain. It is conceivable that a ship could be run by a committee. But it could not possibly survive if its course were determined by bickering tribes that claimed rights without responsibilities.

What about Spaceship Earth? It certainly has no captain, and no executive committee. The United Nations is a toothless tiger, because the signatories of its charter wanted it that way. The spaceship metaphor is used only to justify spaceship demands on common resources without acknowledging corresponding spaceship responsibilities.

An understandable fear of decisive action leads people to embrace "incrementalism"—moving toward reform by tiny stages. As we shall see, this strategy is counterproductive in the area discussed here if it means accepting rights before responsibilities. Where human survival is at stake, the acceptance of responsibilities is a precondition to the acceptance of rights, if the two cannot be introduced simultaneously.

[19.2] LIFEBOAT ETHICS

Before taking up certain substantive issues let us look at an alternative metaphor, that of a lifeboat. In developing some relevant examples the following numerical values are assumed. Approximately two-thirds of the world is desperately poor, and only one-third is comparatively rich. The people in poor countries have an average per capita GNP (Gross National Product) of about $200 per year; the rich, of about $3,000. (For the United States it is nearly $5,000 per year.) Metaphorically, each rich nation amounts to a lifeboat full of comparatively rich people. The poor of the world are in other, much more crowded lifeboats. Continuously, so to speak, the poor fall out of their lifeboats and swim for a while in the water outside, hoping to be admitted to a rich lifeboat, or in some other way to benefit from the "goodies" on board. What should the passengers on a rich lifeboat do? This is the central problem of "the ethics of a lifeboat."

First we must acknowledge that each lifeboat is effectively limited in capacity. The land of every nation has a limited carrying capacity. The exact limit is a matter for argument, but the energy crunch is convincing more people every day that we have already exceeded the carrying capacity of the land. We have been living on "capital"—stored petroleum and coal—and soon we must live on income alone.

Let us look at only one lifeboat—ours. The ethical problem is the same for all, and is as follows. Here we sit, say 50 people in a lifeboat. To be generous, let us assume our boat has a capacity of 10 more, making 60. (This, however, is to violate the engineering principle of the "safety" factor. A new plant disease or a bad change in the weather may decimate our population if we don't preserve some excess capacity as a safety factor.)

The 50 of us in the lifeboat see 100 others swimming in the water outside, asking for admission to the boat, or for handouts. How shall we respond to their calls? There are several possibilities.

[19.3] *One.* We may be tempted to try to live by the Christian ideal of being "our brother's keeper," or by the Marxian ideal[5] of "from each according to his abilities, to each according to his needs." Since the needs of all are the same, we take all the needy into our boat, making a total of 150 in a boat with a capacity of 60. The boat is swamped, and everyone drowns. Complete justice, complete catastrophe.

Two. Since the boat has an unused excess capacity of 10, we admit just 10 more to it. This has the disadvantage of getting rid of the safety factor, for which action we will sooner or later pay dearly. Moreover, *which* 10 do we let in? "First come, first served?" The best 10? The neediest 10? How do we *discriminate*? And what do we say to the 90 who are excluded?

Three. Admit no more to the boat and preserve the small safety factor. Survival of the people in the lifeboat is then possible (though we shall have to be on our guard against boarding parties).

The last solution is abhorrent to many people. It is unjust, they say. Let us grant that it is.

"I feel guilty about my good luck," say some. The reply to this is simple: *Get out and yield your place to others.* Such a selfless action might satisfy the conscience of those who are addicted to guilt but it would not change the ethics of the lifeboat. The needy person to whom a guilt-addict yields his place will not himself feel guilty about his sudden good luck. (If he did he would not climb aboard.) The net result of conscience-stricken people relinquishing their unjustly held positions is the elimination of their kind of conscience from the lifeboat. The lifeboat, as it were, purifies itself of guilt. The ethics of the lifeboat persist, unchanged by such momentary aberrations.

This then is the basic metaphor within which we must work out our solutions. Let us enrich the image step by step with substantive additions from the real world.

REPRODUCTION

The harsh characteristics of lifeboat ethics are heightened by reproduction, particularly by reproductive differences. The people inside the lifeboats of the wealthy nations are doubling in numbers every 87 years; those outside are doubling every 35 years, on the average. And the relative difference in prosperity is becoming greater.

Let us, for a while, think primarily of the U.S. lifeboat. As of 1973 the United States had a population of 210 million people, who were increasing by 0.8% per year, that is, doubling in number every 87 years.

Although the citizens of rich nations are outnumbered two to one by the poor, let us imagine an equal number of poor people outside our lifeboat—a mere 210 million poor people reproducing at a quite different rate. If we imagine these to be the combined populations of Colombia, Venezuela, Ecuador, Morocco, Thailand, Pakistan, and the Philippines, the average rate of increase of the people "outside" is 3.3% per year. The doubling time of this population is 21 years.

[19.3] Suppose that all these countries, and the United States, agreed to live by the Marxian ideal, "to each according to his needs," the ideal of most Christians as well. Needs, of course, are determined by population size, which is affected by reproduction. Every nation regards its rate of reproduction as a sovereign right. If our lifeboat were big enough in the beginning it might be possible to live *for a while* by Christian–Marxian ideals. *Might.*

Initially, in the model given, the ratio of non-Americans to Americans would be one to one. But consider what the ratio would be 87 years later. By this time Americans would have doubled to a population of 420 million. The other group (doubling every 21 years) would now have swollen to 3,540 million. Each American would have more than eight people to share with. How could the lifeboat possibly keep afloat?

All this involves extrapolation of current trends into the future, and is consequently suspect. Trends may change. Granted: but the change will not necessarily be favorable. If—as seems likely—the rate of population increase falls faster in the ethnic group presently inside the lifeboat than it does among those now outside, the future will turn out to be even worse than mathematics predicts, and sharing will be even more suicidal.

RUIN IN THE COMMONS

[19.3, 19.4] The fundamental error of the sharing ethics is that it leads to the tragedy of the commons. Under a system of private property the man (or group of men) who own property recognize their responsibility to care for it, for if they don't they will eventually suffer. A farmer, for instance, if he is intelligent, will allow no more cattle in a pasture than its carrying capacity justifies. If he overloads the pasture, weeds take over, erosion sets in, and the owner loses in the long run.

But if a pasture is run as a commons open to all, the right of each to use it is not matched by an operational responsibility to take care of it. It is no use asking independent herdsmen in a commons to act responsibly, for they dare not. The considerate herdsman who refrains from overloading the commons suffers more than a selfish one who says his needs are greater. (As Leo Durocher says, "Nice guys finish last.") Christian–Marxian idealism is counterproductive. That it *sounds* nice is no excuse. With distribution systems, as with individual morality, good intentions are no substitute for good performance.

A social system is stable only if it is insensitive to errors. To the Christian–Marxian idealist a selfish person is a sort of "error." Prosperity in the system of the commons cannot survive errors. If *everyone* would only restrain himself, all would be well; but it takes *only one less than everyone* to ruin a system of voluntary restraint. In a crowded world of less than perfect human beings —and we will never know any other— mutual ruin is inevitable in the commons. This is the core of the tragedy of the commons.

One of the major tasks of education today is to create such an awareness of the dangers of the commons that people will be able to recognize its many varieties, however disguised. There is pollution of the air and water because these media are treated as commons. Further growth of population and growth in the per capita conversion of natural resources into pollutants require that the system of the commons be modified or abandoned in the disposal of "externalities."

The fish populations of the oceans are exploited as commons, and ruin lies ahead. No technological invention can prevent this fate: in fact, all improvements in the art of fishing merely hasten the day of complete ruin. Only the replacement of the system of the commons with a responsible system can save oceanic fisheries.

The management of western range lands, though nominally rational, is in fact (under the steady pressure of cattle ranchers) often merely a government-sanctioned system of the commons, drifting toward ultimate ruin for both the rangelands and the residual enterprisers.

WORLD FOOD BANKS

[19.5] In the international arena we have recently heard a proposal to create a new commons, namely an international depository of food reserves to which nations will contribute according to their abilities, and from which nations may draw according to their needs. Nobel laureate Norman Borlaug has lent the prestige of his name to this proposal.

A world food bank appeals powerfully to our humanitarian impulses. We remember John Donne's celebrated line, "Any man's death diminishes me." But before we rush out to see for whom the bell tolls let us recognize where the greatest political push for international granaries comes from, lest we be disillusioned later. Our experience with Public Law 480 clearly reveals the answer. This was the law that moved billions of dollars worth of U.S. grain to food-short, population-long countries during the past two decades. When P.L. 480 first came into being, a headline in the business magazine *Forbes*[6] revealed the power behind it: "Feeding the World's Hungry Millions: How it will mean billions for U.S. business."

And indeed it did. In the years 1960 to 1970 a total of $7.9 billion was spent on the "Food for Peace" program, as P.L. 480 was called. During the years 1948 to 1970 an additional $49.9 billion were extracted from American tax-payers to pay for other economic aid programs, some of which went for food and food-producing machinery. (This figure does *not* include military aid.) That P.L. 480 was a give-away program was concealed. Recipient countries went through the motions of paying for P.L. 480 food—with IOU's. In December 1973 the charade was brought to an end as far as India was concerned when the United States "forgave" India's $3.2 billion debt.[7] Public announcement of the debt was delayed for two months: one wonders why.

[19.6] "Famine—1975!"[8] is one of the few publications that points out the commercial roots of this humanitarian attempt. Though all U.S. taxpayers lost by P.L. 480, special interest groups gained handsomely. Farmers benefited because they were not asked to contribute the grain—it was bought from them by the taxpayers. Besides the direct benefit there was the indirect effect of increasing demand and thus raising prices of farm products generally. The manufacturers of farm machinery, fertilizers, and pesticides benefited by the farmers' extra efforts to grow more food. Grain elevators profited from storing the grain for varying lengths of time. Railroads made money hauling it to port, and shipping lines by carrying it overseas. Moreover, once the machinery for P.L. 480 was established an immense bureaucracy had a vested interest in its continuance regardless of its merits.

Very little was ever heard of these selfish

interests when P.L. 480 was defended in public. The emphasis was always on its humanitarian effects. The combination of multiple and relatively silent selfish interest with highly vocal humanitarian apologists constitutes a powerful lobby for extracting money from taxpayers. Foreign aid has become a habit that can apparently survive in the absence of any known justification. A news commentator in a weekly magazine,[9] after exhaustively going over all the conventional arguments for foreign aid—self-interest, social justice, political advantage, and charity—and concluding that none of the known arguments really held water, concluded: "So the search continues for some logically compelling reasons for giving aid. . . ." In other words, *Act now, Justify later*—if ever. (Apparently a quarter of a century is too short a time to find the justification for expending several billion dollars yearly.)

The search for a rational justification can be short-circuited by interjecting the word "emergency." Borlaug uses this word. We need to look sharply at it. What is an "emergency"? It is surely something like an accident, which is correctly defined as *an event that is certain to happen, though with a low frequency*.[10] A well-run organization prepares for everything that is certain, including accidents and emergencies. It budgets for them. It saves for them. It expects them—and mature decision-makers do not waste time complaining about accidents when they occur.

What happens if some organizations budget for emergencies and others do not? If each organization is solely responsible for its own well-being, poorly managed ones will suffer. But they should be able to learn from experience. They have a chance to mend their ways and learn to budget for infrequent but certain emergencies. The weather, for instance, always varies and pe-riodic crop failures are certain. A wise and competent government saves out of the production of the good years in anticipation of bad years that are sure to come. This is not a new idea. The Bible tells us that Joseph taught this policy to Pharaoh in Egypt more than 2,000 years ago. Yet it is literally true that the vast majority of the governments of the world today have no such policy. They lack either the wisdom or the competence, or both. Far more difficult than the transfer of wealth from one country to another is the transfer of wisdom between sovereign powers or between generations.

"But it isn't their fault! How can we blame the poor people who are caught in an emergency? Why must we punish them?" The concepts of blame and punishment are irrelevant. The question is, what are the operational consequences of establishing a world food bank? If it is open to every country every time a need develops, slovenly rulers will not be motivated to take Joseph's advice. Why should they? Others will bail them out whenever they are in trouble.

Some countries will make deposits in the world food bank and others will withdraw from it: there will be almost no overlap. Calling such a depository-transfer unit a "bank" is stretching the metaphor of *bank* beyond its elastic limits. The proposers, of course, never call attention to the metaphorical nature of the word they use.

THE RATCHET EFFECT

[19.7] An "international food bank" is really, then, not a true bank but a disguised one-way transfer device for moving wealth from rich countries to poor. In the absence of such a bank, in a world inhabited by individually responsible sovereign nations, the population of each nation would repeatedly go through a cycle of the sort shown in Figure 1. P_2 is greater than P_1, either in absolute numbers or because a deterioration of the food supply has removed the safety factor and produced a dangerously low ratio of resources to population. P_2 may be said to represent a state of overpopulation, which becomes obvious upon the appearance of an "accident," e.g., a crop failure. If the "emergency" is not met by outside help, the population drops back to the "normal" level—the "carrying capacity" of the environment—or even below. In the absence of population control by a sovereign, sooner or later the population grows to P_2 again and the cycle repeats. The long-term population curve[11] is an irregularly fluctuating one, equilibrating more or less about the carrying capacity.

A demographic cycle of this sort obviously involves great suffering in the restrictive phase, but such a cycle is normal to any independent country with inadequate population control. The third century theologian Tertullian[12] expressed what must have been the recognition of many wise men when he wrote: "The scourges of pestilence, famine, wars, and earthquakes have come to be regarded as a blessing to overcrowded nations, since they serve to prune away the luxuriant growth of the human race."

Only under a strong and farsighted sovereign—which theoretically could be the people themselves, democratically organized —can a population equilibrate at some set point below the carrying capacity, thus avoiding the pains normally caused by periodic and unavoidable disasters. For this happy state to be achieved it is necessary that those in power be able to contemplate with equanimity the "waste" of surplus food in times of bountiful harvests. It is essential that those in power resist the temptation to convert extra food into extra babies. On the public relations level it is necessary that the phrase "surplus food" be replaced by "safety factor."

But wise sovereigns seem not to exist in the poor world today. The most anguishing problems are created by poor countries that are governed by rulers insufficiently wise and powerful. If such countries can draw on a world food bank in times of "emergency," the population *cycle* of Figure 1 will be replaced by the population *escalator* of Figure 2. The input of food from a food bank acts as the pawl of a ratchet, preventing the population from retracing its steps to a lower level. Reproduction pushes the population upward, inputs from the world bank prevent its moving downward. Population size escalates, as does the absolute magnitude of "accidents" and "emergencies." The

Figure 1 The population cycle of a nation that has no effective, conscious population control, and which receives no aid from the outside. P_2 is greater than P_1.

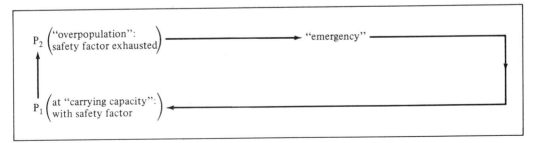

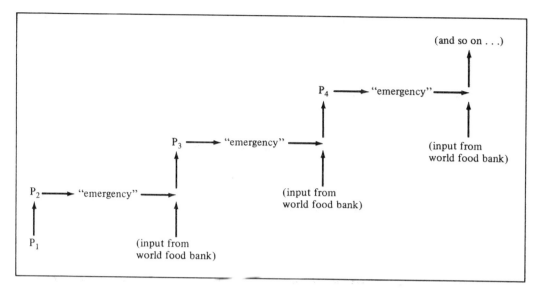

Figure 2 The population escalator. Note that input from a world food bank acts like the pawl of a ratchet, preventing the normal population cycle shown in Figure 1 from being completed. P_{n+1} is greater than P_n, and the absolute magnitude of the "emergencies" escalates. Ultimately the entire system crashes. The crash is not shown, and few can imagine it.

process is brought to an end only by the total collapse of the whole system, producing a catastrophe of scarcely imaginable proportions.

Such are the implications of the well-meant sharing of food in a world of irresponsible reproduction.

I think we need a new word for systems like this. The adjective "melioristic" is applied to systems that produce continual improvement; the English word is derived from the Latin *meliorare*, to become or make better. Parallel with this it would be useful to bring in the word *pejoristic* (from the Latin *pejorare*, to become or make worse). This word can be applied to those systems which, by their very nature, can be relied upon to make matters worse. A world food bank coupled with sovereign state irresponsibility in reproduction is an example of a pejoristic system.

This pejoristic system creates an unacknowledged commons. People have more motivation to draw from than to add to the common store. The license to make such withdrawals diminishes whatever motivation poor countries might otherwise have to control their populations. Under the guidance of this ratchet, wealth can be steadily moved in one direction only, from the slowly-breeding rich to the rapidly-breeding poor, the process finally coming to a halt only when all countries are equally and miserably poor.

All this is terribly obvious once we are acutely aware of the pervasiveness and danger of the commons. But many people still lack this awareness and the euphoria of the "benign demographic transition"[13] interferes with the realistic appraisal of pejoristic mechanisms. As concerns public policy, the deductions drawn from the benign demographic transition are these:

1. If the per capita GNP rises the birth rate will fall; hence, the rate of population increase will fall, ultimately producing ZPG (Zero Population Growth).
2. The long-term trend all over the world (including the poor countries) is of a rising per capita GNP (for which no limit is seen).
3. Therefore, all political interference in population matters is unnecessary; all we need to do is foster economic "development" —note the metaphor—and population problems will solve themselves.

Those who believe in the benign demographic transition dismiss the pejoristic mechanism of Figure 2 in the belief that each input of food from the world outside fosters development within a poor country thus resulting in a drop in the rate of population increase. Foreign aid has proceeded on this assumption for more than two decades. Unfortunately it has produced no indubitable instance of the asserted effect. It has, however, produced a library of excuses. The air is filled with plaintive calls for more massive foreign aid appropriations so that the hypothetical melioristic process can get started.

The doctrine of demographic *laissez-faire* implicit in the hypothesis of the benign demographic transition is immensely attractive. Unfortunately there is more evidence against the melioristic system than there is for it.[14] On the historical side there are many counter-examples. The rise in per capita GNP in France and Ireland during the past century has been accompanied by a rise in population growth. In the 20 years following the Second World War the same positive correlation was noted almost everywhere in the world. Never in world history

before 1950 did the worldwide population growth reach 1% per annum. Now the average population growth is over 2% and shows no signs of slackening.

On the theoretical side, the denial of the pejoristic scheme of Figure 2 probably springs from the hidden acceptance of the "cowboy economy" that Boulding castigated. Those who recognize the limitations of a spaceship, if they are unable to achieve population control at a safe and comfortable level, accept the necessity of the corrective feedback of the population cycle shown in Figure 1. No one who knew in his bones that he was living on a true spaceship would countenance political support of the population escalator shown in Figure 2.

ECO-DESTRUCTION VIA THE GREEN REVOLUTION

[19.8] The demoralizing effect of charity on the recipient has long been known. "Give a man a fish and he will eat for a day: teach him how to fish and he will eat for the rest of his days." So runs an ancient Chinese proverb. Acting on this advice the Rockefeller and Ford Foundations have financed a multipronged program for improving agriculture in the hungry nations. The result, known as the "Green Revolution," has been quite remarkable. "Miracle wheat" and "miracle rice" are splendid technological achievements in the realm of plant genetics.

Whether or not the Green Revolution can increase food production is doubtful,[15] but in any event not particularly important. What is missing in this great and well-meaning humanitarian effort is a firm grasp of fundamentals. Considering the importance of the Rockefeller Foundation in this effort it is ironic that the late Alan Gregg, a much-respected vice-president of the Foundation, strongly expressed his doubts of the wisdom of all attempts to increase food production some two decades ago. (This was before Borlaug's work—supported by Rockefeller—had resulted in the development of "miracle wheat.") Gregg[16] likened the growth and spreading of humanity over the surface of the earth to the metastasis of cancer in the human body, wryly remarking that "Cancerous growths demand food; but, as far as I know, they have never been cured by getting it."

"Man does not live by bread alone"—the scriptural statement has a rich meaning even in the material realm. Every human being born constitutes a draft on all aspects of the environment—food, air, water, unspoiled scenery, occasional and optional solitude, beaches, contact with wild animals, fishing, hunting—the list is long and incompletely known. Food can, perhaps, be significantly increased: but what about forests, and solitude? If we satisfy the need for food in a growing population we necessarily decrease the supply of other goods, and thereby increase the difficulty of equitably allocating scarce goods.[17]

The present population of India is 600 million, and it is increasing by 15 million per year. The environmental load of this population is already great. The forests of India are only a small fraction of what they were three centuries ago. Soil erosion, floods, and the psychological costs of crowding are serious. Every one of the net 15 million lives added each year stresses the Indian environment more severely. *Every life saved this year in a poor country diminishes the quality of life for subsequent generations.*

Observant critics have shown how much harm we wealthy nations have already done to poor nations through our well-intentioned but misguided attempts to help them.[18] Particularly reprehensible is our failure to carry out post-audits of these attempts.[19] Thus have we shielded our tender consciences from knowledge of the harm we have done. Must we Americans continue to fail to monitor the consequences of our external "do-gooding?" If, for instance, we thoughtlessly make it possible for the present 600 million Indians to swell to 1,200 millions by the year 2001—as their present growth rate promises—will posterity in India thank *us* for facilitating an even greater destruction of *their* environment? Are good intentions ever a sufficient excuse for bad consequences?

NOTES

Footnotes have been renumbered—Ed.
1. Susanne Langer, *Philosophy in a New Key* (Cambridge, Mass., 1942).
2. Kenneth Boulding, "The Economics of the Coming Spaceship Earth," in H. Jarrett, ed., *Environmental Quality in a Growing Economy* (Baltimore, Md., 1966).
3. Garrett Hardin, "The Tragedy of the Commons," *Science* 162 (1968), 1243–1248.
4. W. Ophuls, "The Scarcity Society," *Harpers* 248 (1974), 47–52.
5. Karl Marx, "Critique of the Gotha Program," in R. C. Tucker, ed., *The Marx-Engels Reader* (New York, 1972), 388.
6. See W. C. Paddock, "How Green Is the Green Revolution?" *BioScience* 20 (1970) 897–902.
7. *The Wall Street Journal*, 19 February 1974.
8. W. C. Paddock and P. Paddock, *Famine 1975!* (Boston, 1967).
9. K. Lansner, "Should Foreign Aid Begin at Home?" *Newsweek*, 11 February 1974, 32.
10. Hardin, *Exploring New Ethics for Survival: The Voyage of the Spaceship Beagle* (New York, 1972), 81–82.
11. Hardin, in *Biology: Its Principles and Implications*, 2nd ed. (San Francisco, 1966), chap. 9.
12. Hardin, *Population, Evolution, and Birth Control* (San Francisco, 1969), 18.
13. Hardin, *Stalking the Wild Taboo* (Los Altos, CA, 1973), chap. 23.
14. K. Davis, "Population," *Scientific American* 209, no. 3 (1963), 62–71.
15. M. Harris, "How Green the Revolution," *Natural History* 81, no. 3 (1972), 28–30; W. C. Paddock, "How Green is the Green Revolution?"; H. G. Wilkes, "The Green Revolution," *Environment* 14, no. 8, 32–39.

16. A. Gregg, "A Medical Aspect of the Population Problem," *Science* 121 (1955), 681–682.
17. Hardin, "The Economics of Wilderness," *Natural History* 78, no. 6 (1969), 20–27, and "Preserving Quality on Spaceship Earth," in J. B. Trefethen, ed., *Transactions of the Thirty-Seventh North*
American Wildlife and Natural Resources Conference (Washington, D.C., 1972).
18. W. Paddock and E. Paddock, *We Don't Know How* (Ames, IA, 1973).
19. M. T. Farvar and J. P. Milton, *The Careless Technology* (Garden City, NY, 1972).

REFERENCES

Aiken, William, and Hugh LaFollette. *World Hunger and Moral Obligation*. Englewood Cliffs, NJ: Prentice Hall, 1977.
Eberstadt, Nick. "Myths of the Food Crises," in *The New York Review of Books*, 19 February 1976. Reprinted in James Rachels, ed., *Moral Problems*. 3rd ed. New York: Harper & Row, 1979, pp. 292–312.
Hardin, Garrett. *Stalking the Wild Taboo*. Los Altos, CA: William Kauffman, 1978.
Lucas, George R., and Thomas W. Ogletree, eds. *Lifeboat Ethics: The Moral Dilemma of World Hunger*. New York: Harper & Row, 1976.

PROGRESS CHECK 19.1

Instructions: Fill in the blanks with the appropriate responses listed below.

metaphor

tragedy of the commons

Christianity

pejoristic system

ecodestruction

transfer device

errors

misguided

Marxism

ratchet effect

1. Garrett Hardin believes that foreign aid food donations are well-intentioned, but _____ efforts.

2. Producing enough food to feed all of the peoples of the world could reduce or eliminate starvation, but it does not prevent the _____ which results from very high population concentrations existing in relatively small geographic areas.

3. The _____ of a lifeboat is used to portray the human problem of survival as it relates to population and food supply.

4. "From each according to his abilities, to each according to his needs" is a basic principle of _____.

5. The prescription that we "be our brother's keeper" reflects a basic principle of

_____.

6. The ethics of sharing is fundamentally wrong because it leads to the

_____.

7. The concept of an "international food bank" is not intended to be a real bank,

but a disguised one-way _____ for moving wealth from rich countries to poor countries.

8. A world food bank coupled with a country's irresponsibility in human reproduction does not better anything since such a combination is an example of a _____.

9. When rich nations come to the rescue of starving nations which then, in turn, reproduce in such great numbers to again produce an emergency food-shortage situation requiring further assistance, a _____ is created.

10. The problem with Christian–Marxist principles is that they cannot properly handle _____ in the social system, namely, selfish people.

LEARNING EXERCISE 19.2   Completing Syllogisms

Instructions: Complete the following syllogisms.

1. **Value Premise:**   Countries should not get involved in policies which threaten the survival of humanity.

   Factual Premise:

   Conclusion: Therefore, countries should not get involved in food sharing.

2. **Value Premise:**

   Factual Premise: India is a country which is irresponsible about its reproduction rates.

   Conclusion: Therefore, India should not receive aid.

3. **Value Premise:**   Philosophies which do not take into account human imperfections such as greed and dishonesty are naive and therefore not acceptable.

   Factual Premise: Christianity and Marxism are philosophies which do not take into account human imperfections such as greed and dishonesty.

   Conclusion:

4. **Value Premise:**

   Factual Premise: Foreign aid programs exploit taxpayers.

   Conclusion: Therefore, we should not accept foreign aid programs.

5. **Value Premise:**   Diminishing the quality of life for future generations is wrong.

Factual Premise:

Conclusion: Feeding the peoples of overpopulated regions of the world is wrong.

LEARNING EXERCISE 19.3 Testing Principles and Arguments

Instructions: *Evaluate the following principles and arguments looking for logical fallacies and using the role-exchange test, the universalizability and consistency test, the higher-order principle test, and the new-cases test.*

1. The peoples of overpopulated, third-world nations are irresponsible leeches on humanity who deserve their misery and starvation.
2. We shouldn't send aid to Ethiopia. Look what happened to all the aid we sent to India. We were never paid back for our food and resources.
3. We should not send food aid to other lands because this will diminish our own resources and thereby lower the country's standard of living.
4. Threatening human survival is wrong.
5. We should eliminate irresponsible reproduction leading to overpopulation.

20

"KILLING AND STARVING TO DEATH"

James Rachels

EDUCATIONAL OBJECTIVES: After reading this chapter the student will be able to:

20.1 State what Rachels means by the "equivalence thesis."

20.2 Explain the dangers involved with intuitions and prereflective beliefs.

20.3 Demonstrate how our behavior parallels that of the moral monster dubbed "Jack Palance," as he is depicted in the hypothetical example.

20.4 Comment on "spatial location" and its relevance to the world hunger issue.

20.5 Suggest why "numbers of people involved" ostensibly makes Jack Palance's situation different than our own real-life circumstances.

20.6 Paraphrase Rachels' reasons for rejecting spatial location and numbers as significant factors distinguishing Palance's moral position from our own.

20.7 State Rachels' position on the role played by feelings in the moral justification of conduct.

20.8 Explain the purely formal principle relating moral judgments and the reasons for supporting them.

20.9 Provide Rachels' reasons for rejecting philosophers' attempts to give different moral weights to killing and letting die.

20.10 Show how refraining from doing certain acts actually involves action of a type.

20.11 Bring forward counterintuitive evidence to Rachels' thesis.

Reprinted with permission from James Rachels, "Killing and Starving to Death." *Philosophy* 54. Copyright © 1979 Cambridge University Press.

20.12 Outline Rachels' defense against the counterintuitive illustrations.

20.13 Provide Rachels' psychological account for why people are inclined to accept the distinction between killing and letting die.

20.14 Express Rachels' views on "the affluent lifestyle."

FOCUS QUESTIONS

1. How could killing and letting die be seen as different?
2. How could killing and letting die be seen as equivalent?
3. Is the example of Jack Palance and the starving child a fair one to use in this argument? Why or why not?
4. What are some of the reasons why we in affluent countries feel so apathetic and unconcerned about the starving millions in third-world nations? Are we justified in feeling this way? Why or why not?
5. Are we, as individuals, any more or any less responsible for feeding the starving in view of the fact that others who are also affluent do not help? Explain.
6. How are intuitions used in this moral argument about world hunger? Are there any dangers involved with making intuitive appeals?
7. Is it unrealistic to suggest that we have a duty to save all the starving in the world? If so, are we absolved of any and all responsibility to feed the hungry? Explain.
8. Are all wrongdoings by "omission" less morally objectionable than wrongdoings by "commission"? Justify.
9. What is "bad faith" in the context of this discussion? How does it become involved in the argument?
10. Is it wrong to buy records, cars, toys, and fancy clothes when so many others in the world lack basic necessities? What moral assessment can be placed on our affluent society?

SYNOPSIS

The problem of world hunger and the responsibility to do something about it are dealt with in the next essay. In it, James Rachels criticizes the philosophical view that our "positive duty" to give aid to the hungry is weaker than our "negative duty" not to harm them. He presents and defends what he calls the Equivalence Thesis which states that our duty not to let hungry people die is as strong as our duty not to kill them. Moral intuitions that letting die is not as bad as killing are, according to Rachels, based on prereflective beliefs about right and wrong which, in view of more careful rational analysis, must be rejected. Allowing people to die in many cases is much closer to killing than we normally assume.

In support of his thesis, Rachels makes an intuitive appeal himself. He asks us to imagine a situation wherein we find a starving child characterized by a bloated belly and hollow eyes. At our elbow we have a sandwich which we do not need. He says that any decent person would, of course, offer the child the sandwich, or, even better, take the child to a hospital. Such action would not reflect the behavior of a saint. It would not entail going beyond the call of duty (supererogation); nor would the behavior be especially praiseworthy. Intuitively we understand that such action should be taken and we would likely criticize someone who did not take it. Rachels asks us to imagine a man, given the name of "Jack Palance" after the decent-hearted actor who nevertheless plays vile characters, watching indifferently as the starving child dies. The man cannot even be bothered to hand over the sandwich so desperately needed for survival by the child. Most of us would regard such a man as a moral monster.

Rachels believes that there is a striking similarity between this hypothetical situation and our own when we allow people in distant countries to die of starvation. Just as "Jack Palance" could save the child but does not, so too could we save starving people in far-off lands; we choose not to, however, with the result that many die. If most of us do not regard ourselves as moral monsters, then there must be morally relevant differences between Palance and ourselves. Rachels critically examines these assumed differences which permit us not to see ourselves as moral monsters.

It could be argued, for example, that "spatial location" makes a significant difference. Jack Palance is actually in the same room with the starving child, whereas we are quite far away from the starving millions. This fact seems to make a psychological difference in terms of how we feel about our inaction. The problem of starvation becomes somehow more abstract and less emotionally poignant. Rachels asserts, however, that the treatment to which one is entitled does not depend on different longitudinal and latitudinal coordinates. For him, it is absurd to suggest that the child is entitled to help because she is in the room, whereas the starving millions have no right to aid since they are far away. If spatial separation did in fact prevent helping, that would be a different matter. The truth, though, is that we can give to relief agencies as easily as Palance could have given food to the starving child in the room. Nothing prevents us from helping, so the location of the dying is not morally relevant.

It could also be argued that our situation is different from Jack Palance's insofar as he only had one mouth to feed, whereas there are very many we would be forced to look after. Surely we cannot care for all the millions who need assistance. None of us has the resources to care for all of them, and besides, there are many affluent people who could help as easily as we; some are even in a better position to help than we are.

In reaction to this, Rachels admits that nobody alone could save all the starving people of the world. Yet this only means that no one person is responsible for saving everybody; it does not mean that we are absolved from the responsibility to save one starving person or as many as we can. Rejecting Richard Trammell's distinction between killing and letting die, Rachels says we are only morally bound to save those we can. The class of people we are obligated to save is therefore much smaller than the class of people we have an obligation not to kill, as we should refrain from killing all people, including all starving people. Just because we cannot save everybody, that does not mean that our duty with respect to those we can save is any less stringent.

According to Rachels, neither is our duty to help the starving any less stringent just because others, sometimes even those more affluent than ourselves, do not help either. Their inaction may make us feel less guilty or ashamed, but as Rachels points out, "A psychological explanation of our feelings is not a moral justification of our conduct." Had Jack Palance been only one of twenty spectators in the room with him, his guilt would not have been reduced by nineteen-twentieths as some might believe; rather than diminishing Palance's guilt, Rachels claims that all twenty would have become moral monsters. The guilt involved would have increased, not decreased. Thus, the inaction of other affluent people vis-à-vis the starving does not decrease our responsibility or reduce the amount of guilt, but rather responsibility and guilt are increased. Rachels offers a preliminary conclusion at this juncture of the article stating that spatial location and differences in numbers do not make Jack Palance's situation any different from ours. If Palance is judged to be a moral monster, then so too must we judge ourselves in like fashion. Our collective indifference toward the starving, previously based on ignorance and incorrect prereflective intuitions, has now become more blameworthy than before if it continues. With our prior intuitions rejected, it should be clear that letting die is much worse than we have normally assumed, that it is much closer to killing.

In part two of the article, Rachels expands upon his Equivalence Thesis. He qualifies his position by clarifying that not every act of letting die is equally as bad as killing and vice versa. For example, killing a healthy person with malicious intent is worse than allowing a person in irreversible coma to die. Conversely, the act of maliciously allowing an ill person who could be saved to die is probably worse than killing a terminally ill patient upon his request. Thus, whatever rationale can be given for judging one act worse than another, the bare fact that one amounts to killing whereas the other is letting die, is not one of them. By use of a formal principle, Rachels argues that if the same reasons are given for or against A as for or against B, then the reasons in favor of A are neither stronger or weaker than the reasons in favor of B. Therefore A and B become morally equivalent. Neither is preferable to the other. Having stated this formal principle, Rachels then demonstrates that the reasons for why killing and letting die are wrong are identical: the wrongness in each case stems from the fact that a good is lost, that is, one's life. All other reasons are secondary and subordinate. While the basic reasons against killing (A) and letting die (B) are ultimately the same, it follows that both actions are morally equivalent. The fact that killing and letting die are different actions does not in itself make one more or less preferable. The actions are not the objects of comparison, but rather their underlying reasons are. After briefly referring back again to Trammell's concerns about dischargeability of duties, Rachels looks at the presumed difference between killing and letting die in terms of action and inaction. Some would argue that in killing we are actually doing something actively; whereas with letting die we remain passive by doing nothing. Rachels rejects this distinction arguing that letting someone die is in fact a form of action. For example, by not smiling, speaking, or shaking hands, we may insult someone. Similarly, by allowing someone to die, we do not feed the person, we do not give medication, and so forth. Inaction becomes, therefore, a form of action. By not shaking a hand, one has in fact done something; one has actually insulted another. By allowing someone to die, one has again done something; one has permitted the person to expire. Even if this breakdown of the action–inaction distinction is not accepted, Rachels points out that there is no general correlation between it and any sort of moral assessment or evaluation anyway. As he says, we can be found morally blameworthy both for *not* doing things (failing to pay taxes) and for *doing* them (killing); there is nothing intrinsically right or wrong about action and inaction themselves. The action–inaction distinction cannot therefore support letting someone die.

Rachels continues his discussion by rejecting Trammell's "optionality" argument as it refers to the distinction between killing and letting die. Trammell points out that if we fail to save someone, we still allow for the option of someone else coming to the rescue. If we kill, however, the victim is simply dead and no option exists for other possibilities. While Rachels admits that optionality enables one to distinguish between killing and failing to save, it still does not make a difference between killing and letting die. This is illustrated by the Jack Palance example. When he watches the child die, he does not just fail to save the child; he lets the child die. So too, when we fail to send food to the starving and they die, we let them die; we do not just fail to save them. In further rejection of the optionality argument, Rachels explains how it is made in bad faith as an attempt to reduce our guilt and absolve us of the personal responsibility to help the starving.

In part three of Rachels' article, he examines and criticizes further objections to the Equivalence Thesis which are directed at its counterintuitive nature. Again, Rachels cites Trammell who would reject the thesis because of the radical implications it would have for our conduct. Denying the distinction between positive and negative duties would ultimately lead to the conclusion that buying material things like phonograph records, instead of using the money to feed the poor, is always immoral. This perception is counterintuitive since most people do not regard themselves as monsters when they purchase fancy clothes, cars, toys, and so on. In view of this, Rachels asserts that objections to the Equivalence Thesis are not logical or philosophical, but are actually based on the mistaken prereflective belief in the rightness of our affluent lifestyle. Rachels contends that philosophy should not only appeal to intuitions in building arguments, but also question intuitions that are based on pretheoretical assumptions and beliefs, as in the case here. The consequences of adopting Rachels' position are not problematic or embarrassing to him—they are an integral part of his position which maintains that ". . . we are morally wrong to spend money on inessentials, when that money could go to feed the starving. . . ." If the consequences of this position are counterintuitive, then perhaps the intuitions involved should be the objects of criticism, not Rachels' position.

Rachels ends his discussion by quoting and criticizing the views of Daniel Dinello and Richard Trammell, who offer two more counterintuitive examples to his position. Dinello's example is flawed, Rachels claims: what is called "letting die" is not letting die at all. The discussion of how letting die is less bad than killing is therefore misleading. While Rachels has greater difficulty rejecting Trammell's second counterintuitive example, he believes its strength ultimately comes from people's selfishness. People are inclined to accept the distinction between killing and letting die because it is in their self-interest to do so. The implications of accepting the equivalence of the two would force us to take seriously the duty to save the starving. It would necessitate giving up our affluent lifestyles. We could no longer spend on luxurious living while others starved. Since this would be too painful for many of us, it becomes to our own advantage to regard killing as worse than letting die. As Rachels says, "So, both the costs and the benefits encourage us, selfishly, to view killing as worse than letting die. It is to our own advantage to believe this, and so we do."

Although we do not know exactly how many people die each year of malnutrition or related health problems, the number is very high, in the millions.[1] By giving money to support famine relief efforts, each of us could save at least some of them. By not giving, we let them die.

Some philosophers have argued that letting people die is not as bad as killing them, because in general our "positive duty" to give aid is weaker than our "negative duty" not to do harm.[2] I maintain the opposite: letting die is just as bad as killing.[3] At first this may seem wildly implausible. When reminded that people are dying of starvation while we spend money on trivial things, we may feel a bit guilty, but certainly we do not feel like murderers. Philippa Foot writes:

> Most of us allow people to die of starvation in India and Africa, and there is surely something wrong with us that we do; it would be nonsense, however, to pretend that it is only in law that we make a distinction between allowing people in the underdeveloped countries to die of starvation and sending them poisoned food. There is worked into our moral system a distinction between what we owe people in the form of aid and what we owe them in the way of non-interference.[4]

[20.1] No doubt this would be correct if it were intended only as a description of what most people believe. Whether this feature of "our moral system" is rationally defensible is, however, another matter. I shall argue that we are wrong to take comfort in the fact that we "only" let these people die, because our duty not to let them die is equally as strong as our duty not to kill them, which, of course, is very strong indeed.

[20.2] Obviously, this Equivalence Thesis is not morally neutral, as philosophical claims about ethics often are. It is a radical idea which, if true, would mean that some of our "intuitions" (our prereflective beliefs about what is right and wrong in particular cases) are mistaken and must be rejected. Neither is the view I oppose morally neutral. The idea that killing is worse than letting die is a relatively conservative thesis which would allow those same intuitions to be preserved. However, the Equivalence Thesis should not be dismissed merely because it does not conform to all our pre-reflective intuitions. Rather than being perceptions of the truth, our "intuitions" might sometimes signify nothing more than our prejudices or selfishness or cultural conditioning. Philosophers often admit that, in theory at least, some intuitions might be unreliable—but usually this possibility is not taken seriously, and conformity to pre-reflective intuition is used uncritically as a test of the acceptability of moral theory. In what follows I shall argue that many of our intuitions concerning killing and letting die *are* mistaken, and should not be trusted.

I

We think that killing is worse than letting die, not because we overestimate how bad it is to kill, but because we underestimate how bad it is to let die. The following chain of reasoning is intended to show that letting people in foreign countries die of starvation is very much worse than we commonly assume.

[20.3] Suppose there were a starving child in the room where you are now—hollow eyed, belly bloated, and so on—and you have a sandwich at your elbow that you don't need. Of course you would be horrified; you would stop reading and give her the sandwich, or better, take her to a hospital. And you would not think this an act of supererogation: you would not expect any special praise for it, and you would expect criticism if you did not do it. Imagine what you would think of someone who simply ignored the child and continued reading, allowing her to die of starvation. Let us call the person who would do this Jack Palance, after the very nice man who plays such vile

characters in the movies. Jack Palance indifferently watches the starving child die; he cannot be bothered even to hand her the sandwich. There is ample reason for judging him very harshly; without putting too fine a point on it, he shows himself to be a moral monster.

When we allow people in far-away countries to die of starvation, we may think, as Mrs. Foot puts it, that "there is surely something wrong with us." But we most emphatically do not consider ourselves moral monsters. We think this, in spite of the striking similarity between Jack Palance's behavior and our own. He could easily save the child; he does not; and the child dies. We could easily save some of those starving people; we do not; and they die. If we are not monsters, there must be some important difference between him and us. But what is it?

[20.4, 20.6] One obvious difference between Jack Palance's position and ours is that the person he lets die is in the same room with him, while the people we let die are mostly far away. Yet the spatial location of the dying people hardly seems a relevant consideration.[5] It is absurd to suppose that being located at a certain map coordinate entitles one to treatment which one would not merit if situated at a different longitude or latitude. Of course, if a dying person's location meant that we *could not* help, that would excuse us. But, since there are efficient famine relief agencies willing to carry our aid to the far-away countries, this excuse is not available. It would be almost as easy for us to send these agencies the price of the sandwich as for Palance to hand the sandwich to the child.

The location of the starving people does make a difference, psychologically, in how we feel. If there were a starving child in the same room with us, we could not avoid realizing, in a vivid and disturbing way, how it is suffering and that it is about to die. Faced with this realization our consciences probably would not allow us to ignore the child. But if the dying are far away, it is easy to think of them only abstractly, or to put them out of our thoughts altogether. This might explain why our conduct would be different if we were in Jack Palance's position even though, from a moral point of view, the location of the dying is not relevant.

[20.5, 20.6] There are other differences between Jack Palance and us, which may seem important, having to do with the sheer numbers of people, both affluent and starving, that surround us. In our fictitious example Jack Palance is one person, confronted by the need of one other person. This makes his position relatively simple. In the real world our position is more complicated, in two ways: first, in that there are millions of people who need feeding, and none of us has the resources to care for all of them; and second, in that for any starving person we *could* help there are millions of other affluent people who could help as easily as we.

On the first point, not much needs to be said. We may feel, in a vague sort of way, that we are not monsters because no one of us could possibly save *all* the starving people—there are just too many of them, and none of us has the resources. This is fair enough, but all that follows is that, individually, none of us is responsible for saving everyone. We may still be responsible for saving someone, or as many as we can. This is so obvious that it hardly bears mentioning; yet it is easy to lose sight of, and philosophers have actually lost sight of it. In his article "Saving Life and Taking Life,"[6] Richard Trammell says that one morally important difference between killing and letting die is "dischargeability." By this he means that, while each of us can discharge completely a duty not to kill anyone, no one among us can discharge completely a duty to save everyone who needs it. Again, fair enough; but all that follows is that, since we

are only bound to save those we can, the class of people that we have an obligation to save is much smaller than the class of people we have an obligation not to kill. It does *not* follow that our duty with respect to those we can save is any less stringent. Suppose Jack Palance were to say: "I needn't give this starving child the sandwich because, after all, I can't save everyone in the world who needs it." If this excuse will not work for him, neither will it work for us with respect to the children we could save in India or Africa.

The second point about numbers was that, for any starving person we *could* help, there are millions of other affluent people who could help as easily as we. Some are in an even better position to help since they are richer. But by and large these people are doing nothing. This also helps to explain why we do not feel especially guilty for letting people starve. How guilty we feel about something depends, to some extent, on how we compare with those around us. If we were surrounded by people who regularly sacrificed to feed the starving, and we did not, we would probably feel ashamed. But because our neighbors do not do any better than we, we are not so ashamed.

[20.7] But again, this does not imply that we should not feel more guilty or ashamed than we do. A psychological explanation of our feelings is not a moral justification of our conduct. Suppose Jack Palance were only one of twenty people who watched the child die; would that decrease his guilt? Curiously, I think many people assume it would. Many people seem to feel that if twenty people do nothing to prevent a tragedy, each of them is only one-twentieth as guilty as he would have been if he had watched the tragedy alone. It is as though there is only a fixed amount of guilt, which divides. I suggest, rather, that guilt multiplies, so that each passive viewer is fully guilty, if he could have prevented the tragedy but did not. Jack Palance watching the girl die alone would be a moral monster; but if he calls in a group of his friends to watch with him, he does not diminish his guilt by dividing it among them. Instead, they are all moral monsters. Once the point is made explicit, it seems obvious.

The fact that most other affluent people do nothing to relieve hunger may very well have implications for one's own obligations. But the implication may be that one's own obligations *increase* rather than decrease. Suppose Palance and a friend were faced with two starving children, so that, if each did his "fair share," Palance would only have to feed one of them. But the friend will do nothing. Because he is well-off, Palance could feed both of them. Should he not? What if he fed one and then watched the other die, announcing that he has done *his* duty and that the one who died was his friend's responsibility? This shows the fallacy of supposing that one's duty is only to do one's fair share, where this is determined by what would be sufficient *if* everyone else did likewise.

To summarize: Jack Palance, who refuses to hand a sandwich to a starving child, is a moral monster. But we feel intuitively that we are not so monstrous, even though we also let starving children die when we could feed them almost as easily. If this intuition is correct, there must be some important difference between him and us. But when we examine the most obvious differences between his conduct and ours—the location of the dying, the differences in numbers—we find no real basis for judging ourselves less harshly than we judge him. Perhaps there are some other grounds on which we might distinguish our moral position, with respect to actual starving people, from Jack Palance's position with respect to the child in my story. But I cannot think of what they might be. Therefore, I conclude that if he is a monster, then so are we—or at least, so are we after our rationalizations and thoughtlessness have been exposed.

This last qualification is important. We judge people, at least in part, according to whether they can be expected to realize how well or how badly they behave. We judge Palance harshly because the consequences of his indifference are so immediately apparent. By contrast, it requires an unusual effort for us to realize the consequences of our indifference. It is normal behavior for people in the affluent countries not to give to famine relief, or if they do give, to give very little. Decent people may go along with this normal behavior pattern unthinkingly, without realizing, or without comprehending in a clear way, just what this means for the starving. Thus, even though those decent people may act monstrously, we do not judge them monsters. There is a curious sense, then, in which moral reflection can transform decent people into indecent ones: for if a person thinks things through, and realizes that he is, morally speaking, in Jack Palance's position, his continued indifference is more blameworthy than before.

The preceding is not intended to prove that letting people die of starvation is as bad as killing them. But it does provide strong evidence that letting die is much worse than we normally assume, and so that letting die is much *closer* to killing than we normally assume. These reflections also go some way towards showing just how fragile and unreliable our intuitions are in this area. They suggest that, if we want to discover the truth, we are better off looking at arguments that do not rely on unexamined intuitions.

II

Before arguing that the Equivalence Thesis is true, let me explain more precisely what I mean by it. I take it to be a claim about what does, or does not, count as a morally good reason in support of a value judgment: the bare fact that one act is an act of killing, while another act is an act of "merely" letting someone die, is not a morally good reason in support of the judgment that the former is worse than the latter. Of course there may be *other* differences between such acts that are morally significant. For example, the family of an irreversibly comatose hospital patient may want their loved one to be allowed to die, but not killed. Perhaps the reason for their preference is religious. So we have at least one reason to let the patient die rather than to kill him—the reason is that the family prefers it that way. This does not mean, however, that the distinction between killing and letting die *itself* is important. What is important is respecting the family's wishes. (It is often right to respect people's wishes even if we think those wishes are based on false beliefs.) In another sort of case, a patient with a painful terminal illness may want to be killed rather than allowed to die because a slow, lingering death would be agonizing. Here we have a reason to kill and not let die, but once again the reason is not that one course is intrinsically preferable to the other. The reason is, rather, that the latter course would lead to more suffering.

It should be clear, then, that I will *not* be arguing that every act of letting die is equally as bad as every act of killing. There are lots of reasons why a particular act of killing may be morally worse than a particular act of letting die, or vice versa. If a healthy person is murdered, from a malicious motive, while a person in irreversible coma is allowed to die upon a calm judgment that maintaining him alive is pointless, certainly this killing is very much worse than this letting die. Similarly, if an ill person who could be saved is maliciously allowed to die, while a terminal patient is

killed, upon his request, as an act of kindness, we have good reason to judge the letting die worse than the killing. All that I want to argue is that, whatever reasons there may be for judging one act worse than another, the simple fact that one is killing, whereas the other is only letting die, is not among them.

[20.8] The first stage of the argument is concerned with some formal relations between moral judgments and the reasons that support them. I take it to be a point of logic that moral judgments are true only if good reasons support them; for example, if there is no good reason why you ought to do some action, it cannot be true that you ought to do it. Moreover, when there is a choice to be made from among several possible actions, the preferable alternative is the one that is backed by the strongest reasons.

But when are the reasons for or against one act stronger than those for or against another act? A complete answer would have to include some normative theory explaining why some reasons are intrinsically weightier than others. Suppose you are in a situation in which you can save someone's life only by lying: the normative theory would explain why "Doing A would save someone's life" is a stronger reason in favor of doing A than "Doing B would be telling the truth" is in favor of doing B.

However, there are also some purely formal principles that operate here. The simplest and least controversial such principle is this:

(1) If there are the *same* reasons for or against A as for or against B, then the reasons in favor of A are neither stronger nor weaker than the reasons in favor of B; and so A and B are morally equivalent—neither is preferable to the other.

Now, suppose we ask why killing is morally objectionable. When someone is killed, there may of course be harmful effects for people other than the victim himself. Those who loved him may grieve, and those who were depending on him in one way or another may be caused hardship because, being dead, he will be unable to perform as expected. However, we cannot explain the wrongness of killing purely, or even mainly, in terms of the bad effects for the survivors. The primary reason why killing is wrong is that something very bad is done to the victim himself: he ends up dead; he no longer has a good—his life—which he possessed before. But notice that exactly the same can be said about letting someone die. The primary reason why it is morally objectionable to let someone die, when we could save him, is that he ends up dead; he no longer has a good—his life—which he possessed before. Secondary reasons again have to do with harmful effects on those who survive. Thus, the explanation of why killing is bad mentions features of killing that are also features of letting die, and vice versa. Since there are no comparably general reasons in favor of either, this suggests that:

> (2) There are the same reasons for and against letting die as for and against killing.

And if this is true, we get the conclusion:

> (3) Therefore, killing and letting die are morally equivalent—neither is preferable to the other.

The central idea of this argument is that there is no morally relevant difference between killing and letting die, that is, no difference which may be cited to show that one is worse than the other. The argument therefore contains a premise—(2)—that is supported only inductively. The fact that the explanation of why killing is wrong applies equally well to letting die, and vice versa, provides strong evidence that the in-

ductive generalization is true. Nevertheless, no matter how carefully we analyze the matter, it will always be possible that there is some subtle, morally relevant difference between the two that we have overlooked. In fact, philosophers who believe that killing is worse than letting die have sometimes tried to identify such differences. I believe that these attempts have failed; here are three examples:

[20.9] 1. The first is one that I have already mentioned. Trammell urges that there is an important difference in the "dischargeability" of duties not to kill and not to let die. We can completely discharge a duty not to kill anyone; but we cannot completely discharge a duty to save everyone who needs aid. This is obviously correct, but it does not show that the Equivalence Thesis is false, for two reasons. In the first place, the difference in dischargeability only shows that the class of people we have a duty to save is smaller than the class of people we have a duty not to kill. It does not show that our duty with respect to those we *can* save is any less stringent. In the second place, if we *cannot* save someone, and that person dies, then we do not let him die. It is not right to say that I let Josef Stalin die, for example, since there is no way I could have saved him. So if I cannot save everyone, then neither can I let everyone die.

2. It has also been urged that, in killing someone, we are *doing* something—namely, killing him—whereas, in letting someone die, we are not doing anything. In letting people die of starvation, for example, we only *fail* to do certain things, such as sending food. The difference is between action and inaction; and somehow, this is supposed to make a moral difference.[7]

[20.10] There are also two difficulties with this suggestion. First, it is misleading to say, without further ado, that in letting someone die we do nothing. For there is one very important thing that we do: we let someone die. "Letting someone die" is different, in some ways, from other sorts of actions, mainly in that it is an action we perform *by way of* not performing other actions. We may let someone die by way of not feeding him, just as we may insult someone by way of not shaking his hand. (If it is said, "I didn't do anything; I simply refrained from taking his hand when he offered it," it may be replied "You did do one thing—you insulted him.") The distinction between action and inaction is relative to a specification of *what* actions are or are not done. In insulting someone, we may *not* smile, speak, shake hands, and so on—but we *do* insult or snub the person. And in letting someone die, the following may be among the things that are not done: we do not feed the person, we do not give medication, and so on. But the following is among the things that are done: we let him die.

Second, even if letting die were only a case of inaction, why should any moral conclusion follow from *that* fact? It may seem that a significant conclusion follows if we assume that we are not responsible for inactions. However, there is no general correlation between the action-inaction distinction and any sort of moral assessment. We ought to do some things, and we ought not do others, and we can certainly be morally blameworthy for not doing things as well as for doing them—Jack Palance was blameworthy for not feeding the child. (In many circumstances we are even legally liable for not doing things: tax fraud may involve only "inaction"—failing to report certain things to the Department of Internal Revenue—but what of it?) Moreover, failing to act can be subject to all the other kinds of moral assessment. Not doing something may, depending on the circumstances, be right, wrong, obligatory, wise, foolish, compassionate, sadistic, and so on. Since there is no general correlation between the action-inaction distinction and *any* of these

matters, it is hard to see how anything could be made out of this distinction in the present context.

3. My final example is from Trammell again. He argues that "optionality" is a morally relevant difference between killing and letting die. The point here is that if we fail to save someone, we leave open the option for someone else to save him; whereas if we kill, the victim is dead and that is that. This point, I think, has little significance. For one thing, while "optionality" may mark a difference between killing and *failing to save*, it does not mark a comparable difference between killing and *letting die*. If X fails to save Y, it does not follow that Y dies; someone else may come along and save him. But if X lets Y die, it does follow that Y dies; Y is dead and that is that.[8] When Palance watches the child die, he does not merely fail to save the child; he lets her die. And when we fail to send food to the starving, and they die, we let them die—we do not merely fail to save them.

The importance of "optionality" in any particular case depends on the actual chances of someone else's saving the person we do not save. Perhaps it is not so bad not to save someone if we know that someone else *will* save him. (Although even here, we do not behave as we ought; for we ought not simply to leave what needs doing to others.) And perhaps it even gets us off the hook a little if there is the *strong chance* that someone else will step in. But in the case of the world's starving, we know very well that no person or group of persons is going to come along tomorrow and save all of them. We know that there are at least some people who will *not* be saved, if we do not save them. So, as an excuse for not giving aid to the starving, the "optionality" argument is clearly in bad faith. To say of those people, after they are dead, that someone else *might* have saved them, in the very weak sense in which that will be true, does not excuse us at all. The others who might have saved them, but did not, are as guilty as we, but that does not diminish our guilt—as I have already remarked, guilt in these cases multiplies, not divides.

III

[20.11] I need now to say a few more things about the counter-intuitive nature of the Equivalence Thesis.

The fact that this view has radical implications for conduct has been cited as a reason for rejecting it. Trammell complains that "Denial of the distinction between negative and positive duties leads straight to an ethic so strenuous that it might give pause even to a philosophical John the Baptist."[9] Suppose John is about to buy a phonograph record, purely for his enjoyment, when he is reminded that with this five dollars a starving person could be fed. On the view I am defending, he ought to give the money to feed the hungry person. This may not seem exceptional until we notice that the reasoning is reiterable. Having given the first five dollars, John is not free to use another five to buy the record. For the poor are always with him: there is always *another* starving person to be fed, and then another, and then another. "The problem," Trammell says, "is that, even though fulfillment of one particular act of aid involves only minimal effort, it sets a precedent for millions of such efforts."[10] So we reach the bizarre conclusion that it is almost always immoral to buy phonograph records! And the same goes for fancy clothes, cars, toys, and so on. **[20.12]** This sort of *reductio* argument is of course familiar in philosophy. Such arguments may be divided into three categories. The strongest sort shows that a theory entails a contradiction, and, since contradictions cannot be tolerated, the theory must be modified or rejected. Such arguments, when valid, are of course devastating. Second, an argument may show that a theory has a consequence which, while not inconsistent, is nevertheless demonstrably false—that is, an independent proof can be given that the offensive consequence is unacceptable. Arguments of this second type, while not quite so impressive as the first, can still be irresistible. The third type of *reductio* is markedly weaker than the others. Here, it is merely urged that some consequence of a theory is counter-intuitive. The supposedly embarrassing consequence is perfectly consistent, and there is no proof that it is false; the complaint is only that it goes against our unreflective, pretheoretical beliefs. Now sometimes even this weak sort of argument can be effective, especially when we have not much confidence in the theory, or when our confidence in the pretheoretical belief is unaffected by the reasoning which supports the theory. However, it may happen that *the same reasoning which leads one to accept a theory also persuades one that the pretheoretical beliefs were wrong.* (If this did not happen, philosophy would always be in the service of what we already think; it could never challenge and change our beliefs, and would be, in an important sense, useless.) The present case, it seems to me, is an instance of this type. The same reasoning which leads to the view that we are as wicked as Jack Palance, and that killing is no worse than letting die, also persuades (me, at least) that the prereflective belief in the rightness of our affluent life-style is mistaken.[11]

So, I want to say about all this what H. P. Grice once said at a conference when someone objected that his theory of meaning had an unacceptable implication. Referring to the supposedly embarrassing consequence, Grice said, "See here, that's not an *objection* to my theory—*that's* my theory!"[12] Grice not only accepted the implication, he claimed it as an integral part of what he wanted to say. Similarly, the realization that we are morally wrong to spend money on inessentials, when that money could go to feed the starving, is an integral part of the view I am defending. It is not an embarrassing consequence of the view; it is (part of) the view itself.

[20.11] There is another way in which the counter-intuitive nature of the Equivalence Thesis may be brought out. It follows from that thesis that if the *only* difference between a pair of acts is that one is killing, while the other is letting die, those actions are equally good or bad—neither is preferable to the other. Defenders of the distinction between positive and negative duties have pointed out that in such cases our intuitions often tell us just the opposite: killing seems obviously worse. Here is an example produced by Daniel Dinello:

> Jones and Smith are in a hospital. Jones cannot live longer than two hours unless he gets a heart transplant. Smith, who has had one kidney removed, is dying of an infection in the other kidney. If he does not get a kidney transplant, he will die in about four hours. When Jones dies, his one good kidney can be transplanted to Smith, or Smith could be killed and his heart transplanted to Jones . . . it seems clear that it would, in fact, be wrong to kill Smith and save Jones, rather than letting Jones die and saving Smith.[13]

And another from Trammell:

> If someone threatened to steal $1000 from a person if he did not take a gun and shoot a stranger between the eyes, it would be very wrong for him to kill the stranger to save his $1000. But if someone asked from that person $1000 to save a stranger, it would seem that his obligation to grant this request would not be as great as his obligation to refuse the first demand—even if he has good reason for believing that without his $1000 the stranger would certainly die. . . . In this particular example, it seems plausible to say that a person has a greater obligation to refrain from killing

someone, even though the effort required of him ($1000) and his motivation toward the stranger be assumed identical in both cases.[14]

The conclusion we are invited to draw from these examples is that, contrary to what I have been arguing, the bare difference between killing and letting die *must be* morally significant.

[20.12] Now Dinello's example is badly flawed, since the choice before the doctor is not a choice between killing and letting die at all. If the doctor kills Smith in order to transplant his heart to Jones, he will have killed Smith. But if he waits until Jones dies, and then transfers the kidney to Smith, he will *not* have "let Jones die." The reason is connected with the fact that not every case of not saving someone is a case of letting him die. (Josef Stalin died, and I did not save him, but I did not let Stalin die.) Dinello himself points out that, in order for it to be true that X lets Y die, X must be "in a position" to save Y, but not do so.[15] (I was never in a position to save Stalin.) Now the doctor is in a position to save Jones only if there is a heart available for transplantation. But no such heart is available—Smith's heart, for example, is not available since Smith is still using it. Therefore, since the doctor is not in a position to save Jones, he does not let Jones die.[16]

Trammell's position is not quite so easy to dismiss. Initially, I share the intuition that it would be worse to kill someone to prevent $1000 from being stolen than to refuse to pay $1000 to save someone. Yet on reflection I have not much confidence in this feeling. What is at stake in the situation described is the person's $1000 and the stranger's life. But we end up with the *same* combination of lives and money, no matter which option the person chooses: if he shoots the stranger, the stranger dies and he keeps his $1000; and if he refuses to pay to save the stranger, the stranger dies and he keeps his $1000. It makes no difference, either to the person's interests or to the stranger's interests, which option is chosen; why, then, do we have the curious intuition that there is a big difference here?

I conceded at the outset that most of us believe that in letting people die we are not behaving as badly as if we were to kill them. I think I have given good reasons for concluding that this belief is false. Yet giving reasons is often not enough, even in philosophy. For if an intuition is strong enough, we may continue to rely on it and assume that *something* is wrong with the arguments opposing it, even though we are not sure exactly what is wrong. It is a familiar remark: "X is more certain than any argument that might be given against it." So in addition to the arguments, we need some account of why people have the allegedly mistaken intuition and why it is so persistent. Why do people believe so firmly that killing is so much worse than letting die, both in fictitious cases such as Trammell's, and in the famine relief cases in the real world? In some ways the explanation of this is best left to the psychologists; the distinctly philosophical job is accomplished when the intuition is shown to be false. However, I shall hazard a hypothesis, since it shows how our intuitions can be explained without assuming that they are perceptions of the truth. **[20.13, 20.14]** Human beings are to some degree altruistic, but they are also to a great degree selfish, and their attitudes on matters of conduct are determined by what is in their own interests, and what is in the interests of the few other people they especially care about. In terms of both the costs and the benefits, it is to their own advantage for people in the affluent countries to regard killing as worse than letting die. First, the *costs* of never killing anyone are not great; we can live very well without ever killing. But the cost of not allowing people to die,

when we could save them, would be very great. For any one of us to take seriously a duty to save the starving would require that we give up our affluent life-styles; money could no longer be spent on luxuries while others starve. On the other side, we have much more to *gain* from a strict prohibition on killing than from a like prohibition on letting die. Since we are not in danger of starving, we will not suffer if people do not regard feeding the hungry as so important; but we would be threatened if people did not regard killing as very, very bad. So, both the costs and the benefits encourage us, selfishly, to view killing as worse than letting die. It is to our own advantage to believe this, and so we do.

NOTES

1. For an account of the difficulties of getting reliable information in this area, see Nick Eberstadt, "Myths of the Food Crisis," *New York Review of Books,* 19 February 1976, 32–37.
2. Richard L. Trammell, "Saving Life and Taking Life," *Journal of Philosophy* 72 (1975), 131–137, is the best defense of this view of which I am aware.
3. This article is a companion to an earlier one, "Active and Passive Euthanasia," *New England Journal of Medicine* 292 (9 January 1975), 78–80 [reprinted in the present volume, 1–6], in which I discuss the (mis)use of the killing/letting die distinction in medical contexts. But nothing in this article depends on the earlier one.
4. Philippa Foot, "The Problem of Abortion and the Doctrine of the Double Effect," *Oxford Review* no. 5 (1967); reprinted in *Moral Problems,* 2nd ed. (New York, 1975), 66.
5. On this point, and more generally on the whole subject of our duty to contribute for famine relief, see Peter Singer, "Famine, Affluence, and Morality," *Philosophy & Public Affairs* 1 (Spring 1972), 232.
6. Trammell, 133.
7. This argument is suggested by Paul Ramsey in *The Patient as Person* (New Haven, Conn., 1970), 151.
8. This difference between failing to save and letting die was pointed out by David Sanford in a very helpful paper, "On Killing and Letting Die," read at the Western Division meeting of the American

Philosophical Association, in New Orleans, on 30 April 1976.

9. Trammell, 133.
10. Ibid., 134.
11. There is also some independent evidence that this prereflective belief is mistaken; see Singer, "Famine, Affluence, and Morality."
12. Grice made this remark several years ago at Oberlin. I do not remember the surrounding details of the discussion, but the remark seems to me an important one which applies to lots of "objections" to various theories. The most famous objections to act-utilitarianism, for example, are little more than

descriptions of the theory, with the question-begging addendum, "Because it says *that*, it can't be right."

13. Daniel Dinello, "On Killing and Letting Die," *Analysis* 31, no. 3 (January 1971), 83, 86.
14. Trammell, 131.
15. Dinello, 85.
16. There is another way to meet Dinello's counterexample. A surprisingly strong case can be made that it would *not* be any worse to kill Smith than to "let Jones die." I have in mind adapting John Harris's argument in "The Survival Lottery," *Philosophy* 50 (1975), 81–87.

FURTHER READINGS

Aiken, William, and Hugh LaFollette. *World Hunger and Moral Obligation.* Englewood Cliffs, NJ: Prentice Hall, Inc., 1977.

Hardin, Garrett. *Stalking the Wild Taboo.* Los Altos, CA: William Kauffman, 1978.

Singer, Peter. "Famine, Affluence, and Morality." In *Moral Problems,* ed. James Rachels. New York: Harper & Row, 1979, 263–278.

PROGRESS CHECK 20.1

Instructions: *Fill in the blanks with the appropriate responses listed below.*

psychological explanation
good reason
discharge
optionality
counterintuitive

lifestyles
bad faith
intuitions
distinction
positive–negative

1. _____ are prereflective beliefs about what is right and wrong.
2. A _____ of how we feel does not constitute an ethical justification for our conduct.
3. The _____ between action and inaction does not lead to any necessary moral assessment about what is or is not done.
4. If there is no _____ for performing some action, then it is not true that one ought to do it.
5. The fact that we cannot completely _____ a duty to save everyone needing aid does not mean that our duty to save those we can is any less stringent.
6. For Richard Trammell, _____ makes letting die less bad or wrong than killing, since others may choose to save the starving, even if we do not.

7. Arguments which lead to _____ conclusions are not always wrong or inadequate. The intuitions involved may be based on false assumptions.

8. Daniel Dinello accepts the _____ distinction among duties.

9. Taking seriously our responsibility to feed the starving of the world would require that we abandon our affluent _____.

10. When we rationalize our lack of action to save the hungry by pointing to others who could but don't help, we are guilty of _____, according to Rachels.

LEARNING EXERCISE 20.2

Instructions: *Complete the following syllogisms.*

1. **Value Premise:** Anyone who allows a starving child to die when he or she could be saved is a moral monster.

   Factual Premise:

   Conclusion: Therefore, Jack Palance is a moral monster.

2. **Value Premise:**

   Factual Premise: Letting die is an action closely approximating killing.

   Conclusion: Therefore, letting die is wrong.

3. **Value Premise:** Spending money on nonessentials while others go hungry is wrong.

   Factual Premise: Living an affluent lifestyle involves spending money on nonessentials.

   Conclusion:

4. **Value Premise:**

   Factual Premise: Many prereflective beliefs about our responsibilities toward the hungry stem from moral intuitions based on incorrect assumptions and facts.

   Conclusion: Therefore, many prereflective beliefs about our responsibilities toward the hungry should be questioned.

5. **Value Premise:** Actions for which the reasons are the same are morally equivalent.

   Factual Premise:

   Conclusion: Therefore, killing and letting die are morally equivalent.

LEARNING EXERCISE 20.3

Instructions: *Evaluate the following arguments and principles for their acceptability. Check for logical errors and fallacies. Also where appropriate,
use the new-cases, higher-order principle, role-exchange tests, as well
as the universalizability and consistency tests.*

1. I'm not going to contribute to any foreign aid agencies. The people in third-
world nations are simply too stupid to practice birth control effectively. If they
only cut down on their numbers, there wouldn't be any food shortages. The way
I look at it, I'm doing the world a favor by not contributing to food banks.
Nature will take its proper course in determining what the planet's population
should be.
2. It doesn't matter if I don't contribute to food charities; others certainly will.
3. I'm not giving to Food-Aid, Band-Aid, Farm-Aid, or any other kind of aid. Those
who administer the contributions are crooked. So much gets siphoned off that
the truly needy get very little. Look at Ethiopia. So much food was stolen and
then sold on the black market that the starving Ethiopians got hardly anything
at all.
4. Give to foreign aid? No way. I'm saving to buy a fancy sportscar. Everything I'm
earning right now should go to that end.
5. I hate all those television appeals for donations to food-bank charities designed
to make one feel guilty. How dare those Hollywood celebrities try to lay a guilt
trip on me. When they give up their homes and luxuries, then I'll contribute.
Not until then.

21

"IS PORNOGRAPHY BENEFICIAL?"

G. L. Simons

EDUCATIONAL OBJECTIVES: After reading this chapter the student will be able to:

21.1 Paraphrase Simons' criticisms of the antipornography position.

21.2 Explain how pleasure serves as a justification for pornography.

21.3 Cite evidence and authoritative sources on the relationship between pornography and normal sexual development.

21.4 Illustrate the benefits of "sex by proxy," which pornography provides.

21.5 Comment on how pornography can act as a catharsis.

21.6 Tell what the relationship is between reading salacious pornographic literature and committing sexual crimes.

21.7 State Simons' conclusion on making pornography available.

FOCUS QUESTIONS

1. In what way is the onus or burden of proof in this debate on the antipornographers?

2. Arguments in favor of and against the availability of pornography refer heavily to alleged positive and negative consequences? Could the debate rest on other considerations? If so, what might they be?
3. What role does pleasure play in human life? Is it necessarily good or bad? How so?
4. By rejecting pleasure as a justification of pornography, does one necessarily buy into a "cult of puritanism" or "fanatical asceticism"?
5. Is it not always desirable to help people develop a normal sex drive? If so, why? If not, why not?
6. How can pornography act as a catharsis? What benefits does it have as a catharsis?
7. Is it not proper to satisfy people's sexual appetites? Why?
8. What is the apparent causal connection between pornography and sex crimes?
9. Are there any good reasons for regarding pornography as inherently or axiomatically wrong? If so, what are they?

SYNOPSIS

In this article, G. L. Simons builds an argument against the censorship of pornography. He believes that censorship in this instance represents an indefensible restriction of human freedom. He argues that imposing restrictions on individual liberty, in this case the censorship of pornography, is justifiable only if what is being restricted produces harm—and that harm must be significant.

For Simons, it is not enough to demonstrate that some harm has come from pornography, since some harm comes from many things, such as overzealous patriotism or the carcinogenic properties of cigarettes. The harm must be quite substantial. It must also be weighed against any other positive consequences or benefits produced. The harm should be indisputable as well, clearly a result of the activity in question. Therefore, if pornography is to be censored, then the onus is upon the antipornographers to show evidence that harm does indeed flow from pornography and that the harm produced is considerable, outweighing other positive considerations.

In defense of his position, Simons cites the U.S. Report of the Commission on Obscenity and Pornography which concluded that pornography cannot be linked to any significant negative consequences. The report stated: "... if a case is to be made out against 'pornography' it will have to be made on grounds other than demonstrated effects of a damaging personal or social nature...." In further rejection of the antipornography position Simons refers to Danish Professor E. T. Rasmussen, who goes beyond arguing for mere harmlessness by suggesting that pornography may even be beneficial in certain circumstances.

The claim that pornography can be beneficial is supported in several ways. First of all, it is mentioned that pornography produces pleasure. It is something enjoyed, as evidenced by the simple fact that people buy it. Of course, pleasure is not its own justification, but neither should it be seen as inherently evil, as fanatical puritans and ascetics would have it. In view of the pleasure produced, if the bad effects of pornography are small or nonexistent, then pornography should be accepted, if not encouraged. For Simons, it is not enough for antipornographers to point to pornography's possible ill effects; they must demonstrate that these effects are in fact forthcoming.

A second argument favoring pornography stems from the fact that it can aid rather than frustrate normal sexual development. For example, a study done by the Danish Forensic Medicine Council concluded that neurotic and sexually shy individuals may be liberated from some of their anxiety regarding sex by reading pornographic descriptions of normal sexual activity. Through reading pornographic materials individuals can become freer and less frustrated about sexuality.

A third supporting argument is based on the idea that pornography can serve as a replacement for actual sexual activity involving others. This "sex by proxy" certainly has benefit for lonely and deprived people unable to make normal sexual contact. The fantasizing arising from pornography may also help those unable to seek sexual satisfaction with a spouse or loved one due to illness, travel, or bereavement. Fantasizing through pornographic literature is probably also preferable to engaging in sexual activities that would be regarded as illegal, or at least immoral. Some would say that it is a better alternative to prostitution and adultery.

A fourth related argument favoring pornography is based on its cathartic effect. Simons suggests that pornography can neutralize "aberrant" sexual inclinations and thereby reduce the incidence of some sex crimes and immoral conduct. Simons does not believe this reduction must be proven. It would be sufficient for him only to demonstrate that a repeal of antipornography laws will not cause an increase in sexually related crimes. Nonetheless, Simons does cite the U.S. Commission's report which notes that those who read "salacious literature" are less likely to commit sexual crimes than those who do not. What evidence does exist seems to suggest that the availability of pornographic materials reduces the amount of sex crime, not the converse. As Simons points out, the best the antipornographers can do is argue that the present evidence is inconclusive. If this is admitted, however, then the case for repressive legislation falls apart. In a free society where social phenomena are, like individuals, innocent until proven guilty, activities should be allowed unless there is convincing evidence of their harmful consequences. In this regard Simons reminds us of Bertrand Russell, who was initially opposed to sadistic pornography. When informed of the likely cathartic value of such pornography and when told of the fact that there was at that time no preponderance of evidence demonstrating either the evils or the benefits of pornography, Russell concluded that we should uphold the overriding principle of free speech. The general conclusion this leads to seems to be that in the absence of evidence of harm, we should be permissive, not restrictive.

In conclusion, Simons establishes several criteria: if pornography produces enjoyment or pleasure, if this enjoyment is not to be condemned, and if there is no evidence to show serious countervailing harm, then the case for making pornography available is unassailable.

[21.1] It is not sufficient, for the objectors' case, that they demonstrate that some harm has flowed from pornography. It would be extremely difficult to show that pornography had *never* had unfortunate consequences, but we should not make too much of this. Harm has flowed from religion, patriotism, alcohol and cigarettes without this fact impelling people to demand abolition. The harm, if established, has to be weighed against a variety of considerations before a decision can be reached as to the propriety of certain laws. Of the British Obscenity Laws the Arts Council Report comments[1] that "the harm would need to be both indisputable and very dire indeed before it could be judged to outweigh the evils and anomalies inherent in the Acts we have been asked to examine."

The onus therefore is upon the anti-pornographers to demonstrate not only that harm is caused by certain types of sexual material but that the harm is considerable: if the first is difficult the second is necessarily more so, and the attempts to date have not been impressive. It is even possible to argue that easily available pornography has a number of benefits. Many people will be familiar with the *catharsis* argument whereby pornography is said to cut down on delinquency by providing would-be criminals with substitute satisfactions. This is considered later but we mention it here to indicate that access to pornography may be socially beneficial in certain instances, and that where this is possible the requirement for anti-pornographers to *justify* their objections must be stressed.

The general conclusion[2] of the U.S. Commission was that no adequate proof had been provided that pornography was harmful to individual or society — "if a case is to be made out against 'pornography' [in 1970] it will have to be made on grounds other than demonstrated effects of a damaging personal or social nature. . . ."

The heresy (to some ears) that pornography is harmless is compounded by the even greater impiety that it may be beneficial. Some of us are managing to adjust to the notion that pornography is unlikely to bring down the world in moral ruin, but the idea that it may actually do good is altogether another thing. When we read of Professor Emeritus E. T. Rasmussen, a pioneer of psychological studies in Denmark, and a government adviser, saying that there is a possibility "that pornography can be beneficial," many of us are likely to have *mixed* reactions, to say the least. In fact this thesis can be argued in a number of ways.

[21.2] The simplest approach is to remark that people enjoy it. This can be seen to be true whether we rely on personal testimony or the most respectable index of all in capitalist society — "preparedness to pay." The appeal that pornography has for many people is hardly in dispute, and in a more sober social climate that would be justification enough. Today we are not quite puritan enough to deny that *pleasure* has a worthwhile place in human life: not many of us object to our food being tasty or our clothes being attractive. It was not always like this. In sterner times it was *de rigueur* to prepare food without spices and to wear the plainest clothes. The cult of puritanism reached its apotheosis in the most fanatical asceticism, where it was fashionable for holy men to wander off into a convenient desert and neglect the body to the point of cultivating its lice as "pearls of God." In such a bizarre philosophy pleasure was not only condemned in its sexual manifestations but in all areas where the body could conceivably take satisfaction. These days we are able to countenance pleasure in most fields but in many instances still the case for *sexual* pleasure has to be argued.

Pleasure is not of course its own justification. If it clearly leads to serious malaise, early death, or the *dis*pleasure of others, then there is something to be said against it. But the serious consequences have to be demonstrated: it is not enough to condemn certain forms of pleasurable experience on the grounds of *possible* ill effect. With such an approach *any* human activity could be censured and freedom would have no place. In short, if something is pleasurable and its bad effects are small or nonexistent then it is to be encouraged: opposition to such a creed should be recognized as an unwholesome antipathy to human potential. Pleasure is a good except where it is harmful (and where the harmfulness is *significant*). . . .

That pornography is enjoyable to many people is the first of the arguments in its favor. In any other field this would be argument enough. It is certainly sufficient to justify many activities that have—unlike a taste for pornography—demonstrably harmful consequences. Only in a sexually neurotic society could a tool for heightening sexual enjoyment be regarded as reprehensible and such as to warrant suppression by law. The position is well summarized[3] in the *first* of the Arts Council's twelve reasons for advocating the repeal of the Obscenity Publications Acts:

> "It is not for the State to prohibit private citizens from choosing what they may or may not enjoy in literature or art unless there were incontrovertible evidence that the result would be injurious to society. There is no such evidence."

[21.3] A further point is that availability of pornography may *aid*, rather than frustrate normal sexual development. Thus in 1966, for example, the New Jersey Committee for the Right to Read presented the findings of a survey conducted among nearly a thousand psychiatrists and psychologists of that state. Amongst the various personal statements included was the view that "sexually stimulating materials" might help particular people develop a normal sex drive.[4] In similar spirit, Dr. John Money writes[5] that pornography "may encourage normal sexual development and broadmindedness," a view that may not sound well to the anti-pornographers. And even in circumstances where possible dangers of pornography are pointed out conceivable good effects are sometimes acknowledged. In a paper issued[6] by The Danish Forensic Medicine Council it is pointed out that neurotic and sexually shy people may, by reading pornographic descriptions of normal sexual activity, be freed from some of their apprehension regarding sex and may thereby attain a freer and less frustrated attitude to the sexual side of life. . . .

[21.4] One argument in favor of pornography is that it can serve as a substitute for actual sexual activity involving another person or other people. This argument has two parts, relating as it does to (1) people who fantasize over *socially acceptable* modes of sexual involvement, and (2) people who fantasize over types of sexual activity that would be regarded as illegal or at least immoral. The first type relates to lonely and deprived people who for one reason or another have been unable to form "normal" sexual contacts with other people; the second type are instances of the much quoted *catharsis* argument.

One writer notes[7] that pornography can serve as a substitute for both the knowledge of which some people have been deprived and the pleasure in sexual experience which they have not enjoyed. One can well imagine men or women too inhibited to secure sexual satisfaction with other adults and where explicit sexual material can alleviate some of their misery. It is facile to remark that such people should seek psychiatric assistance or even "make an effort": the factors that prevent the forming of effective sexual liaisons are just as likely to inhibit any efforts to seek medical or other assistance. Pornography provides *sex by proxy*, and in such usage it can have a clear justification.

It is also possible to imagine circumstances in which men or women — for reasons of illness, travel or bereavement — are unable to seek sexual satisfaction with spouse or other loved one. Pornography can help here too. Again it is easy to suggest that a person abstain from sexual experience, or, if having *permanently* lost a spouse, seek out another partner. Needless to say such advice is often quite impractical — and the alternative to pornography may be prostitution or adultery. Montagu notes that pornography can serve the same purpose as "dirty jokes," allowing a person to discharge harmlessly repressed and unsatisfied sexual desires.

In this spirit, Mercier (1970) is quoted by the U.S. Commission:

"... it is in periods of sexual deprivation — to which the young and the old are far more subject than those in their prime — that males, at any rate, are likely to reap psychological benefit from pornography."

And also Kenneth Tynan (1970):

"For men on long journeys, geographically cut off from wives and mistresses, pornography can act as a portable memory, a welcome shortcut to remembered bliss, relieving tension without involving disloyalty."

It is difficult to see how anyone could object to the use of pornography in such circumstances, other than on the grounds of a morbid anti-sexuality.

[21.5] The *catharsis argument* has long been put forward to suggest that availability of pornography will neutralize "aberrant" sexual tendencies and so reduce the inci-

dence of sex crime or clearly immoral behavior in related fields. (Before evidence is put forward for this thesis it is worth remarking that it should not be necessary to demonstrate a *reduction* in sex crime to justify repeal of the Obscenity Laws. It should be quite sufficient to show that an *increase* in crime will not ensue following repeal. We may even argue that a small increase may be tolerable if other benefits from easy access to pornography could be shown: but it is no part of the present argument to put this latter contention.)

[21.6] Many psychiatrists and psychologists have favored the catharsis argument. Chesser, for instance, sees[8] pornography as a form of voyeurism in which — as with sado-masochistic material — the desire to hurt is satisfied passively. If this is so and the analogy can be extended we have only to look at the character of the voyeur — generally furtive and clandestine — to realize that we have little to fear from the pornography addict. Where consumers are preoccupied with fantasy there is little danger to the rest of us. Karpman (1959), quoted by the U.S. Commission, notes that people reading "salacious literature" are less likely to become sexual offenders than those who do not since the reading often neutralizes "aberrant sexual interests." Similarly the Kronhausens have argued that "these 'unholy' instruments" may be a safety-valve for the sexual deviate and potential sex offender. And Cairns, Paul and Wishner (1962) have remarked that *obscene materials* provide a way of releasing strong sexual urges without doing harm to others.

It is easy to see the plausibility of this argument. The popularity of all forms of sexual literature — from the superficial, *sexless*, sentimentality of the popular women's magazine to the clearest "hard-core" porn — has demonstrated over the ages the perennial appetite that people have for fantasy. To an extent, a great extent with many single people and frustrated married ones, the fantasy constitutes an important part of the sex-life. The experience may be vicarious and sterile but it self-evidently fills a need for many individuals. If literature, as a *symbol* of reality, can so involve human sensitivities it is highly likely that when the sensitivities are *distorted* for one reason or another the same sublimatory function can occur: the "perverted" or potentially criminal mentality can gain satisfaction, as does the lonely unfortunate, in *sex by proxy.* If we wanted to force the potential sex criminal on to the streets in search of a human victim perhaps we would do well to deny him his sublimatory substitutes: deny him fantasy and he will be forced to go after the real thing. . . .

The importance of this possibility should be fully faced. If a causal connection *does* exist between availability of pornographic material and a *reduction* in the amount of sex crime — and the evidence is wholly consistent with this possibility rather than its converse — then people who deliberately restrict pornography by supporting repressive legislation are prime architects of sexual offenses against the individual. The anti-pornographers would do well to note that their anxieties may be driving them into a position the exact opposite of the one they explicitly maintain — their commitment to reduce the amount of sexual delinquency in society.

The most that the anti-pornographers can argue is that at present the evidence is inconclusive. . . . But if the inconclusive character of the data is once admitted then the case for repressive legislation falls at once. For in a *free* society, or one supposedly aiming after freedom, social phenomena are, like individuals, innocent until proven guilty — and an activity will be permitted unless there is clear evidence of its

harmful consequences. The point was well put — in the specific connection with pornography — by Bertrand Russell, talking[9] when he was well over 90 to Rupert Crawshay-Williams.

After noting how people beg the question of causation in instances such as the Moors murders (where the murders and the reading of de Sade *may* have a common cause), Russell ("Bertie") said that on the whole he disapproved of sadistic pornography being available. But when Crawshay-Williams put the catharsis view, that such material might provide a harmless release for individuals who otherwise may be dangerous, Russell said at once — "Oh, well, if that's true, then I don't see that there is anything against sadistic pornography. In fact it should be encouraged. . . ." When it was stressed that there was no preponderating evidence either way Russell argued that we should fall back on an overriding principle — "in this case the principle of free speech."

Thus in the absence of evidence of harm we should be permissive. Any other view is totalitarian. . . .

[21.7]   If human enjoyment *per se* is not to be condemned then it is not too rash to say that we *know* pornography does good. We can easily produce our witnesses to testify to experiencing pleasure. If in the face of this — and no other favorable argument — we are unable to demonstrate a countervailing harm, then the case for easy availability of pornography is unassailable. If, in such circumstances, we find some people unconvinced it is futile to seek out further empirical data. Once we commit ourselves to the notion that the evil nature of something is axiomatic we tacitly concede that evidence is largely irrelevant to our position. If pornography never fails to fill us with predictable loathing then statistics on crime, or measured statements by careful specialists, will not be useful: our reactions will stay the same. But in this event we would do well to reflect on what our emotions tell us of our own mentality. . . .

NOTES

1. *The Obscenity Laws*, André Deutsch, 1969, p. 33.
2. *The Report of the Commission on Obscenity and Pornography*, part three, II, Bantam Books, 1970, p. 169.
3. *The Obscenity Laws*, André Deutsch, 1969, p. 35.
4. Quoted by Isadore Rubin, "What Should Parents Do about Pornography?" *Sex in the Adolescent Years*, Fontana, 1969, p. 202.
5. John Money, contribution to "Is Pornography Harmful to Young Children?" *Sex in the Childhood Years*, Fontana, 1971, pp. 181–185.
6. Paper from The Danish Forensic Medicine Council to The Danish Penal Code Council, published in The Penal Code Council Report on Penalty for Pornography, Report No. 435, Copenhagen, 1966, pp. 78–80, and as appendix to *The Obscenity Laws*, pp. 120–124.
7. Ashley Montagu, "Is Pornography Harmful to Young Children?" *Sex in the Childhood Years*, Fontana, 1971, p. 182.
8. Eustace Chesser, *The Human Aspects of Sexual Deviation*, Arrow Books, 1971, p. 39.
9. Rupert Crawshay-Williams, *Russell Remembered*, Oxford University Press, 1970, p. 144.

FURTHER READINGS

Berger, Fred R. *Freedom of Expression*. Belmont, CA: Wadsworth, 1980.
Clor, Harry M. *Obscenity and Public Morality*. Chicago: University of Chicago Press, 1965.
Dyal, Robert. "Is Pornography Good for You?" *Southwestern Journal of Philosophy*, 7 (Fall 1976): 95–118.
Simons, G. L. *Pornography without Prejudice*. London: Abelard-Schuman Ltd., 1972.

PROGRESS CHECK 21.1

Instructions: *Fill in the blanks with the appropriate responses listed below.*

sexual development	inconclusive
pleasure	consequences
catharsis	sex by proxy
causal connection	aberrant
onus	overriding principle

1. The _____ is upon antipornographers to demonstrate that pornography produces harm and that the harm is significant.
2. The evidence seems to suggest that there is a _____ between the availability of pornographic material and a reduction in the amount of sex crime.
3. In 1966, the New Jersey Committee for the Right to Read presented findings suggesting that pornography may in fact promote normal _____, not hinder it.
4. On the matter of sadistic pornography, Bertrand Russell argued that because there was no preponderance of evidence pointing to its condemnation, we should appeal to the _____ of free speech.

5. Those favoring pornography and the liberalization of pornography laws frequently present the _____ argument which states that pornography allows for an emotional release or discharge of sexual tendencies, thereby reducing the chances of sex crime and other immoral behaviors.

6. Antipornographers claim that pornography produces harmful _____.

7. _____ is good and desirable except in cases where significant harm is produced.

8. For those unable to have relations—because of illness, travel, or bereavement, for example—pornography allows for _____.

9. Pornography may neutralize _____ sexual tendencies.

10. The evidence about the positive and negative consequences of pornography is _____.

LEARNING EXERCISE 21.2   Completing Syllogisms

Instructions: Complete the following syllogisms.

1. **Value Premise:** Activities having indeterminate results should not be condemned.

   Factual Premise:

   Conclusion: Pornography should not be condemned.

2. **Value Premise:**

   Factual Premise: Pornography reduces sexual crime.

   Conclusion: Pornography is good.

3. **Value Premise:** Producing pleasure in people's lives is desirable.

   Factual Premise: Pornography produces pleasure in people's lives.

   Conclusion:

4. **Value Premise:** That which contributes to normal sexual development should be accepted.

   Factual Premise:

   Conclusion: Therefore, pornography should be accepted.

5. **Value Premise:**

   Factual Premise: Some antipornographers refuse to examine the empirical evidence on pornography.

   Conclusion: Therefore, some antipornographers are irrational.

LEARNING EXERCISE 21.3

Instructions: *Identify the following as either factual statements (F) or value judgments (V).*

_____ 1. Sexually stimulating material helps people to develop a normal sexual drive.

_____ 2. Pornography provides "sex by proxy."

_____ 3. Those opposed to pornography are puritanical zealots.

_____ 4. Pleasure without harm is good in itself.

_____ 5. Pornography is inherently evil.

_____ 6. The current evidence on pornography is inconclusive.

_____ 7. If something is pleasurable and its bad effects are small or nonexistent, then it is to be encouraged.

_____ 8. Pornography neutralizes aberrant sexual tendencies.

_____ 9. The principle of free speech should override conservative sexual values.

_____ 10. Many witnesses can be produced to testify that pornography produces pleasure.

22

"PORNOGRAPHY AND RESPECT FOR WOMEN"

Ann Garry

EDUCATIONAL OBJECTIVES: After reading this chapter the student will be able to:

22.1 Demonstrate how pornography violates the moral principle of respect for persons.
22.2 Give examples of how pornography is degrading and exploitive.
22.3 Explain how traditional respect for women is unacceptable from a feminist's perspective.
22.4 List Garry's reasons for rejecting the treatment of women as sex objects.
22.5 Explain why the sex-harm connection makes it worse to treat women as sex objects than to treat men as sex objects.

FOCUS QUESTIONS

1. What does it mean to dehumanize? How are women dehumanized by contemporary pornography?

This article first appeared in *Social Theory and Practice* 4 (Summer 1978), pp. 395–421. It is reprinted here as it appears in Sharon Bishop and Marjorie Weinswey, eds., *Philosophy and Women* (Wadsworth, 1979). Reprinted by permission of the author.

2. What is meant precisely by the principle of respect for persons?

3. Garry distinguishes between being treated as a sex object and being treated as a sex object in a degrading manner. What is the difference?

4. Garry objects to the contemporary content of pornography. Could one object to pornography for its own sake? If so, on what basis would one's objections rest?

5. How does the distinction between good and bad women point to the fact that men's respect for women is sexist?

6. What reasons could women give for resenting treatment as sex objects?

7. How is sex related to harm in pornography?

8. Why would the treatment of both men and women only as sex objects in pornography be morally unacceptable?

9. How is contemporary pornography sexist?

10. What conditions would have to be met in order for pornography to be considered morally acceptable from a feminist perspective?

SYNOPSIS

This essay offers a moral assessment of pornography from a feminist perspective. Its author, Ann Garry, presents the view that pornography is morally reprehensible insofar as it "exemplifies and recommends behavior that violates the moral principle to respect persons." Nonetheless, she does believe that it is possible to produce morally acceptable pornography which is nonsexist and nondegrading.

In part one of her essay, Garry objects morally to pornography not because of its effects upon people, but because pornography itself illustrates and recommends conduct violating the moral imperative to show respect for persons. It is the content, therefore, not the results, which is found objectionable. For Garry, the content of pornography treats women as sex objects to be exploited and manipulated. Treating women as sex objects is not the central point, however; what is still more important is that they are treated as sex objects in a degrading manner. Examples are provided.

Garry criticizes the concept of respect as it has traditionally applied to women. She points out that the "respect" men have had for women in the past is a respect which can be lost. It is not an all-encompassing respect for persons as autonomous beings. The respect men have shown toward women is an outgrowth of a double standard. Pure, fragile, and delicate women are described as good and they are the ones who are respected, whereas women without these qualities are described as bad, not deserving respect. The respect which is won and lost is defined, awarded, and withdrawn by men. Thus, even good women who are respected and placed on a pedestal do not occupy an equal place with men. Their whole being is not being respected. Women are treated as a special class of inferior beings whose "respectfulness" hinges on one dimension of their lives, that is, their sexuality. The respect men have shown toward women in the past is not a

". . . wholehearted respect for full-fledged human beings but half-hearted respect for lesser beings, some of whom they feel the need to glorify and purify." From the feminists' perspective, all women are full-fledged people deserving respect regardless of whether they are labeled good or bad, treated as sex objects, or think of themselves as sex objects.

Garry's concerns about treating women as sex objects do not come from any worry that sex is dirty. She objects on the ground that women are treated only as sex objects, in the same way that she would resent being treated only as a baker of chocolate chip cookies. In these cases, only one talent or attribute is being valued. Second, Garry objects to the possibility that others, believing that sex is dirty, could treat her as a sex object, though she may believe sex is healthy. Third, Garry dislikes being treated as any type of object. She would prefer to be a partner over an object.

Garry's fourth reason for disliking being treated as a sex object stems from Robert Baker's observations of the sexual double standard and the evidence from language that we associate the notion of sex with the concept of harm. Slang terms make the male the subject who does something to the female object. Words like "fuck" and "screw" possess two connotations, harming and having sex. Garry says, "Because in our culture we connect sex with harm that men do to women, and because we think of the female role in sex as that of harmed object, we can see that to treat a woman as a sex object is automatically to treat her as less than fully human." The situation is different for men, Garry claims. Because of prior conditioning and cultural history, it is more difficult for heterosexual men to assume the role of "harmed object." Men do not understand very well as a result how it is undesirable to be treated as a sex object. Some men would even like to be treated in this fashion.

Ann Garry further objects to contemporary pornography because it is male-oriented and designed to turn a profit through appealing to male fantasies. These male fantasies are based on stereotypical sex roles whereby women cater to male desires. Women's pleasure is seldom emphasized for its own sake. The woman's job is to service the man. As Garry puts it, ". . . very little contemporary pornography goes against traditional sex roles. This is certainly no significant attempt to replace the harmer/harmed distinction with anything more positive and healthy. In some stag movies, of course, men are treated sadistically by women, but this is an attempt to turn the tables on degradation, not a positive improvement."

In part two of her article (not included here), Garry outlines a form of pornography which would be morally preferable to the extent that it is nonsexist and nondegrading with respect to content. In order for pornography to have acceptable content, it must sever the connections between sex and harm. To do this, changes in people's attitudes and feelings will be required. Second, nonsexist pornography would have men and women treated as equal sex partners. No one gender would control the circumstances or positions in which sex took place. There would also be no suggestion of a power play or conquest on the man's part. Furthermore, the primary objective of sexual intercourse would not be male ejaculation. To extinguish sexism in pornography, Garry also suggests that men and women be shown in equally valued roles wherein sexual equality would mean more than merely the possession of equally functional genitalia. In this case, characters would treat each other respectfully and with consideration. No attempts would be made to treat men and women with brutality or without thought. If such recommendations were enacted, then nonsexist pornographic films could be appreciated in the proper spirit.

[22.1] The . . . argument I consider is that pornography is morally objectionable not because it leads people to show disrespect for women, but because pornography itself exemplifies and recommends behavior which violates the moral principle to respect persons. The content of pornography is what one objects to. It treats women as mere sex objects "to be exploited and manipulated" and degrades the role and status of women. In order to evaluate this argument I first clarify what it would mean for pornography itself to treat someone as a sex object in a degrading manner. I then deal with three issues which are central to the discussion of pornography and respect for women: how "losing respect" for a woman is connected with treating her as a sex object, what is wrong with treating someone as a sex object, and why it is worse to treat women rather than men as sex objects. I argue that today the content of pornography is sometimes in violation of the moral principle to respect persons. . . .

To many people, including [Susan] Brownmiller and some other feminists, it appears to be an obvious truth that pornography treats people, especially women, as sex objects in a degrading manner. And if we omit "in a degrading manner," it seems hard to disagree: how could pornography not treat people as sex objects?

[22.2] First, is it permissible to talk about either the content of pornography or pornography itself degrading people or treating people as sex objects? It is not difficult to find examples of degrading content in which women are treated as sex objects. There are unnamed movies conveying the message that all women really want to be raped, so don't believe them when they struggle against you. By portraying women in this manner, the content of the movie degrades women. Degrading women is morally objectionable. Seeing the movie need not cause anyone to imitate the behavior shown. We can call the content degrading to women because of the character of the behavior and attitudes it recommends. The same kind of point can be made about films (books, or TV commercials) with other kinds of degrading, thus morally objectionable, content, for example, racist messages.

The next step in the argument is to infer that because the content or message of pornography is morally objectionable, we can call pornography itself morally objectionable. Support for this step can be found in an analogy. If a person takes every opportunity to recommend that men rape women, we would think not only that his recommendation is immoral but that he is immoral too. The objection to making the inference from that which is recommended to that which recommends in the case of pornography is that we ascribe such predicates as "immoral" differently to people than to objects such as films, books, and so on. A film which is the vehicle for an objectionable message is still an object independent of its message, its director, its producer, those who act in it, and those who respond to it. Hence one cannot make an unsupported inference from "the content of the film is morally objectionable" to "the film is morally objectionable." Because the central points in this paper do not depend on pornography itself (in addition to its content) being morally objectionable, I will not try to support this inference. The question about the relation of the content to the work itself, is of course, extremely interesting; but in part because I cannot decide which side of the argument is more persuasive, I will pass.[1] Certainly one appropriate way to evaluate pornography is in terms of the moral features of its content. If a pornographic film exemplifies and recommends attitudes or behavior which are morally objectionable, then its content is morally objectionable.

Let us turn to the first of the remaining three questions about respect and sex objects: what is the connection between losing respect for a woman and treating her as a sex object? Some people who have lived through the era in which women were taught to worry about men "losing respect" for them if they engaged in sex in inappropriate circumstances, find it troublesome or at least amusing that feminists, supposedly "liberated" women, are outraged at being treated as sex objects, either by pornography or in any other way. The apparent alignment between feminists and traditionally "proper" women need not surprise us when we look at it more closely.

[22.3] The respect which men traditionally believed they had for women, hence which they could lose, is not a general respect for persons as autonomous beings, nor is it respect that is earned because of one's personal merits or achievements. It is respect that is an outgrowth of the "double standard." Women are to be respected because they are more pure, delicate, and fragile than men, have more refined sensi-

bilities, and so on. Because some women clearly do not have these qualities, thus do not deserve respect, women must be divided into two groups—the good ones on the pedestal and the bad ones who have fallen from it. One's mother, grandmother, Sunday school teacher, and usually one's wife are "good" women. The appropriate behavior to express respect for good women would be, for example, not swearing or telling dirty jokes in front of them, giving them seats on buses, and other "chivalrous" acts. This sort of respect for good women is that which adolescent boys in back seats of cars used to "promise" not to lose. Note that men define, display, and lose this kind of respect. If women lose respect for women, it is not typically loss of respect for (other) women as a class, but loss of self-respect.

It has now become commonplace to acknowledge that although a place on the pedestal might have advantages over a place in the "gutter" beneath it, a place on the pedestal is not at all equal to the place occupied by other people, that is, men. "Respect" for those on the pedestal was not respect for whole, full-fledged people, but for a special class of inferior beings.

If someone makes two traditional assumptions—that (at least some) sex is dirty and that women fall into two classes, good and bad—it is easy to see how this person might think that pornography could lead people to lose respect for women or that pornography is itself disrespectful to women.[2] Pornography describes or shows women engaging in activities which are inappropriate for good women to engage in, or at least inappropriate for them to be seen by strangers engaging in. If one sees these women as symbolic representatives of all women, then all women fall from grace with these women. This fall is possible, I believe, because the "respect" men had for women was not genuine wholehearted respect for full-fledged human beings, but half-hearted respect for lesser beings some of whom they felt the need to glorify and purify.[3] It is easy to fall from a pedestal. Can we imagine 41% of men and 46% of women answering "yes" to the question, "Do movies showing men engaging in violent acts lead people to lose respect for men?"

Two interesting asymmetries appear. The first is that it is more difficult to lose respect for men as a class (men with power, typically Anglo men) than it is to lose respect for women or ethnic minorities as a class. Anglo men whose behavior warrants disrespect are more likely to be seen as exceptional cases than are women or minorities (whose "transgressions" may be far less serious). Think of the following: women are temptresses; Blacks cheat the welfare system; Italians are gangsters; but the men of the Nixon administration are exceptions—Anglo men as a class did not lose respect because of Watergate and related scandals.

The second asymmetry concerns the active and passive roles of the sexes. Men are seen in the active role. If men lose respect for women because of something "evil" done by women (such as appearing in pornography) the fear is that men will then do harm to women, not that women will do harm to men. Whereas if women lose respect for male politicians because of Watergate the fear is still that male politicians will do harm, not that women will do harm to male politicians. This asymmetry might be a result of one way in which our society thinks of sex as bad—as harm men do to women (or to the person playing a female role, for example, in a homosexual rape). Robert Baker calls attention to this point in " 'Pricks' and 'Chicks': A Plea for 'Persons.' "[4] Our slang words for sexual intercourse, "fuck," "screw," or older words such as "take" or "have" not only can mean harm but traditionally have taken a male subject and a female object. The active male screws, harms, the passive female. A "bad" woman only tempts men to hurt her further.

One can understand why one's proper grandmother would not want men to see pornography or lose respect for women. But feminists reject these "proper" assumptions: there are not good and bad classes of women and sex is not dirty (though many people believe it is). Why then are feminists angry at women's being treated as sex objects, and some feminists opposed to pornography?

[22.4] The answer is that feminists as well as proper grandparents are concerned with respect. However, there are differences. A feminist's distinction between treating a woman as a full-fledged person and treating her as merely a sex object does not correspond to the good–bad woman distinction. In the latter distinction "good" and "bad" are properties applicable to groups of women. On the feminist view, all women really are full-fledged people, it is just that some are treated as sex objects and perhaps think of themselves as sex objects. A further difference is that although "bad" women correspond to those who have been thought to deserve to be treated as sex objects, good women have not corresponded to full-fledged people: only men have been full-fledged people. Given the feminist's distinction, she has no difficulty at all saying that pornography treats women as sex objects, not as full-fledged people. She can object morally to pornography or anything else treating women as sex objects.

One might wonder whether any objection to being treated as a sex object implies that the person objecting still believes, deep down, that sex is dirty. I don't think so. Several other possibilities emerge. First, even if I believe intellectually and emotionally that sex is healthy, I might object to being treated *only* as a sex object, in the same spirit that I would object to being treated only as a maker of chocolate chip cookies or as a tennis partner — only a few of my talents are being valued. Second, perhaps I feel that sex is healthy, but it is apparent to me that you think it is dirty; so I don't want you to treat me as a sex object. Third, being treated as any kind of object, not just a sex object, has an unappealing ring to it. I would rather be a partner (sexual or otherwise) than an object.

[22.5] Fourth, and more plausible than the first three, is Robert Baker's view mentioned above. Both (i) our traditional double standard of sexual behavior for men and women and (ii) the linguistic evidence that we connect the concept of sex with the concept of harm, point to what is wrong with treating women as sex objects. As I said earlier, in their traditional uses, "fuck" and "screw" have taken a male subject, a female object, and have had at least two meanings: harm and have sexual intercourse with. (In addition, a prick is man who harms people ruthlessly; and a motherfucker is so low that he would do something very harmful to his own dear mother.)[5] Because in our culture we connect sex with harm that men do to women and think of the female role in sex as that of harmed object, we can see that to treat a woman as a sex object is automatically to treat her as less than fully human. To say this does not imply that no healthy sexual relationships exist; nor does it say anything about individual men's conscious intentions to degrade women by desiring them sexually (though no doubt some men have these intentions). It is merely to make a point about the concepts embodied in our language.

Psychoanalytic support for the connection between sex and harm comes from Robert J. Stoller. Stoller thinks that sexual excitement is linked with a wish to harm someone (and at least a whisper of hostility).

The key process of sexual excitement can be seen as dehumanization (fetishization) in fantasy of the desired person. He speculates that this is true in some degree of everyone, men and women, with "normal" or "perverted" activities and fantasies.[6]

Thinking of sex objects as harmed objects enables us to explain some of the first three reasons why one wouldn't want to be treated as a sex object. (1) I may object to being treated only as a tennis partner, but being a tennis partner is not connected in our culture with being a harmed object. (2) I may not think that sex is dirty and that I would be a harmed object; I may not know what your view is; but what bothers me is that this is the view embodied in our language and culture.

Awareness of the connection between sex and harm helps us to explain other interesting points. Women are angry about being treated as sex objects in situations or roles in which they do not intend to be thought of in that manner, for example, serving on a committee or attending a discussion. It is not merely that a sexual role is inappropriate for the circumstances, it is thought to be a less fully human role than the one in which they intended to function.

Finally, the sex-harm connection makes it clear why it is worse to treat women as sex objects than to treat men as sex objects, and why some men have had difficulty understanding women's anger about the matter. It is more difficult for heterosexual men than for women to assume the role of "harmed object" in sex; for men have the concept of themselves as sexual agents, not as passive objects. This is also related to the point I made earlier about the difference in the solidity of respect for men and for women: respect for women is more fragile. Although there are exceptions, it is generally harder to degrade men sexually or nonsexually than to degrade women. Men and women have grown up with different patterns of self-respect and expectations about the extent to which they will be respected and the extent to which they deserve respect or degradation. The man who doesn't understand why women do not want to be treated as sex objects (because he'd sure like to be) would not think of himself as being harmed by that treatment: a woman might. Pornography, probably more than any other contemporary institution, succeeds in treating men as sex objects.

Having seen that the connection between sex and harm helps to explain both what is wrong with treating someone as a sex object and why it is worse to treat a woman in this way, I want to use the sex–harm connection to try to resolve a dispute about pornography and women. Recall Brownmiller's view that pornography is "the undiluted essence of antifemale propaganda" whose purpose is to degrade women.[7] Some people object to Brownmiller by saying that since pornography treats both men and women as sex objects for the purpose of arousing the viewer, it is not sexist, not antifemale, not designed to degrade women. It just happens that degrading women arouses some men. How can the dispute be resolved?

Suppose we were to rate the content of all pornography from most morally objectionable to least morally objectionable. Among the most objectionable would be the most degrading, for example, "snuff" films or movies which recommend that men rape women, molest children and puppies, and treat nonmasochists very sadistically. Next we would find a large number of cases, probably most pornography, which are not quite so blatantly offensive. In these cases it is relevant to appeal to the analysis of sex objects given above. As long as sex is connected with harm done to women, it will be very difficult not to see pornography as degrading to women. We can agree with Brownmiller's opponent that pornography treats men as sex objects, too, but maintain that this is only pseudo-equality: such treatment is still more degrading to women.

In addition, pornography often exemplifies the active–passive, harmer–harmed object roles in a very obvious way. Because pornography today is male oriented and supposed to make a profit, the content is designed to appeal to male fantasies. Judging from the content of the most popular legally available pornography, male fantasies still run along the lines of stereotypical sex roles and, if Stoller is right, include elements of hostility. In many cases the women's purpose is to cater to male desires, to service the man or men. Her own pleasure is rarely emphasized for its own sake; she is merely allowed a little heavy breathing, perhaps in order to show her dependence on the great male "lover" who produces her pleasure. In addition, women are clearly made into passive objects in still photographs showing only close-ups of their genitals. Even in movies which are marketed to appeal to heterosexual couples, such as "Behind the Green Door," the woman is passive and undemanding (and in this case kidnapped and hypnotized as well). Although there are many kinds of specialty magazines and films for different sexual tastes, very little in contemporary pornography goes against traditional sex roles. There is certainly no significant attempt to replace the harmer–harmed distinction with anything more positive and healthy. There are, of course, stag movies in which men are treated sadistically by women; but this is an attempt to turn the tables on degradation, not a positive improvement. . . .

NOTES

1. In order to help one determine which position one feels inclined to take, consider the following statement: It is morally objectionable to write, make, sell, act in, use, and enjoy pornography; in addition, the content of pornography is immoral; however, pornography itself is not morally objectionable. If this seems extremely problematic, then one might well be satisfied with the claim that pornography is degrading because its content is.
2. The traditional meaning of "lose respect for women" was evidently the one assumed in the Abelson survey cited by the Presidential Commission. No explanation of its meaning is given in reporting the study. See H. Ableson et al., "National Survey of Public Attitudes toward and Experience with Erotic Materials," *Tech Report* 6, 1–137.
3. Many feminists point this out. One of the most accessible references is Shulamith Firestone, *The Dialectic of Sex: The Case for the Feminist Revolution* (New York: Morrow, 1970); see especially 128–132.

4. In Richard Wasserstrom, ed., *Today's Moral Problems* (New York: Macmillan, 1975), 152–171. See 167–171.
5. Baker, 168–169.
6. "Sexual Excitement." *Archives of General Psychiatry* 33 (August 1976): 899–909, expecially 903. The extent to which Stoller sees men and women in different positions with respect to harm and hostility is not clear. He often treats men and women alike, but in *Perversion: The Erotic Form of Hatred* (New York: Pantheon Books, 1975), 89–91, he calls attention to differences between men and women, especially regarding their response to pornography, lack of understanding by men of women's sexuality, and so forth. Given that Stoller finds hostility to be an essential element in male-oriented pornography and given that women have not responded readily to it, one can think of possibilities for women's sexuality; their hostility might follow a different scenario; they might not be as hostile, and so on.
7. Susan Brownmiller, *Against Our Will: Men, Women and Rape* (New York: Simon and Schuster, 1975), 394.

FURTHER READINGS

Devlin, Patrick. *The Enforcement of Morals.* New York: Oxford University Press, 1965.
Holbrook, David (ed.). *The Case against Pornography.* New York: Library Press, 1973.
The Report of the Commission on Obscenity and Pornography. Washington, DC: Government Printing Office, 1970.

PROGRESS CHECK 22.1

Instructions: *Fill in the blanks with the appropriate responses listed below.*

morally objectionable	sex–harm
attitude	roles
respect for persons	degrading
sex objects	inferior beings
equal	spirit

1. According to Ann Garry, much of contemporary pornography violates the principle of _____.
2. Pornography views women unidimensionally as _____.
3. Even a modified, ethically acceptable pornography must be appreciated by the audience in the proper _____.

4. In order to make pornography less sexist and morally objectionable, the _____ link must be broken.

5. When men place "good" women on a pedestal, they still treat them as _____ whose human value can be withdrawn at any time.

6. Feminists would prefer men and women to be _____ partners in pornographic scenarios.

7. Some pornography is exploitive and _____ insofar as it conveys the message that women really wish to be raped and hurt.

8. If a pornographic film exemplifies and recommends ethically offensive attitudes or behaviors, then its content must be considered _____.

9. Garry is cautious about giving wholehearted approval to any pornography viewed today because of the possibility that audience _____ may be inappropriate.

10. Along with treating men and women as equals with respect to functioning genitalia, acceptable pornography would display men and women in equally valued social _____.

LEARNING EXERCISE 22.2   Completing Syllogisms

Instructions: Complete the following syllogisms.

1. **Value Premise:**   Degrading and exploiting human beings is morally objectionable.

   Factual Premise:

   Conclusion: Therefore, much of contemporary pornography is morally objectionable.

2. **Value Premise:**

   Factual Premise: Exploitive pornography shows disrespect for women.

   Conclusion: Therefore, exploitive pornography is wrong.

3. **Value Premise:**   Viewing people unidimensionally does violence to their humanity.

   Factual Premise: Pornography views people unidimensionally as sex objects.

   Conclusion:

4. **Value Premise:**   Treating men and women as equals is good.

   Factual Premise: Nonsexist pornography treats men and women as equals.

   Conclusion:

5. **Value Premise:**

   Factual Premise: Some pornography perpetuates the myth that women like to be hurt.

   Conclusion: Some pornography is unacceptable.

LEARNING EXERCISE 22.3   Evaluating Principles and Arguments

Instructions: *Evaluate the following principles and arguments using the tests for adequacy. Look for any incorrect logic and logical fallacies.*

1. What do you mean my views are chauvinistic? How can anyone agree with all those feminists opposed to pornography? They're opposed to a lot of traditional institutions which made this country great. Why, some are even choosing to be single mothers out of wedlock. I don't see how you can trust the judgment of someone who would undermine the Judeo-Christian concept of the nuclear family.

2. I disagree with women who oppose pornography. Opponents are usually ugly anyway. It's in their interest to draw attention away from human beauty.

3. Exploiting and degrading people is wrong.

4. All pornography is unacceptable. If we allow for soft pornography, hard pornography will shortly follow. From kissing and handholding, we're sure to move on to heavy petting and intercourse and then on to bestiality and homosexual acts.

5. Pornography is good because it provides pleasure and enjoyment.

23

"IN DEFENSE OF WAR"

William Earle

EDUCATIONAL OBJECTIVES: After reading this chapter the student will be able to:

23.1 Define the principle of pacifism.

23.2 State William Earle's thesis in regard to pacifism.

23.3 Identify the strategy used to argue against pacifism.

23.4 List the contributors that feed fuel to the pacifist's fire.

23.5 Provide the causal explanation for war, when viewed as some form of distorted conduct.

23.6 Explain Earle's objections to and criticisms of the causal explanations for war.

23.7 Paraphrase Earle's argument intended to show that war is both moral and rational.

23.8 Clarify what is meant by "individuation" and how this process is relevant to discussions of war.

23.9 Identify and explain so-called false dichotomies which lend support to the pacifist's position.

23.10 Outline "popular" objections to war and give Earle's reasons for rejecting them.

23.11 Show how suffering has acted as an argument against war.

Reprinted by permission, William Earle, "In Defense of War," copyright © 1973, *The Monist*, LaSalle, IL. Reprinted from Vol. 57, No. 4, October 1973.

23.12 State Earle's views on the value of life and its relationship to honor and dignity.

FOCUS QUESTIONS

1. What is pacifism? What assumptions do pacifists make about human nature? Do you think they are correct? Why or why not?
2. Is Earle's description of antiwar advocates as baby doctors, neurotic poets and novelists, psychoanalysts, ministers, and confused philosophers neutral? Is he simply making a statement of fact or is he building something else into his description?
3. What are Earle's reasons for rejecting the pathological causes of war? Do you agree with them? Can you see any problems contained in his rejections? If so, explain.
4. What is the relationship between the concepts of "justification" and "cause" in the context of war?
5. Why does Earle consider rational solutions to conflict ineffective and inappropriate?
6. How is Earle's justification of war tied to existence? What does Earle mean by existence? How is individuation related to existence? Are there other ways of conceiving human existence?
7. Is there anything wrong with going to war for reasons of material interest? What do pacifists say? How does Earle respond? Do you agree with his response?
8. What are Earle's views on abstract concepts like equality and justice?
9. Does Earle respect "popular" objections to war? Why or why not?
10. How does Earle understand the relationship between the government and the ordinary voting citizen? Do you agree with his assessment of their respective responsibilities?
11. How does Earle view suffering as a reason for not going to war?
12. How could it be irrational and morally deplorable not to go to war?

SYNOPSIS

William Earle's basic aim in this article is to show that the principle of pacifism is "practically absurd and morally deplorable." He supports his position by exposing and criticizing the underlying presuppositions of pacifism, as well as by tracing the harmful consequences of it.

Pacifism is described at the outset of the article as principled opposition to war. From the idealistic perspective of pacifism, war is regarded as inherently evil and peace as inherently good. To Earle's disapproval, much fuel has been fed to the pacifist's fire by television and by people he describes as retired baby doctors, neurotic poets and novelists, psychoanalysts, ministers, and confused philosophers. For him, all of such people, as he identifies them, claim some kind of "special insight" qualifying them to speak for suffering humanity. The net result is the elimination of careful political thought and the emergence of preposterous slogans supported by elevated passions, parades, demonstrations, and the exchange of loud insults.

After defining pacifism, Earle proceeds to examine the causal explanations of war provided by a type of individual he dubs "the sloganeer with a smattering of pop-culture." For the "sloganeer" there can be no moral justification for war whatsoever. Since the presupposition is held that man is naturally good and war is evil, a cause must be found for man's distorted conduct. If war were, or ever could be, morally justifiable, then there would be no need to look for pathological explanations. The justification for war would become its cause. War would not be indicative of pathology or aberrant behavior. Regarding war as intrinsically evil, however, the pacifist does try to give causal account for the occurrence of it. The causal explanations point to biological origins, distorted family histories, selfishness, warlike instincts, capitalist societies, and glory-seeking presidents or national leaders. Earle offers reasons for rejecting all of these causal accounts. He believes that war can be justified and that its proponents do not need treatment, therapy, reconditioning, or character education.

In criticizing the pacifist's position, Earle questions the assumption that all men are good. He cautions us of the consequence of holding and acting upon this assumption. Earle intimates that not all men will be good or at least that not all men will envisage the good in the same way. Those few left who turn out to be wicked will in the end suppress the good people who are unwilling to fight for their ideals and lives. The practical consequences of not fighting, therefore, is that evil forces will dominate and rule. The brutal reality is that humans have throughout history found it necessary to engage in hostilities unto death in order to preserve and protect dignity, autonomy, and life. Refusing to fight would mean that the forces of evil would control the world.

William Earle apparently finds resorts to violence in settling disputes as necessary. He rejects the philosopher's attempt to correct the problem of war through "right reasoning." From the philosophical viewpoint, if rational men fight, and if war is irrational, then there must be a rational solution to it. Pacifists adopting the philosophical approach choose the medium of reason and praise it for its applications in the verbal solution to hostilities. The product of the rational route is the "treaty." Earle is quick to remind us that in the last 350 years approximately 85 percent of the treaties signed in the Western world have been broken. In view of this, it is not prudent in his view to entrust the security of one's country to treaties. Simply put, rational solutions to conflicts do not work. Even the ultimate rational solution to war—a super United Nations—is fraught with the dangers of totalitarianism, ones which Earle would prefer not to face.

In the second section of the article, Earle outlines his justification for war. This justification is intended to illustrate both the morality and rationality of war, thereby making any proscription of war in principle both irrational and ethically deplorable. According to Earle, the basic justification of war rests on "existence." War is a means and condition for the possibility of human existence. By existence, Earle means life; however, he does not limit life to mere survival. He also includes in his definition of existence those things that make life worth living. Existence incorporates all of those concrete values imbedded in laws, customs, religions, and institutions which illuminate and glorify life.

A fundamental fact about existence is that it entails a process of individuation. As Earle puts it, "Existence or life individuates itself; when it can speak it says 'I,' and what it possesses, 'mine.'" While concepts and ideas can be shared by everybody as abstract and universal meanings, that which actually exists in the individuated world cannot. This impossibility is important to note for the fact that "I am not you, or we are not they, is the ineluctable ground for war. . . ." Since existent things cannot be shared by all, a ground for conflict is created. There are simply not enough resources to go around though we all want them.

Earle admits to using terms like "existence" or "existential" over "material" because of the negative connotations associated with the latter. Pacifists frequently believe that if they can prove that nations have gone to war for reasons of material self-interest, then it is proven that the war is immoral. Earle argues that rejecting war on material grounds stems from a false contrast which juxtaposes the material and the ideal. He asks: "Is the health of a nation 'material' or 'ideal'?" (We are to suppose that it is ideal.) He then points out that the health of a nation (an ideal) depends on its wealth (a material consideration). In view of this, he then asks the question about whether the pursuit of wealth is ideal or materialistic and crass. For Earle, materialistic considerations of wealth allow for the possibility of nations to achieve the ideal of health. Seeing a very close relationship between the material and the ideal, Earle believes that discussing and pursuing ideals of human life, justice, and autonomy as totally independent of material considerations is wrongheaded. For him, there is nothing wrong therefore in fighting for reasons of material self-interest.

In further defense of war, Earle draws our attention to another so-called false dichotomy—the one between egoism and altruism. He attempts to demonstrate the inconsistency of altruism by asking what would be the consequences of everyone deciding that his or her life were less preferable than everyone else's. Whose life would be preferable in the end? Furthermore, Earle rejects the idea that it is selfish for one to protect his or her own life, and the lives of family, friends, and compatriots. To affirm any form of life is to affirm the means to preserving it.

In the third section Earle examines some objections to war. The first is based on what "people" think of war. Earle underscores the fact that people's opinions of war are shaped largely by reporters and the media who show only the horrors of war and therefore give a one-sided account. For Earle, it is no wonder that most are against war. Nonetheless, Earle argues the citizens of a country have a political duty to observe the decisions of their leaders. Earle states: ". . . war and peace are decisions which obviously fall to the national government and not to miscellaneous groups, random interests, or ad hoc political rallies. Nor, least of all, to the private opinions of reporters interviewing a few people, usually those with the least opportunity to consider and weigh what is at stake." Despite the fine characters of housewives, factory workers, farmers, and other ordinary people, they are in no position to consider the wisdom of the political decisions upon which their lives depend, according to Earle. He claims that, "What the people think is simply the repetition of slogans derived either from campaigning politicians or their favorite newspapers." Earle apparently has little respect for public opinion and cautions us that nothing is more dangerous than the enthusiasm of the people.

Another popular objection to war is based on the fact that soldiers do not know their enemies personally. In war, one stranger kills another. Earle believes this is the way it must be in war and suggests that taking personal interest in the lives of soldiers is undesirable for a number of reasons. Presumably, generals would become less effective and soldiers would be transformed from men doing their duty to murderers.

Other popular objections to war are psychological in nature. The underlying motives of political and military leaders have been held suspect. In reaction to this, Earle states that wars cannot be shown to be justified or unjustified in terms of the private motives of the leaders involved. Policy decisions in war must be measured by their probable costs and effects, not by the intentions of those who prosecute the war.

Finally, Earle criticizes objection to war based on the suffering of people. Media exhibitions of death, injury, disease, poverty, and destruction are little more than foul kicks below the moral belt of reason. According to Earle, reasonable moral judgment can never be a simple reaction to our emotions and sentiments. Horrific images represent no arguments against anything. Using images of surgical operations and vivid color photographs accompanied by screaming, wailing, and crying, the prospect of life itself could be presented as disgusting.

In conclusion to his article, Earle makes a positive statement. While acknowledging that life is important and suffering is terrible, there is no moral obligation, he says, to live at all costs under any condition. There is, however, a moral obligation to live honorably. He contends that men find honor ". . . in defending unto death what they take to be more valuable than sheer existence, namely a human life dedicated to excellence and dignity." Earle goes on to say, "There will always be occasions when human freedom and dignity are threatened; there will always be occasions then for a justifiable war, and the pacifist argument fails. To attack the very idea of war is to attack something fundamental to the preservation of any honorable life, and to offer under the flag of idealism or humanitarianism the very substance of cowardice."

A philosophical consideration of political affairs has the disadvantage of being incapable, in and of itself, of implying any specific practical action or policy. It would, then, seem useless except for the accompanying reflection that specific policy undertaken without any attention to principles, is mindless; and mindless action can have no expectation either of practical effect or of intellectual defense. No doubt the relation of principles to action is complex indeed; but at least it can be said that practical principles without reference to possible action are vacuous, and action which can not be clarified by principle is aimless commotion. Principled action offers us then the best that can be hoped for. That, however, is the work not of philosophy but of statesmanship, a faculty which is as theoretically clear as it need be but also skilled by experience in reading the existing political scene. Accordingly my present remarks aim only at some principles involved in the understanding of war, focusing on those which seem conspicuously absent in contemporary discussion, and not at defending any specific judgments about the current war. Examples of incoherent principles will be drawn from present discussions; but any other war might have served equally well. No judgment about the present war can be derived from these remarks on principles; and if most of the false principles are quoted from the antiwar side, it is only because that side has been more vocal.

[23.1, 23.2, 23.3] The villain of the present essay is *pacifism*, by which I mean a principled opposition to all war. Since it is a principled opposition, any appropriate opposition to pacifism must itself be a matter of principles. That pacifism is a principle and not a specific opposition to this war is sufficiently indicated by the suffix "ism," as well as by the arguments it mounts to make its principle plausible: it is war itself which is evil, and peace itself good under no matter what terms. Pacifism thinks it is sufficient to declare these ideals to win all hearts and minds; and if to some these pacifist principles seem impractical or indeed immoral, that can only be because the unconverted are hard of heart, slow of comprehension, or the world itself not yet ready for such a glory. That pacifism itself is practically absurd and morally deplorable is the chief burden of these present remarks. The argument will be by way of excavating the presuppositions and tracing the consequences of pacifism, and exhibiting them to the reader for his free choice. That pacifism itself is evil does *not*, needless to say, imply that the *persons* who hold that view are evil; a radical distinction between the character of persons and the character of their articulated views is the very basis of this or any other civilized discussion. If human beings could not be decent while their views are absurd, then all of us would fall into the abyss.

[23.4] In any event, the first casualty of the present war seems to have been philosophy itself. The transition was easy: from an opposition to the war on whatever ground, a portion of the public mind rose to what it thought was the proper principle of that opposition: pacifism, the sentiment that war was itself evil. And its arguments proceeded down from that height. Flattering itself for its "idealism," it could only survey the home reality it had left with high indignation: *we were killing!* Children were trotted forth on TV to ask: why must men kill one another? Can we not all love one another, the child asks, having immediately forgotten his fight with his brother off-screen. Having been illuminated by the purity and innocence of children, the new pacifist can but flagellate himself in public remorse. Not merely must this war be stopped at once, but all war and forever; we must recompense our enemies for the damage wrought upon them; we must ask their forgiveness, for are they not really our friends and our friends our enemies? and as the confusion multiplies and moral passion inflames itself, nothing appears as too severe a punishment for ourselves; impeachment of our leaders and finally the impeachment of ourselves and our history seem too gentle. These public outbursts of moral self-hatred are, of course, not unknown in history; let Savonarola stand for them all. Today the uproar is orchestrated by retired baby-doctors, neurotic poets and novelists, psychoanalysts, ministers and confused philosophers, each of whom, armed with the authority of his special "insight," seeks to speak for suffering humanity. The message to be read through the tear-stained faces is the same: we must stop killing! Regardless of how one reads the present war, what is *said* publicly for or most usually against it, presents something like the eclipse of political thought. And with the eclipse of thought, we are left with some of the most preposterous slogans ever to find utterance. When supported by high passion, parades and demonstrations, insults in loud voices, we find ourselves once again in the theater of the absurd.

WHY WAR?

[23.5] Why indeed, asks the child? Why can not everyone love one another? Settle all disputes "rationally," so that all men could live as brothers, already having forgotten the first brothers, Cain and Abel? Thrashing around for "explanations" of the horrid fact that men can indeed be hostile to one another, the sloganeer with a smattering of pop-culture finds some answers ready to hand. War has a biological origin; it arises from an excess of testosterone in the male; maybe there is a biological solution, something like castration? That Indira Gandhi and Golda Meir have conducted their wars very successfully, is already forgotten. Or maybe they are men in disguise? Or the impulse to fight arises from some distorted family history, a son conditioned by a father who in turn was conditioned by his father to conceive war as particularly masculine, an expression of *machismo*; but that could be remedied by "treatment." Perhaps drugs, suggested a recent president of the American Psychological Society. Or perhaps war arises from selfishness, a moral flaw which could be remedied by a turn of the heart, that hoped for by a Quaker who during World War II looked Hitler straight in the eye and said: Thou art an evil man! If there is a warlike "instinct," maybe it could be diverted into harmless games like chess or the Olympics. And then maybe there is no such instinct? Animals like the gazelle or lamb may be found which are not particularly aggressive; why not take them for our ideal? Or, if not an animal "instinct," then surely it is generated by the capitalist society, which as everyone knows, fosters aggression, competition, acquisitiveness, imperialism. But then even the most casual glance sees that communist societies are even more imperialist and aggressive than the capitalist. And does not the stock market fall with each new bombing? Or, finally, it is all caused by presidents, who wish to be mentioned in the history books, or be re-elected by the Veterans of Foreign Wars. The presidency should, accordingly, be abolished; policy should be turned over to the people. But which people? Those people who have been treated, have had a change of heart, who take flowers and gentle animals for their ideal, in a word, the saving remnant who through their dictatorship, will save the world from every war except that against themselves.

The generating assumption of this system of explanations is of course that there can be no *moral justification* for war at all. It is simply an evil; and since man is "naturally good," one must look for a "cause" of his distorted conduct. If war were morally justifiable, then that justification would remove any occasion for looking for pathological explanations. If one does not seek for "causes" for a man doing good works other than the goodness of the work itself, neither need one seek biological, psychological, cultural, sociopolitical causes for a justifiable war. The justification *is* the cause in this case.

And so then the question, why war? would be answered if any moral justification for it were forthcoming. A "justifiable war?" Is that not a contradiction in terms, or is it the pacifist who represents a living contradiction in terms?

[23.6] This first answer to the question, why war, assumes at the start that it *is* evil, assumes that men are or could be "naturally good," meaning "peaceful," but since in point of fact they are not, the "explanation" is to be found in an artificial distortion of their passionate nature. The elimination of war will result from a correction of that passionate nature, through treatment whether physiological, psychological, social or rhetorical. In a word, either their bodies or their characters must be changed by whatever treatment promises success. The lion will lie down with the lamb, indeed will be indistinguishable from him. He will abandon pride, greed, egotism, the desire to display power, to intimidate, to coerce; he will at the end of history at last be good. But, of course, absolutely *all* men must be good; for if even a few are left who do *not* so envisage the good, our "good" men will be, of course, good-for-nothing, and their peace will be the peace determined by the wicked. Unwilling to fight for their lives or ideals, they are suppressed and at that point the whole

of human history recommences as if there had been no interlude, or at best an interlude within common sense. The lamb who lies down with the lion may indeed be good for the lion when his appetites return; and if he is good in any other sense, it could only be on a mystic plane not exactly pertinent to the practical moral plane of existence. It is not surprising then that advocates in the church of the kingdom of heaven, do indeed place it in heaven, but never advocate it as political policy. After all, by definition, heaven has already expelled or refused admittance to the wicked, hence is hardly faced with problems commensurate with ours on earth. What does a lion *eat* in heaven? Men, needless to say, are not animals *simpliciter*, but rational or spirited animals; but neither reasons nor spirit so long as they remain living can *contradict* animal needs.

That rational animals engage in hostilities unto death has always seemed a scandal to those philosophers who neglect existence. If one stamp of moralist finds both the cause and solution to war in some alteration in body or character, many philosophers of abstractions find both the cause and solution to war in *thought* to be corrected by right reasoning. If rational men still fight, and if war is irrational, then there must be a rational solution to it. The medium of reason is the word, so we can expect this stamp of pacifist to praise the verbal solution to hostilities: the treaty. Would it not be reasonable to prevent or terminate hostilities by calculation, agreements, and solemnly pledged words? It is easy to forgive philosophers and the educated in general for their touching confidence in the power of words; they exercise a magical power in and over the mind; but perhaps that is their proper place. However, it is an outrageous neglect to fancy that they have any power except that over the mind, mind moreover which itself has the *obligation* to superintend the very existential conditions of its own life. Who then is surprised when he reads that in the last 350 years, something like 85 percent of the treaties signed in the Western world have been broken? But the treaty theory of peace can then congratulate itself on the fact that now a culprit can be identified, declared to be an aggressor, and, while the aggressor is condemned by the "enlightened goodwill of mankind," he nevertheless proceeds to enjoy his dinner, and later may be celebrated as a benefactor of mankind; he will certainly not hesitate to sign new treaties. Our question is what to do: wring one's hands over men's irrationality or rethink the meaning of war? In all of this, one can easily agree that treaties exercise some slight restraining power over the more rapacious inclinations; but would it not be criminal neglect to entrust the security of one's country to treaties? And in fact, does any responsible leader ever do it? No doubt, the lambs, since they have nothing better to work with.

And eventually, as the final rational "solution" to the problem of war, there is the idea of a single superstate, whether an enlargement of one of those now extant, such as the USA, Russia or China — or conceived as a super United Nations. This convulsive, "final solution" to the war problem particularly appeals to those who have little "negative capability" as Keats put it, little tolerance for the uncertain, for risk, for in fact the most fundamental characteristics of free human life. When put in the form of a super United Nations, it almost looks harmless. But it can more properly be put in uglier terms; if it were indeed to be a Super State, it could be nothing short of a Super Totalitarianism. The historical totalitarianisms we have all witnessed would be as nothing compared with this monstrosity; and, as has often been remarked, they grew in precisely

the same spiritual soil, a certain inability to face risk, death, war or confusion, in a word, the existential conditions of a free life with dignity. Everything must be put *in order!* And if the World is not now in order and never has been, then the order will be imposed, imposed in fact by the very Force which once seemed so odious. A new order of the World; but now *its* dissidents become World-enemies and where are they to flee? Do they have a right to life itself? Are they not enemies of the World? In this abstract fantasia, the first thing lost sight of is a small annoying matter, a point of logic: any Order is also only itself a *specific* order. Law and Order, of course, are only universal abstractions, whose proper medium of existence is the word. In existence itself, it is always this or that order, that is, *somebody's* order; and then there is always a somebody else, who believes honestly in another order, one perhaps more favorable to himself or his ideal. Again the eternal hostilities break out, now however with a difference: hostilities between nations have not been eliminated, but only redubbed: each is now a *civil* war within the World State. Perhaps the candid observer will be excused if he fails to perceive the difference, except in the new savagery now morally permitted. And as for the individual? He has been forgotten for a long time in his prison or madhouse. He must be given therapy.

Many serious persons, of course, are sensitive to these paradoxes, and yet finally in desperation cling to the solution of a world state or world dictatorship as the only preventative of world destruction through nuclear holocaust. It is one thing to be willing to give one's own life for one's nation, but it is qualitatively different to destroy the habitable parts of the globe for "nothing but" freedom and dignity. For our present discussion, we shall assume that some such thing is possible now or in the not-too-distant future. The possibility raises questions, obviously, of an ultimate order. But I do not think it unambiguously true that some such possible world catastrophe compels assent to world totalitarianism. In any event, for the moment, it might seem that here, at last, pacifism becomes sanity; and that any acceptance of world destruction is the very essence of evil and immorality. I shall revert to this question at the end and touch upon it now only to complete this first part surveying various sentiments which find war, as such and in principle, intolerable with the ensuing effort to formulate a solution or eliminate the cause.

II. THE JUSTIFICATION OF WAR

[23.7] The attitudes so far considered begin, as we have seen, by assuming war to be unjustifiable; *if* it is unjustifiable, then its cause must be found, in biological, psychological, social or moral distortions of an inherently peace-loving human nature; the cure is always some form of therapy. Or those who conduct war must have reasoned badly or given up the hope that rational discussion with its eventual treaty would be effective. Wars are "irrational," no philosophical justification of any is possible; thought will find the rational "solution." But on the other hand, if war is justifiable, then the search for its causes in either distortions of the passionate nature of man, or in errors or failures of reason, is downright foolish. The justification removes the premise of the search for causes and cures. The justification of war as a form of moral and rational excellence may seem scandalous to the pacifist, and yet it is that scandal I should like to defend. And as for talk about the greater or lesser of two evils, I shall try to

avoid this ambiguous, slippery and ultimately meaningless effort to calculate the incalculable. The justification of war aims at showing both its morality and its rationality; if therefore there are occasions when a moral and rational man must fight, then a proscription of war in principle must be itself irrational and ethically deplorable.

In a word, the justification of war is existence; to will to exist is to affirm war as its means and condition. But perhaps the term "existence" puts the matter too abstractly. In the present context, and in its most abstract sense, existence is a synonym for life, and nonexistence for death. Wars then are justified as means taken to assure life and death. And yet little has been said; the life and death of what? Bare life measured by the beating of the heart, is hardly life at all; it would be prized only as the supporter and condition of a life *worth living*. Obviously men have always thought it justifiable to fight not merely to preserve their physical being, but also for those additional things which make that life worth living, fertile lands, access to the sea, minerals, a government of their choice, laws and customs and religions, and finally peace itself. Existence then is hardly bare survival but an existence in the service of all those concrete values which illuminate and glorify existence. They too must exist; it is almost by definition that values, in and of their intrinsic meaning, *demand existence*. Justice would misunderstand itself if it were content to remain abstract and merely ideal.

So much might easily be granted until another reflection arises, that perhaps the goods of existence could be shared by all men. This utopian notion is much beloved of *philosophers* or *art critics* who look upon the diversities of thought and cultural style as so many advantages and opportunities for spiritual growth. And indeed they are;

but then those values are not exactly what war is about. If the library can house every book in peaceful coexistence, or if the museum can calmly exhibit the styles of the world, why must men themselves fight? Could the world not be like an international congress of philosophy or perhaps a quieter meeting of UNESCO: would this not be the civilized thing? Would it not be better if nations conducted themselves according to the model of a genteel conversation, where views are advanced and withdrawn without anger, and where men say "excuse me for interrupting?"

[23.8] But elementary reflection is sufficient to dispel these dreams. Existence or life individuates itself; when it can speak it says "I," and what it possesses, "mine." Nothing is changed logically in this respect when the I becomes a We, and mine, Ours. That I am not you, or we are not they, is the ineluctable ground of war; individuation is essential to existence. That which is not individuated does not exist, but subsists as a universal or abstract meaning. Consequently the meaning of a book or cultural artifact can be shared by all; but the existent book or existent painting can not, and could supply a ground for conflict. No wonder philosophers or scientists or critics, accustomed to living in the domain of abstractions and ideal meanings which are not, like quantities of matter, diminished progressively by each man who partakes of them, find something scandalous and primitive about war or anything else appropriate in the domain of existence and life. Nothing is easier than for the spirit to neglect the conditions of its own existence, or indeed be outraged by them.

[23.9] I have used the term "existential" intentionally in spite of its abstractness to avoid at all costs what might seem to be its more common equivalent, "material." Some sentimental pacifists think it sufficient to prove that a nation has gone to war for "material" interests to conclude, with cheers from their audience, that such a war is *immoral*. The idealism should find itself opposed to "matter," or its equivalent, life and existence, would certainly not have surprised the Buddha or Nietzsche, both of whom accurately perceived that the only surcease of war and public sorrow is in nothingness, Nirvana or eternity. And, as President Truman remarked, those who can not stand the heat should get out of the kitchen.

But of course, what the sentimental pacifist wants is nothing so radical as the genuine alternative of a Buddha; he wants an *existent* heaven, perpetual peace-on-earth, a mishmash which has never been or never will be seen, violating as it does patent ontological differences subsisting between existence and the abstract. The exposure of this error is not difficult. At what precise point do material interests become ideal? Is the health of a nation "material" or "ideal?" But its health depends, of course, upon its wealth; is the pursuit of that wealth ideal or materialistic and crass? Is the culture of a nation an ideal or material value? and is its culture dependent or not upon the wealth available for education and leisure? Is the wealth devoted to such tasks materialistic or idealistic? Money versus human life! All these false contrasts need not be multiplied to perceive the vacuity of any argument against war based upon "idealistic" as opposed to "materialistic" principles.

[23.9] Functioning according to the same false logic is another simplistic contrast, also beloved of pacifists: that thought to exist between egoism and altruism. The highminded rhetoric poured out against "selfishness" is laughable indeed when not taken seriously. Is it "selfish" for me to protect my own life, or those of my family, friends, or compatriots? And, moreover, not merely our physical existence, but our human life with its wealth, customs, laws, institutions, languages, religions, our autonomy? Or to protect the "material," i.e., economic conditions which support all these values? To affirm any form of life at all is at the same time to affirm the means to it; what *could* be more confused than to will our life and also to will the life opposed to it? The ultimate pacifist who would do nothing even to protect his own life for fear of killing another, is simply a case of self-hatred; but both nature and logic combine to guarantee that this particular illness never becomes widespread. Has or could there ever be a defense for the idea that everyone else's life is preferable to my own, particularly when adopted in turn by everyone else? To be bound together in friendship is certainly preferable to being torn apart by hostility; but is it not clear that neither the friendship of all nor the hostility of all is possible; the line to be drawn which assures the provisional existence of any state is to be drawn by practical statesmanship judging in its time for its time, and not by abstract, would-be idealistic principles, which by hoping to be valid for all times are pertinent to none.

Excursus on Equality. No doubt it will have been noted that war here has *not* been justified as a means of securing justice or equality. It has been justified as a means necessary to any nation to secure or preserve its own social good, and as such, is held to be eminently reasonable and honorable. However, the social life of a nation is not itself to be further judged by means of abstract categories such as justice or equality. Hasty thought frequently identifies justice with equality, particularly since justice is elusive and protean in its applications, whereas the notion of equality, being mathematical and abstract, is within the grasp of all. I either do

or do not have as much as another; if I do not, am I not wronged? Can not anyone see this? and indeed they can, but what can not be so immediately seen is whether such inequality is also *ipso facto* unjust.

These confusions pour into those discussions which, for example, would justify any war at all against the United States; since we have more than anyone else, we could never have a right to defend that more. To have more is to be guilty before the abstract bar of Equality. But this last gasp of the French Revolution, amplified by Marxist bellows, blows against certain existential realities. Those realities are simply that the earth itself is differentiated by rivers, climates, flora and fauna, mountains, valleys and plains. Not all can live everywhere nor is this an injustice to them. And, to belabor the obvious, men are not equal, having very different temperaments, tastes, ideals, and histories. Not merely are men not equal, they are not unequal either, the category of "equality" being quantitative whereas a man or a nation is not a quantity of anything, but rather an individual or communal person aiming at a definite form of excellent life. Since nations and men are always already in a differentiated possession of the goods of the world, differentiated forms of excellence, differentiated histories and memories, the desire to equalize all is equivalent to the desire to obliterate history as well as the individuated free choices of nations and men. Computerized thought might delight in such simplicities, but is there any a priori reason why a truly just mind must accept it?

If I have not used the notion of justice in any abstract form to justify war, again, it is for the simple reason that it leads nowhere. Wars are fought *over* differing notions of justice; does any party to war ever think itself unjust? Justice in the abstract therefore is useless for purposes of condemnation or justification. Victory in war equally does not decide what is abstractly just, but which form of justice will prevail.

III. OBJECTIONS TO WAR

[23.10]   *I. What the "people" think of war.* I shall use this title for a slippery mass of appeals increasingly popular in the mass media. Reporters, seemingly getting the "objective" facts, can always ask some fleeing peasants : "do you want war?" Of course, the bewildered peasant replies that he only wishes to live in peace, that war has destroyed his family, his rice fields, that it is caused by "government," that he could live equally well under any regime, that in fact he does not know the enemy, or does, having relatives among them, etc., all of which is pathetic as much for the sufferings of the peasant as for the mindlessness of the reporter who imagines himself to be presenting an ultimate argument based upon "humanity."

Television, since it can not picture any thought about war, is confined to showing what can be shown: the dismembered, burned, legless, eyeless, as if to say: this is what war really is. And when the dead or wounded are little children, women, or old men, the very heart recoils; the argument is decisive. But not yet: the soldiers must be asked; have they not seen it first hand, fought it with their lives, seen their comrades fall before their very eyes? Any number can be rounded up to swear they haven't the faintest idea what all the killing is about, that it must be immoral or absurd, probably conducted by munition makers or politicians seeking reelection, in a word by all that "establishment" in which they never had much participation even during peace. Their own virtue is to be resigned or, if they "think," to wearing peace symbols.

As for the ideal component in war, the honor and courage of the soldier, that too is immediately debunked. "There's nothing heroic about war" says the soldier who may just yesterday have risked his life to save a comrade. War is nothing but living in the mud and rain, with poor food, disease, fatigue, danger and boredom; is that heroic? His reticence about "heroism" is admirable; but we need not believe what he says. Since heroism is doing one's duty or going beyond it under extreme conditions, it is difficult to see how the difficulties diminish the accomplishment; without those difficulties, genuine heroism would be nothing but parade-ground heroics. But let us look in more detail at these arguments of the people.

The "People": who are they? They are either citizens of their country or not; if not, they have no political right to complaint. If so, then their government is indeed theirs, and they have every political duty to observe its decisions or try to alter them legally. In any event, the people are all the people, not merely the peasants, and they are in their collective capacity *already* represented by their government, whose decisions they must respect as made by their legal representatives. If the people are in no way represented by their government, then the question shifts itself away from war to that of forming a representative government. In any event, war and peace are decisions which obviously fall to the national government and not to miscellaneous groups, random interests, or *ad hoc* political rallies. Nor, least of all, to the private opinions of reporters interviewing a few people, usually those with the least opportunity to consider and weigh what is at stake. To suggest opinion polls or referenda on these questions every month or so, simply offers us the idea of another form of government altogether, an unheard-of-populism which in effect negates representative government altogether and substitutes for it the ever-shifting voice of the street. And since that in turn clearly reflects the overwhelming influence of propaganda, immediate "democracy" of this order shifts the decision from government to the directors and voices of "news" media. It is hardly surprising that this prospect delights the media, but it is surprising that so many otherwise sensible citizens wish to shift their allegiance from their own duly elected representatives to the directors of news media whom they have not elected and for the most part hardly know, all the while imagining that this offers them an opportunity themselves to direct the course of events.

The truth is, unwelcome as it may be, that the "people," ordinary housewives, factory workers, farmers, etc., as fine as they may be personally, are in no position whatsoever to consider the wisdom of that very politics upon which their own lives depend. It is, naturally, for this reason that very few nations at all, and none of any importance, are run on any such scheme. It is precisely the responsibility of representatives of the people to occupy themselves with such questions, inform themselves and circumspectly weigh the possibilities. The limits of experience and political habits of thought which more or less make the ordinary private citizen private, at the same time warn us against encouraging any immediate or undue influence of his opinions on matters of state. What the people think is simply the repetition of slogans derived either from campaigning politicians or their favorite newspaper. For some researchers, the popular mind is a pool of infinite wisdom and goodness; the truth is it is nothing but an ephemeral reflection of popular songs, sandwich-board slogans, newspaper headlines and clichés. For the popular mind "thought" is what can be written on a placard or

shouted at a rally; for the reflective, thought is precisely what eludes this form of expression. Who has the wind to shout a *qualified* thought?

Nothing could be more dangerous than the enthusiasms of the people. Mad joy at the beginning of hostilities; and rage when the bodies are brought in, the expenses reckoned up. But of course this is precisely what is to be expected from the people, suggestible, flighty, and unused to either foresight or circumspection. As for the shallow notion that the people want only peace, that all peoples love one another as brothers, and that war therefore is imposed upon them from above — could one find any stretch of history or any segment of the world where these notions are significantly illustrated? The natural brotherhood of man? The natural goodness of the people? Indeed! One could far better argue that there is nothing whatsoever "natural" in man; the natural is exactly what man *decides*.

When we substitute for the people, the common soldier, all the same applies. Their experience is always tempting to novelists, looking for the "reality" of war. The reality in question, it should be remembered, is the one they are best equipped to express with vividness: the day-to-day life in the foxhole, or in the pouring rain, the mudholes, the terror, sickness, ambiguities of fighting life. It is easy for novelists to enter into the mind of the G.I. who is presented as seeing only what lies before his eyes: a dead friend. *That* is the reality of war; meanwhile at headquarters, the colonels are arrogant, incompetent, not really suffering but instead well provided with booze and whores, no doubt profiteering from the PX, and in cahoots with the government, known to be corrupt. No doubt all this is true enough from time to time, and no doubt anyone at all can sympathize with the sentiments involved.

And no doubt at all, the same structure can easily be found in any civil society that ever was in peace time as well. The question however concerns the exact pertinence of such considerations, to the justification or lack of it for any given war. Since wars are not fought in the first place to make common soldiers comfortable, nor to make generals live the same lives as privates, nor to remove corruption in the armies involved, the only pertinence of such observations when true would be to improve the army, not to stop the war. And that a platoon leader does not know the whole strategy from his experience, that a general can not perform his legitimate functions in the same state of exhaustion as the G.I., nor carry his maps and codes into the foxholes, nor subject himself to the same risks as the ordinary soldier, is all obvious but no doubt at times escapes the full approval of the G.I. which is why the G.I. is not a general.

Related, is the curious popular objection that war is immoral because the soldier does not know his enemy *personally*. A German soldier of World War I in *All Quiet on the Western Front* receives a shock when after killing a Frenchman, he realizes he never knew him personally. However he would have received a greater shock upon recovering his wits when he realized that if he *had* known him personally and acted out of personal rage, his act would be radically transformed in meaning. From being a soldier doing his *duty*, he would be transformed into a *murderer*. But no doubt this distinction is too fine for those who love to talk of war as "mass murder," oblivious to all distinctions between on the one hand the legitimate duties of the police and soldiers, and on the other punishable murder. This essential distinction is obliterated in that higher pacifistic fog where all "taking of human life" is immoral. There could hardly be anything more obscurantist than the desire

to obliterate all distinctions of roles and offices of men into that warm, personal, brotherly unity of "the personal." Generals receive criticism for not taking a "personal" interest in each of their troops; I, for one, would demote any who did. If some such thing is the philosophy of the best seller, it is easy to predict that of the worst seller: the wise general and the stupid G.I. In all of this, it would hardly take a Nietzsche to perceive the influence of that old, popular motive, the resentment of authority. In the present instance it feeds pacifism.

Popular thought loves to "psych" its political leaders. In this, has it not been aided and abetted by the rise of psychological novels where the plot sinks into insignificance and the psychological analysis of motives occupies the stage, usually a popular version of Freud. Psychologizing has, undoubtedly, a limited relevance to political decision; national policies are at the same time policies of leaders, whose characters and temperaments are significant factors in their actions and reactions. Roosevelt and Churchill both considered the personalities of Hitler and Stalin in this fashion, and if their judgments left something to be desired, at least the pertinence of the question is undeniable; political personality is unquestionably a factor in objective policy. Which items in announced policy are sticking points, and which negotiable? Which remarks made to the inner constituency, and which to the outer world? Generals also try to sense the temperament of their opponents, as one factor in the whole.

On the other hand, what could be more ludicrous than the popular effort to assess policy through a judgment of the character and assumed private motives of the initiators of that policy? Antiwar finds nothing but reprehensible private motives at the root of the matter; prowar finds nothing but heroic strength; reflection finds both irrelevant. Wars are neither justifiable nor unjustifiable in terms of the private motives of the leaders; wars are not personal acts of rage and revenge, but as von Clausewitz showed, an extension of policy by other means. Policies are measured by their probable costs and effects, and not by the motives of the agents.

The weighing of policy properly belongs in the hands of those responsible and thoughtful men who are experienced in such matters. It is not in any conspicuous sense the experience of pastors in their morality, poets with their sensitivity, the young with their "idealism," psychoanalysts with their probings of emotions, or news reporters with their "scoops."

The distressing thing about popular psychologizing is its confidence; it *knows* the black heart inside the political leader, and is certain that anything more complex or even favorable is "naive." All of which reflects the failure of both psychology and the psychological novel to make their point; should not popular wisdom at least be sensitive to the difficulties and ambiguities of searching out the motives of the human heart? If I can only seldom if ever be confident I know my own motives, how can I be so sure I know those of others?

I conclude that the "people" must take their chances in war, do not represent a pool of persons separate from the organized body of citizens with a government, and that their perception, judgment and analysis of public policy is sound only by accident. Public policy is beyond the scope of private people; since it is, the common people revert to something they imagine themselves to be expert in, the psychological motives of leaders; but alas, even that is beyond their or anyone else's proper grasp. At which point we have nothing to do but return to where we should never have left, the objective consideration of policy by those competent to consider it.

[23.11] 2. *The Sufferings of the People.* A final set of criticisms against war again purports to rest upon humanitarian or idealistic grounds: its argument is the simple exhibition of death, injuries, disease, poverty, destruction, the ravaging of both countryside and cities. Television makes it as vivid as possible, and the color photographs in *Life* magazine are almost enough to sicken the heart of the bravest and to shake the firmest judgment. Indeed this is their overt intention, and it is not long before they end up on pacifist posters as ultimate arguments. But of course arguments they are not, at best facts to be considered; but then who hasn't already considered them? Is there anyone who imagines war to be anything but killing? The decision to fight is the decision to kill; such a decision, needless to say, is never easy although it may frequently be justified. If *justified*, what service is performed by such direct appeals to vital instinct and sentiment? At best they would enfeeble our powers of judgment, never too strong, so that we would choose the unjustifiable rather than the wise course.

These images thought to be decisive, are in reality nothing but kicks below the belt and from behind; reasonable moral judgment can never be a simple reaction to our emotions and sentiments; the emotions and sentiments themselves are more than enough for that; but it is the role of policy and judgment to judge *over* these forces. The job is no doubt the most difficult man faces; it is hardly made easier by the daily flood of images of suffering in the media.

The image in itself is no argument against anything. It would be easy indeed by vivid color photographs, accompanied by recordings of screaming, wailing and crying, to sicken anyone of the very project of living. Surgical operations would never be undertaken, women would be afraid to give birth to children; images of the old, sick and senile would convince us that life itself is folly; and some such thing is the conclusion of transcendental ascetics. But then such an ethic, by intention, is not pertinent to public policy, necessarily committed to not merely life, but the good life.

[23.12] The humanitarian argument drawn from ruins and suffering, aims at a higher idealism; but with a suddenness which would have delighted Hegel, turns into its opposite, a crass materialism. If human life is justifiable in terms of its excellence, where is the idealism in locating that excellence in a clinging to cities and fields? Or finally, in clinging to mere life itself as our highest value? The founder of Western philosophy, Socrates, disdained to use arguments resting upon such sympathies in his own defense, and did *not* bring his wife and children to court to plead for him. Nor did he conjure up imaginative pictures of his own suffering. No doubt, this is old-fashioned. . . .

Since one dies anyway, the sole question would seem to be *how* one dies, with honor or not. There is no moral obligation to live at all costs and under any conditions; there is no moral obligation to live at all; there is a moral obligation to live honorably if one lives at all. What that obligation dictates under specific historical concrete circumstances clearly can not be decided for all and in general; but it can dictate that under some circumstances, some men must find their honor in defending unto death what they take to be more valuable than sheer existence, namely a human life dedicated to excellence and dignity. Human lives whose chief moral defense is that they have kept themselves alive, have at the same stroke lost *all* moral defense. Such is the age-old paradox of life.

Traditionally, the man who chose life and personal safety under any conditions was regarded as a coward, and his condition that of a slave. Do we now have new reasons for reversing this decision? Which is not to say that some have not tried; what other judgment could be pronounced upon the current rash of movies and novels all celebrating the *antihero* as a new form of excellence; sometimes it is even thought to be "authentic" or "existential!" What is it but mediocrity and cowardice? It follows that some are authentic cowards, but need we admire them? A footnote to the present confusion is the argument that war "brutalizes" the troops. The brutalization is rarely spelled out although hovering around the attack is the suspicion that troops are brutalized in their coarse speech, their terms of contempt for the enemy, their failure personally to consider the "justice" of every order, to bring their superiors before the bar of their own private conscience, their fondness for booze and camp followers above lectures and the opera. Well! But if brutalization means a willingness to kill the enemy, I for one fail to perceive the fault; that's what they are there for in the first place, and who is closer to the brute, a man afraid to kill the enemy, or one who will kill and die to preserve the freedom and dignity of himself or his compatriots?

There will always be occasions when human freedom and dignity are threatened; there will always be occasions then for a justifiable war, and the pacifistic argument fails. To attack the very idea of war is to attack something fundamental to the preservation of any honorable life, and to offer under the flag of idealism or humanitarianism, the very substance of cowardice. Having already denounced Soviet injustice, what could be a worse capitulation than Bertrand Russell's slogan: "Better Red than dead"?

IV. WHAT WAR DECIDES

Needless to say, victory does not always fall to the just. And if not, then victory is no measure of the justice of the cause, a truth commonly recognized by the respect accorded to the defeated. For while they were indeed defeated with regard to the immediate occasion of the dispute, they were not defeated, if they fought well, with regard to something far more important, that infinite self-respect which defines their humanity. The morale of a nation, that is, its self-respect, is certainly tested by the war, and is that factor which nullifies the old Chinese warlord "solution" to the problem of war, much beloved of computer thinkers. Why not, the argument goes, have the leaders meet on a neutral ground, calculate their resources, and decide victory without bloodshed, as the story says the warlords did. Is this not the essence of "rationality"? If the idea seems preposterous is it not because there remains one *incalculable* factor, the morale of the troops and the nations behind them? No doubt, this factor was negligible when the troops in question were mercenaries without any morale whatsoever except that for their pay or "professional" reputation. And no doubt one can easily find battles when the odds are so unequal as to render armed resistance suicidal. But even such "suicidal" resistances *win something,* namely, the enacted courage unto death of the men fighting them; to think nothing of

this or to regard it as pure folly is itself a judgment proceeding out of little but crass materialism. To offer it as a rational *idealism* is a betrayal of everything noble in the defeated. A man is not necessarily ignoble because he was defeated; but he is if there is nothing he will fight for except his own skin.

Courage then, about which little is said today without an accompanying smirk, is a virtue whose analysis quickly carries us into transcendental realms. It looks like madness or vanity or an "ego-trip" to those who imagine the issues of life settled, and settled into the values of biology, economics, or fundamentally *pleasure.* But courage puts all those values into question, discloses that as always, men today put to themselves a goal and destiny which has no common measure with mere life, mere well-being, or mere comfort. These things may properly be fought over, but they are not *in themselves* the full story of what is involved. That full story can never be told, but at very least it must include what here is called the transcendental, the domain of freedom and dignity which is never compromised by mere death, poverty, or defeat; but most certainly is compromised by a certain deafness to its claims. Wars are not fought to prove courage, but they do prove it all the same.

FURTHER READINGS

Narveson, Jan. "Violence and War." In *Matters of Life and Death,* ed. Tom Regan. New York: Random House, 1980, pp. 109–147.

Walzer, Michael. *Just and Unjust Wars.* New York: Basic Books, 1977.

Wasserstrom, Richard (ed.). *War and Morality.* Belmont, CA: Wadsworth, 1970.

PROGRESS CHECK 23.1

Instructions: Fill in the blanks with the appropriate responses listed below.

moral justification   altruism
rational   material

totalitarianism   pacifism
existence   pathological consequences
biological origin   individuation
private motives   emotions and sentiments
dignity and excellence   cowardice

1. The principle that war is inherently evil and therefore unjustified is known as
   _____.

2. _____ means more than survival; it entails dignity and all those things for
   which life is worth living.

3. Pacifists believe that no _____ can be given for war.

4. Those who believe that war is irrational and symptomatic of disordered conduct have looked for the _____ of war.

5. The only form of life worth living is one with _____.

6. Analyzing the _____ of generals and statesmen has little or nothing to do
   with the justification of the war process.

7. Reference to testosterone levels in those who engage in armed conflict points
   to the possibility of a _____ to war.

8. Human existence entails a process of _____. whereby we begin to appreciate our uniqueness and separateness from others.

9. The false dichotomy between the _____ and the ideal serves as a basis for
   the pacifists' antiwar arguments.

10. The principle of _____ is inconsistent as not everyone can regard others'
    lives more important than their own.

11. Under the guise of humanitarianism, those who refuse to fight for life's dignity
    and autonomy are hiding their own _____.

12. Horrific television images of war's suffering are irrelevant to discussions of its
    acceptability, for _____ play no role in the justification of the war
    process.

13. There is no _____ solution to war.

14. The idea of a super United Nations to govern the world's affairs and safeguard
    its peace will in the end lead to a dangerous form of _____.

LEARNING EXERCISE 23.2   Completing Syllogisms

Instructions: Complete the following syllogisms.

1. **Value Premise:**   That which threatens human freedom and dignity is wrong.

   Factual Premise:

   Conclusion: Refusing to engage in war is wrong.

2. **Value Premise:** Principles based on faulty presuppositions should be rejected.

   Factual Premise: Pacifism is a principle based on faulty presuppositions.

   Conclusion:

3. **Value Premise:**

   Factual Premise: Philosophers and pacifists are people who think there is a rational solution to war.

   Conclusion: Therefore, philosophers and pacifists are naive and unrealistic.

4. **Value Premise:** That which protects our vital interests is good.

   Factual Premise: War protects our vital interests.

   Conclusion:

5. **Value Premise:**

   Factual Premise: Refusing to fight under the pretense of humanitarianism is a cowardly action.

   Conclusion: Therefore, refusing to fight under the pretense of humanitarianism is deplorable.

LEARNING EXERCISE 23.3   Identifying Statements

Instructions: *Identify the following statements as factual claims (F) or value-judgments (V).*

_____ 1. Pacifism is morally deplorable.

_____ 2. Tendencies to war are generated by capitalism which promotes competition and aggressiveness.

_____ 3. Pacifists believe there is no moral justification for war at all.

_____ 4. Rational animals have always engaged in hostilities unto death.

_____ 5. A life without dignity and honor is not worth living.

_____ 6. The establishment of a super United Nations to prevent international hostilities will only lead to civil war.

_____ 7. There are occasions when a moral and rational person must fight.

_____ 8. Wars are justified as a means to ensure existence.

_____ 9. Limited resources and universal demand supply a ground for conflict.

_____ 10. Those opposed to war are cowards.

24

"NUCLEAR ILLUSION AND INDIVIDUAL OBLIGATIONS"

Trudy Govier

EDUCATIONAL OBJECTIVES: After reading this chapter the student will be able to:

24.1 Provide a rationale for why the nuclear problem is the most pressing issue of our time.

24.2 Explain how the nuclear problem is relevant to philosophy.

24.3 Discuss the role "silence" has played in the arms race.

24.4 Give reasons why social reality cannot be properly interpreted independently of nuclear issues.

24.5 State the Catholic position on nuclear deterrence.

24.6 Paraphrase the argument against nuclear arms by Archbishop Hunthausen of Seattle.

24.7 Explain how the "nation-state" is a potential threat to world survival.

24.8 Raise questions regarding our responsibilities to future generations of people.

24.9 Relate the nuclear issue to existential problems concerning the meaning of life.

24.10 Describe the role self-deception has played in the proliferation of nuclear arms.

24.11 Outline Trudy Govier's views on individual responsibility in the face of a global nuclear threat.

From the *Canadian Journal of Philosophy*, 13 (1983): 483–492. Reprinted by permission of the author and the publisher.

FOCUS QUESTIONS

1. Why is the nuclear arms issue important? Cannot we continue to live our daily lives without preoccupying ourselves with the unpleasant thoughts arising from it? Shouldn't we concern ourselves with more concrete problems?

2. Instead of raising such a fuss about nuclear arms, wouldn't it be better if we all just forgot about the matter and remained silent? Why?

3. Can't we understand the world and our place in it without involving nuclear issues? Explain.

4. How could the nuclear arms issue be treated from a religious perspective?

5. Isn't patriotism good? Shouldn't we use nuclear arms if necessary to protect national interests? Have nation-states always existed? Will they always continue to exist? Comment.

6. Should we care what the world looks like in the year 2050? Do we have any obligations regarding the future of the planet?

7. How does nuclear war impact on the meaning of life?

8. What is the desirability or undesirability of self-deception when it comes to the nuclear issue?

9. Can we, as individuals, do anything about the nuclear arms race? Should we even try?

10. What role can philosophers and philosophy play in the nuclear arms debate?

SYNOPSIS

Trudy Govier begins her article by introducing the danger of nuclear war as the most pressing problem of our time. She places this problem in a philosophical context by pointing out that discussions of moral values and political structures are absurd if they ignore the nuclear threat. A nuclear holocaust would quickly bring to an end most, if not all, human values and problems. Govier urges that philosophers address the nuclear war threat, since their silence may implicitly convey the message that they condone the nuclear status quo. Silence, Govier believes, is what allowed the world to move from a position in 1945 where there were only three nuclear weapons to a point today where we find fifty thousand. She contends that as teachers of ethics, applied ethics, and political philosophy, philosophers occupy a special role in ending the dangerous silence. Apart from the inherent perils of nuclear proliferation, Govier contends we should also increase our awareness of nuclear issues since the arms race is a powerful force behind the economies, technologies, ideologies, and scientific research programs of our day. If we choose to ignore the military developments associated with nuclear arms, we risk developing a distorted and inaccurate view of social reality.

After underscoring the philosophical relevance of nuclear arms and the gravity of nuclear war for humankind, Govier proceeds in her article to examine the nuclear problem from the vantage point of (1) occupational ethics, (2) nation-states, (3) future generations, (4) the meaning of life, and (5) self-deception. On the issue of nuclear arms production from the occupational-ethics perspective, Govier refers to the pastoral letter of America's Catholic bishops on nuclear weapons. In that letter conditional endorsement of nuclear deterrence is given provided every effort is made to eliminate reliance on nuclear arms. Specific mention is made of Archbishop Hunthausen of Seattle, who argues that the manufacturing of nuclear arms is wrong as it involves an implicit threat which, if carried out, would kill noncombatants. Catholic bishops who abide by the just-war theory are opposed to killing innocent people in war. Since nuclear detonations almost necessarily involve killing others besides soldiers, their use in war is virtually always immoral, according to Hunthausen.

On the subject of nation-states, Govier apparently agrees with Jonathan Schell who contends that the nation-state is a temporary historical entity whose value is not worth preserving if it jeopardizes the survival of mankind as a whole. Schell believes that since any war now has the potential of becoming a nuclear confrontation and because wars are typically fought to preserve and protect the interests of nation-states, national sovereignty must be abolished if nuclear security is to be made possible. Govier points to a number of concerns and problems which can be identified in Schell's position, but nonetheless believes that Schell's views warrant further thought and discussion within political philosophy.

Govier believes that the nuclear arms issue also has particular relevance for future generations. She raises a number of questions about the moral status of people who have not yet been born. A central question pertaining to the moral status of future generations is whether we, the living, have any duties or obligations to work to ensure their existence and well-being on this planet. The related question is also asked, "Would the annihilation of the human species be a tragedy? If so, to whom?" The nuclear arms issue certainly has implications for the meaning of life. As Govier states: "Discussions of the meaning of life have largely ignored the constant possibility that human life on this planet could end." The fact is that the threat of nuclear war casts a dark shadow of meaninglessness over all activities having a future orientation. The spectre of nuclear holocaust undermines the meaningfulness of many human activities and pushes into new relief perennial questions about the meaning of life itself. To the extent that philosophers regard interpreting the meaning of life as part of their task, it is incumbent upon them therefore to acknowledge the nuclear threat and to endeavor to make sense of it.

Govier suspects that self-deception on a society-wide basis may have contributed greatly to the proliferation of nuclear arms. To the extent this is true, she recommends that we reevaluate the belief that self-deception can sometimes be good. It is probably the case that public illusions and ignorance about the nature and role of nuclear weaponry have been a necessary condition of the perpetuation of the nuclear arms race.

Concluding her essay, Govier examines the role of individual responsibility in view of the global nuclear threat. She rejects the argument that individuals have no obligations to try to change the course of world events, at least as they pertain to nuclear issues. The factual claim imbedded in this argument is that ordinary individuals have little chance to make a difference. In rejection of this claim, Govier draws our attention to people like Gandhi and Bertrand Russell who, as individuals, did make a difference to the world. Although not all of us have their special talents and abilities, it still is not true that ordinary people can make no difference. As Govier suggests, a collection of 50 million individuals in the peace movement could make a significant difference. The impact of any individual's actions will hinge on how others act. An individual is important taken in isolation, but powerful as one of a larger group. Quoting Annette Baier, Govier illustrates how individual responsibility is largely based on a type of secular faith. This faith entails the belief that other people will have the moral concern to make our own moral commitments practically significant. Despite the fact that an individual's actions can succeed only if enough people act in similar ways, the individual ought to undertake actions to reduce the threat of nuclear war in any event. Although there is no inductive or deductive proof that people will abide by the moral code leading to the reduction or abolition of nuclear arms, believing that they will ultimately serves as a foundation both for action and for the social and moral order.

[24.1, 24.2] If we ask why philosophers as such should contribute to public understanding of nuclear problems, answers are readily forthcoming. Fundamentally, the danger of nuclear war is the most pressing problem of our time. If there is a global nuclear war most (if not all) of the other human problems will entirely disappear. Any which remain will appear in a radically different context. Global nuclear war would, in all likelihood, end human social life as we know it. It could end the human race altogether and might even result in the death of virtually all mammalian life on the planet.[1] A discussion of moral values and political structures which ignores this pervasive threat is in a sense absurd, for the threat could eliminate all those things we value. And it is a real one. There is a genuine persistent risk of nuclear war and virtually all adult citizens are at some level aware of this risk. To "apply" ethics to such problems as abortion, sexism, and capital punishment and ignore the nuclear arms race is to suggest that these less cosmic

problems are more real and pressing than the problem of global peace or war. It may also suggest to students and the public at large that philosophers who have studied moral theory, competing ideologies, and principles of probability and strategy, condone the nuclear status quo.

[24.3] Secondly, if we do not discuss the nuclear arms race and related dangers, we contribute to the suppression of thought about the issue which has been such a dominant feature of the nuclear age. Public silence through much of the period between 1945 and the present has enabled the superpowers to move from a position where there were three nuclear weapons in 1945 to one where there are more than 50,000 today. Now, that silence is ending; awareness is increasing. And philosophers, especially in their role as educators, can play their part in ending the silence.

[24.4] An additional point is that the nuclear arms race and the enormous accumulations of conventional arms weapons are important forces behind the economies, technologies, ideologies, and scientific research programs of our time. These military developments (said by some to occupy forty percent of the scientists and engineers on the earth) contribute to the world political and social scene in many ways. By ignoring them, we risk an analysis of social reality which is seriously distorted and inaccurate.

Obviously the reason for philosophers as people to become knowledgeable about nuclear problems is that their very survival is at stake. But the reason for philosophers as philosophers to do this is that they have special opportunities to educate people on the topic, and they have special obligations to do so, especially insofar as they teach ethics, applied ethics, and political philosophy.

To show that issues pertaining to nuclear arms are related to other matters which are already recognized to be legitimate topics of philosophical study, we go on to mention some specific topic areas.

OCCUPATIONAL ETHICS: DEFENSE PRODUCTION

[24.5] In the American Catholic bishops' pastoral letter on nuclear weapons, a very conditional endorsement of (strict?) nuclear deterrence is given. Maintaining a nuclear arsenal for deterrence is allowed to be morally acceptable for some period of time provided that all efforts are made to eliminate reliance on this arsenal for national defense. The bishops conclude that the traditional just war theory could not justify the use of nuclear weapons, for just war theory requires a strict distinction between combatants and civilians in war. The distinction cannot hold up when nuclear weapons are used. Their conclusion, then, is that it could never be morally acceptable to detonate nuclear weapons against targets in populated areas. Nuclear weapons can never be used.

[24.6] Given this conclusion, some bishops (notably Archbishop Hunthausen of Seattle) went much further, developing the following argument: If it is not right to use nuclear weapons, then it is not right to threaten to use them. If it is not right to threaten to use them, then it is not right to possess them; possession itself might be said to constitute some kind of implicit threat or implicit intention to use. If it is not right to possess nuclear weapons, then it is not right to manufacture them. On this analysis those participating in the design, manufacture or testing of nuclear weapons are participating in immoral activities, and have an obligation to change their occupation. Hunthausen's view went further than that of the majority of bishops; many disagreed with him as to the soundness of the inference "if doing X is wrong, then threatening to do X is wrong." The argument raises some important and fascinating problems which should certainly be discussed by philosophers interested in occupational ethics.[2]

[24.7] NATION STATES

In *The Fate of the Earth,* Jonathan Schell argues that the only way to eliminate the risk of nuclear war is to eliminate nation states. He says that the knowledge of nuclear weaponry is now a permanent feature of the human condition, and given this, any war will retain the potential for becoming a nuclear war. Thus nuclear weapons make *all* war obsolete as a means of resolving disputes. Yet, Schell claims, the ability to wage war in pursuit of its interests and in its own self-defense is an intrinsic feature of the sovereign nation state. For nuclear security to be possible, national sovereignty must go.[3]

There are many issues central to the appraisal of this argument. Among them are conceptual issues as to how we understand the nation state and national sovereignty. Also involved are evaluative issues. What is the value of nation states, as such? If they possess real cultural and social/psychological value, is the preservation of this value worth some attendant risks? Could it be worth the risk of global nuclear war? Of limited nuclear wars? Schell's instinct—shared by the present author—is to think that the nation state is a comparatively transient historical entity which does not possess a value worth preserving at jeopardy to the very survival of mankind as a whole. The question is arguable, however; if the risk of nuclear war is believed to be very small and the value of nation states very large, a different judgment would likely be made. A number of reviewers reacted with great hostility to Schell's conclusion that the world—the international order, in particular—would have to be "reinvented" in order to eliminate the risk of nuclear war. Suggestions of the necessity of some kind of world government struck them as utopian at best; Orwellian at worst. Yet the issues raised clearly bear thinking about, and should be central topics in political philosophy.

[24.8] FUTURE GENERATIONS

Philosophers have discussed the question of what kind of moral status people who do not yet exist, but will or may exist, should have. How should they count in our moral decision-making, when we come to weigh the consequences of our actions? Equally with existing people? Or not at all, since they are not real at the time that a decision is made? Neither answer seems quite right, and compromise positions tend not to work

very well.[4] Philosophers have also discussed reproductive morality: whether the interests of a prospective child should be taken into account when he or she is still nonexistent and an agent is deciding whether or not to produce him or her.

These topics are important and difficult to resolve, but the questions raised avoid yet another question. Will there be any future generations of humans? It is not certain that even a global nuclear war would end the era of human beings on the planet earth, but there is a very good chance that it would. There are indications that a large number of nuclear detonations would destroy the earth's protective ozone layer. If this were to happen, human and animal life could be entirely destroyed. Part of the problem about the moral status of future generations, then, is whether we have any obligation to work to ensure that they *can* persist on our globe. If there is such an obligation, it is rather different from others which have been discussed in the context of the moral status of future people. These have fallen into two categories: obligations to take into account the interests of people who will (or likely will) exist; and obligations pertaining to reproductive decision-making. Obligations to ensure that some future people can exist on this globe would be another subject.

Would the annihilation of the human species be a tragedy? If so, to whom? If it were a tragedy would this be so only because those who were already alive wanted to live longer and (in some cases) suffered greatly in dying.[5] Or would there be a less person-related tragedy: the death of the species as a whole? To the last question most of us would probably give an instinctive affirmative answer. But we might not know just why. Such an answer is not easily made coherent with the individualistic ontology of such common moral theories as utilitarianism and contractarianism. Ecologically minded philosophers have reflected on whether and why it would be a bad thing for such species as the whale and the whooping crane to become extinct. The same questions can, alas, be extended to our own species.

[24.9] THE MEANING OF LIFE

Discussions of the meaning of life have largely ignored the constant possibility that human life on this planet could simple end. The real possibility of a nuclear catastrophe at any time can cast a dark shadow of meaningless over all mundane activities which have a future orientation. For many, that simply means all mundane activities. (It need not, if one interprets and values activities in terms of their internal actions rather than in terms of their goals and results, but such an attitude is not common in western culture.) The prospect of the extinction of our social world is more radically disruptive psychologically than the prospect of our own individual death. Individual death is inevitable; social or (worse yet) species death is not. Individual death permits the survival of descendants and of valued projects; social or species death does not. All future-oriented meaning is in jeopardy when the very survival of our social world is at risk. Psychiatrist Robert Lifton has long argued that the pervasive and unspoken threat of nuclear disaster has been profoundly damaging to the psyche of post-war generations.[6] He believes that it is responsible for hedonistic and self-interested attitudes, for irresponsibility to the biosphere, and for the low birth rate in many industrialized countries.

Lifton's claims would be extremely difficult to verify. Yet there is a basic sense in

which the nuclear threat does undermine the meaningfulness of many human activities and forces into new relief old questions about the very meaning of life itself. Many philosophers are still willing to acknowledge that reflection on the meaning of life is a fundamentally philosophical task. If this is so, then a central part of this task is to acknowledge the nuclear threat and try to make sense of it. For the time being, this is a fact about our world, and one which we cannot will away.

[24.10] SELF-DECEPTION

Intricate articles have been written trying to make logical and psychological sense of self-deception. Traditionally, philosophers argued that self-deception was morally wrong, for all people in all circumstances. Recently some have revised this stance, contending that self-deception can be excusable or even admirable in some circumstances.[7] The nature of nuclear arms and the risks and nature of nuclear war are topics on which we may well have society-wide self-deception. The psychological need to repress information and to highlight any optimistic prospects is very great. For several decades between the early nineteen sixties and the present time, the arms race accelerated, billions were spent, accidents occurred, nuclear threats were made, and scarcely anyone thought much about it. Looking back, this hardly seems possible. Was this a case of society-wide self-deception? Does that idea make sense? What are the social, political, and linguistic strategies which a society employs in order to deceive itself? If we decide that societies have in fact deceived themselves about the role of nuclear weapons and the threat of nuclear war, this may make us want to re-examine the recent more charitable view of self-deception which allows that it can sometimes be a good thing. Public illusions and ignorance about the nature and role of nuclear weaponry have been a necessary condition of the perpetuation of the dangerous nuclear arms race.

[24.11] INDIVIDUAL RESPONSIBILITY IN THE FACE OF A GLOBAL THREAT

Many people believe that no ordinary individual has a chance to make any difference to the unfolding of global events. If this is so, then individuals would have no obligation to try to affect the course of such events. They would not be morally responsible, either, when things go wrong. The traditional principle of "ought implies can" will give us these comfortable conclusions, provided of course that it is true that an individual cannot make a difference. In an obvious sense whether this principle is true will depend on which individual you are. Mohatma Gandhi, Bertrand Russell, Albert Einstein, and (more recently) Helen Caldicott and Rosalie Berthell *have* made some difference. But then we do not all have their special abilities and opportunities.

A more general point is that whether an individual can make a difference to the prospects of nuclear peace or nuclear war depends on how many other individuals are trying to make a difference. To say that a single person cannot make a difference may be true. But to say that a very large number of single persons cannot is obviously false. An energetic peace movement of 50,000,000 people within the United States could certainly do a very great deal to reduce the risk of nuclear war. A peace movement of 1,000,000 dedicated people in that country would have some chance of doing

this, as would a movement of 100,000 dedicated people in Canada or another allied country.[8] Three or four hundred people would have a very limited chance of having any influence, unless they were in positions of special power and importance. In general, the impact of one person's actions will depend on how other people act. He or she will be impotent alone, but powerful as one of a number.

What we are able to do will depend, then, on what others do. Following on the "ought implies can" principle, it appears that what we are obliged to do will depend on what others do. How are we obligated to act when we do not know what others will do?

At this point we have reached an impasse familiar in moral philosophy. The problem is a dramatic version of that which arises whenever an agent questions an obligation to act at possible personal cost in a moral community which can offer no guarantee that all or most of its members will abide by moral rules. Though interest may be foregone to no avail unless a sufficient number of others abide by the rules, this does not appear to be an excuse for ignoring the obligation. At least, from the moral point of view it is not commonly taken to be an excuse. Plato, Hobbes, Gauthier and many others have wrestled with this problem, trying to show how a commitment to moral principles can be made rational in the sense of being in an agent's ultimate self-interest.

In a beautifully expressed essay entitled "Secular Faith," Annette Baier approached the problem differently. She made no attempt to justify moral action on the basis of reason alone: whether it be reason understood as enlightened pursuit of self-interest, or on some other model. Rather she argued that an individual's commitment to a project whose success requires the actions of a number of other individuals requires, in the end, *faith* in other people.

Baier wrote:

> If everyone insisted on knowing in advance that any sacrifice of independent advantage which they personally make, in joining or supporting a moral order, will be made up for by the return they will get from membership in that moral order, that moral order could never be created, nor, if miraculously brought about, sustained.[9]

For social life to continue we need to have a secular faith—the faith that enough other people will have the moral concern to make our own moral commitments practically significant.

It is such faith in other people that is needed in order to vindicate the individual sacrifices of time and valued projects which will be necessary for individuals to work to reduce the risk of nuclear war. The work is bound to go slowly and the task will be accomplished (if at all) only in many small stages. A large part of this work consists in seeking very basic changes in public attitudes toward nuclear weapons and their historical and present role. The illusion that these weapons have kept us safe, serve only to deter, and are being well-managed by people who know what they are doing has made the nuclear arms race possible. This illusion must be eliminated, and this is no easy task. No one person can do this alone; yet all are obliged to do their part.

Baier does not discuss the problem of global war but she makes a number of remarks which seem very appropriate to it.

> . . . the alternative, giving up on that crucial part of the moral enterprise which secures cooperation, must eventually lead to an outcome disastrous to all—although those with a taste for gun-running may make a good profit before doomsday dawns.

A morally serious person has no alternative to trying in such contexts though he has no guarantee that a sufficient number of others will make the effort. Although his action *can* succeed only if a substantial number of other people act in similar ways, he *ought* to undertake the action in any event. It is faith in other people which bridges the gap. It replaces the faith in God which played an analogous role for earlier generations. Instead of believing in a god who will reward the virtuous and punish the wicked (thus making morally good actions which turn out to be futile on earth "pay off" for the individual in heaven), we are to believe in the capacity of other people for those virtuous actions which we ourselves undertake, so that our own moral commitments may lead to the desired goals right here on this earth. We do not *know* that enough other people will abide by the moral code for this goal to be realized. No deductive or inductive argument can prove this either, given the nature of the problem. Our faith in other people is not rational in the sense of being warranted by proof or evidence. Yet it is rational in the broader sense of serving an overall purpose: it is the foundation of the social and moral order.

If secular faith is, as Baier argued, the necessary foundation for much moral action, then there is no special basis for denying the responsibility of individuals for the global nuclear situation. Although we cannot, as individuals, control what happens, collectively people do have an impact. And this collective capacity is a sufficient basis for individual commitment. Any single action taken by an individual toward the goal of reducing risks of nuclear war is likely to appear solitary and futile, the means seeming grotesquely disproportionate to the end. The action needs to be set in a context where many other people act in similar and related ways. In this context, it appears in a framework where people are working to do something they can do: stop the nuclear arms race and reduce the risks of nuclear war.

We need hope and a will to believe to remain within the moral order. So far as nuclear peace or war is concerned, we have had both. But they have been sadly misused. We have placed our hope in the political and military leaders whose sanity and responsibility we have trusted beyond all evidence. And we have willfully ignored the risks of nuclear disaster, while failing to place our confidence and trust in the moral capacities of our fellow human beings. Those of us who are students and teachers of moral philosophy can play our own small part in changing this situation, and should now be convinced that we have a special obligation to do so.*

April, 1983.

NOTES

*An earlier version of this paper was presented at the annual meeting of the Society for Women in Philosophy, London, Ontario, October 1982.

1. The grisly details are amply described in Schell's *The Fate of the Earth*. Precise predictions are obviously not possible, due to possible variations in numbers of weapons used, reliability of weapons, performance of weapons over a North-South route, weather conditions, and pertinent gaps in scientific knowledge.

2. For some discussion of the bishops' debate, see R. G. Hoyt. "The Bishops and the Bomb," *Christianity and Crisis*. August 9, 1982: Michael Novak, "Nuclear Morality." *America*, 147 (1982): 5–8; J. A. O'Hare, "One Man's Primer on Nuclear Morality," *America*. 147 (1982): 9–12; Francis X. Winters. "Catholic Debate and Division on Deterrence." *America*, 147 (1982): 127–131. Also relevant is Walter Wink. "Faith and Nuclear Paralysis." *Christian Century*, 99 (1982): 234–237.

3. Schell, *The Fate of the Earth*. part 3. This part of the book has been strongly criticized.

4. This comment applies to my own paper. "What Should We Do about Future People?" *American Philosophical Quarterly*, 16 (1979): 105–113. An indication as to just how complex these problems have become may be gleaned from Derek Parfit. "Future Generations: Further Problems." *Philosophy and Public Affairs*, 11 (1982): 113–172.

5. Schell dwells on these questions in a manner quite metaphysical in Part II of his book. They have also been addressed by John Leslie in "Why Not Let Life Become Extinct?", a paper presented at the Canadian Philosophical Association meetings in Montreal, June 1980. See also John Leslie, *Value and Existence* (Totowa, NJ: Rowman and Littlefield 1979).

6. See R. J. Lifton and Richard Falk. *Indefensible Weapons* (Toronto: CBC Publications 1982). Lifton's discussion of psychological effects of nuclear weapons comprises Part I of this work.

7. This view has been defended by Bela Szabados in "Self-Deception," *Canadian Journal of Philosophy*, 4 (1974): 41–49.

8. Moral perspectives on nuclear issues, and potential for political action to alter the status quo, vary considerably depending upon whether one is a citizen within a super-power or a citizen within an allied country. The difference in perspective is often blurred by uses of "we" which fail to make clear whether the point of view taken is that of the U.S., of Canada, or of any country within the NATO alliance.

9. Annette Baier. "Secular Faith." *Canadian Journal of Philosophy*, 10 (1980): 131–148.

FURTHER READINGS

Cohen, Avner, and Steven Lee (eds.). *Nuclear Weapons and the Future of Humanity*. Totowa, NJ: Rowman and Allenheld, 1984.

Kavka, Gregory. "Nuclear Deterrence: Some Moral Perplexities." In *The Security Gamble: Deterrence Dilemmas in the Nuclear Age*, ed. Douglas MacLean. Totowa, NJ: Rowman and Allanheld, 1984.

Hardin, Russell. "Unilateral versus Mutual Disarmament." *Philosophy and Public Affairs* 12(3) (1983): 255.

Lackey, Douglas. "Ethics and Nuclear Deterrence." In *Moral Problems: A Collection of Philosophical Essays*, 3rd ed., ed. James Rachels. New York: Harper & Row, 1979, pp. 426–442.

PROGRESS CHECK 24.1

Instructions: *Fill in the blanks with the responses listed below.*

public silence
responsibility
absurd
threat
secular faith

conditional endorsement
self-deception
nation-states
awareness
distorted

1. It is not correct to say that individuals have no personal _____ to do anything about the nuclear arms race.
2. Philosophical discussions of moral values and political structures which ignore the nuclear threat are in some respects _____.
3. _____ for the last 40 years or so has greatly contributed to the proliferation of nuclear arms.
4. _____ are according to Jonathan Schell merely transient historical entities.
5. _____ is a means for coping with the horrors associated with nuclear holocaust.
6. In the American Catholic bishops' pastoral letter, a _____ of nuclear deterrence is given.
7. According to Archbishop Hunthausen, if doing X is wrong, then making a _____ to do X is also wrong.
8. Acting responsibly as an individual hinges partly on a _____ which leads us to believe that others will act morally and that the moral concern of others will make our own moral commitments practically significant.
9. Philosophers have a special obligation to increase the public _____ of nuclear issues and to point out the moral implications of nuclear war.
10. Any interpretation of social reality which ignores the role and influence of nuclear arms is seriously inaccurate and _____.

LEARNING EXERCISE 24.2   Completing Syllogisms

Instructions: *Complete the following syllogisms.*

1. **Value Premise:**   That which could end all social life as we know it is a pressing issue that should be dealt with immediately.

Factual Premise: Nuclear confrontation could end all social life as we know it.

Conclusion:

2. **Value Premise:**   Threatening human survival is wrong.

   Factual Premise:

   Conclusion: Therefore, public silence is wrong.

3. **Value Premise:**   Distorting our understanding of social reality is wrong.

   Factual Premise: Ignoring the nuclear arms race issue distorts our understanding or social reality.

   Conclusion:

4. **Value Premise:**

   Factual Premise: Using nuclear arms endangers the health and welfare of
   future generations.

   Conclusion: Therefore, using nuclear arms is morally unacceptable.

5. **Value Premise:**   Hiding from a horrifying reality is not beneficial.

   Factual Premise:

   Conclusion: Therefore, self-deception is not beneficial.

LEARNING EXERCISE 24.3   Evaluating Principles and Arguments

Instructions: *Evaluate the following principles and arguments. Look for fallacies,
check for logic, and use the ethical tests of adequacy.*

1. I am opposed to nuclear arms proliferation because the Catholic bishops
   oppose it.
2. We should get rid of nation-states. They are the cause of wars. Look at what
   happened as a result of Hitler's nationalistic aspirations.
3. Threatening the survival of the human species is wrong.
4. Future generations don't count in our moral calculations.
5. I'll let everyone else worry about the nuclear problem. I have more practical
   matters to worry about. Besides, there's no effect I can have, so why should I
   bother.

Appendix

HOW TO WRITE A MORAL PHILOSOPHY PAPER

OVERVIEW

Step One: Identify a controversial moral value issue and formulate a thesis or moral position on it.

Step Two: Recognize that moral argument is dialectical.

Step Three: Present arguments in favor of your thesis or position.

Step Four: State objections to your position.

Step Five: Provide criticisms of arguments against and objections to the thesis defended.

Progress Check

Learning Exercises

Summary

References

Notes

EDUCATIONAL OBJECTIVES: After reading this chapter the student will be able to:

A.1 State reasons why students experience difficulty writing moral philosophy papers.

A.2 List four basic formats which can be used in writing moral philosophy papers.

A.3 Explain what kinds of topics are ideal for, or not particularly suited to, the writing of ethics papers.

A.4 State the characteristics of moral thesis statements.

A.5 Characterize the dialectical nature of moral argumentation.

A.6 Develop arguments in favor of, and opposed to, moral theses using the guiding questions "Why?" and "So What?"

A.7 Explain the ways in which arguments can be criticized.

A.8 Give reasons why the recommended order and structure of presenting papers could be changed.

A.9 Construct and complete an Argument Assembly Chart.

FOCUS QUESTIONS

1. Why could the task of writing a moral philosophy paper be difficult?
2. What are the various aims and formats of moral thesis papers?
3. What exactly is a moral thesis? How does it differ from any other kind of thesis? How does one know if one's thesis is stated properly?
4. How does one go about selecting an appropriate topic for a moral philosophy paper?
5. In moral argumentation, must one simply present one's own moral viewpoint, or is more required?
6. How does one begin to articulate arguments?
7. How does one know if arguments in favor of or against a thesis are adequate?

A.1   Students asked to write their first moral philosophy paper frequently become worried and confused, if not terrified. Sometimes the students have never studied philosophy before, or have never been asked to write a philosophy paper. In this case, the task is completely foreign to them. Philosophy teachers sometimes assume that simply by listening to class lectures and by reading classical ethics texts, students will learn through **osmosis** to understand philosophy and to write philosophical papers properly. Occasionally, some of the brighter, more interested, or talented students do learn how to write good philosophical essays through reading and by example of the teacher. However, for many students the process of osmosis simply does not work. Because of their unfamiliarity with the subject, students may not be able to identify what is philosophically important. They may also be unable to follow the highly complex and technical nature of the teacher's lectures. In addition, assigned readings in moral philosophy may have different and varied formats so that no regularities in structure and organization are apparent.

Students struggling to construct arguments according to the proper form may therefore become uncertain about how they ought to proceed. Without explicit instructions from teachers about how papers should be written, students are often forced to write by trial and error, hoping that what they submit is what the instructor wants. The purpose of this chapter is to eliminate the guesswork for the student assigned the task of writing his or her first ethics paper.

A.2 To begin with, there is more than one correct way to write an ethics paper. Since the purposes of ethics papers differ, so do their formats. There are at least four basic types of moral philosophy papers one could write.[1] One entails the **comparison** of two or more theories. Here, one is interested in determining which theory arrives at the best conclusion on a particular moral problem like evil or responsibility. If neither theory presents an adequate conclusion, an alternative may be offered. A second type of paper involves the **criticism** of a single argument or theory. In this case one might be questioning unfounded assumptions, for example, or inconsistencies in reasoning. A third paper involves **defending** another philosopher's position against criticism or attack. For instance, one could demonstrate how opponents of a particular philosopher's position are guilty of misrepresenting the position or committing the straw-man fallacy. The fourth type of paper entails presenting and **defending a thesis** or position of one's own. It is this type of paper which will concern us here. If you wish to criticize or defend other theories and ethical positions, you must first be skilled in presenting cogent arguments of your own—otherwise, your criticisms and defenses will be undermined. The following suggests a process and format that allow students to present and defend a thesis in a highly structured and organized way.

STEP ONE: IDENTIFY A CONTROVERSIAL MORAL VALUE ISSUE AND FORMULATE A THESIS OR MORAL POSITION ON IT

A.3 The student writing a thesis or position paper in moral philosophy first needs to identify a **controversial issue** involving moral value concerns. There is certainly no point arguing about what is self-evident or obvious to all. Wife-battering, for instance, is probably not a very good topic to select for a moral thesis paper, though an examination of its causes and impact might be ideal for a psychology or sociology essay. Wife-battering would make a poor ethics topic since virtually all rational and moral thinkers are likely to be opposed to it; there appears to be little dispute about the immorality of assaulting one's wife. This is not to deny that wife-battering has moral implications, only that few if any serious and plausible arguments could be put forward in favor of it. By contrast, topics like abortion, capital punishment, and animal vivisection are sufficiently controversial and bound up with moral value concerns to be relevant for thesis papers. Positions both for and against can be presented and argued for by referring to reasonable and defensible moral principles.

A.4 Once you have identified a controversial moral value issue, after some careful consideration, you must articulate the thesis you wish to advance and defend. This thesis should be expressed clearly and simply as a **normative** statement, not as an empirical claim. Remember that a normative statement is a value judgment. It prescribes or proscribes action, or it says something about what is good or bad, right or wrong, praiseworthy or blameworthy. "Abortion is always wrong" is an example of a normative thesis statement. "Abortion will desensitize us to the value of life" is not normative but empirical, since it makes a causal claim. Though causal and other empirical claims will no doubt become a part of moral argumentation, they will be used as factual premises in support of conclusions which follow if specified value premises are accepted. Whereas factual empirical claims can be proven or verified to be true or false in principle by methods of observation and controlled experiment, normative moral thesis statements cannot. Moral theses must be supported and defended by **rational argument,** requiring appeals to things like intuition and higher-order principles.

Once you are certain that your moral thesis is worded as a normative statement, you should be careful to avoid other pitfalls. First, never mix up or combine with your thesis an argument or any portion thereof. The thesis, "Marijuana should be legalized because it would generate government revenue," does just this. This actual thesis should be "Marijuana should be legalized." The factual claim that it would generate government revenue is an argument in support of the thesis. By combining the two claims, one is guilty of conflating a **stated position** with a **supporting argument.** Unless these two things are clearly separated, it may become unclear whether criticisms of the thesis are directed against the position itself or only against a specific argument supporting the position.

In formulating a thesis statement, one must also be careful not to combine two or more theses or positions, since each requires its own defense. The following normative claim combines two theses: "Rock music should be banned in college cafeterias and anyone who listens to such music is profoundly evil." In this case, one could argue in favor of banning rock music in cafeterias without accepting the notion that those who listen to it are evil. There are two distinct claims being made here. If they are combined and not argued for separately, confusion is likely to result.

In summary, then, the statement of a moral thesis should be normative. Second, it should not mix up arguments with the stated position. Finally, it should not contain more than one position or claim. If these general rules of thumb are followed, and if thesis statements are expressed clearly and simply, you are much more likely to express them in a proper fashion.

STEP TWO: RECOGNIZE THAT MORAL ARGUMENT IS DIALECTICAL

A.5   Obviously, controversial moral issues give rise to opposing viewpoints and conflicting prescriptions for action. Students writing a moral thesis paper should not expect to get by with a one-sided discussion that takes into account only those positive arguments in favor of the thesis being advanced. You must also account for the possible objections and refutations of the position for which you are arguing. Thus you must anticipate such objections and refutations and prepare countercriticisms and rebuttals to deal with them. The strategy is much like a chessgame's. When contemplating a move in chess, a player does not remain oblivious to the probable move the opponent will make in reaction to his own move. Possible alternative moves by the opponent are considered in advance and ways of responding to each alternative are carefully considered and evaluated even before one's own move is made. Choosing to remain blind to the reasoning, moves, and strategy of one's opponent is likely to bring about defeat in chess. Choosing to remain blind to others' arguments and criticisms in moral debate is likely to weaken the defended position considerably, not strengthen it.

Of course, when writing an ethics paper, an opponent is not usually present. The act of writing is typically a very personal and private affair. To facilitate the argumentative, dialectical nature of reasoning required for a moral philosophy paper, you should conduct a **hypothetical debate** within your imagination. The writer of the paper becomes both the **arguer** for the position advanced and the **questioner** or **skeptic** of that position in the process of solitary inquiry. In short, an imaginary debate is conducted "in your head." As you construct arguments, counterarguments, and rebuttals pertinent to the thesis, you must alternate back and forth between the two roles of arguer and questioner. This alternating back and forth underscores the **dialectical** nature of moral inquiry, and of thesis writing in particular. The simplest form of dialectical reasoning may be summarized in the following fashion.

Dialectical Reasoning

1. Present one argument which has the claim/thesis in question stated as its conclusion (support for the claim/thesis).
2. Present one argument which has the denial of the claim/thesis in question stated as its conclusion (argument in opposition to the claim/thesis).
3. Present one argument which has as its conclusion a criticism of one argument against the claim/thesis (a refutation of the critical argument against the claim/thesis).[2]

In the context of paper writing, the process of dialectical reasoning can become much more complex than the above indicates. More than one argument is typically presented in support of a thesis, just as more than one objection can usually also be presented in opposition to the thesis. This in turn could necessitate several rebuttals and refutations of arguments against the claim put forward. Nonetheless, this dialectical structure of reasoning always entails presenting arguments in favor of the thesis, arguments against the thesis, and criticisms refuting arguments against the thesis.

When offering arguments in support of your thesis or claim, you should be careful that the value premises are acceptable, that the factual premises are correct, and that the conclusions follow logically from preceding premises. You must also be sure that arguments are free of logical fallacies. Otherwise your arguments in favor of particular theses can come under attack, thereby complicating the dialectical process even further. Before proceeding to refute arguments in opposition to your thesis, you would be forced to defend your own argument first. It is also important that your refutations of opposing arguments be faultless. Otherwise, you are placed in a position of having to refute the criticisms of your refutations.

STEP THREE: PRESENT ARGUMENTS IN FAVOR OF YOUR THESIS OR POSITION

A.6   Once a controversial moral issue has been selected and a thesis statement articulated; and once you appreciate that dialectical nature of the reasoning process which will be used in support of the thesis, then you are ready to being presenting positive arguments in favor of the position advocated. It is at this point that the argument starts. You might begin by asking yourself the question, "Why?" What are the strongest reasons that can be given in support for holding the position that you do? Let us say that the issue is immigration. Let us also assume that one reason given in support of the thesis, "Further immigration should be stopped," is that immigrants take jobs away from North Americans. The reason given here is factual. The factual claim made could be true or it could be false. The truth or falsity of this claim could in principle be verified by an appeal to the facts. Assuming that you can prove the truth of the empirical, factual claim, you must then ask yourself "So what?" Such a self-directed question demands that the arguer for the claim provide an underlying value premise relevant to the factual claim, which ultimately allows the arguer to arrive at the conclusion, "Further immigration should be stopped." A plausible value premise in this instance could be, "Whatever takes away jobs from North Americans should be stopped." With this underlying value premise now made explicit, you can construct a practical syllogism which acts as a positive argument in favor of the thesis being put forward.

> Value Premise: *Whatever takes away jobs from North Americans should be stopped.*
> Factual Premise: *Further immigration will take jobs away from North Americans.*
> Conclusion: *Further immigration should be stopped.*

It is likely that as the arguer you will have more than one argument in favor of the thesis. Other arguments could be developed by asking the basic questions "Why" and "So what." The "Why" question can be used to identify factual premises supporting the thesis, whereas the "So what" question can help to uncover the underlying value premises of the argument. Once these questions are answered, additional practical syllogisms can be constructed.

After arguments in favor of a particular thesis have been constructed in syllogism form, you should test them by subjecting the value premises to the role-exchange, consistency, universalizability, new-cases, and higher-order principle tests. You should also make certain that positive arguments are free of fallacies and that conclusions obtained follow logically from premises. In short, the process of constructing your arguments in support of a thesis requires self-questioning and evaluation of your own claims, whether they be factual, logical, or normative. This task can be quite difficult as it requires objectivity and detachment from your own preferred viewpoint. You must eliminate subjective preferences, and egocentric and ethnocentric thinking. You must step out of your own shoes, as it were, and examine your arguments and claims from afar.

STEP FOUR: STATE OBJECTIONS TO YOUR POSITION

Having completed the first step of the dialectical process of reasoning—that is, stating positive or affirmative arguments in favor of your thesis—you must now consider objections to the position being defended. At this stage, you must state the strongest arguments possible which oppose the thesis at issue. These objections or negative arguments will do one of two things. They will either present as their conclusion the statement that one's own conclusion is false or unacceptable, or they will present conclusions that, if true or acceptable, are incompatible with the original thesis advanced, namely, the one you for which you are arguing.

When considering arguments against your own position, care should be taken to state them fairly and completely. If objections to your own thesis are misrepresented or worded unfairly, then a "straw man" is set up. If, in the process of dialectical reasoning and in defense of a thesis, you simple set up and refute straw-man counterarguments and objections, the cogency of your position is probably undermined. Certainly, nothing is added to that cogency. Your argument likely becomes less persuasive than would be the case if objections to a thesis were first fairly stated and then rejected on rational grounds.

STEP FIVE: PROVIDE CRITICISMS OF ARGUMENTS AGAINST
AND OBJECTIONS TO THE THESIS DEFENDED

The dialectical process of reasoning is completed when **antithetical arguments** are criticized and rejected. Reasons must be provided why objections to and criticisms of the defended thesis are themselves inadequate, unjustifiable, or unacceptable. Of course, you should keep in mind that the criticisms of your position are self-constructed while playing the role of questioner in the hypothetical debate. Nonetheless, these self-directed objections and criticisms are meant to be like those which could be held by others if the thesis were debated publicly.

A.7   As with all syllogistic, deductive arguments, evaluation may occur at three levels. Countercriticisms of your imaginary questioner or opponent may occur at the level of the conclusion. Perhaps it does not follow logically from what precedes. Or, its wording may be incorrect. At a second level, antithetical arguments may be based on false or highly **questionable factual premises**. Common sense, scientific research, or sensory observation might be used to refute objections based in part on unfounded empirical claims. Third, you might apply the aforementioned tests of adequacy to the value premises to ensure their acceptability. With respect to arguments as a whole, you should also be wary about making psychological or emotional appeals in the form of **diversionary** or **intimidation tactics.** This usually indicates the presence of logical fallacies or unacceptable modes of philosophical reasoning.

A.8   In closing, remember that the process recommended here for developing a moral argument is not based on any hard and fast rules. On occasion, depending on the subject and the target audience one wishes to persuade, arguments against a thesis could be presented first and rejected before positive arguments in favor of the thesis are laid out. This reversal of order might be advisable to persuade listeners who are otherwise clearly convinced that the advocated position is false. By first attacking the arguments of your adversaries, the listeners' predispositon to dismiss your position without much reflection is weakened.[3] Once those hostile to your position have been made more receptive, you might then begin to present positive arguments in favor of a disliked, unpopular thesis or proposition.

A.9   It is helpful if one's arguments and objections are structured and organized using what can be called an Argument Assembly Chart. The chart allows one to assemble—and state in deductive, syllogistic form—the basic arguments for and objections to the thesis defended. The chart thus provides the "bare bones" upon which the body of the text can be placed.

At the top of the chart is found the thesis statement. Below the thesis statement are two headings: (1) supporting positive arguments, and (2) objections. Under each of these headings are placed appropriate syllogisms. The argument assembly chart should be completed prior to the actual writing of your paper, since the detailed content of the paper depends on what arguments are summarized in the chart. Though you cannot say in advance how many supporting and objecting syllogisms should be included in each column, including at least two or three on each side will allow you to build a substantial dialectical argument. On page 335 is an example of a completed chart. It illustrates how the chart should be designed.

ARGUMENT ASSEMBLY CHART

Thesis: Smoking in Public Places Should Be Prohibited

SUPPORTING POSITIVE ARGUMENTS

Value Premise	Factual Premise	Conclusion
Argument 1		
That which endangers the health of others should be prohibited.	Smoking in public places endangers the health of others.	Therefore, smoking in public places should be prohibited.
Argument 2		
That which increases health care costs should be discouraged.	Smoking in public places increases health care costs.	Smoking in public places should be discouraged.
Argument 3		
Violating the rights of others is wrong.	Smoking in public places violates the rights of others.	Smoking in public places is wrong.

OBJECTIONS

Conclusion	Factual Premise	Value Premise
		Objection 1
Therefore, we should not enforce public smoking regulations.	Public smoking regulations interfere with everyday business practices.	We should not enforce public regulations which interfere with everyday business practices.
		Objection 2
Public smoking regulations are wrong.	Public smoking regulations limit individual choice.	Limiting individual choice is wrong.

Criticisms of Objections

Objection 1
a. Logic and Conclusion *Acceptable.*
b. Factual Premise *Correct.*
c. Value Premise *Unacceptable.* Fails new-cases test (e.g., regulations governing industrial wastes and car emissions interfere with business and profit maximization, yet we're in favor of them).
d. Fallacies: *None.*

Objection 2
a. Logic and Conclusion: *Acceptable.*
b. Factual Premise: *Acceptable.*
c. Value Premise: *Unacceptable;* individual choice is acceptable only insofar as other's rights are not violated.
d. Fallacies: *None.*

Adapted from the Association of Values Education and Research, *Value Reasoning Series*, the University of British Columbia, 1978–1981.

PROGRESS CHECK A.1

Instructions: *Insert the appropriate responses in each of the blanks.*

factual premise	argument assembly chart
controversial	target audience
osmosis	diversionary
normative	moral assumption
imaginary debate	factual
skeptic	dialectical
straw-man fallacy	prescription
questionable	empirical
intimidation	self-evident
subject	cogent
value premise	antithetical

1. Sometimes ethics teachers do not explicitly tell students how moral philosophy papers should be written. They erroneously assume that all students will learn by _____.
2. Another way of saying an argument is persuasive is saying it is _____.
3. When two or more opposing positions on an issue can be identified, one can say that the issue is _____.
4. The statement 2 + 2 = 4 is _____.
5. A moral thesis is _____.
6. The statement, "Wife-battering occurs most frequently in homes occupied by alcoholics" is _____.
7. A statement of obligation or one about what ought to be done is a _____ of action.
8. In writing a moral philosophy paper, a(n) _____ is carried on with oneself. One assumes both the role of arguer and questioner.
9. One who questions and rejects a position taken, criticizes it, and demands further justification is a _____.
10. An argument which goes "back and forth"—that is, begins with positive arguments in favor of a thesis, then proceeds with negative antithetical ones, and finally concludes with criticisms of the negative arguments—is _____.
11. Tests of adequacy (e.g., role-exchange) are applied to the _____ of an argument.
12. Empirical claims made to support the conclusion of an argument are found at the level of the _____ in a practical syllogism.

13. When developing arguments either in favor of or against a particular thesis, asking the initial question, "Why is one in favor or against?" helps one to establish _____ reasons for holding one's position.

14. The follow-up question—that is, the "So what?" question—helps one to uncover the underlying ethical principle or _____ upon which the argument is based.

15. Misrepresenting the arguments of an opponent and then rejecting them makes one guilty of the _____.

16. An argument which is diametrically opposed to one's position is _____.

17. An empirical claim which is highly improbable is _____.

18. Logical fallacies typically indicate that _____ and _____ tactics are being used.

19. The order of presentation in an argument may depend on the _____ and the _____.

20. A helpful aid in preparing one's first ethics paper is the _____.

LEARNING EXERCISE A.2

Instructions: *Below is a list of statements. Some statements could properly be used as moral theses for ethics papers, while others would not be suitable. Beside the suitable statements, place the letter "T." Next to those which are not suitable, place the letters "N/S."*

_____ 1. Christians are obligated to attend church on Sundays.

_____ 2. The Moral Majority is opposed to abortion.

_____ 3. Capital punishment should be reinstated.

_____ 4. Corporations pollute because it is in their material self-interest.

_____ 5. Men and women should be treated equally and fairly.

_____ 6. To compensate for past injustices, visible minorities should be hired over others.

_____ 7. Canada should participate in the development of Star Wars technology.

_____ 8. Homosexuals should not be allowed to teach in public schools.

_____ 9. Allowing homosexual teachers to teach endangers the psychological well-being of young, impressionable children.

_____ 10. Girls from broken homes tend to engage in premarital sex more frequently than girls from traditional nuclear families.

_____ 11. Rock-n-roll music is inherently evil.

_____ 12. Scientists place toxic substances on the eyelids of baby rabbits to determine tolerance levels.

_____ 13. The use of animals in cosmetics research is wrong.

_____ 14. Humans have the conditional right to exploit the resources of the planet.

_____ 15. We should be willing to kill and die for democracy.

LEARNING EXERCISE A.3

Instructions: *Complete an Argument Assembly Chart stating a moral thesis of your own. Provide three positive supporting arguments and two objections to the thesis advanced. Also give countercriticisms of opposing arguments, indicating the level at which they are unacceptable.*

Argument Assembly Chart
Thesis

Supporting Positive Arguments	Objections
Argument One VP _____ FP _____ Conclusion _____	*Objection One* VP _____ FP _____ Conclusion _____
Argument Two VP _____ FP _____ Conclusion _____	*Objection Two* VP _____ FP _____ Conclusion _____
	Criticisms of Objections
Argument Three VP _____ FP _____ Conclusion _____	*Argument One* Logic: FP: VP: Fallacies: *Argument Two* Logic: FP: VP: Fallacies:

LEARNING EXERCISE A.4

Instructions: *Using the recommended process of writing moral thesis papers, practical syllogisms must be extracted from the Argument Assembly Chart and expanded into sentence and paragraph form. Take any valid practical syllogism and transform it into a one-page discussion of an argument. To do this, one ought to elaborate on the exact meaning of the value premise, explaining and clarifying it in detail. Justification for the value premise should be offered as well. Factual premises must be supported by referring to scientific research, illustrations, or everyday observation. Some assurance must be given to the skeptic that the factual premise is correct, or at least highly probable. Finally, make it explicit how the conclusion of the argument follows necessarily if the preceding premises are accepted. Be sure not to include any logical fallacies.*

SUMMARY

1. Problems with Learning How to Write Moral Philosophy Papers

   Initial worry, confusion, or terror.

   Not everybody can learn through osmosis (lectures can be difficult; assigned readings may have inconsistent formats).

2. Types of Paper Formats

   Comparison of two or more theories or positions.

   Critique of a single theory or position.

   Defense of another's theory, position, or thesis.

   Presentation of one's own thesis or position.

3. An Appropriate Thesis:

   Must involve a controversial issue.

   Must entail moral value concerns.

   Must be normative.

   Must be worded clearly and succinctly.

   Must not confuse a stated position with a supporting argument.

   Must not combine two or more positions or theses.

4. Dialectical Nature of Moral Argument

   Moral arguments should become much like imaginary debates, with the writer playing the roles of arguer and questioner.

   Moral arguments are a "back and forth" process.

   Involves at least a three-part progression, i.e., a presentation of supporting arguments, a presentation of objections and, lastly, a criticism of those objections.

5. Arguments Can Be Evaluated and Criticized in Four Ways:

   Value premises can be questioned.

   Factual premises can be questioned.

   The logic and conclusion can be questioned.

   The argument may be examined for the possible presence of logical fallacies.

6. Arguments Can Be Constructed Using Two Helpful Questions:

Why? — The answer to this question provides factual claims to support the conclusion.

So What? — This question serves to uncover implicit value premises.

7. Order of Argument Presentation May Vary Depending

On the Subject.

On the target audience.

8. Argument Assembly Chart.

Practical syllogisms should be constructed and assembled in chart form.

Countercriticisms of objections should also be included.

REFERENCES

Coombs, Jerrold, Leroi Daniels, and Ian Wright. "Introduction to Value Reasoning." In *Prejudice: Teacher's Manual*, Value Reasoning Series. Toronto: The Ontario Institute for Studies in Education, 1978.

Johnson, Ralph H., and J. Anthony Blair. *Logical Self-Defense*. 2nd ed. Toronto: McGraw-Hill Ryerson, Ltd., 1983.

Woodhouse, Mark B. *A Preface to Philosophy*. 3rd ed. Belmont, CA: Wadsworth, 1984.

NOTES

1. Mark Woodhouse, *A Preface to Philosophy*, 3rd ed., (Belmont, CA: Wadsworth, 1984).
2. Adapted from R. H. Johnson and J. A. Blair, *Logical Self-Defense*, 2nd ed., (Toronto: McGraw-Hill Ryerson, Ltd., 1983), p. 192.
3. Ibid., p. 198.

Index